RESEARCH HANDBOOK ON MENTAL HEALTH POLICY

To my wife – Barbara

Research Handbook on Mental Health Policy

Edited by

Christopher G. Hudson

Professor Emeritus, School of Social Work, Salem State University, USA

EE Edward Elgar
PUBLISHING

Cheltenham, UK • Northampton, MA, USA

Published by
Edward Elgar Publishing Limited
The Lypiatts
15 Lansdown Road
Cheltenham
Glos GL50 2JA
UK

Edward Elgar Publishing, Inc.
William Pratt House
9 Dewey Court
Northampton
Massachusetts 01060
USA

A catalogue record for this book
is available from the British Library

Library of Congress Control Number: 2022944608

This book is available electronically in the **Elgar**online
Sociology, Social Policy and Education subject collection
http://dx.doi.org/10.4337/9781800372788

MIX
Paper | Supporting
responsible forestry
FSC
www.fsc.org   FSC® C013604

ISBN 978 1 80037 277 1 (cased)
ISBN 978 1 80037 278 8 (eBook)
Printed and bound by CPI Group (UK) Ltd, Croydon, CR0 4YY

Contents

Figures

Tables

Biographical sketches

John R. Belcher is Professor of Social Work at the University of Maryland School of Social Work in Baltimore, Maryland. His research interests include mental health, homelessness, and financialization. The author can be contacted at Jbelcher@ssw.umaryland.edu.

Patrick W. Corrigan is Distinguished Professor of Psychology at the Illinois Institute of Technology. Prior to that, he was Professor of Psychiatry at the University of Chicago where he directed its Center on Psychiatric Rehabilitation. His research examines psychiatric disability, substance use disorder, and social disadvantage. Currently, he is principal investigator of the Chicago Health Disparities Center. Funded by the National Institute on Minority Health and Health Disparities and the Patient Centered Outcomes Research Institute, this work examines how ethnic and income disparities further lessen the opportunities of those with serious mental illness. He is also principal investigator of the National Consortium on Stigma and Empowerment, supported by the National Institutes of Health (NIH) for about 20 years. He has written more than 450 peer-reviewed articles, is editor emeritus of the *American Journal of Psychiatric Rehabilitation*, and editor of *Stigma and Health* published by the American Psychological Association (APA). Corrigan has authored or edited 20 books, most recently, *The Stigma Effect* published by Columbia University Press. He is recipient of numerous awards including APA's Alexander Gralnick award for his research on serious mental illness and the Presidential Medal from the Royal College of Psychiatrists.

Liron David, Policy and International Relations Chief Officer at Enosh – The Israeli Mental Health Association. Vice-Chair of Keystone Human Services International and a member of the World Health Organization Technical Advisory Group (TAG) on the mental health impacts of COVID-19 in the WHO European Region. Liron's research focuses on the connections between law and social work, mental health disability rights access to justice, and The non-take up of social rights.

Eva Dragomirecká is a Senior Researcher at the Faculty of Arts at Charles University, Prague. Her main fields of interest are social and psychological aspects of health, transformation of social and health care, service research, and development and validation of assessment methods.

Mencía R. Gutiérrez-Colosía is a senior researcher and Head of the Department of Psychology at Universidad Loyola Andalucía, Spain. Her research interests are social and health service provision; development and application of decision support systems for mental health policy and practice. Further information can be found at https://www.uloyola.es/oferta -cientifica/personal-investigador/mencia-ruiz-gutierrez-colosia.

Hilla Hadas, Executive Director of Enosh – The Israeli Mental Health Association. A member of the board of directors of The Israeli Psychiatric Rehabilitation Association (ISPRA), a member of the board of trustees of The Academic College of Tel Aviv-Yafo, a member of the international advisory committee of the Jewish Agency's Partnership2Gether (P2G) program. She is a member of the Advisory Committee to the Israeli Commissioner for Equal Rights of

Persons with Disabilities in the Israeli Ministry of Justice and the co-chair of the Israeli Prime Minister Cross-sector Roundtable.

Jared M. Hirschfield is a student at Yale Law School and graduate of Northeastern University, where he studied biology and political science. Guided by research interests at the intersection of law, public policy, and public health, he studies health system reform and its potential impact on geographic and racial health disparities in the United States.

Christopher G. Hudson is Professor Emeritus at Salem State University, Salem, Massachusets. He has B.A. and M.A. degrees from the University of Chicago and a Ph.D. from the University of Illinois at Chicago. His career includes 35 years as a professor of social work. He is author of over 60 professional publications, including four books, on mental health policy, homelessness, complex systems, psychiatric epidemiology, mental health finance, and related areas. He is also recipient of two William J. Fulbright awards. See https://directory.salemstate.edu/profile/christopher.hudson.

Emily Ihara is Associate Professor and Chair of the Department of Social Work at George Mason University. Her research focuses on interventions, policies, and system changes necessary to eliminate health and mental health inequities for older adults and non-dominant populations. Current projects include using agent-based modeling to address the complexity of dementia caregiving, examining creative arts intervention for individuals living with dementia and their caregivers, and evaluating workforce education initiatives.

Hugo Kamya is the Social Work Alumni Fund Endowed Chair and Professor at Simmons University School of Social Work. His research has focused on the social determinants of health, health disparities, social networks, community capital, transactional sex, HIV risk for youth and adolescents, as well as refugee and immigrant health. He also does research on youth health and development, youth transitions into adulthood, using youth-led focus groups, and community-based participatory research. More information can be found at https://www.simmons.edu/academics/faculty/hugo-kamya.

John Karavatas, has a B.A. from Howard University, and is currently an MSW student at George Mason University.

Carla D. Kundert is a Ph.D. student in Rehabilitation Counseling Education at the Illinois Institute of Technology in Chicago. Her current research interests include understanding and combatting the stigma of behavioral health conditions, health equity among people with serious mental illness, and the value of peer support for people with lived experience of mental health and substance use.

Max Lachman is Associate Professor Haifa University (Community Mental Health Department), Consultant of the Laszlo N. Tauber Family Foundation in Israel, member of the Steering Committee of ISPRA – Israel Association of Psychiatric Rehabilitation, Member of the Board Committee of the World Association of Psychiatric Rehabilitation (WAPR), with 18 years of work in the Israeli Ministry of Health (Mental Health Department) and more than 40 years of experience in practice, policy, management, and research in mental health.

JoAnn Lee is Associate Professor in the Department of Social Work at George Mason University. She uses quantitative and computational methods in her research, which is focused on improving child welfare and juvenile justice systems to better facilitate the transition to adulthood for all youth.

Jonathan Lukens is Associate Professor in the School of Social Work at Salem State University, Salem, Massachusets, where he teaches courses in social welfare policy, health and mental health policy and service delivery systems, applied research, agency leadership, and ethics. Lukens has published widely in the academic literature on the topics of mental health policy and services and clinical and professional ethics.

Ronald W. Manderscheid serves as Adjunct Professor at the Bloomberg School of Public Health, Johns Hopkins University, and the Suzanne Dworak-Peck School of Social Work, University of Southern California. Until recently, he was President/CEO, National Association of County Behavioral Health and Developmental Disability Directors and National Association for Rural Mental Health. Concurrently, Manderscheid serves on the boards of the American Academy of Social Work and Social Welfare, the National Grand Challenge for Social Work Initiative, the Danya Institute, and the NASMHPD Research Institute.

Ondřej Pěč is a psychiatrist and Director of the ESET Clinic in Prague. He also works as a psychoanalyst. He is Assistant Professor at the First Faculty of Medicine at Charles University in Prague. His scientific interests include psychotherapy in psychoses, psychiatric rehabilitation and community care. Previously, Pěč was also consultant in the Centre for Mental Health Development in Prague.

Shulamit Ramon is Professor of Social Inclusion and Wellbeing at the University of Hertfordshire, UK. A registered social worker and a chartered clinical psychologist, Ramon has specialized in developing the perspective of mental health recovery in theory, research, and practice, often through an international dimension. This has included projects and many publications on the closure of psychiatric hospitals, the development of alternative services, systematically involving service users as co-researchers and co-trainers, and pioneering shared decision making in mental health through action research projects in two UK National Health Service (NHS) trusts.

David A. Rochefort is Arts & Sciences Distinguished Professor of Political Science and Public Administration at Northeastern University. A specialist in mental health policy analysis, Rochefort's books include *From Poorhouses to Homelessness: Policy Analysis and Mental Health Care*, 2nd edition (1997), and *Mental Health and Social Policy*, 6th edition, with David Mechanic and Donna McAlpine (2013), among other titles. His articles have appeared in such journals as *The Milbank Quarterly*, *International Journal of Health Services*, *Health Affairs*, *Public Administration Review*, and *Annual Review of Sociology*.

Sebastian Rosenberg is Senior Lecturer, Brain and Mind Centre, University of Sydney, and Adjunct Associate Professor at the Mental Health Policy Unit, University of Canberra, Australia. Rosenberg's research interest focuses on accountability for mental health, attempting to understand if what is done to people is helping.

Jose A. Salinas-Perez is a Senior Researcher in the Department of Quantitative Methods at Universidad Loyola Andalucía. He holds a Ph.D. in Geography and his areas of interests are spatial data statistics and epidemiology, health indicators and development of mental health care atlases for decision making in health planning. More information can be found under https://www.uloyola.es/oferta-cientifica/personal-investigador/jose-alberto-salinas-perez.

Luis Salvador-Carulla is Professor and Deputy Head of the Health Research Institute, Faculty of Health, University of Canberra, Australia. His field of interest is support decision systems and policy in long-term care, disability and mental health, and intellectual developmental disorders. Salvador-Carulla is honorary member of the World Psychiatry Association and Secretary of the WPA section "Classification, Diagnostic Assessment and Nomenclature." He has been advisor to the Spanish Ministry of Health, the European Commission (EC) and the World Health Organization (WHO).

Russell K. Schutt is Professor of Sociology at the University of Massachusetts Boston, Lecturer (part-time) in Psychiatry at the Harvard Medical School, and Clinical Research Scientist I at the Beth Israel Deaconess Medical Center. Schutt's research interests are the social environment and mental health, service preferences, and service program organization and impact, with current research on the social impact of the COVID-19 pandemic and on psychosocial programs to improve social and community programs in persons diagnosed with schizophrenia-spectrum disorders. For more information see https://blogs.umb.edu/russellkschutt/.

Phyllis Solomon is the Kenneth L.M. Pray Chair, Professor of Social Work and Associate Dean for Research in School of Social Policy & Practice, University of Pennsylvania. Her primary research focus is on psychiatric rehabilitation/mental health services, service systems, including behavioral health, criminal justice and child welfare, and service interventions for persons with severe mental illness and their families.

Sylvia Tessler-Lozowick is the Executive Director of the Laszlo N. Tauber Familiy Foundation, which focuses on supporting innovative and ground-breaking projects in mental health. Former chair of Soteria Israel – Short Term Acute Residential Treatment (START) homes ("balancing homes"), current chair of ISPRA, The Israel Psychiatric Rehabilitation Association, and of MOSHE – words that make a difference – for the prevention of suicide.

Yvonne Vissing is Professor of Healthcare Studies and Director of the Center for Childhood & Youth Studies at Salem State University, Salem, Massachusetts. She was a NIMH Post-doctoral Research Fellow and is the US policy chair for the UN Convention on the Rights of the Child. Author of 14 books, Vissing focuses on child wellbeing, human rights, homelessness, child abuse prevention, and community & organizational development.

Amy Ward is the Social Work Program Director and Assistant Professor at East Central University in Ada, Oklahoma. Before entering academia, she served as a frontline social worker in a tribal community, specializing in the Indian Child Welfare Act. Recently, Ward received the Western Social Sciences Association award for the outstanding graduate paper, this work was entitled "Tribal Family Healing Court: A Culturally Sensitive Approach to Child Welfare in Tribal Communities." In 2020, she was awarded ECU's prestigious teaching excellence award.

Jaap van Weeghel is a social scientist. Until February 2021 he was the scientific director of Phrenos, a national center of expertise on the recovery and treatment of persons with severe mental illnesses in the Netherlands. Currently he is working at Phrenos as a Senior Advisor. He is also Emeritus Professor in Psychiatric Rehabilitation and Social Inclusion at Tilburg University, Department Tranzo, Tilburg, the Netherlands. More information can be found under http://www.research.tilburguniversity.edu/en/persons/jaap-van-weeghel.

Michael Wolf-Branigin is Professor of Social Work at George Mason University. His research focuses on complex adaptive systems and their application to social work practice. Specifically, these applications include developing new program evaluation methods, investigating the built environment using spatial analytic methods, and facilitating the discipline to move toward a complex systems orientation. His substantive areas primarily include behavioral health and disabilities.

Echo Yuet Wah Yeung is Associate Professor in Research at the University of Hertfordshire, UK. Yeung's professional background is social work. Her research interests are in health and social care of people from Chinese backgrounds and other minority ethnic communities. Other research interests include practice education in social work. More information about her research profile and publications can be found under: https://www.researchgate.net/profile/Echo-Yeung-2.

Reginald O. York is Adjunct Professor, School of Social Work, University of North Carolina Wilmington. Previously York served on the faculties of East Carolina University and the University of North Carolina Chapel Hill. He is the author of five books on human service research methods and statistics, one book on human service planning, and more than 30 journal articles on a myriad of topics. Among his key interests are evidence-based practice, research methods, organizational leadership, and organizational decision making.

Preface

This Handbook is an outgrowth of a variety of studies I have conducted in the field of mental health policy and services since the 1980s. These have involved evaluations of spending patterns on the state level, projects which have sought to model the need for psychiatric hospitalization both globally and within the US, and studies on the impact of sociocultural conditions on the risk of serious mental illness, predictors of the growth of populations' homeless persons, to mention some of the most significant areas of this research. My research, in turn, has been the outcome of my earlier practice as a clinical social worker in inpatient and outpatient mental health settings, as well as my involvement over the course of my career in various mental health boards and related projects. All of these experiences have not only reinforced my belief in the centrality of empirical research in the design of mental health service systems, but also impressed me with the formidable challenges of planning, conducting, and disseminating research in a way which assures its adoption in practice.

This Handbook, therefore, has been written as a guide to the design and use of research in mental health policy from an international perspective. It focuses on public mental health, but also includes quasi-public and private policies in those nations with significant private sectors. Mental health policies reviewed include not only those pertinent to psychiatric treatment and care, but those concerned with substance abuse, developmental disabilities, forensic care, as well as other populations or settings such as primary care. The research reviewed covers a wide range of mental health topics, such as that on particular interventions, which is relevant to mental health policy, as well as more specific studies on mental health policy issues.

Some of the most timely themes explored in this Handbook involve both the processes and methods of research in the field, as well as a range of actual findings on the types of services, practices, and policies which are most efficacious. There is widespread agreement on the part of the various authors about the importance of integrating both qualitative and quantitative methods, and in general pursuing a multi-perspectival and multimethod approach to both research and policy development. By doing so, substantial headway can be made toward overcoming the well-known gap between research and policy making. A theme highlighted by several authors is the importance of elevating the voice of consumers, including those of children and adolescents, in the design of services. While grounding mental health policies in data on what works and doesn't work is important, so is it of critical importance to ground it in analyses of ethical dilemmas and fundamental human rights, most notably the protection of individual civil liberties when consumers are experiencing mental breakdown and may require hospitalization. Such issues have been particularly germane to debates regarding psychiatric deinstitutionalization, on whether there is any remaining role for psychiatric inpatient care, a topic addressed in chapter 11 – as well as parts of several other chapters. The Handbook also emphasizes an emerging approach to this problem involving the ideal of a balanced service system, one that implements an optimal response to a range of principles such as the need for continuity of care, consumer choice, treatment in the least restrictive environment, accessibility of services, equity in service provision, to mention a few. Finally, a central theme is the importance of grounding policy development with research on the sociocultural environment and psychiatric epidemiology.

Each chapter explores some combination of the achievements and limitations of mental health policy development, as well as the conduct and methods of research, along with their pros and cons, for facilitation such development. Chapters on individual nations or regions also delve into relevant history and recent achievements in the attempt to build balanced mental health service systems. A few of the chapters advocate for particular policies, such as shared decision making or the inclusion of children in research and policy development. These are written for anyone who wishes to conduct research with the aim of developing more accessible, effective, and equitable systems of care, especially policy makers, administrators, and post-graduate students.

Christopher G. Hudson
Editor

PART I

INTRODUCTION

1. Introduction to the *Research Handbook on Mental Health Policy*

Christopher G. Hudson

An ongoing challenge in the mental health field has been to assure that its guiding policies are grounded on the best possible research. The fragmentation of the field, including its diverse practices, agencies, and policies, is evidence that popular fads, political expediency, simplistic rules, and even guesswork too often guide policy decisions. Barriers to the use of research in decision making involve its availability, relevance, and quality; the values and expertise of policy makers and their advisors; and the urgency of emergent problems and opportunities. A critical barrier involves the lack of fit between, on one hand, current mental health policies and systems, and, on the other hand, available research, including its data, methods, and the skills of researchers.

This Handbook is designed to address this lack of fit between the needs for better information on existing mental health policies and systems and the opportunities and limitations inherent in the existing body of mental health research. In both the case of mental health policies and research, this Handbook seeks to bridge considerations of what actually exists, and the associated processes for developing enhanced policies and more useful research. In both cases, a critical bridge between these domains consists of our evolving understanding of decision-making processes. A related theme is the need for multiple methodologies for research and policy development, especially the use of diverse perspectives and voices on the part of current and recovered patients, families, practitioners, administrators and policy makers, and the larger public.

This Handbook also examines mental health policy in an international context, one that is reflected in an emerging body of research in the field of global mental health.[1] This includes the completion of psychiatric epidemiology surveys in 28 of the nations participating in the World Mental Health Survey Initiative (see Kessler & Üstün, 2008). These studies have highlighted the high global burden of disease attributable to psychiatric, neurological, and substance abuse disorders, 14.7 percent by 2020 (Murray & Lopez, 1996). In total, neuropsychiatric conditions constitute the most important cause of disability across the world, accounting for 37 per cent of years lived with disability among those 15 and older (Mathers, Ezzqati, & Lopez, 2007). This research has also highlighted stark disparities between developed and developing nations, not only in terms of prevalence of major mental disorders (Kohn et al., 2004), but also in respect to access to services (see *World Health Report 2001*).

While much research on national mental health systems has been driven by calls for system development, there are some who are skeptical about the impact of well-coordinated and systematized services to enhance outcomes, believing that what is most important is instead the implementation of empirically based practice models at the local level, whatever the organizational context. One such research group is Rosenheck and his colleagues (2002) who examined 18 communities in the US, comparing the nine with integrated mental health authorities with those without. They found no evidence that efforts to better coordinate mental health services enhanced service outcomes. There were, however, limited statistical controls used in this research, and thus, the results should be regarded as, at best, suggestive.

Research on national mental health systems has been the exception and the results have unfortunately not been cumulative. A plethora of editorials on this research have been supplemented by case studies of single nation mental health systems and qualitative comparisons of two to five nations, with only an occasional descriptive study or quasi-experimental analysis. Editorials in psychiatric journals have often highlighted the dramatic disparities between the mental health systems of developed and developing nations. Discussions of the sparsity of resources in the developing nations repeatedly urge the need for better integration of mental health into the work of primary care medical practitioners, given the sparsity of mental health professionals in many such developing nations. Along these same lines is the recommendation for improved public education, more creative use of non-professional staff, and improved access to psychotropic drugs, all viewed as cost-effective measures. Comparative studies on a more favorable course of schizophrenia in developing countries (Hopper & Wanderling, 2000) have been interpreted as support for a more effective engagement of natural and family supports in these nations (Law, 1985). Finally, such editorials regularly urge more consistent and rigorous collection of data on epidemiology, services, and outcomes. Such commentators increasingly recommend more research on mental health systems, for instance, Minas and Cohen (2007) argue that "While mental health research attention and funds are devoted predominantly to neuroscience and clinical research, we believe that the highest global mental health research priority is mental health systems research."

Single and comparative national case studies date back many years, most notably to Donna Kemp's compendium, *International Handbook of Mental Health Policy* (1991). More recent studies such as Lurie's (2005) comparison of the systems in the UK, US, Canada, and New Zealand have highlighted themes of recovery, stigma reduction, developing services for particular client populations, for example, children and older adults, use of new technologies, workforce training, improved performance measurement and research. Increasingly, governments are no longer being expected to provide services, but rather to just fund and regulate them. A comparison (Liu et al., 2008) of the systems in Australia and China has highlighted the need for developing nations not to rely exclusively on institutional services, and to emulate those nations, such as Australia, which have moved more aggressively toward the creation of community mental health service systems. Particular barriers, relevant to China and many developing nations, include the lack of professionals and services in rural areas, in part, due to problems inherent in the poor economies of scale in service development in such environments. Just as is the case with the editorial literature, national case studies have not lent themselves to the development of a cumulative knowledge base, given the diversity of systems, issues, and data sources that they have examined.

PROBLEMS ADDRESSED BY MENTAL HEALTH POLICY

The policies reviewed in this Handbook represent a diverse array of responses to substantial levels of mental illness and disability in most countries, including substance abuse, and developmental disabilities. Mental illnesses occur around the world with substantial frequency. The World Health Organization (WHO) estimates that in 2019 approximately 970 million people world-wide have mental health conditions. Such conditions range from depression (more than

280 million people at any time) to schizophrenia (approximately 24 million people) (WHO, 2022). In the US, the National Comorbidity Study found that 46.5 percent of the adult population has had a diagnosable mental disorder at some point in their life, with 23.5 percent having such a disorder in the prior year. In addition, 5.3 percent has a serious mental disorder involving a significant level of disability.[2] Given such levels of need, there has been, at best, an uneven level of availability of services, both inpatient hospital as well as community mental health services. Gaps in community services involving emergency care, day programs, supported housing, and forensic services for mentally ill individuals involved with the criminal justice system are particularly acute.

Inadequate service coverage either leads to or exacerbates a range of problems involving unjust service disparities and inaccessibility, ineffectiveness, and lack of confidence both on the part of patients and the general public in the mental health system. Limited budgets undermine the implementation of evidence-based services, through low salaries, inadequate training, large caseloads, and scant staff supports. The presence of numerous service gaps, along with limited service effectiveness, generates a range of dysfunctional service patterns, with discontinuities between the various types of service modalities involving, on one hand, service gaps for those with the most severe needs, and on the other hand, duplication of services for patients who have greater resources. Some of the most important discontinuities involve traditional counseling services and physical health, substance abuse, and especially services involving concrete supports such as income, housing, employment, and training. In recent years, an increasing awareness of gaps in these areas has stimulated sporadic attempts to develop integrated services.

All of the above problems have eroded public confidence and, thus, political support for mental health services, undermining the ability of many jurisdictions to adequately budget for the required services. This problem has, in turn, been severely aggravated by that of ignorance and stigma associated with severe mental illness. Too often the attitude "Out of sight, out of mind" has led either to isolation in institutional services or to difficulties in developing community services located close to recipients' homes.

An important conflict affecting mentally ill persons is that between, on one hand, the pervasive individual focus of many mental health professionals who attribute mental illness exclusively to either psychological or biological breakdowns, and on the other hand, the results of hundreds of sociocultural studies which have documented the impact of low socioeconomic status, economic inequality, geographic isolation, and related conditions in generating and perpetuating disproportionate levels of mental illness (see Silva, Loureiro, & Cardoso, 2016). While it is still not fully understood what the respective roles are of social stress and social selection in explaining these effects, a growing consensus is that social stress and lack of social supports contribute substantially, although some individuals with the most severe conditions such as schizophrenia may be "socially selected" into impoverished conditions due to downward geographic and socioeconomic drift. For this reason, most mental health services are not designed to assist with concrete needs, whether they involve income, employment, housing, or education, that are central challenges for a substantial proportion of the mentally ill.

Development of policy responses to the foregoing problems are complicated by the fact that such problems are embedded in the perennial conundrums of social policy, those involving conflicts between competing social and philosophical positions for which there are no solutions that are optimal. A sampling of these is discussed below and illustrated in Figure 1.1, with the interconnecting lines indicating implications of how the solutions to each complicate the solutions to the others listed.

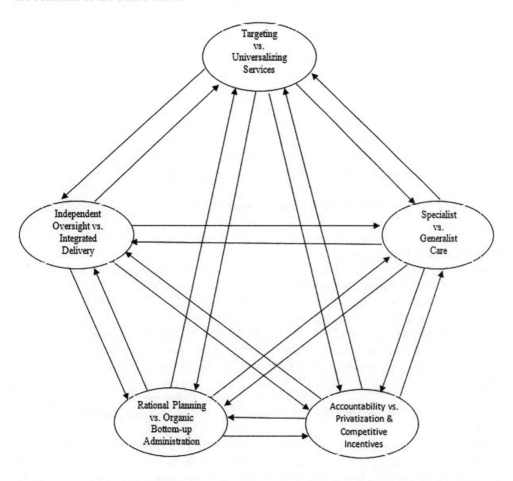

Figure 1.1   Examples of the perennial conundrums of social and mental health policy

Targeting vs. Universalization

Strong arguments can be made for targeting or restricting eligibility criteria for various mental health services to only those in greatest need, such as the seriously and persistently mentally ill (SPMI) who often cannot care for themselves, experience considerable levels of personal dis-tress, and for whom family ties often fall by the wayside. Limited resources are often cited as a key argument for such targeting. Yet, compelling arguments are also made for making access to such services as non-restrictive as possible, available to all in need, so as not to discourage the provision of support at early stages in the development of such conditions when there is a more favorable prognosis. It should not be necessary for clients to have total breakdowns before receiving services.

Specialist vs. Generalist Services

On one hand, the complexity of mental health problems calls for high levels of training on the part of mental health professionals requiring substantial specialization. Yet, it is well known that so many mental health clients are confronted by multiple, interlocking problems involving legal issues, housing, employment, social relations, and profound intrapsychic, biological, and neurological dysfunctions, all calling for the ability to skillfully orchestrate multiple interventions without overwhelming the client, based on a generalist or biopsychosocial perspective. There have been various efforts to reconcile these demands, for example, in social work's advanced generalist model of practice (Roy & Vecchiolla, 2004).

Rational Planning vs. Organic Bottom-up Administration

Mental health professionals are under considerable pressure to base not only their practice interventions but their agency service designs on the best available scientific results and to do this in a planful and systematic manner. Yet, the many limitations in both the availability and relevance of such results create pressures to involve many stakeholders in mental health decision making. Many decisions are often deferred or periodically updated, and often the strategy is one of an iterative or successive approximation to goal achievement. Such practices capitalize on a bottom-up emergent approach to decision making. The primary challenge in many contexts involves deciding on the best possible way of balancing and integrating rational planning methods with organic, bottom-up approaches, for example, through advocacy planning models.

Transparency and Accountability vs. Privatization and Competitive Incentives

Some service systems, especially those publicly operated, often optimize the transparent provision of information and public accountability through such means as freedom-of-information laws and advisory boards. In contrast, when services are contracted out or otherwise privately provided, the privatization of service delivery often minimizes such accountability, but maximizes professional autonomy. When financial or other incentives for productivity and outcomes are enhanced, transparency and public accountability may be further diminished. What the optimal balance is for public accountability and private autonomy and competition is by no means clear, and undoubtedly will vary between cultures and service systems.

Independent Oversight vs. Integrated Service Delivery

Whether one is concerned with a direct practice such as case management, or the design of service systems, an important decision involves the degree of independence of those who regulate or provide oversight to the services. For example, in certain models of case management, the case managers abstain from directly providing services, but instead focus on brokering and monitoring them, so as to oversee them as objectively as possible. In contrast, other models of case management encourage the case managers to provide counseling and various other services themselves so as to most effectively coordinate them and engage with clients who often have difficulty with split roles, referrals, and multiple providers. Again, the challenge is designing the system and professional roles in a way that optimally balances objective oversight with the need for client engagements and service integration.

How any of these conundra are resolved in a particular service system design both influence and are influenced by the resolutions of various related dilemmas. For example, strengthening integrated service delivery will create a pressure for generalist practitioners and more universal, less targeted eligibility criteria. Universalizing services in turn can lead to some fragmentation as diverse providers have the flexibility to skew their services – often unintentionally – to those problems and diagnoses that are well reimbursed, and avoiding those that are not. Such developments would then create pressure to identify parties and lead agencies that can provide systematic planning and independent oversight. In every case involving the conundra depicted in Figure 1.1, one can identify not only intended but unintended effects of any given solution. It is for this reason that the development of research-based solutions to such mental health policy problems requires a broad lens for their discovery.

As difficult as such conundra may be to resolve, there are both practical steps that are known for designing workable mental health policies for particular national or local environments, as well as recognized criteria for evaluating such solutions. One critical reminder is that such conundra can be understood as representing continua in which solutions can be integrated, and are regarded as matters of degree. Rarely do they represent either/or issues, but often may amount to both/and integrated strategies when creative and practical solutions are found.

Discovering these solutions requires moving beyond ideologically framed positions and grounding such plans on the results of actual research whenever possible. For example, in allocating resources between institutional and community services, what data can be marshalled to decide on the number of patients and service units, along with their particular needs, that will be needed for the types of inpatient and community services proven to be most efficacious? Guiding both the search for data, and its use in planning, are conceptual models of professional interventions and service system design. But most important is the need for engaging visions, derived from practitioners, consumers, and others as to what such services and systems would actually look like when fully implemented. With luck, exemplars may be discovered in other communities or nations, but when not available, the imagination of stakeholders will be particularly needed and should be unduly tethered to research and a variety of practical decisions.

Two other elements are also needed in such planning and development initiatives. One is confidence building, sometimes through incremental steps, so as to assure the continued involvement of such stakeholders in the process. Also, it is often important to plan ahead for periods of service innovation, and is particularly needed in the period between such planning initiatives when fiscal austerity prevails. One of many ways of doing this may be through a kind of preliminary identification or "stockpiling" of ideas, ready to go when new imperatives and resources emerge.

Both system design and the evaluation of particular services that have been implemented need to be guided by relevant and clear criteria. The literature on program and policy evaluation, both in mental health and beyond, has typically emphasized the importance of the various generic criteria listed in Table 1.1. Those selected for a particular initiative need to be defined and tailored to the relevant goals, values, and other features of the initiative, as well as being conceptually meaningful and measurable. For example, effectiveness for a day hospital program might be defined to include development of social and vocational skills, minimiza-

Table 1.1   Common criteria for evaluation of policies and programs

1. Accessible	Are the services provided in a manner that is maximally accessible, geographically, economically, linguistically, and socially to the target population?
2. Balanced	Does the mix of services correspond with the mix of needs in the population covered?
3. Client-centered	Are the client assessments and the services themselves oriented to client needs?
4. Comprehensive	To what extent does the policy address a range of needs?
5. Continuity of care	Are the provided services carefully linked together so that they assure seamless transitions for clients, as needed, between the most restrictive to the least restrictive?
6. Culturally sensitive	Is the design of the policies and program, and their management and delivery, done in a way that is sensitive to the various cultural groups involved?
7. Efficient and cost-effective	Is the system and its services managed in a way that makes the best possible use of available resources?
8. Effective	Do the services mostly succeed in achieving the goals sought, in resolving the problems addressed?
9. Engaged	Is the system and the component services delivered in a manner that attract and interest clients?
10. Equitable	Are the services provided in a fair and just manner, without favoritism, or consideration of irrelevant client characteristics such as race, age, gender, political or religious affiliations?
11. Individualized	Are the service plans tailored to the specific needs of individual clients?
12. Integrated	Are there effective provisions for coordinating services on the client, agency, and policy levels, both within the system, and with other service systems?
13. Responsive	Is the design of the system and its services flexible and adaptable to changing client and community needs and characteristics?
14. Science-based	Are the services provided based on the best available research data?
15. Transparent	Are policies, procedures, and relevant information concerning the system and its outcomes, both positive and negative, easily available to all interested?

Note: The above are a sampling (in alphabetical order) of the most important and commonly used criteria for the evaluation of mental health policies and programs.

tion of psychiatric symptoms, stabilization of functioning, finalization of housing arrangements, improved quality of life, or improved self-monitoring, or some combination. Selection of criteria is typically based on the most important legal mandates and official purposes of the services, as well an effort to address the interests of consumers, staff, and other stakeholders in the community. For this reason, it is important not to unduly restrict the range of criteria to only one or two, but conversely, not to be overly ambitious in attempting to satisfy a wide variety of criteria.

Clarity regarding criteria for the evaluation of policies and programs is of crucial importance in the development of solutions for the various conundra and problems reviewed above. Also, of central importance are the strategies that developers of mental systems can employ in this regard. Thus, we will now turn to discussing both generic strategies which have been used around the world, as well as ideas that should be considered in the mental health field.

POLICY DEVELOPMENT STRATEGIES

Efforts to improve public health programs have historically involved a number of strategies, ones that have been extensively reviewed elsewhere. Most notable is the review of Pallasa et al. (2012) of 181 studies that identified seven broad strategic domains of change: standards and guidelines; organizational structure and governance; human resource knowledge and skill; process re-engineering and technology development; use of incentives; organizational culture;

and leadership and management. Their identification of the pros and cons of such approaches forms the basis of their arguing for a prescriptive model for the selection of optimal strategies that is contingent on the answers to questions involving an analysis of the causes of performance deficits, feasibility and environmental fit, use of best practices, and organizational capability. Several of these involve the decentralization of decision making, which is a strategy that is increasingly used in contexts involving professional services. Decentralization often accompanies psychiatric deinstitutionalization and typically involves an expansion in the range of stakeholders such as community agencies, professionals, consumers, and families of the mentally ill who seek to influence the service delivery system.

In contrast, Bossert (1998) specifically reviewed research on decentralization in health care in developing nations. He draws on the traditional typology of types of decentralization used in public administration, which include deconcentration, delegation, devolution, and privatization, and focuses on the use of principle agent theory from econometrics, most commonly involving the application of financial incentives as a means for central public health administrations to retain some control over peripheral units or organizations within a newly decentralized service system.

Much of the existing theory and research suggests that the success of mental health reform initiatives hinges on the ability of a nation's mental health authority, such as a ministry of health, to navigate the complexities and tradeoffs involved in shared decision making under an increasingly decentralized structure. Within the mental health field, increasing attention has been paid to incorporating various models of shared decision making as a means of assuring maximal responsiveness to the needs of diverse constituencies (see Chapter 17 and Ramon, Zisman-Ilani, & Kaminsky, 2017). Strategies to improve decision making may focus on any of several system levels. A common focus has been one involving the relationship of mental health professionals and their clients revolving around intervention planning. But also, in many systems concerted efforts have been made to improve both administrative and policy decision making through enhanced involvement of clients and a range of constituencies, often through such mechanisms as advisory boards and the like.

Another strategy for the improvement of decision making has involved the long history of efforts to integrate research into both practice and policy (Brown, 2019). These have included requirements for needs assessments, program evaluations, and other forms of research. Such efforts have had a minimal level of success, too often resulting in merely including research into the rhetoric surrounding mental health programs. Research is expensive, and most mental health professionals are ill prepared to undertake it, and otherwise prioritize other activities as either more lucrative or ones that provide greater visibility. When quality research is produced, the challenge has been disseminating it, and finding the means to translate its results into practice. One means by which system-wide research has been promoted has been through the establishment of system-wide registries of mental patients and the services they receive. Such data depositories permit highly generalizable studies of a wide variety of patients and services, often over extended periods of time. Several European nations, such as Israel, have implemented such systems. In the US, the Commonwealth of Massachusetts utilizes an inpatient registry that is referred to as a casemix system. Such systems enhance the possibilities for public monitoring and integration of the mental health system, but even when they exist, they are often underutilized. Data from these systems are optimally suited to enable the development of easily used "report card" systems in which either mental health authorities or advocacy groups can benchmark and regularly rate various facets of the service system, such as its coverage, quality, effectiveness, and other indicators in a manner that is easily accessible and understood by administrators and advocates, thus enhancing its transparency.

There are a wide variety of strategies for using research in system development, and these range from improvements in training and workforce development, agency-level requirements, and funding and stimulating of independent research. An emerging area involves integrating research generation into computerized management and clinical information systems so as to partially automate its management, analysis, and report generation in real-time. One lesson that is often forgotten is the frequent admonition to involve mental health practitioners and all users in the design of such systems, as they are the ones who experience the greatest burden of data entry, accountability, and scrutiny. Academics have for many years now complained about the minimal efforts in these areas, but too often do not consider the social and cultural dimensions of research generation and use and the training and acculturation of many practitioners that mitigate against the conduct and use of research.

There are a variety of other strategies for system development that go beyond decision making, consumer involvement, and integration of research. There is an extended history of experiments with approaches to improved service coordination, too extensive to fully review here. One idea that was developed as part of the Community Support Program (CSP) in the US is that there should be three levels of interlinked service coordination. Client-level service coordination, involving coordination on behalf of a particular client, has often involved the work of case managers, but a variety of other professional practices have also been used for this purpose, such as regular staff meetings, team work, or clinical information systems for data sharing. Agency-level coordination includes efforts to coordinate both with an agency, between its staff and programs, and with other providers in the local community. Approaches used include interagency agreements, appointment of staff representatives to other agencies, and monthly meetings of representative staff and clients. Finally, policy-level coordination involves such efforts at the regional, district, state, or national level. Much of such efforts have been undertaken by funding and regulatory organizations, such as state or national mental health authorities or ministries of health.

Many of the policy-level coordinative efforts have been implemented via development and monitoring of regulations, and, especially, through funding. When such units provide funding, they have the option to capitalize on the incentives that such funding creates for providers, whether these involve the proverbial "carrot" or "stick." Economists have become increasingly interested in understanding such incentives, using what is known as agency theory (see Eisenhardt, 1989), in understanding how different types of funding mechanisms affect service provision. One insight that has come out of this field is that whereas funding that involves capitation, typically advanced fixed payments per person, often encourages service minimization, payment systems that involve set fees for particular service units, such as a hospital night, a course of ECT, or a psychotherapy appointment, paid after the service is delivered, have the effect of maximizing services, of encouraging providers to generate as many such payments as possible, whether or not needed. In reality, many systems employ complex hybrid funding models, sometimes with payment mechanisms with incentives that work at cross purposes with one another. Perhaps some of the most important lessons emerging from this experience is that funding and its resulting incentives need to be used judiciously, in a planned manner, in a way that minimizes extreme unintended consequences, preserves a needed degree of professional autonomy, yet is able to incentivize interagency and professional collaboration. On the organizational level, the use of salaries, supplemented by modest incentives, and on the system level, use of set grants and contracts, also supplemented by some incentives for quality, may be the most promising approaches to achieving such a balance.

Another finance strategy that has been periodically pursued is the establishment of funding systems that permit funds to flexibly "follow the client," whether he or she is hospitalized or is a recipient of community services. This contrasts with systems in which such services receive fixed allocations, thus, generating a system in which clients "follow the funds," in which they may typically be referred to the best funded services, whether needed or not. Client-level funding through various forms of insurance sometimes can achieve this, as long as the repertory of insurance benefits is comprehensive and well designed.

An increasingly popular strategy in many western nations has involved the privatization of services, especially community mental health services. This approach has been attractive to many public administrators as the contracting out of services to the public sector often proves to be less expensive, and to circumvent many regulations, including union protections of staff, common in services directly provided by public authorities. Such administrators see such purchase of service systems as providing them considerably greater flexibility in adapting services to local needs. Debates on the pros and cons of such approaches have been contentious and often ideologically driven, with limited data to enlighten such decisions. For this reason, mental health authorities need to pay considerable attention to the design of such systems, and to instituting a variety of protections and oversight mechanisms. A key principle is that services should only be privatized when such protections have been developed and when there is a sufficient body of agencies available that are fully competent in the services privatized. Such development is best accomplished in stages over several years, with public support with modest grants or contracts.

An ongoing problem in the development of mental health service systems is that of enhancing access to services. Some systems may have multiple points of possible entry in which clients can select from a wide range of providers. Such systems risk a lack of coordination, especially when there is insufficient information for clients to make prudent decisions. In contrast, other systems rely on a restricted array of entry points, perhaps a panel of assigned doctors, a case management program, or an information and referral unit. While such systems are better positioned to assure the coordination of services, they potentially complicate the effort of clients to freely access services. Critical is finding a balance of client freedom of choice with professional discretion, a balance that may vary in various cultures.

An alternative set of strategies seeks to improve mental health systems indirectly, through the development of better accreditation of agencies and licensing or certification of professionals. This often represents a bottom-up strategy in which resulting improvements on the micro or mezzo levels are expected to improve the larger policy systems. These kinds of improvements typically involve more stringent standards, or even higher levels of licensing that call for greater levels of educational preparation. A related strategy consists of the redesign of jobs so as to attract more qualified staff and minimize their burnout, ineffectiveness, and turnover. Sometimes such changes involve adding the possibilities for new service provision for professional groups which have not seen them previously, such as highly qualified social workers being permitted to engage in the private mental health practice, or nurse practitioners and doctoral-level psychologists being allowed to prescribe psychotropic medications.

PREVIEW OF HANDBOOK

These strategies, beginning with the integration of research in mental health policy making, will be explored in greater detail throughout the various chapters of this Handbook. Part II involves an examination of the conduct or process of research. Research examined will include its methodologies and their implications for administrators and policy makers tasked with translating the results into optimal practices, programs, and policies. Chapters about the process and conduct of research in Part II cover research formulation and planning, based on both theory and the needs of practitioners; qualitative methodologies, such as focus groups and concept mapping; quantitative studies, including epidemiological designs, and both quasi-experimental and experimental evaluations; and include one that introduces several state-of-the-art emerging methodologies. This will include the problem of adapting research to the needs of diverse populations based on such considerations as gender, race, ethnicity, and age.

Part III of the Handbook presents overviews of key research results that will be of interest to many students and professionals. The two initial chapters involve problems of disseminating and implementing research results, an area that that has come to be known as implementation science. These will be organized by system level, starting with research with children, the sociology of mental illness, and psychiatric commitment. An important focus of the chapter on children involves their inclusion in the formulation, design, and conduct of research and that of partnering with local communities in this regard. The chapter on psychiatric commitment cuts across large and small systems and involves mental health laws, for example, assisted outpatient treatment, the right to treatment and to refuse treatment, competency and guardianship, advanced directives, and privacy issues. The next chapter covers psychiatric deinstitutionalization, including both the driving forces behind such policies as well as their effects on service delivery. The remaining chapter in Part III covers some of the outgrowths of deinstitutionalization such as the recovery movement and psychiatric rehabilitation and several associated service models. Part IV then reviews some of the most important results of mental health research relevant to a sampling of nations and regions, specifically, Australia, Europe, Israel, the UK, and the US. It focuses on policy development in these areas and the research methods that are being employed to support these efforts.

Part V summarizes the Handbook and reviews the various cross-cutting themes and lessons from the preceding chapters. It concludes with several recommendations pertinent to both continued policy development and the research that is needed to support it.

NOTES

1. Parts of this section have been adapted from Hudson (2010).
2. Computed from US Comorbidity Replication Study, 2003, Longform data downloaded from Interuniversity Consortium for Social and Economic Research (October 2007). Retrieved August 13, 2022 from http://www.icpsr.umich.edu/CPES/

REFERENCES

Bossert, T. (1998). Analyzing the decentralization of health systems in developing countries: Decision space, innovation and performance. *Social Science & Medicine,* 47(10), 1513–27.

Brown, M. (2019). Constructing accountability: The development and delegation of outcome evaluation in American social work. *Social Service Review,* 93(4), 712–63.

Eisenhardt, K.M. (1989). Agency theory: An assessment and review. *Academy of Management Review,* 14(1), 57–74.

Hopper, K. & Wanderling, J. (2000). Revisiting the developed versus developing country distinction in course and outcome in schizophrenia: Results from ISoS, the WHO collaborative followup project. *Schizophrenia Bulletin,* 26(4), 835–46.

Hudson, C.G. (2010). A predictive model of the development of national mental health systems. *Journal of Mental Health Policy and Economics,* 13, 175–87.

Kemp, D., Ed. (1991). *International handbook of mental health policy.* New York: Praeger.

Kessler, R.C. & Üstün, T.B. (2008). *The World Health Organization mental health survey.* Cambridge, UK: Cambridge University Press.

Kohn, R., Saxena, S., Levav, I., & Saraceno, B. (2004). The treatment gap in mental health care. *Bulletin of the World Health Organization,* 82(11), 858–66.

Law, M. (1985). Mental health: A shared concern of the international community. *Canadian Psychology,* 26, 275–81.

Liu, T., Chee, N., Ma, H., Castle, D., Hao, W., & Li, L. (2008). Comparing models of mental health service systems between Australia and China: Implications for the future development of Chinese mental health service. *Chinese Medical Journal* (Engl), 121(14), 1331–8.

Lurie S. (2005). Comparative mental health policy: Are there lessons to be learned? *International Review of Psychiatry,* 17(2), 97–101.

Mathers, C.D., Ezzati, M., & Lopez, A.D. (2007). Measuring the burden of neglected tropical diseases: The global burden of disease framework. *PLoS Neglected Tropical Diseases,* 1(2), e114.

Minas, H. & Cohen, A. (2007). Why focus on mental health systems? *International Journal of Mental Health Systems,* 1(1), 1.

Murray, C.J. & Lopez, A.D. (1996). *The global burden of disease: A comprehensive assessment of mortality and disability from diseases, injuries, and risk factors in 1990 and projected to 2020.* Cambridge, MA: Harvard School of Public Health.

Pallasa, S.W., Curry, L., Bashyala, C., Bermanb, P., & Bradley, E.H. (2012). Improving health service delivery organisational performance in health systems: A taxonomy of strategy areas and conceptual framework for strategy selection. *International Health,* 4(1), 20–9.

Ramon, S., Zisman-Ilani, Y., & Kaminsky, E. (2017). Shared decision making in mental health. *Mental Health Review Journal,* 22, Special Issue (3), 149–51.

Rosenheck, R.A., Lam, J., Morrissey, J.P., Calloway, M.O., Stolar, M., & Randolph, F. (2002). ACCESS National Evaluation Team. Service systems integration and outcomes for mentally ill homeless persons in the ACCESS program. Access to community care and effective services and supports. *Psychiatric Services,* 53(8), 958–66.

Roy, A.W. & Vecchiolla, F.J. (Ed.). (2004). *Thoughts on an advanced generalist education. Models, readings and essays.* Peosta, IA: Eddie Bowers Publishers.

Silva, M., Loureiro, A., & Cardoso, G. (2016). Social determinants of mental health: A review of the evidence. *European Journal of Psychiatry,* 30(4), 259–92.

World Health Organization (WHO). (2001). *The World Health Report 2001 – Mental health: New under-standing, new hope.* Geneva: World Health Organization.

World Health Organization. [WHO]. (2022). Mental Disorders. Website: https://www.who.int/news-room/fact-sheets/detail/mental-disorders, last accessed 9/28/2022.

PART II

THE CONDUCT OF MENTAL HEALTH POLICY RESEARCH

2.   Formulation of mental health policy research problems
Christopher G. Hudson

The successful resolution of most problems requires the best information available. Likewise, the development of mental health policies requires thorough analysis that employs the most complete information possible. When such information is not available through easily accessible sources, new research is often needed, the usefulness of which critically depends on the quality of its initial formulation and design. This chapter on the planning of mental health policy research, which launches Part II of this Handbook, will therefore focus on its formulation or conceptualization involving decisions on the problems addressed and the aims of the research, and especially the specific questions or hypotheses and the dimensions for which understanding is most needed to facilitate policy development.

The relevant literature includes extensive work on both policy research as well as policy development. This chapter will review key ideas from this work and will focus primarily on its intersection, that is, on the formulation of research that is specific to mental health policy development and implementation. This will be done with the aid of several lenses. Both research and policy development are understood as intersecting decision-making processes, both formal and informal, on the part of individuals, groups, and institutions. Such decisions build on one another and typically intersect in complex and unpredictable ways. Thus, a central challenge is orchestrating the coordination of research planning and policy development, making sure that planned research is maximally attuned to the needs of policy development.

Orchestrating these diverse decision processes highlights the complexity of the tasks involved, which usually derive from the complexity of the underlying social problems and the history of the multiple attempts to address them. The scholarly literature has often described these problems as not only complex, but also as "messy," "fuzzy," or "wicked" (Mitroff & Featheringham, 1974; Mitroff & Mason, 1980). One of the implications of this is that both research and policy processes are best understood as approximately circular rather than as linear simple step-by-step protocols, and often resistant to clear definition. They often progress in parallel streams that are only loosely linked together.

Such complexity and uncertainty can be overwhelming for those involved. However, there are fortunately several key areas of intersection of these activities that highlight strategic opportunities for intervention. One involves the identification of "windows of opportunity," times during which policy development is moving ahead, or is expected to imminently and clearly demand the attention of researchers. The other is the possibility that insightful participants can analyze the relevant problems and systems and identify the salient points of overlap of stakeholders' motivations, opportunities to pursue them, and capacities that can be mobilized. This chapter will, therefore, begin by considering the role of research in mental health policy making, and continue from there to discuss the identification, definition, development, and theoretical refinement of mental health policy research questions. It will conclude with a brief discussion of several specialized techniques for accomplishing the foregoing.

THE ROLE OF RESEARCH IN POLICY MAKING

The academic literature includes extensive discussion, reviews, and research on how research is employed in the development of mental health and other types of social policies. Perhaps the most agreed upon observations are not only the importance of research in the development and evaluation of needed policies, but also the pervasive inadequacy of this linkage. Blame is cast on both researchers and policy makers. Much research may involve problems that policy makers are not interested in, it may be too technical or even "statistical" to be easily explained, poorly timed, or better suited for obscure publications. It may be overly descriptive, or, conversely, overly focused on advocacy for particular solutions without sufficient methodological rigor to elicit confidence in the results. On their part, policy makers may be more committed to satisfying powerful stakeholders, adopting fashionable fixes, advancing their careers, or more interested in "quick and dirty" data collection efforts, than in securing quality research.

Central to these mismatches are two critical issues. Most researchers are often trained to avoid normative questions involving what should be, and restrict themselves to describing what is. They may not be aware of the many ways that research can reveal the outcomes of past interventions, both the costs and benefits, and establish a firm foundation for decisions on needed and actionable interventions, as much as values and ethics may be the final lynchpins in such decisions. Along these lines, researchers need to carefully assess the state of knowledge in a given area, whether they need to focus more on understanding problems or if enough is known about the problems, on evaluating possible interventions.

How researchers handle these limitations and opportunities affects the roles they are able to play in policy making. William Dunn (1981) summarized two common perspectives regarding such roles. Many believe that researchers and policy analysts can merely function to rubber stamp decisions that policy makers arrive at through political means, a viewpoint known as the *technocratic counsel perspective*. On the other hand, Dunn points out that some believe that researchers can actually influence decisions as to needed policies, a viewpoint known as the *technocratic guidance perspective* (pp. 26–8). Both may be true in alternative contexts, depending on how controversial the particular policies may be and how skillfully the individuals involved manage the research-policy interface. Researchers can enhance their influence both by improving the quality and relevance of their research, and by better managing the dissemination and translation of their results and their relationship with policy makers. Yet, they need to recognize the diverse sources of information that policy makers use, and the many considerations that need to be taken into account in developing mental health policies beyond what their research can address.

Early in the formulation process, researchers need to carefully assess the policy-making landscape in the field of interest, both the existing and emergent issues that most need to be addressed, as well as decision making and institutional structures and stakeholders through which policy making and implementation occurs. The focus might be a local community and mental health board; a state mental health authority and its related stakeholders; or relevant national agencies, governmental branches, and associations. Are the target problems and policies primarily private, or ones that governmental agencies can best address, whether through executive, legislative, or judicial means? At the same time that researchers are reviewing the literature, writing proposals, and planning their studies, they must also be thinking ahead and assessing target audiences, and the needs and interests of particular policy makers.

The role of research in policy making depends on how both research and policy making are conceptualized. In both cases, these activities are often presented as single linear sequences of staged tasks. For example, policy development may be thought of as the sequence of agenda-setting policy formulation, adoption, implementation, and assessment. Yet, most commentators recognize that these are idealized or textbook explanations, with no shortage of obvious limitations. Somewhat more sophisticated models present these sequential tasks instead as circular, involving either a single or multiple feedback loops, perhaps involving the recognition that the successes and failures of prior policies determine in part the beginning of the next cycle of agenda setting and policy development. An even more complex rendition involves the idea that research and policy development happen not only in feedback cycles, but sometimes in independent streams, parallel or conflicting.

Before considering policy research specifically, we will turn to several of the ways that policy development is often conceived. Moloughney (2012) conducted a systematic review of frameworks of policy development and the extent of their use, informed by a body of empirical research involving mostly case studies. He argues that the possibility of using research in policy development requires an understanding of how such development proceeds.

The traditional approach, which he terms the "stages heuristic," involves the simple stages already noted: (i) agenda setting, often through public discourse and media; (ii) policy formulation, the identification and elaboration on key goals and options; (iii) policy adoption, whether through legislative action, or executive or judicial decrees; (iv) policy implementation, whether by public or private bureaucrats and service providers; and finally (v) policy assessment, both informal and formal evaluations.

The Institutional Analysis and Development Framework of policy development considers the successive interactions of both rational individuals and various material interests. The analysis of the many interactions typically involves: (i) the various stakeholders, either individuals or groups; (ii) the positions of power that such stakeholders occupy; (iii) allowable actions; (iv) potential outcomes; (v) levels of control that are available; (vi) existing information; and (vii) the costs and benefits of actions and outcomes.

A more nuanced approach is referred to as the Multiple Streams Framework, which was first introduced by Cohen, March, and Olsen (1972) as the "garbage can model of choice." It explains how policies are made under conditions of ambiguity, often in separate arenas or streams. For example, a problem recognition stream usually involves agenda setting, as well as fluctuation in attention given to changing issues. A policy stream typically includes various competing proposals. Their technical feasibility and popular acceptance increase the chance of their survival; however, ideas that do not align with prevailing ideological currents or those that are not engaging are at risk of floundering. A politics stream is often influenced by shifting public opinion, pressure-group campaigns and administrative/legislative turnover. A key notion is that policy choices are eventually made when the various streams involving problems, policies, and politics are coupled at critical windows of opportunity, which are also times when participants may be most open to relevant research results.

The Punctuated-Equilibrium Framework adapts a theory from evolutionary biology (see Eldredge & Gould, 1972) to understanding policy development. It involves the idea that development may plateau for extended periods, then suddenly proceed swiftly due to the convergence of multiple positive feedback loops, until it plateaus again. The sociologist Amitai Etzioni (1967) builds on this idea through his notion of Mixed Scanning, in which long periods involving the use of incremental decision making are periodically interrupted by a period of massive reform involving more rational and comprehensive approaches. Such possibilities, if and when they occur, suggest the importance of the preliminary preparation of research results ready for use when such a convergence of forces happen, often suddenly and unpredictably.

Moloughney (2012) also identifies the Advocacy Coalition Framework. This approach was developed to understand substantial conflicts involving policy goals, technical disputes, across multiple levels of government, especially when coalitions have developed between key stakeholders. It purposely avoids a linear description of the policy development process, and seeks to understand the interplay between cooperation and competition so common when multiple levels of government have shared responsibilities.

The case studies that Moloughney (2012) reviewed suggested that the multiple streams model may be the most commonly used approach. He emphasizes that once a problem is identified, it is important to begin with a descriptive analysis, before proceeding to explanatory analysis of causes and consequences. It also highlights the importance of tailoring any anticipated research to the perceived needs of policy makers, the stage or stages of development of the understanding of problems and policy options, and the presence of any windows of opportunity regardless of the particular developments in the policy environment.

Perhaps one of the more useful descriptions of the Multiple Streams Framework is provided by De Leeuw and Peters (2015) in an article in which they present key questions for incorporating health considerations in all policies. They outline a series of questions associated with the various traditional stages of policy development: defining the problem, evaluating existing policies, gathering information, establishing policy logic based on social determinants, development of alternatives, analysis of costs and benefits, assessment of power and interest landscape, consideration of political strategy, and planning of implementation. But instead of treating these in a simple sequential fashion, they use the metaphor of juggling to characterize these tasks as separate balls, the motion of each must be maintained in a coordinated fashion. Likewise, it may be assumed that researchers need to assess the state of motion of several of these balls, and decide on the most important contributions they might make in advancing the balls or tasks of interest.

Further direction for researchers in respect to influencing the policy-making process can be obtained by considering the wide range of reasons for conducting policy research. Those proposed are the following (CCD, 2021):

1. To show that there is a need for funding or intervention on a particular issue.
2. To show that a need or issue exists and to assure it is actually addressed.
3. To assure that what's addressed is, in fact, what needs to be addressed.
4. To support or discredit a specific method or practice.
5. To identify and advocate for an appropriate policy in a given situation.
6. To point out incompetence or corruption in government, business, or elsewhere that affects the public interest.
7. To protect the public health and safety.
8. To give yourself a solid base for advocacy.
9. To maintain your integrity and make sure that you're doing the right thing.

Each of these reasons, when applied to the field of mental health policy, suggests particular types of research, whether they involve needs assessment, program evaluation, or cost-benefit analysis, that researchers may wish to pursue.

Others have proposed alternative ways that research can influence policy making. Whiteford (2001) concludes affirmatively to his question, "Can research influence mental health policy?" He emphasizes the interaction of social filters, which inform the agenda-setting process, and issue entrepreneurs, who together produce patterns of problem definition. He notes the conflicts involved when these miss one another, for example, in debate about needle exchange problems to combat drug addiction. He concludes by noting that

> Policy development, adoption and implementation is often seen as a political and bureaucratic exercise. However research can impact on all these levels by providing options which are scientifically validated and data which allow decisions to be made more on the basis of fact and less on the basis of political expediency and ideology. In doing this it is necessary for the information to be available and communicated to the right people at the right time. (p. 433)

Other breakdowns in the incorporation of research into policy formulation are suggested by Clancy, Glied, and Lurie (2012) who identify four ways this can happen: researchers can fail to identify critical problems; research the benefits and harms of policy solutions; estimate the costs and consequences of policy proposals; or actively participate in the policy process to aid real-time decision making. They argue that simply producing rigorous and precise results about important problems is not enough to assure the successful use of research. Instead, they advise that policy researchers need to be informed by knowledge of the institutional context, and when they are, they will be much more likely to contribute to the policy process especially if they understand the environment in which they are working. Researchers, who spend time deeply immersed with policy problems and the policy process, are most likely to succeed in influencing policy.

Given such observations, a critical consideration for any researcher is his or her particular role, whether it be as an academic researcher in a university, an employee of an advocacy association, an analyst for an executive or legislative unit of the government, an independent researcher-advocate, or some combination. Each role is informed by varying levels of academic freedom, as well as alternative standards and expectations. Even though the academic researcher has considerable latitude in the choice of problems and methodologies employed, they may be constrained by the expectations of funders; their insulation from the policy process; and the particular theoretical lenses through which they view mental health problems and interventions. Likewise, those in all other roles have their own unique set of constraints and capabilities. For this reason, it is critically important that mental health policy researchers, whatever their role, develop active and collaborative relationships with those who work in alternative environments so as to effectively formulate the most needed topics, and decide on the best designs for their research.

IDENTIFICATION OF RESEARCH PROBLEMS

Decisions on the topics of mental health policy research derive from many sources. These range from the curiosity and personal issues of the researcher; the concerns of colleagues, students, and supervisors; to their assessment of the needs of the field, either in general or of the local providers, advocates, and other stakeholders with which the researcher is connected. As such, these decisions represent complex and dynamic processes, ones that are informed by observation and listening, reading, and often the results of preliminary studies. Examples of these can be small interview surveys, case studies, focus groups, or policy Delphi studies (which will be discussed in the conclusion to this chapter). At the root of all of such decisions is the imperative to conduct research that will be needed, that will have the greatest impact possible in improving the lives of people.

A wide variety of studies has been conducted with the aim of identifying what should be priorities for future researchers, a few examples of which will be discussed here. Zhou et al. (2018) reviewed 93 studies from the international mental health literature, ones that covered nine policy domains: service organizing, service provision, service quality, human resources, legislation and human rights, advocacy, administration, surveillance and research, and financing and budgeting. Whereas high-income countries (HICs) have built considerable knowledge bases in all of these domains, middle- and low-income countries (MLICs) have only started to do so since the 1990s. Whereas the main problems that HICs have focused on are primarily related to service organizing and provision, MLICs have been most concerned with financing and budgeting, administration, and human resources, all significant problems in these nations. For example, lack of funding in many MLICs was so severe that their formulation of mental health policies was contingent on international funding and its loss greatly impacted the sustainability of their programs. Zhou et al. (2018) conclude that "Global mental health policy developments present a process of diversification and enrichment. The process in HICs is long and incremental through centuries. Based on HICs' experience, MLICs have quickly developed mental health policies covering domains as comprehensive as HICs, in the recent three decades" (p. 6). They advise that future efforts are best aimed at assisting MLICs in developing their overall policies, as well as promoting the effective implementation, especially administration and staffing of programs in MLICs' local context.

In contrast, Townsend and his colleagues (2004) reviewed the literature and developed a template to guide the development of successful mental health policies. They also sought to validate this template through extensive consultations with experts in six World Health Organization (WHO) regions of the world. This framework builds on an earlier one proposed by Tansella and Thornicroft (1998) which involves a matrix model that outlines the key issues that need to be considered in planning and implementing services. This template is based on the identification of four domains:

1. **Context.** The Context domain describes the prevailing social, economic, cultural, and political contexts that impact on mental health and in which mental health policy is to be formulated.
2. **Resources.** The Resources domain includes all specific health and non-health elements that are inputs to the mental health system.
3. **Provision.** The Provision domain includes all mental health and related services that are or should be provided to the community in order to prevent and treat mental illness and promote mental health and well-being.
4. **Outcomes.** Outcomes are indicators of the impact of the mental health policy, system, or services applied at both individual and population level. Outcome measurement has the potential to provide policy makers with reliable data on the efficiency and effectiveness of services and interventions.

These domains suggest critical areas of mental health policy research that may focus on the preconditions or determinants, requisite resources or inputs, service and organizational processes, and especially the measurement of outcomes. The details and definition of these, and the particular questions and hypotheses, will be highly influenced by the history and current aspirations of key stakeholders in each context.

DEFINING RESEARCH PROBLEMS

Ideas for topics for research usually start out vague and excessively broad. These topical phrases – such as schizophrenia, effectiveness of psychotherapy, adjustment of adolescents, or impact of mental health parity – need to eventually be formulated as more specific problem statements. Problem statements, typically either a sentence or a short paragraph, encapsulate the aim, central question, and/or the overall issue of an anticipated project, and sometimes, the major dimensions and delimitations of the study. Problem statements may be presented formally, but more often they are integrated into the introductory content of research proposals, reports, and empirical articles. An example of a problem statement for a mental health policy research project is as follows (Hudson, 2020, p. 15):

> the current project aims to develop international benchmarks on optimal levels of inpatient care that not only incorporate such [international] data but are also comparable to results developed by previous researchers, who have in recent years used alternative methodologies. Specifically, this study employs predictive analytics (Finlay, 2014) for the purpose of identifying useful benchmarks for needed levels of inpatient psychiatric care on a national level.

Definitions of research problems commonly proceed from such topical phrases, to problem statements, and listings of more specific questions and hypotheses, along with conceptual and operational definitions of the key terms used in the foregoing. This process, sometimes referred to as operationalization, is often contingent on the completion of considerable literature review, and perhaps consultations with others, and even preliminary studies. Researchers are often reluctant to formulate questions and definitions that depart dramatically from what is already being used in the field. Considerable value is placed on extending the knowledge-building efforts initiated by earlier researchers, to confirm or test, or even invalidate prior results, or investigate the extent to which such results can be generalized to new groups not yet studied. In addition, the extent that the researcher departs from definitions already developed and widely used will severely limit the degree to which results from diverse studies can be compared and aggregated, whether these involve definitions of populations, problems, or interventions.

Depending on the level of prior knowledge development, the problem statement may be elaborated into a set of more detailed questions or hypotheses. If not much is already known, often open-ended questions are preferred, such as: What are the major pathways by which mentally ill individuals become homeless? In contrast, a more specific question might be: To what extent have young mentally ill homeless individuals (age 18–35) previously been involved with a foster care system that did or did not provide transitional services? For studies that focus on correlation and causation, and seek to quantify such relationships, the custom is to orient the research around specific hypotheses, such as, "It is hypothesized that the provision of discharge planning from psychiatric hospital care that adheres to professional standards will enhance community adjustment and minimize the likelihood of rehospitalization." While specific definitions and hypotheses are an invaluable guide to useful research, they are not always possible, and much valuable exploratory research can still be conducted even when one begins with only difficult to define concepts, such as consciousness, stigma, or support. Careful research may succeed in identifying the key dimensions, and perhaps even definitions and questions involving such concepts.

Commentators have provided no shortage of advice on the process of research definition and operationalization. It has been advised that research questions should not have one-sentence or factual answers, contain a lot of proper nouns, have a single correct answer, and focus on overly specific measures or indicators of a concept. Others advise that they should eschew terms such as "should" and "ought," and also avoid overly broad unanswerable questions, yet not be so specific as to minimize the possibility of generalizing results. In many ways, research definition is as much an art as a science, and should always consider questions of, so what? Problem definition represents the first part of research operationalization or the development of research problems, to which we will now turn.

DEVELOPING RESEARCH PROBLEMS

Defining questions, hypotheses, and their terms, as important as this is, leaves many questions unanswered. These involve both conceptual issues as well as those involving research design or the logic by which the questions will be answered or the hypotheses tested. Key decisions involve the level or the aim of the research, whether it will be primarily Exploratory, involving an effort to identify key variables, develop theories, or decide on the direction of future research; Descriptive, focused on describing the parameters of some phenomenon, numbers of people involved, their circumstances and experiences; Quasi-experimental, to approximate experiments and answer correlational questions through higher level surveys or longitudinal studies; or Explanatory studies, designed to test hypotheses regarding causation, either the causes or the consequences of some phenomenon, service, or policy outcome, often through experiments or other studies involving random assignment.

In the later instances, it becomes increasingly critical to define the intervention and outcomes of interest. Unless one fully defines the intervention, it will not be possible to be sure that any benefits or other outcomes detected are in fact due to the intervention. An important decision involves the specificity of this definition, whether it will involve an entire program or package of interventions, or some particular method or technique used as part of a program. Both possibilities present challenges and considerable benefits if an adequate design can be found for it.

A very difficult set of decisions involves the outcomes or dependent variables to be explored, described, or evaluated. Will the project focus only on the official or formal outcomes sought, perhaps sobriety in a program involving substance abuse? Or, will it also examine surrounding benefits, often sought by staff, clients, or families, perhaps involving social functioning, quality of life, or insight? One way to flexibly capture the most important outcomes is to evaluate the attainment of whatever goals that the worker or team agree to work on with the client. Too often neglected is an effort to understand any negative effects and costs of an intervention, whether they involve further breakdowns, financial costs, stigma, or undue loss of liberty. Other decisions, ones involving research design, include the length of the follow-up period. Whereas the urgency for obtaining results may require only an immediate post-test after receipt of the services, responsible evaluations of services and policies involve medium and long-term follow-up and data collection anywhere from three to six months, to many years after the completion of the intervention.

Other key design issues need to be initially addressed at the stage of problem formulation. A very important one involves who the data will be collected from, that is, clients, staff, administrators, or others? Critical issues in this regard include privacy matters and the question of who can most reliably and validly provide the needed information. When possible, researchers increasingly like to take a multi-method and a multi-perspectival approach and consider the viewpoints of multiple stakeholders. But in doing so, they are often confronted with difficult problems of how to integrate the diverse sources of information collected. Whereas workers are often quite positive about their efforts, clients are often more critical of their actual goal attainment, even while they may be appreciative of staff efforts to assist them. Some instruments are designed with parallel versions for various parties, for example, the Child Behavior Checklist has similar versions for children, parents, and teachers.

Early in problem formulation, researchers need to review prior research and theoretical literature on their topic from the relevant academic and professional literatures (see Galvin, 2013), including government documents and the "gray" literature of unpublished memoranda and other materials. This serves multiple purposes, namely, to properly situate the anticipated research within the body of knowledge already developed and to identify questions that have yet to be answered. Previous research reports will contain invaluable information on methodologies which have been productive, on instruments that have proven reliable and valid, as well as identifying important variables and their definitions that the planned research may do well to incorporate. There are various types of reviews, some of which may represent separate preliminary studies. At the most basic level is the thematic literature review in which the researcher develops a narrative describing the existing literature and its most salient themes and findings, along with a critique of the strengths and weaknesses of the main studies reviewed. It is particularly important in such reviews that they are focused primarily on material relevant to the questions, variables, and methods of interest. Such reviews are increasingly being viewed with skepticism because of their inherent subjectivity and questions about how the various studies might be interpreted and weighted, especially when they are not in agreement.

Increasingly, researchers are using a more structured approach, involving specific standards, to conduct systematic reviews in which the various relevant studies are formally compared with one another, often using various tabular presentations (see Muka et al., 2020). A more sophisticated form of review may include the results of a meta-analysis in which the reported statistical indices from multiple studies are analyzed in aggregate, so as to generate inferential statistics on the generalizability of the overall or aggregated body of results (see Wolf, 1986). A considerable body of work has employed such methods, with specialized techniques developed to control for possible sources of bias, such as the file drawer effect involving the non-publication of non-significant results. And only rarely is it possible to actually combine the raw data from multiple studies, in what is called a mega-analysis, to arrive at an aggregated analysis of the data from the various studies considered. This typically requires the use of the same measuring instruments in each of the included studies. Some reports may include a combination of thematic and systematic reviews, and perhaps meta- or mega-analyses.

As noted earlier, those who seek to develop and elaborate their problem formulation must juggle a number of balls, including input from policy makers, the review of the literature, arrangements with funders, the securing of permissions from human subjects committees, and making initial decisions about what may be required from a research design perspective. Throughout this process, the researchers need to also analyze their own positionality, that is, the ways that their background and biases may skew their framing of the problem and decision regarding the design. Walt et al. (2008) specifically urge that

> Greater reflexivity on the part of researchers, that involves an analysis of their own institutional power, resources and positions (in much the same way they would analyse actors in the policy process) and their role in defining research agendas and generating knowledge (rather than assuming themselves to be "objective" and "independent"). Greater attention to policy research team composition and roles, including insiders and outsiders, which can relate to nationality but also to multiple roles. (p. 315)

THEORETICAL REFINEMENT

Central to both the formulation of the problem statement and the review of the literature is an examination and decisions about any theory that is relevant to the project. Not all mental health policy research projects involve theory, especially those which are exploratory or descriptive. However, if relevant theory can be identified, the capacity to generalize the findings, and to integrate them with the wider body of work on the subject is greatly enhanced. When little is known in advance about the subject of the envisioned research, it is sometimes the case that the best the researcher can do is to take an exploratory approach, so as to inductively derive needed principles and theories to guide policy research and development. Yet, for most research topics relevant to mental health policy there is a considerable body of theory available, whether it is formal academic theories, or informal theories of the researchers or policy developers. Seeking to validate hypotheses derived from such theories, and even to falsify them, provides an invaluable check on pre-existing biases and a restraint on the tendency to post hoc fit conclusions to such biases (see Popper, 1935). While there are some who minimize the importance of theory in policy research (Thyer, 2001), increasingly commentators advise integrating theory with policy and practice research, so that truly theory-free research may be an impossibility (Marsh, 2004).

The first step in the use of theory in mental health policy research involves its critical review. Although some researchers are not explicit in naming any theory used, often they will identify it at least in passing, or discuss it informally, sometimes in terms of global frameworks such as "empowerment," "participation," or "systems." Essential in the consideration of key theories for a particular project is an adequate summary of them. This will at a minimum include a description of the theory's assumptions, its central concepts, and the various propositions that link these concepts. There is a considerable diversity of opinion in the literature as to the appropriate criteria to be used in such a critical review of theory. Some of the major criteria include the following (Hudson, 2010, pp. 113–15):

1. Its underlying values
2. Relevance or potential usefulness
3. Comprehensiveness
4. Clarity and coherence
5. Reasonableness
6. Parsimoniousness
7. Empirical basis

8. Explanatory ability
9. Predictive ability
10. Heuristic value

Whereas examples of theories that inform micro-level mental health research are plentiful, and involve such fields as psychoanalytic theory, cognitive and behavioral approaches, humanistic and positive psychology theories, macro-level theories are not used as frequently. Examples of these include agency theory from economics, various sociocultural theories from sociology, theories of reasoned and planned action, and a range of political and economic theories of decision making. Rather than simply using some global framework or perspective, such as ecological or psychoanalytical theory, to "dress-up" a research proposal or report, much more useful is the decision to use a specific model, perhaps one derived from a global framework or other broad theory. Such models not only represent operationalized applications of the framework as it applies to a particular phenomenon or problem, but often provide specific testable hypotheses to guide the research. Many such models are graphically illustrated through path diagrams. When it is used, theory is too often employed merely as a general guide to research, and as a way of conferring legitimacy to it and aiding in the interpretation of the results. However, a far better use of theory in research takes place when it is possible to actually test the theory, especially as a whole, and in relation to other competing theories that are relevant to questions of need and of mental health service and policy effectiveness.

SPECIAL TECHNIQUES

In addition to the standard approaches to formulating and designing research projects, involving literature review and consultation, researchers and policy developers will sometimes employ specialized techniques, perhaps as discrete preliminary projects. These are often best undertaken by collaborations of researchers and policy makers and their staff. Examples include the following:

1. **Exploratory studies** can take many forms, commonly case studies, small interview studies of 10–30 knowledgeable individuals, perhaps consumers, providers, or policy makers. These may be conducted by phone or in-person, supplemented by document analysis. Participant observation studies are sometimes conducted that could involve researchers taking part in day programs, activities of homeless individuals, or legislative sessions. Another example involves the content analysis of textual material, perhaps comments of families of disabled children who participate in online discussions (see Mills, Durepos, & Wiebe, 2010). Chapter 3 will discuss qualitative and exploratory methods in greater depth.
2. **Listening Projects** often involve policy makers meeting, in-person or in-group, with a wide range of constituents to hear their concerns regarding issues of interest to them (see Mullen, 2016).
3. **Focus Groups** consist of small groups of 5–20 individuals who are brought to together to participate in moderated conversions, guided by general questions designed to probe for the participants' underlying thinking regarding any expressed needs or concerns that the moderator manages to elicit. Such groups are often used in need assessment studies (see Kitzinger, 1995).

4. **Concept Mapping** employs a wide variety of techniques with small conference-sized groups to aid in the identification of key concepts as well as the comparison and contrast of the key concepts. The participants are often either policy makers, providers, or academics. It is designed as a strategy not only for identifying the concepts, but understanding how the chosen experts understand and interrelate those concepts. Such exercises are usually conducted in multiple stages, and employ various graphical devices and computer programs to tabulate and present the system of concepts that is identified (see Trachim & Kane, 2005).

6. **Policy Delphi** studies employ a systemic set of procedures to anonymously elicit feedback from a panel of identified experts regarding some need, intervention, or issue, usually in two or three stages. At the end of each stage, the feedback of the experts, both of a structured and qualitative type, is anonymously summarized and provided to all the other participants who then, in the next stage, are invited to update their ratings and feedback on the matter of concern. Through repetition of such steps, the goal is to develop a consensus among the experts, one that is not influenced by the social standing of the participants or of personal considerations that may cause some to be unduly positive or negative regarding the feedback provided. The final stage may be an open presentation of the final results and discussion (see Niederberger & Spranger, 2020).

The results of such preliminary studies are often presented in reports or published articles and used to design larger-scale policy research projects, often ones that seek to quantify key relationships that have been provisionally identified. If the focus involves a policy or program evaluation of outcomes, the results of such studies may also be used to formulate logic models that seek to systematically and graphically interrelate the inputs, intervening processes, and outputs of a program so as to guide both the implementation of the program and the selection of variables for its monitoring and evaluation.

CONCLUSIONS

The challenges of formulating and designing mental health policy research are compounded by diverse considerations related to policy development and the range of mental health problems that need to be addressed. Because of the diversity of considerations, and the various decisions involved, regarding overall aims, topics, questions and hypotheses, variables, theories to be used, and research strategy, it is rarely possible to proceed with these in a simple linear fashion. Rather, work must often be undertaken in parallel streams, in a way that is akin to juggling, with multiple feedback loops included. Particularly important is the need for researchers to include policy makers and implementors, and especially key stakeholders such as consumers, in such tasks, and learn of their needs and perspectives regarding the anticipated research. Throughout this process, problem definition and development, including decisions about use of theory, are of central importance. In many respects, the process is also driven by what the researcher will learn as part of the review of the existing research and professional literature. Orchestrating these multiple tasks of conceptualization, literature review, research design, and consultation with policy makers and stakeholders demands considerable skill of the researcher who is forced to function as both a scientist and artist.

REFERENCES

Center for Community Development (CCD). (2021). Chapter 31, Section 10. Understanding the policy making process. University of Kansas. Retrieved June 28, 2021 from ctb.ku.edu/en/table-of-contents/advocacy/ advocacy-research/influence-policy/main

Clancy, C.M., Glied, S.A., & Lurie, N. (2012). From research to health policy impact. *Health Services Research*, 47(1 Part 2), 337–43. https://doi.org/10.1111/j.1475-6773.2011.01374.x

Cohen, M.D., March, J.G., & Olsen, J.P. (1972). A garbage can model of organizational choice. *Administrative Science Quarterly*, 17(1), 1–25.

De Leeuw, E., & Peters, D. (2015). Review: Nine questions to guide development and implementation of Health in All Policies. *Health Promotion International*, 30(4), 987–97. https://doi.org/10.1093/heapro/dau034

Dunn, W.N. (1981). *Public policy analysis. An introduction.* Englewood Cliffs, NJ: Prentice-Hall.

Eldredge, N., & Gould, S.J. (1972). Punctuated equilibria: An alternative to phyletic gradualism. In T.J.M. Schopf (Ed.), *Models in paleobiology* (pp. 82–115). San Francisco: Freeman Cooper. Reprinted in N. Eldredge, *Time frames* (pp. 193–223). Princeton, NJ: Princeton University Press, 1985.

Etzioni, A. (1967). Mixed-scanning: A "third" approach to decision-making. *Public Administration Review*, 27(5), 385–92.

Galvin, J.L. (2013). *Writing literature reviews.* 5th ed. Glendale, CA: Pyrczak Publishers.

Hudson, C.G. (2010). *Complex systems and human behavior.* Chicago, IL: Lyceum Books.

Hudson, C.G. (2020). Benchmarking psychiatric deinstitutionalization: Development, testing, and application of a model through predictive analytics. *Best Practices in Mental Health*, 16(1), 13–32.

Kitzinger, J. (1995, July 29). Qualitative research. Introducing focus groups. *BMJ: British Medical Journal*, 311(7000), 299–302.

Marsh, J.C. (2004). Theory-driven versus theory-free research in empirical social work practice. In H.E. Briggs & T.L. Rzepnicki (Eds.), *Using evidence in social work practice: Behavioral perspectives* (pp. 20–35). Chicago, IL: Lyceum Books.

Mills, A J., Durepos, G., & Wiebe, E. (2010). *Encyclopedia of case study research* (Vols. 1-0). Thousand Oaks, CA: Sage Publications.

Mitroff, I.I., & Featheringham, T.R. (1974). On systematic problem solving and the error of the third kind. *Behavioral Science*, 19, 383–93.

Mitroff, I.I., & Mason, R. (1980). Structuring ill-structured policy issues: Further explorations in a methodology for messy problems. *Strategic Management*, 1, 331–42.

Moloughney, B. (2012). *The use of policy frameworks to understand public health-related public policy processes: A literature review final report.* Peel Public Health, October, 1–61. Retrieved August 13, 2022 from https://www.peelregion.ca/health/library/pdf/Policy_Frameworks.PDF

Muka, T., Glisic, M., Milic, J., Verhoog, S., Bohlius, J., et al. (2020). A 24-step guide on how to design, conduct, and successfully publish a systematic review and meta-analysis in medical research. *European Journal of Epidemiology*, 35(1), 49–60.

Mullen, F. (2016). The community listening project. The Catholic University of America, Columbus School of Law.

Niederberger, M., & Spranger, J. (2020). Delphi technique in health sciences: A map. *Frontiers in Public Health*, 8, 457. https://doi.org/10.3389/fpubh.2020.00457

Popper, C. (1935). *The Logic of scientific discovery.* London: Hutchinson. English translation of *Logik der Forschung*, Vienna: Springer.

Tansella, M., & Thornicroft, G. (1998). A conceptual framework for mental health services: The matrix model. *Psychological Medicine*, 28, 503–8.

Thyer, B.A. (2001). What is the role of theory in research on social work practice? *Journal of Social Work Education*, 37(1), 9–25. https://doi.org/10.1080/10437797.2001.10779034

Townsend, C., Whiteford, H., Baingana, F., et al. (2004). The mental health policy template: Domains and elements for mental health policy formulation. *International Review of Psychiatry*, 16(1–2), 18–23. https://doi.org/10.1080/09540260310001635069

Trachim, W., & Kane, M. (2005). Concept mapping: An introduction to structured conceptualization in health care. *International Journal for Quality in Health Care*, 17(3), 187–91. https://doi.org/10.1093/intqhc/mzi038

Walt, G., Shiffman, J., Schneider, H., Murray, S.F., Brugha, R., & Gilson, L. (2008). "Doing" health policy analysis: Methodological and conceptual reflections and challenges. *Health Policy and Planning*, 23(5), 308–17. https://doi.org/10.1093/heapol/czn024

Whiteford, H. (2001). Can research influence mental health policy? *Australian and New Zealand Journal of Psychiatry*, 35(4), 428–34. https://doi.org/10.1046/j.1440-1614.2001.00919.x

Wolf, F.M. (1986). *Meta-analysis. Quantitative methods for research synthesis*. A Sage University Paper, No. 59. Beverly Hills, CA: Sage Publications.

Zhou, W., Yu, Y., Yang, M., Chen, L., & Xiao, S. (2018). Policy development and challenges of global mental health: A systematic review of published studies of national-level mental health policies, *BMC Psychiatry*, 18(1), 1–9. https://doi.org/10.1186/s12888-018-1711-1

3.   Qualitative and exploratory methods in mental health policy research
Hugo Kamya

The conduct of mental health policy research ought to be seen in the general context of research. Such context involves the formulation of a research problem, the methodologies used in examining a research problem, the strategies for the dissemination and application of policies, and inherent ethical issues. Several approaches abound in the conduct of mental health policy research. These approaches include traditional quantitative methodologies, and qualitative and exploratory methods among new and emerging research strategies.

This chapter will explore some qualitative and exploratory methods in the conduct of mental health policy research. Qualitative inquiry needs to be seen in context. The chapter begins by highlighting the definition of qualitative research and anchoring qualitative research in key paradigms of inquiry. It will then discuss the epistemological understandings that undergird qualitative research. These will include philosophical approaches that support qualitative research. The impact of qualitative research and its ability to transform the view of the world's problems will be discussed. The chapter then explores what researchers think about, and the participation of consumers in the doing of research. The importance of context when cultivating knowledge and designing interventions with gang affiliated adolescents will be explored. Finally, the chapter asks what is missing and examines the challenges and vicissitudes of doing qualitative research. When might one want to use qualitative methods exclusively or in conjunction with other methods as part of a strategy involving mixed methods or triangulation? If, and when, qualitative methods are used as part of a larger mixed methods strategy, how might the differences in results be integrated or reconciled, if at all?

PARADIGM OF INQUIRY: POSITIVISM, REALISM, AND CONSTRUCTIVISM

Research is often anchored in theoretical lenses from the social sciences. Guba and Lincoln (2005) define paradigm as an overarching model that guides theory, research, and professional practice. Broadly defined, it is a philosophical or theoretical framework or lens. It is a set of fundamental assumptions that influence how people think and how they perceive the world. Guba and Lincoln (2005) propose five paradigms of inquiry: positivism, postpositivism, critical theory, constructivism, and participatory.

Positivism, realism, and constructivism are three major theoretical lenses or interpretative frameworks. Most writing on qualitative inquiry is situated in a constructivist paradigm. While this is true, it is important to note the differences and similarities within these three paradigms. The differences help to illustrate key theoretical underpinnings.

Positivism has its roots in the Enlightenment, a time period that heavily emphasized science and the notion that humans could possess "right" and fixed knowledge such as absolute truth and facts (Kovach, 2015). Realism asserts that there is no absolute truth, or pure foundation of knowledge. Rather, knowledge is ever-evolving and unfinished (House, 1991). Constructivism holds that individuals' knowledge of the world is informed by their observations and experiences of the contexts in which they live, and that this knowledge is subjective (Creswell & Creswell, 2017).

Positivists believe there are truths that are uninfluenced by culture, or contextual experiences (Kovach, 2015). Realists believe that there are endless intricacies and complexity as realism relates to knowledge and the world. As research is completed, the knowledge that is accumulated generates more questions and unknowns to be further explored (House, 1991). Constructivists believe that reality is relative and local, and emphasize open-ended questions specific to individuals' own life experiences, the social context in which they exist, and on culture and values (Staller, 2012).

Positivism is highly aligned with the scientific method and employs the use of close-ended questions, looking for absolute truth in knowledge (Creswell & Creswell, 2017). Realism contends that knowledge and truth are informed socially and through history; however, knowledge can be furthered by developing and testing theories through rational methods and critical reasoning (House, 1991). Constructivism puts emphasis on participants' views, and participants' meaning-making, which is formed through interactions, experience, and respective cultural norms and practices (Creswell & Creswell, 2017).

Positivist researchers use theory as a starting point, and then use deductive reasoning to attempt to prove or disprove the theory through the scientific method and hypothesis testing (Ravitch & Riggan, 2016). Realism also employs deductive reasoning, asserting that the task of research is to suggest theories of how the world works, in which theories should then be tested through scientific reasoning. No "proof," however, is forever set in stone, and theories can be further challenged (House, 1991). Constructivism uses inductive reasoning, where researchers accumulate observations of subjects and patterns to develop a theory, rather than using a theory as a starting point (Creswell & Creswell, 2017). Positivist researchers do not consider the social or cultural environment of the researcher as it relates to what is being researched. In positivism, there is a focus on operational definitions, objectivism, and little room for individualized variance based on context (Staller, 2012).

While researchers consider their own experiences of reality and knowledge-making, realism does not emphasize researcher bias. Instead, realism pushes the researcher to ask more questions, and conduct further observation, to get closer to underlying patterns and causations (House, 1991). Researchers informed by the constructivist worldview are mindful of their own background, biases, and culture, and how these elements interact with and relate to what is being researched (Staller, 2012).

Creswell and Poth (2018) propose the use of a transformative framework that goes beyond postpositivism (p. 25). Building on Mertens' (2003) work, they note that a transformative framework acknowledges that knowledge is "not neutral and it reflects the power and social relationships within society" (Creswell & Poth, 2018, p. 25). Qualitative research is seen as containing an action agenda for reform of people's lives. Similarly, any policy research ought to further this action agenda for the peoples who are affected by the policies that are enacted. Such policy research therefore attends to examining issues such as oppression, inequity, alienation, isolation, and discrimination. Ultimately, policy research attends not only to addressing injustices but also creating opportunities for those that these policies affect. Within these interpretative frameworks are pragmatic approaches that examine what is useful, practical, and what works. They also include critical theory, critical race theory, feminist theory, queer theory, and disability theory. These theorists engage in an inquiry that interrogates the status quo. These interpretative frameworks build on various forms of data that acknowledge differences, contexts, social justice issues, feminist views, class, gender, race, racism, and power, an invitation to engage in decolonizing ideologies (Smith, 2021).

Philosophical Assumptions

The interpretative frameworks must be understood in the context of philosophical assumptions. These assumptions include ontology, epistemology, axiology, and methodology as key premises used in the interpretative frameworks for qualitative research. Qualitative inquiry as it relates to mental health policy research asks ontological and epistemological questions: What is real? How is reality defined? These questions reveal that reality is in a dynamic state of flux. To capture what is real one must engage a framework that values process and immersion as reality is understood and as it unfolds. This assumption underscores the fact that there are multiple realities. Different researchers seek to capture reality from multiple perspectives. While psychometricians seek to measure reality, experimentalists seek to control it, interviewers ask questions about it, observers watch it, statisticians count it, evaluators evaluate it, and qualitative inquirers find meaning in it.

At an epistemological level, qualitative inquirers ask about what constitutes knowledge. How is knowledge defined and how does one know? In the case of mental health policy research, questions as to how we know what we know provide deep insight in the construction of meaning and developing a policy. They also inquire about how policy makers know what they know, raising even more questions. Is seeing enough? Is acquaintance alone knowledge? What are the requirements of knowing something rather than just believing it? Indeed, what research supports policy stances that ultimately affect people's lives? Why do some policies have a longer lifespan than others? Subjective knowledge constitutes a major contribution to the subject of knowing.

A key epistemological need in mental health policy research is the examination of ways of knowing that highlight subjective and local knowledges. Attention to subjective and local knowledge raises even more questions. How is knowledge known? How might the type of research speak to the extent of involvement of different parties involved in the research? This assumption becomes crucial especially in working or doing research with indigenous populations. Mental health policy research therefore needs to attend to the subjective experiences of those for whom it serves. Field studies and explorations seek to address near experiences for those who are studied.

Beyond ways of knowing, mental health policy research ought to acknowledge that research is value laden (Creswell & Poth, 2018). Owning and identifying researchers' positionality that recognizes the standpoints of such policy research is key. Positionality takes into account history, context, and social location, as well as their changing nature. Mental health policy research must take into account an analysis of values to better understand the meanings, characteristics, origins, purposes, and influences of people's daily experiences. All of these contribute to the construction of knowledge.

It is not enough to name these viewpoints. The perspectives and standpoints of mental health policy researchers need to be closely interrogated and scrutinized. It is best that the conduct of research engages a critical inquiry that interrogates what research has previously been done: Whose interests have been attended to? What contexts have been engaged? Responsible conduct of research must continually ask what is missing. Such interrogation must examine common sense understandings that are associated with those issues. For example, one might want to examine common sense understanding or taken-for-granted ideas around policies that address gangs, maternal health, immigrant children, policy makers' response to research. Similarly, any policy research needs to deconstruct the hegemonic processes that have characterized previous research. It is most effective to include the voices of the parties involved. This raises the question of who speaks for whom and how marginalized voices find spaces to be heard. Any mental health policy research needs to center the particular ways of knowing, doing, and valuing that which connects to those who are to be affected by the policies. Through it all, such policy research ought to consider social, historical, and political contexts which shape the lives and experiences of the people involved. Ultimately, the importance of decentering dominant voices and allowing the centering of marginalized voices cannot be overstressed. Decentering hegemonic voices in mental health policy research is key.

Creswell and Poth (2018) highlight the importance of contextualizing research in global and international contexts. They underscore the importance of seeing method as process and theory as product. They also highlight the importance of interrogating the logic of inquiry and the philosophical stances used. They caution about viewing approaches as fluid, interactive, and open ended. This is important in doing policy research. Any policy research cannot be seen as an end in itself. It also means noting different ways of collecting data and engaging in inquiry.

Policy research needs to engage a social justice inquiry lens. Such attention to social justice sharpens the scope of inquiry and constantly calls into sharp focus issues of justice, fairness, equality, equity, individual and collective rights and obligations. Such research aims at building good societies and creating a collective sense of responsibilities. Constructs of power are constantly interrogated. All in all, it is best when policy research attends to the local voices of those affected by the policies. It is effective when it attends to local knowledges, data and cultural contexts. These contexts also need to be seen as constantly changing and evolving.

COLLECTION OF DATA IN QUALITATIVE INQUIRY

The collection of data in qualitative inquiry is key to research. Qualitative researchers build complex and holistic pictures through the analyses of words and reports of participants. Ethnographic studies, case studies, and grounded theory provide methodological approaches to the collections of data. Other approaches include narrative, phenomenological studies, constructivist studies, and participatory action research. Tesch (1990) notes four ways of categorizing qualitative research based on the continuum from highly structured and concrete to less structured and interpretive. These include how language is characterized, how patterns and regularities are analyzed, how meaning and action are comprehended, and finally how reflection is expressed.

Crabtree and Miller (1992) categorized qualitative approaches based on the methods embraced. They include quasi-statistical methods, template approaches, editing approaches, and immersion approaches. Qualitative inquiry relies on observation and data collection and yields conclusions based on data collection. According to Crabtree and Miller (1992), qualitative inquiry seeks to enter into the subject's insider position. The insider position provides added value to policy research especially in such cases when little is known about the subject or when the topic of inquiry requires sensitivity and greater emotional depth, to capture the "lived experience" of subjects and to merge advocacy with research through participatory action research. While a lot is known about mental health there is still a paucity of knowledge on the manifestation of mental health among different populations. The questions that surround different mental health issues among alternative populations suggest a careful analysis of those issues as they relate to those populations to address their lived experiences. Such attention bears witness, brings forth subjected knowledges and silenced voices, paving a way to generate and disseminate new and useful knowledge and to create policies that represent those populations. Attention to the formulation of the research question is key. It drives the paradigm of inquiry and fuels the methodological approaches to data collection and analysis leading to the interpretation of how the analysis answers the overall question.

It is important to decide on appropriate data to collect. Such data may include live individual interviews, focus groups, documents, artifacts, videos or photographs, observations and field notes, online data, and secondary data. Representation using purposeful sampling is important. Creswell and Poth (2018) provide a typology of sampling strategies in qualitative inquiry. Types of sampling include: maximum variation, homogeneous, critical case, theory based, confirming or disconfirming cases, snowball or chain, extreme or deviant case, typical case, random purposeful, stratified purposeful, criterion, opportunistic, combination or mixed, convenience (Creswell & Poth, 2018, p. 159). For mental health policy research, sampling can co-occur with data collection. Beginning with a broad and open approach, relational sampling can be done to allow concepts to emerge. Cases are sought to explore variation, co-occurrences, patterns and exceptions. This is key especially among populations where voices have been silenced or marginalized. Finally, discriminate sampling helps to confirm or disconfirm categories and relationships to support or challenge viewpoints. The adequacy of a sample occurs when no additional data are needed to capture participants' experiences and meanings. Achieving this point of saturation requires a researcher's utmost patience.

The ethics of conducting research with vulnerable populations cannot be overstressed. Indeed, mental health policy research compels researchers to protect participants from the abuses of power related to research, while including them as experts of their stories.

MENTAL HEALTH POLICY RESEARCH: THE CASE OF GANG-INVOLVED ADOLESCENTS

This section explores research with gang-involved adolescents as a key example of qualitative mental health policy research. This includes the problem of adapting research to the needs and views of gang-involved adolescents. An important theme in this section involves the inclusion of consumers in the formulation, design, and conduct of research and that of partnering with local communities in this regard.

Background: The Importance of Context

Like many stigmatized groups, gang-affiliated adolescents have been largely homogenized within the context of research, programming, and policy development in the United States (Hughes, 2005). "Street gangs" in America date back to the end of the Revolutionary War, and since that time have shifted in reputation, patterns of behavior, and nature of membership

(Flores, 2016). Beginning in the 1980s, the United States has seen a surge in gang prevalence, and gang-related crimes – including drug sales, assaults, robberies, homicides, with the recent increase in the availability of firearms (Flores, 2016). Over the past four decades, quantitative research approaches have driven the collection of gang-related data, yielding staggering numbers related to prevalence, crime, and incarceration rates. These findings circulate in the public discourse, and contribute to the dominant narrative about the nature of gang-involved youth (Flores, 2016). For many reasons, it is challenging to capture accurate statistics on the prevalence of active adolescent gang members in the United States; however, most recent statistics from federal data suggest there are an estimated 850,000 adolescent active gang members across primary urban cities in the United States, with approximately 90 per cent of active members identifying as male, and 83 per cent identifying as Latino or African-American (Egley, Howell, & Harris, 2014). Perhaps just as staggering are the rates of traumatic exposure, mental health disparities, and barriers to successful de-affiliation and reintegration seen amongst gang-affiliated adolescents (Quinn et al., 2017).

It is important to deconstruct gang membership, examine risk factors associated with adolescent gang affiliation, and explore the influence that gang affiliation is seen to have on adolescent mental health – which perpetuates systems of violence, traumatization, and ultimately, the marginalization of this vulnerable population. Qualitative approaches to examining gang membership will be reviewed for strengths and limitations, and the ways that qualitative inquiry engages research findings, dissemination, and influence on public discourse will be explored. Through the consideration of a cornerstone qualitative research study, the discussion will explore best practices for working with gang-affiliated adolescents, and discuss how findings from research on best practice techniques can support future practice and policy formation. Furthermore, ethical considerations that must be considered when working with gang-affiliated adolescents will be discussed (Quinn et al., 2017).

Adolescent Gang Involvement

Research regarding adolescent gang affiliation repeatedly finds that adverse childhood experiences, particularly traumatic exposure, are among the leading risk factors for future affiliation (Quinn et al., 2017). For adolescents, a history of violent victimization and future delinquency are mutually reinforcing, and many findings regarding cycles of violence and intergenerational trauma support the relationship between youth victimization and future perpetration (Loeber, Kalb, & Huizinga, 2001). This relationship is compounded and often strengthened by other risk factors such as conflictual family dynamics, low socioeconomic status, prevalence of community violence, and perceptions of school and other social spaces as being "unsafe" (Quinn et al., 2017). Research suggests that the highest-risk youth show "stepping stone" patterns of behavior from ages as young as 3–4. Such behavior is classified as "conduct issues," followed by school-based challenges, and "delinquency" around the onset of 12 years old (Howell & Egley, 2005). Within the context of trauma theory, each of these behaviors is understood to be indicative of childhood exposure to trauma – particularly, hyper-arousal symptoms, reactivity, and limited development of internalized self-soothing strategies (Herman, 2015). Frequently, existing systems respond to such behavioral challenges, particularly when exhibited by African-American children, with punitive and further marginalizing responses (Fenning & Rose, 2007). Examples of this are particularly evident within the context of school systems, where the most vulnerable students – affected by factors such as sexual orientation, race, and socioeconomic status – are pushed from public mainstream institutions to underfunded, and underperforming, alternative schools at a greater rate than white-identifying peers (Mizel et al., 2016). These punishment-oriented systems perpetuate existing stereotypes, disadvantages, and isolation from pro-social supportive structures, which are noted to contribute to the risk factors for potential gang involvement (Mizel et al., 2016).

In studies examining mental health among gang-involved youth, poly-victimization – the experience of two or more types of trauma – is found to be uniquely associated with the development of ongoing, profound mental health challenges, particularly post-traumatic stress disorder, depression, and anxiety (Quinn et al., 2017). Behavioral implications associated with traumatic exposure often serve as a barrier for gang-affiliated adolescents to engage with pro-social systems such as education or vocational opportunities, which, if accessed, would serve as protective factors from further entrenchment and victimization (Nydegger et al., 2019).

When considering the influence of chronic traumatic exposure, and the associations between trauma and delinquency and future exposure to violence, it is unsurprising that longitudinal research suggests that adolescent gang affiliation frequently leads to prolonged delinquent behavior, and cyclical affiliation with gangs throughout early and middle adulthood (Pyrooz et al., 2016). Retraumatization throughout the life course has lasting psychological, spiritual, and biological impacts on gang-affiliated adolescents, and the intrapsychic effects of chronic traumatization are compounded by the predominant discourse which conveys demonizing and homogeneous messages about gangs and those affiliated (Nydegger et al., 2019). Many of these messages have been informed by statistics from quantitative research approaches, which yield data regarding crime, violence, drug sales, imprisonment, and recidivism (Hughes, 2005). However important, this knowledge derived from standard quantitative research is critically disconnected from knowledge gained from qualitative research – which tends to provide a more comprehensive story about the origins, activity, and experiences of gang-involved adolescents.

Disconnects between Qualitative and Quantitative Research

During the surge of gang activity seen in America during the 1980s and 1990s, a wide range of quantitative studies were conducted in attempts to better understand factors associated with gang involvement (Hughes, 2005). An analysis of quantitative research shows that such research methods often involve surveying law enforcement officials, reviewing court documentation, and self-report samples from involved youth. Language throughout surveys is seen to center on terms such as "violent," "delinquent," "criminal," "antisocial," or "drug activity" when characterizing a group of majority Black or Hispanic youth (Hughes, 2005). In addition, quantitative studies have also been successful in identifying trends of risk factors that are specific for gang-affiliated adolescents, such as family composition, economic circumstances, and experience with the education system (Thornberry & Krohn, 2003). However, quantitative methodologies typically fail to capture holistic nuances regarding the environmental context which may have led to affiliation, which cannot be accounted for numerically. Quantitative approaches have been critiqued as creating a misleading, stereotype-reinforcing image of gangs, reflected and reinforced by racist practices in the criminal justice system (Hughes, 2005). This concern is evident in Klien's reflection of programming efforts when working with gang-affiliated youth in Los Angeles (Hughes, 2005). Klein noted that prevention and reformation programs have been largely ineffective, particularly when workers assigned to programs spent little time in direct contact with involved youth, and when community support for programming was lacking. These limitations are driven by inadequate time being spent centering programmatic work on the initiative, input, and experience of those directly involved. These programs' inadequacies of capturing effective and comprehensive knowledge about a subject parallel the limitations of quantitative research as it relates to gang activity, as methodologies of gathering information often fail to understand, and honor, the complexity of the dynamics of gang-related activity – and the interacting contributions that lie beyond the bounds of what can be reported uniformly through measures (Hughes, 2005).

Qualitative, or mixed methods research approaches, do not dispute quantitative research findings that display the disproportionate numbers of gang-related crime, when compared with non-affiliated adolescents. However, the approaches and methodologies applied provide a larger, more subjective understanding of the push and pull factors involved in highly nuanced and complex situations (Hughes, 2005). By engaging in research practices that reduce the distance between researcher and participant, using environmentally and historically informed frameworks, qualitative research can drive efforts to combat existing and marginalizing perceptions through the proper analysis and denomination of findings in a way that centers on the formation of more suited prevention and treatment interventions, as opposed to control-oriented and legal interventions (Hughes, 2005).

Qualitative approaches, including ethnographic studies, in-depth interviews, and field studies, have yielded results which explore the daily realities of adolescent gang members, and portray gangs differently from what has been historically depicted in research and the dominant narrative (Hughes, 2005). Qualitative studies are found to indicate that many aspects of gang life and activity are in fact "ordinary," and reflect behavior expected of an adolescent peer group, with pockets of violence and antisocial behavior, which by and large are not representative of the general functioning of gang affiliation.

Qualitative Study, Benefits of Utilizing Semi-structured Interviews

A qualitative study, completed by Quinn et al. (2019), was conducted to examine adolescent gang members' "lived experience," prior to affiliation. Results from this study exemplify the strength of qualitative research and its propensity for gaining the facts that researchers are interested in, as well as the contextual underpinnings necessary for a comprehensive understanding of topics, particularly as they relate to vulnerable populations. In Quinn's 2019 study, 58 semi-structured interviews were conducted with male and female-identifying adolescent gang members. Two researchers – one who identified as an African-American woman and one a Latino male – completed the interviews. The interviews were conducted in a community-based setting, and lasted between an hour and an hour and a half. The setting, and time duration of each interview, honor the importance of participants feeling comfortable, in their own space and community, and provide an amount of time to generate a natural flowing conversation. Interview questions included information about family history, drug and sexual risk behaviors, experience with violence, and future aspirations (Quinn et al., 2019).

The findings of the study were deeply personal, and spoke to the complex and cumulative traumatic experiences of the adolescent participants. Clear themes arose throughout the research, such as adolescents' feelings of having limited choice in affiliating, informed by the economically deprived, disenfranchised, and often violent communities where they lived. For many, there was a belief that through affiliation, they would be offered protection and support that was often lacking in their homes, school systems, and communities at large. Consistently, adolescents spoke of their exposure to community or domestic violence prior to affiliating, and ongoing exposure throughout their years of affiliation, as violence was frequently utilized as a way to prove loyalty, and avoid retribution. When asked about their future, teens struggled to envision a path for themselves that did not involve an early death, or incarceration (Quinn et al., 2019). Findings from the semi-structured interviews, when considered through a developmental and trauma-informed lens, speak to the perpetuating influence of violence and trauma, which is particularly profound during adolescent development (Herman, 2015). This knowledge provides context, and greater understanding of the challenges that adolescents face prior to gang affiliation, as well as the vulnerabilities that lend themselves to affiliation, and how the perceived and actual threats to safety make it challenging to disaffiliate – particularly in the absence of supportive protective factors.

The findings from this study promote the use of semi-structured interviews as a best practice methodology for working with gang-affiliated youth. A semi-structured interview format allows researchers to keep within the scope of their research intention, and this structure is understood to provide a sense of safety and containment for those being interviewed, while permitting enough flexibility to establish an authentic, and dynamic conversation with the research subject (Biddle et al., 2013). Participants of this study have been affected by varying forms of violent, interpersonal, systematic trauma. The implications of this chronic exposure on the ability to form trust is profound. In spite of this, researchers were able to establish enough of a rapport, in a relatively short period of time, to engage in a conversation that was highly vulnerable and personal. Throughout Quinn's findings, there was a breadth of information gathered, and excerpts from dialogue showed that researchers never imposed their own understanding or knowledge onto participants being researched (Quinn et al., 2019).

Through respecting the adolescents involved as the experts of their own lives, channels of communication were opened that otherwise may not have been – and rich findings are evidence of this. Findings from this study speak to the power of a trauma-informed semi-structured interview as an effective qualitative approach that has the capacity to effectively engage vulnerable populations in a way that encourages respect, and yields results that can be directly utilized for practice and policy formation to better serve gang-affiliated adolescents. For ethically sound research involving gang-involved youth, this is imperative.

Implications for Dissemination and Application

The research study presented above is thematically similar to other qualitative semi-structured interview studies that have been conducted with gang-involved youth. As a whole, qualitative findings offer rich implications on the micro and macro levels (Raymond-Flesch et al., 2017). Research findings honor the individual's experience, and can deconstruct the homogenizing and criminalizing implications which can be deduced from statistically driven quantitative findings, which, by not providing personal context, run the risk of legitimizing stereotypes that typecast gang-involved adolescents as "dangerous" and in need of legal disciplinary responses. Furthermore, findings reveal how limited safe options serve as a massive barrier to de-affiliating from gangs.

When considering where research findings should be disseminated, it is important to think of the communities that are most affected by the social determinants of health identified as contributing to risk factors for adolescent gang involvement (Quinn et al., 2019). In addition, spaces that serve youth and families, such as pediatricians' offices, community health care centers, schools, and recreation spaces, should be informed of risk factors for children they serve. The importance of available and responsive programming, especially during the developmental period from childhood to adolescence, is necessary to provide opportunities for pro-social engagement, through the development of social networks in safe, responsive, accessible spaces – where mastery as it relates to developing strengths can be formed. The accessibility of such programming is rare in systematically disenfranchised communities, and noted to be one of the greatest challenges for children and families (McKenzie et al., 2013).

Perhaps equally as important as preventive strategies are the use of participants' responses from qualitative research to inform reintegration programs. By specifically speaking to gang-involved adolescents about environmental factors that contribute to their perceived, and actual, limited alternative options to continued affiliation, existing programs can be enhanced, and future programs developed specifically to address these needs. It is understood that by taking these steps to extrapolate key findings to build programs, possibilities would open up for gang-involved adolescents that have the possibility to change the trajectory of their lives – and have cascading effects on circles of influence, families, and communities at large.

Experience of Gang Members Using Mental Health Services and Navigating Service Systems

Multiple factors serve as barriers to accessing mental health services, particularly for marginalized communities. The influence of social determinants of health as factors that disproportionately undermine the health and wellbeing of marginalized communities frequently serve as a barrier for accessing services, with similar intensity the need for services they create (Armstead, Wilkins, & Nation, 2021). Multiple interacting forces, such as economic instability, access to education, neighborhood composition, and discrimination, have cascading effects on inequalities, and profound implications on the mental health of those living in disenfranchised neighborhoods (Reiss, 2013). For children and adolescents, parental involvement is a protective factor associated with assisting adolescents in connecting to treatment facilities. For gang-involved adolescents, family dysfunction and limited parental support have been identified as a pertinent risk factors (Quinn et al., 2017). Considering this, gang-involved adolescents may not have parental support to aid them in accessing treatment. This has implications for different modalities that treatment can make accessible, for example, embedding services into accessible systems such as school facilities (Green, Dvorsky, & Langberg, 2020). In addition to parental involvement, information for accessing available programs and treatment facilities is often not readily available, difficult to find, and challenging to navigate – particularly for proven-risk youth, whose "behavior," or in some cases the presence of previous criminal charges, may make them ineligible for protective programming and services (Knight et al., 2018).

In addition to barriers, stigma around receiving mental health treatment, particularly for adolescents whose identity is informed by group membership, is a considerable barrier. Christine Crawford, of McLean Hospital, discusses the additional stigma faced by communities of color in discussing and receiving support as it relates to mental health challenges. Crawford suggests that this stigma has historical roots, and can be traced back to slavery and its offshoots – and the disavowment of African-American's experience of depression, post-traumatic stress, and anxiety (Crawford, 2021). The intersectionality of race, socioeconomic status, gender, and ethnicity, all must be considered when thinking about where and how research findings would be of the most benefit for gang-affiliated adolescents.

ETHICAL CONSIDERATIONS

In the United States and in many other parts of the world, there has been a considerable history of egregious unethical research, at the expense of marginalized populations. Civil rights violations in the infamous Tuskegee experiment brought to attention the need for specific consideration of ethical research principles, such as informed consent, remaining mindful of coercive processes, and constantly analyzing risk-benefit ratios (Shivayogi, 2013). Such history must inform work related to mental health policy, particularly when considering the particular sensitivity of working with vulnerable populations. In clinical research, the term "vulnerable," in the context of research subjects, includes children, prisoners, pregnant women, and persons who are handicapped, mentally disabled, economically disadvantaged, or educationally disadvantaged (Ruof, 2004). For the purposes of working with gang-involved adolescents, particularly youth involved with the criminal justice system, considerations about their mental health disparity, and potential education and/or economic disadvantages, need to be considered.

Additionally, while using the proposed best practice of semi-structured interviews, it is important to consider how interviews may take a turn to probe areas that were unexpected at the forefront of the interview. For this reason, it is challenging to get a full informed consent prior to the beginning of the interview. Through the consideration of the sensitive nature of many adolescent gang members' personal histories, it is important to remain mindful of the potential emotional harm that interview questions could induce. However important this is to consider, research suggests that the therapeutic benefit to youth from sharing stories through research interviews outweighs any potential harm (Corbin & Morse, 2003). Lastly, it is important to consider the beneficence principle, which asserts the importance of maximizing the benefits for participants involved in the research process (Pieper & Thomson, 2016). This principle is paramount when working with gang-affiliated youth, and informs what should be done with research findings as it relates to practice and policy formation that is responsive to the stated needs of adolescent gang members – their personal needs, their families' needs, and their communities.

VALUING QUALITATIVE INQUIRY IN POLICY RESEARCH

It is important to ask not only what works but what works for whom and under what circumstances. Qualitative inquiry offers a great entry in answering this question. It attends to the participants' lived experiences and promises to honor those lived experiences. Lived experiences help bridge the gap between the nature of research evidence and goals of research versus the insider's knowledge, especially as it affects vulnerable populations. Qualitative research methods help to address the disconnect between the goals and language of policy makers and researchers. Such inquiry attends to data quality which includes data collection, measurement, and analysis. Participant responses provide important information that can contribute to making evidence-based research more accessible to policy makers. Qualitative inquiry also facilitates understanding between researchers and relevant stakeholders about research methods, standards for interpretation of research-based evidence, and its use in evaluating mental health policies. It also invites researchers and policy makers to keep asking the question: What is missing? Indeed, when all is said and done, how might people's lives, especially vulnerable populations, be improved?

CONCLUSION

When might one want to use qualitative methods exclusively or in conjunction with other methods as part of a strategy involving mixed methods or triangulation? If, and when, qualitative methods are used as part of a larger mixed methods strategy, how might the differences in results be integrated or reconciled, if at all? The choice of qualitative methods may be driven by a number of things including how much is known about a topic. Mental health policy research can be complex. Sometimes, little is known about a topic. Some topics require sensitivity and emotional depth. There are topics that require entering into the "lived experience" of the people affected. To understand policy, one might need to get on the inside of practice, programs, and interventions. In some cases, to merge advocacy with research through participatory action research one might need to use qualitative research. One might need to use qualitative inquiry when other methods, such as quantitative research, have reached an impasse.

A choice for a method might need to examine the purpose of the inquiry, the questions to guide the inquiry, the data to illuminate the inquiry and the resources available to support the inquiry. It is best then to triangulate the data from all available sources. In doing so, qualitative inquiry in mental health policy research seeks to bear witness, bringing forth subjected knowledge and silenced voices. Such an approach then seeks to describe, understand, tell and generate new and useful knowledge. But there are challenges too. To do this, mental health policy researchers need to be willing to immerse themselves, use themselves, and deal with risk and ambiguity, while maintaining ethical boundaries and owning their reflexivity. Ultimately, it is best if mental health policy research is related to the people who are being affected, is connected to the culture and wellbeing of those people, and to the struggle and issues of justice that affect those populations.

REFERENCES

Armstead, T.L., Wilkins, N., & Nation, M. (2021). Structural and social determinants of inequities in violence risk: A review of indicators. *Journal of Community Psychology, 49*(4), 878–906. https://doi.org/10.1002/jcop.22232

Biddle, L., Cooper, J., Owen-Smith, A., Klineberg, E., Bennewith, O., Hawton, K., Kapur, N., Donovan, J., & Gunnell, D. (2013). Qualitative interviewing with vulnerable populations: iIndividuals' experiences of participating in suicide and self-harm based research. *Journal of Affective Disorders, 145*(3), 356–62. https://doi.org/10.1016/j.jad.2012.08.024

Corbin, J., & Morse, J.M. (2003). The unstructured interactive interview: Issues of reciprocity and risks when dealing with sensitive topics. *Qualitative Inquiry, 9*(3), 335–54. https://doi.org/10.1177/1077800403009003001

Crabtree, B.F. & Miller, W. (1992). *Doing qualitative research.* 2nd ed. Sage Publications.

Crawford, C.M. (2021). *How can we break mental health barriers in communities of color?* Retrieved November 26, 2021 from https://www.mcleanhospital.org/essential/how-can-we-break-mental-health -barriers-communities-color

Creswell, J.W., & Creswell, J.D. (2017). *Research design: Qualitative, quantitative, and mixed methods approaches.* 5th ed. Sage Publications.

Creswell, J.W., & Poth, C.N. (2018). *Qualitative inquiry and research design: Choosing among five approaches.* 4th ed. Sage Publications.

Egley, A. Jr., Howell, J.C., & Harris M. (2014). Highlights of the 2012 national youth gang survey. *OJJDP Juvenile Justice Fact Sheet.* Retrieved November 26, 2021 from http://www.ojjdp.gov/pubs/ 248025.pdf

Fenning, P., & Rose, J. (2007). Overrepresentation of African American students in exclusionary discipline: The role of school policy. *Urban Education, 42*(6), 536–59. https://doi.org/10.1177/ 0042085907305039

Flores, E. (2016). The history of street gangs in the United States: Their origins and transformations. *Contemporary Sociology, 45*(6), 751–3. https://doi.org/10.1177/0094306116671949x

Green, C.D., Dvorsky, M.R., & Langberg, J.M. (2020) The impact of social determinants of health on the efficacy of school-based interventions for adolescents with ADHD. *School Mental Health, 12*(3), 580–94. https://doi.org/10.1007/s12310-020-09367-w

Guba, E.G., & Lincoln, Y.S. (2005). Paradigmatic controversies, contradictions, and emerging con-fluences. In N.K. Denzin & Y.S. Lincoln (Eds.), *The Sage handbook of qualitative research* (pp. 191–215). Sage Publications.

Herman, J.L. (2015). *Trauma and recovery: The aftermath of violence – from domestic abuse to political terror.* Basic Books.

House, E.R. (1991). Realism in research. *Educational Researcher, 20*(6), 2–9. https://doi.org/10.3102/ 0013189X020006002

Howell, J., & Egley, A. Jr. (2005). Moving risk factors into developmental theories of gang membership. *Youth Violence and Juvenile Justice, 3*(4), 334–54. http://dx.doi.org/10.1177/1541204005278679

Hughes, L. (2005). Studying youth gangs: Alternative methods and conclusions. *Journal of Contemporary Criminal Justice, 21*(2), 98–119. https://doi.org/10.1177/1043986204272875

Knight, A., Maple, M., Shakeshaft, A., Shakehsaft, B., & Pearce, T. (2018). Improving the evi-dence base for services working with youth at-risk of involvement in the criminal justice system: Developing a standardised program approach. *Health & Justice, 6*(1), 8. https://dx.doi.org/ 10.1186/ s40352-018-0066-5

Kovach, M. (2015). Emerging from the margins: Indigenous methodologies. In L. Brown & S.S. Strega (Eds.), *Research as resistance.* 2nd ed. (pp. 43–64). Canadian Scholars' Press.

Loeber, R., Kalb, L., & Huizinga, D. (2001). Juvenile delinquency and serious injury victimization. *OJJDP Juvenile Justice Bulletin.* Retrieved from https://www.ojp.gov/pdffiles1/ojjdp/188676.pdf

McKenzie, T.L., Moody, J.S., Carlson, J.A., Lopez, N.V., & Elder, J.P. (2013). Neighborhood income matters: Disparities in community recreation facilities, amenities, and programs. *Journal of Park and Recreation Administration, 31*(4), 12–22.

Mertens, D.M. (2003). Mixed methods and the politics of human reseatch: The transformative-emancipatory perspective. In A. Tashakkori & C. Teddlie (Eds.), *Handbook of mixed methods in social & behavioral research* (pp. 135–64). Thousand Oaks, CA: Sage Publications.

Mizel, M.L., Miles, J.N.V., Pedersen, E.R., Tucker, J.S., Ewing, B.A., & D'Amico, E.J. (2016). To educate or to incarcerate: Factors in disproportionality in school discipline. *Children and Youth Services Review, 70*, 102–11. https://doi.org/10.1016/j.childyouth.2016.09.009

Nydegger, L.A., Quinn, K., Walsh, J.L., Pacella-LaBarbara, M.L., & Dickson-Gomez, J. (2019). Polytraumatization, mental health, and delinquency among adolescent gang members. *Journal of Traumatic Stress, 32*(6), 890–8. https://doi.org/10.1002/jts.22473

Pieper, I., & Thomson, C.J.H. (2016). Beneficence as a principle in human research. *Monash Bioethics Review, 34*(2), 117–35. https://doi.org/10.1007/s40592-016-0061-3

Pyrooz, D.C., Turanovic, J.J., Decker, S.H., & Wu, J. (2016). Taking stock of the relationship between gang membership and offending: A meta-analysis. *Criminal Justice and Behavior, 43*(3), 365–97. https://doi.org/10.1177/0093854815605528

Quinn, K., Pacella, M.L., Dickson-Gomez, J., & Nydegger, L.A. (2017). Childhood adversity and the continued exposure to trauma and violence among adolescent gang members. *American Journal of Community Psychology, 59*(1–2), 36–49. https://doi.org/10.1002/ajcp.12123

Quinn, K., Walsh, J.L., & Dickson-Gomez, J. (2019). Multiple marginality and the variation in delinquency and substance use among adolescent gang members. *Substance Use Misuse, 54*(4), 612–27. doi: 10.1080/10826084.2018.1528465

Ravitch, S.M., & Riggan, M. (2016). *Reason & rigor: How conceptual frameworks guide research.* 2nd ed. Sage Publications.

Raymond-Flesch, M., Auerswald, C., McGlone, L., Comfort, M., & Minnis, A. (2017). Building social capital to promote adolescent wellbeing: A qualitative study with teens in a Latino agricultural community. *BMC Public Health, 17*, 177. https://doi.org/10.1186/s12889-017-4110-5

Reiss, F. (2013). Socioeconomic inequalities and mental health problems in children and adolescents: A systematic review. *Social Science & Medicine, 90*, 24–31. https://doi.org/10.1016/j.socscimed.2013.04.026

Ruof, M.C. (2004). Vulnerability, vulnerable populations, and policy. *Kennedy Institute of Ethics Journal, 14*(4), 411–25. https://doi.org/10.1353/ken.2004.0044

Shivayogi, P. (2013). Vulnerable population and methods for their safeguard. *Perspectives in Clinical Research, 4*(1), 53–7. https://doi.org/10.4103/2229-3485.106389

Smith, L.T. (2021). *Decolonizing methodologies: Research and indigenous people.* 3rd ed. Zed Books.

Staller, K.M. (2012). Epistemological boot camp: The politics of science and what every qualitative researcher needs to know to survive in the academy. *Qualitative Social Work, 12*(4), 395–413. https://doi.org/10.1177/1473325012450483

Tesch, R. (1990). *Qualitative research: Analysis types and software tools.* Falmer Press.

Thornberry, T.P., & Krohn, M.D. (2003). *Taking stock of delinquency: An overview of findings from contemporary longitudinal studies.* Kluwer Academic/Plenum Publishers.

4. Quantitative methods for mental health research

Reginald O. York

Mental health research is often conducted using methods that are either quantitative, qualitative, or mixed methods. Quantitative research variables are measured as either numbers (e.g., age measured in years) or categories (e.g., male or female). With qualitative research, the data are in the form of words taken from such sources as notes from interviews or answers to open-ended questions on a questionnaire. Mixed methods research employs both quantitative and qualitative methods. This chapter will focus on quantitative research methods.

In the first section of this chapter, we will examine the nature of quantitative research as contrasted with the qualitative and mixed methods alternatives. In it, we will see some of the contributions to quantitative methods to mental health policy. A few examples illustrate this mechanism. In addition, some key concepts will be discussed, such as causation, evidence-based practice, and chance as an alternative explanation of data using statistics as the means of analysis.

The purposes and *processes* of mental health research is the focus of the second section of this chapter. We will see presentations on the purposes of description, explanation, evaluation, and exploration. The steps in the scientific process of quantitative research are also enumerated along with issues inherent in each step.

Designs for mental health research is the theme of the third section of this chapter. The design of the research study depicts the structure whereby data are collected. For example, one evaluative research design requires the measurement of clients one time before treatment begins and another time at the end of the treatment period. Descriptive research, however, normally requires the collection of data at one point in time. Evaluation designs include the categories of pre-experimental, quasi-experimental, and experimental. A key concept in explanatory research is correlation, a depiction of the relationships between variables.

A subsequent section examines the statistical analysis of quantitative data. Both descriptive and inferential statistics are described with examples. Effect size is presented as a vehicle for the examination of data, especially in evaluative research, particularly in the meta-analysis in mental health research.

THE NATURE OF QUANTITATIVE RESEARCH FOR MENTAL HEALTH POLICY

There is a great deal of quantitative evidence that informs mental health policy. For example, a group of researchers conducted a systematic review of evidence on various studies of interventions for street-connected youth. Here are the conclusions of that review:

There is a dearth of evidence from controlled trials on interventions to improve integration of street-connected children and young adults into society and providing skills-based education. The evidence from health interventions aimed at engaging in safe sexual practices, and at improving mental health vary widely and are inconclusive as to their effectiveness. Some of the interventions aimed at reducing the risk of substance abuse may be effective. Further research in this area will be useful in understanding the effectiveness of these approaches and validating the effect of some of the interventions that are supported by moderate evidence. (Coren, Hossain, Pardo, & Bakker, 2016)

The main policy lesson from the above conclusion suggests that priority in treatment should focus on those interventions for substance abuse that have been found to be effective, and that treatments for other behaviors should take a back seat until further evidence is forthcoming.

Knapp and others (1990) conducted a study to help predict the community costs of closing community psychiatric hospitals in England. More than 100 discharged patients were studied in regard to the outcomes of the discharge. They discovered that patients with social withdrawal, flattened emotions, and speech problems had been the most difficult to place in the community. A potential policy lesson from this study is the need to focus more attention upon this part of the population.

Quantitative, Qualitative, and Mixed Methods Research

Measurement in quantitative research takes the form of numbers or categories, such as age measured as years, or category of political party affiliation. Measurement in qualitative research, on the other hand, takes the form of words to be examined. These words may come from the researcher's notes from interviews, or answers to an open-ended question on a survey. Mixed methods research includes both quantitative and qualitative measurements.

An advantage of quantitative measurement is precision, and is best achieved with larger sample sizes. You might need to know the mean age of a group of clients or the proportion who are female. You might need to know if self-esteem is better than school grades at predicting recovery from substance abuse. An advantage of qualitative research is discovery of patterns among less known phenomena. For example, you might want to study the stages of moral decline among at-risk youth. You would first examine the literature to see what has been theorized. From this review you might develop a specific research question that has not been adequately researched.

Mixed methods research is employed when the strengths of both quantitative and qualitative measurement are needed. Palinkas and others (2011) examined research studies that had employed mixed methods from a variety of sources and found that a great number of mixed methods research focused upon the nature of services being examined or newly developed. Another focus was the assessment of need. Both of these aspects of mental health services lend themselves to both quantitative and qualitative methods.

Need should be measured in regard both to number and nature. How many people have this need? What is the nature of this need? The number is better studied by quantitative methods and the nature is better suited with qualitative research. Need could be measured as a dichotomy (either Yes or No), as a frequency (How often does it happen?), as duration (How long does it last?), or as magnitude (How severe is it?).

Causation in Quantitative Research

In both explanatory and evaluative research, the issue of causation is a key theme. Are school grades caused by self-esteem, depression, academic motivation, or all of these? Are improvements in the clients' scores for depression caused by the intervention or something else? Is gender a cause of salary?

Causation refers to the effect of one variable upon another. One variable causes another variable to be the way it is. There is the cause and the effect. There are three conditions for the determination of causation, one of which is the relationship between the variables. A second criterion for causation is time-order. A change in the cause must occur before a change in the effect. A third criterion is ruling out other causes of the effect.

Let's take work motivation and work productivity as an example. Is work motivation the cause of work productivity? To examine this question comprehensively, you need to find that (a) work motivation has a positive relationship (i.e., correlation) with work productivity, (b) changes in work motivation have been found to precede changes in work productivity in time-order, and (c) you have adequately ruled out some of the other causes of work productivity. Therefore, you would compute a correlation between scores for work motivation and scores for work productivity. You would also measure both of these variables at different times and examine these time-order relationships. It is possible that work productivity is a cause of work motivation rather than the other way around. Finally, you would examine the relationship between work productivity and work motivation with other possible causes of work productivity in the analysis to see if motivation is related to productivity when the potential effect of the other variables is controlled.

As you can see, the comprehensive examination of causation is a tall order. We seldom have the ability to do this, so we have to settle for something less than comprehensive, and accept the limitations of our work. A caveat is in order: you may have seen the statement "Correlation is not causation." A better statement would be "Correlation is one of the three conditions for determining causation." The first statement is misleading: it suggests that correlations have nothing to do with causation. When you have established correlation, you have engaged in an incomplete examination of causation, not an irrelevant one. If you examine correlation and fail to show a relationship between a given cause and a given effect, you have ruled out causation in this case. Therefore, correlation is highly relevant to causation.

Some might assert that theory has a role to play in the examination of causation because it is designed to explain things. Traditionally, causation has been examined in quantitative research studies related to the three conditions mentioned above. But some researchers might examine theory to explain the relationships found in research studies. If you found that scores for self-esteem were positively related to grades in school, you might search for a theory that would explain why self-esteem is a cause of grades. Does higher self-esteem result in higher motivation for achievement? Does higher motivation for achievement result in higher grades? This analysis could depend both on the logical examination of concepts as well as the empirical examination of them.

Evidence-Based Practice

Evidence-based practice has emerged as a central theme in intervention research in mental health. It promotes the use of evidence in making practice decisions. There are many definitions of evidence-based practice, including the following:

> Evidence-based practice harnesses recent advances in clinical epidemiology, biostatistics, and information science to produce a coherent and comprehensive approach to allow clinicians to base their practice on the best available evidence. (Geddes, Reynolds, Steiner, Szatmari, & Maynes, 1998, p. 1484)

A definition given by York (2020, p. 80) provides more specifics for the clinical mental health practitioner: "Evidence-based practice in mental health employs the judicious use of the best available evidence, along with considerations of client preferences and therapist expertise, in making practice decisions."

The above definition is a slight revision of a definition from York (2020) and is consistent with most definitions of this concept given in many sources. It suggests there are three components of evidence-based practice: client preference; practitioner competence; and evidence. In other words, the practitioner and client decide on the model of therapy after consideration of each of these components. If any of these considerations is absent in a given process of mental health therapy, evidence-based practice has not been implemented fully. Evidence-based programs would be those that have been found to be effective in the accomplishment of a mental health goal.

In evidence-based practice, evidence refers to scientific studies, preferably ones with sound methods. It does not include opinions and eschews the practice of cherry-picking of data that supports a given assertion. In other words, it must employ evidence that has been acquired through the spirit of scientific inquiry and critical thinking.

Evidence-based practices are clinical practices (e.g., cognitive-behavioral therapy) for a given client behavior (e.g., depression) that have noteworthy support from scientific studies. The concept of noteworthy support will depend upon the standards you employ when examining scientific evidence. There are many sources of evidence where standards have been implemented and practices have been asserted as being evidence-based for a given client behavior. Some of these sources provide guides for how to employ evidence-based practices. A statement from the American Psychological Association provides guidance on the basis upon which a given practice for a given behavior should be considered an evidence-based practice:

> Generally, evidence derived from clinically relevant research on psychological practices should be based on systematic reviews, reasonable effect sizes, statistical and clinical significance, and a body of supporting evidence. The validity of conclusions from research on interventions is based on a general progression from clinical observation through systematic reviews of randomized clinical trials, while also recognizing gaps and limitations in the existing literature and its applicability to the specific case at hand (APA, 2002). Health policy and practice are also informed by research using a variety of methods in such areas as public health, epidemiology, human development, social relations, and neuroscience. (American Psychological Association, n.d.)

It should be clear that a single supportive study would not be sufficient for declaring a given practice an evidence-based practice. There must be much more. The systematic review of evidence is the best source. It typically employs at least one meta-analysis whereby data from several studies are calculated in such a way as to generate an effect size that depicts the overall effect of the treatment on the outcomes for all studies included. However, some practices have not been subjected to a systematic review. At a minimum level, the number of good supportive research studies must significantly outnumber the number of unsupportive research studies.

PURPOSES AND PROCESSES OF MENTAL HEALTH RESEARCH

Studies that have used quantitative methods have supported a variety of practice and policy actions. For example, a systematic review of research provided support for the use of cognitive-behavioral treatment for the recovery of children who had suffered sexual abuse (MacDonald et al., 2012). Predictive analytics was used by Hudson to predict the optimal number of psychiatric hospital beds needed in a community per 100,000 population (Hudson, 2020).

Mental health research can be classified according to purpose. Some studies have the purpose of describing phenomena. The above-mentioned study by Hudson is an example. It had a descriptive question: How many psychiatric hospital beds does a community need based on population? Another purpose of research is explanation. This type of research examines the relationships between variables in order to see if one might explain another. An example is a book by Loeber and others (1998) that reported research on variables that explain various antisocial behaviors in children and adolescents. Evaluation is a third type of mental health research when we categorize it by purpose. The evaluative study seeks to determine the effects of mental health interventions. For example, a systematic review of research suggested that web-based mindfulness interventions were effective in the treatment of a variety of mental health disorders (Sevilla-Llewellyn-Jones, 2018). A fourth purpose of mental health research is exploration, where the researcher is seeking new understandings from a relatively unknown topic. McDaid and Delaney (2011) undertook a qualitative study of the experiences of clients in the mental health system to explore their perceptions of decision-making processes in treatment. These persons highlighted the issue of power and powerlessness in describing how incapacity is determined in mental health services. While quantitative studies are sometimes undertaken with exploration as a purpose, most of this type of research uses qualitative methods because of the need for flexibility when the subject is not well known.

A quantitative study that was exploratory in nature was conducted by Kessler et al. (2014). His team conducted an exploratory study designed to predict the incidence of PTSD (post-traumatic stress disorder) using s sample of 47,466 patients from 24 countries, utilizing data from the World Health Organization. His research team found that various socio-demographic data predicted PTSD diagnosis. Also included in their predictive model were the incidence of prior traumatic exposures, and DSM-IV diagnoses.

In addition to the purposes of mental health research that are discussed in this section are the processes that guide this research. In this regard, we are speaking of the steps that are normally undertaken when quantitative mental health research is normally conducted.

While the steps in mental health research can be categorized in many ways, only four major steps in this process will be presented in this chapter. Each step has a major function. The first step is the development of the research question and the knowledge base that is relevant. A given research study should contribute to the existing knowledge in regard to the relevant theme. This requires an examination of the existing knowledge on the theme so that gaps in knowledge can be addressed. You don't want your study to be an attempt to reinvent the wheel!

The research question and knowledge base will inform the second step in the research process – the development of research methods. The research methods will include the type of sample selected, the tools used to measure variables, and the design of the study. If your research question is whether your cognitive-behavioral treatment is effective in the reduction of depression for your clients, you will know that depression is one of the variables you must measure when you determine your study methods.

The sampling method refers to the means that were employed in the selection of the study subjects (the sample) from the study population. This task will help us to address the issue of generalization of findings. Generalization refers to the extent that we are confident that a repeat of the current study with a new sample, selected in the same manner as the current one, would generate similar findings. In other words, are these findings relevant to people who were not included in this study?

The method of measurement deals with the issue of validity, or accuracy. You must measure depression in an accurate way if you conduct a study with a particular depression scale. If your depression scale does not correlate with the assessment of clients by therapists, you would not have evidence that your tool is accurate – either your tool is not accurate or your therapists are not accurate, or both. So, you would be advised to use a different tool for measuring depression, one that has been well tested for validity.

Research design is the third aspect of the research step of study methods. One research design measures a group of clients on client outcome one time before treatment begins (pretest) and once again after treatment has been completed (posttest), with the gains for each person calculated. This design is classified as pre-experimental. Another research design would call upon you to measure a comparison group that did not have the intervention and compare the gains of the two groups. The second design, using a comparison group, would be superior to the first in regard to the issue of causation. If you used the comparison group design you would be in a better position to assert that it was the intervention, not other things, that caused the measured client growth. This research design would be classified as quasi-experimental. A more sophisticated research design is one of several research designs that are classified as experimental. Each experimental design uses random assignment of people to their status as a group that gets treatment or a group that does not.

The collection and analysis of data is the third step in the quantitative research process. Data analysis will typically employ statistics, descriptive statistics for descriptive studies and inferential statistics for either explanatory or evaluative research. Inferential statistics deal with the issue of chance and generalizability. The question is whether the measured data would occur by chance at a certain level.

The final step in the research process is the drawing of conclusions based on the results of the study. It portrays a summary of the study findings along with a discussion of the implications of these findings. For example, do the results of this study support the assertion that African-American males should be the primary focus of criminal justice reform because this group is the one most at risk? Do the results of this study support the assertion that cognitive-behavioral therapy is effective in the reduction of depression for recently divorced women? Do the results of this study support the conclusion that strengths-based tutoring is better than problem-based tutoring in the enhancement of the grades of middle school students most at risk of dropping out of school?

DESIGNS FOR QUANTITATIVE MENTAL HEALTH RESEARCH

The design of the quantitative research study portrays the structure whereby data are collected and analyzed. Data can be collected on a retrospective basis, where existing data are analyzed, or on a prospective basis, where data are designed to be collected in the future in the pursuit of a mental health question. Retrospective studies are often used for descriptive studies, such as the use of census data to determine population trends in the past several decades. On the other hand, if you decided to administer an anxiety scale to all clients who are seeking your agency's help due to anxiety, you would be conducting research on a prospective basis.

There are numerous research designs for two general types of mental health research that will be examined here: epidemiologic research and intervention research. Epidemiology is a type of research that typically is either descriptive or explanatory and deals with large populations. You might want to know the distribution of depression among the peoples of North America and South America, or the incidence of child abuse in parts of Africa. These would be examples of epidemiologic research.

Intervention research examines the extent that a given treatment has been effective in regard to a given target behavior. Such a study may pursue the question of whether grades improved after the implementation of a special tutoring intervention, or whether depression scores improved after the implementation of cognitive-behavioral therapy.

Epidemiology

According to the Centers for Disease Control and Prevention, epidemiology is the study of the distribution of health-related states in specific populations and the application of knowledge to the control of health problems. Scientific methods are the basis for its inquiry. It is data-driven, systematic, and unbiased in the collection and analysis of data (Definition of Epidemiology, 2020). For a complete examination of the evolution of the definition of epidemiology during the past few decades, see Frérot et al. (2018).

An example is an article on mental disorders in children and adolescents (Merikangas, Nakamura, & Kessler, 2009). This article presents information on the magnitude of mental disorders in children and adolescents from various places in the world. It presents a summary of evidence from prior reviews of epidemiologic research. Reviews were limited to studies that apply the DSM-IV criteria and included direct structured interviews of children and reports regarding child symptoms from a parent or caregiver. The summary revealed that approximately one-quarter of youths had experienced a mental disorder during the past year and about one-third experienced it for a lifetime. Anxiety disorders were found to be most prevalent followed by behavior disorders, mood disorders, and substance abuse disorders. Fewer than one-half had received mental health treatment.

The European Study of the Epidemiology of Mental Disorders is another example of epidemiology. It was a large-scale survey of data on prevalence, risk factors, disability and the use of health care services for mood, anxiety, and alcohol-related disorders throughout Europe (Alonso & Lépine, 2007). More than 20,000 adults were included in this major study. A lifetime presence of a mental disorder was reported by 25.9 percent of these study subjects and 11.5 percent had experienced a disorder during the past year. Females, younger participants, the unmarried, and the unemployed were found to be more at risk than others. Of those with a mood disorder, only 36.8 percent had sought help.

Epidemiology can be helpful in mental health policy in several ways. For example, one article provides suggestions on how it can help in the delivery of mental health services for children and adolescents (Costello, Burns, Angold, & Leaf, 1993). As noted in this article, epidemiology can provide information on need for services, availability of services, and effectiveness of services. It can inform us about such things as the developmental course of psychiatric disorders in this population. Information on incidence and prevalence can be useful for mental health planning. In addition, information about causation and outcome can guide the development of successful mental health services.

As you will see in the next section of this chapter, intervention research designs can be classified into the categories of non-experimental research, quasi-experimental research, and experimental research. Epidemiology can employ these same types of designs but are more likely to use designs that are more descriptive in nature. Munnangi and Boktor (2020) have identified several types of research designs for epidemiology in public health. One design is the case-control study which can be employed to determine the degree of associations between various risk factors and outcomes. Another design is the case-crossover study which can identify triggers within an individual when the client is experiencing a transient exposure or risk factor. Cross-sectional studies are observational in nature and give a snapshot of the characteristics of study subjects in a single point of time. Ecological studies are used when data at an individual level are unavailable or when large-scale comparisons are needed to study the population-level effect of exposures on a disease condition.

Intervention Research

The intervention research designs discussed in this section are prospective in nature and especially useful for the evaluation of mental health services or policies. There are many research designs and there are many ways to classify them. A classification system by Campbell and Stanley (1963) will be used here because it remains the clearest way to characterize these designs. There are three general categories in this system: pre-experimental, quasi-experimental, and experimental.

The better your research design, the better you are in a position to assert that the intervention was the cause of the measured outcome rather than something else, such as normal growth over time. There are several conditions, such as normal growth over time, that might explain the measured client growth in a given study. These conditions have been labeled "threats to internal validity." Maturation is the label given to normal growth over time as one threat to internal validity, that is, an alternative explanation for measured client growth. Changes in the client's environment is another of these conditions. This threat to internal validity is referred to as history. Testing is a third threat to internal validity. It refers to the experience of being tested as an influence on measured client growth. For example, if knowledge is your intended outcome and you have measured knowledge at pretest, it is possible that clients' posttest scores will be influenced by what the client remembered from the pretest, rather than the knowledge that was gained due to the intervention.

There are 13 threats to internal validity identified by Campbell and Stanley (1963) but only a few will be mentioned here. The main point is that the greater that your design controls for threats to internal validity, the better is your position to claim that it was the intervention that caused the measured client growth rather than something else.

The pre-experimental category is the lowest of the three in regard to causation. It calls for the measurement of client target behavior but fails to control for any of the threats to internal validity. The quasi-experimental category is next because it employs some controls for threats to internal validity, such as by comparing the growth of clients to the growth of a group of people who have not had the treatment. The experimental designs are at the highest level because they control for threats to internal validity in an optimal way – by the assignment of people (clients and non-clients) to their group on a random basis.

Pre-experimental designs
Intervention research designs that provide for the measurement of target behavior but do not control for any threats to internal validity are labeled "pre-experimental designs." An example is the *one-shot case study* whereby a group of clients are measured only after they have received the intervention. This shows their condition at posttest time but fails to show if they have achieved any growth because their behavior before treatment is not known.

The *one-group pretest-posttest design* is another example of a pre-experimental design. It calls for the measurement of client behavior for a group of clients both before and after the intervention and the assessment of their growth on it. However, there is no comparison group with which this growth is compared; therefore, this design does not control for any of the threats to internal validity, but it does provide for the measurement of client growth.

Here is the graphic depiction of this design using the symbol of O_1 for observation (i.e., measurement) at time 1 (e.g., the pretest), the symbol X for treatment, and the symbol O_2 for observation at time 2 (e.g., the posttest).

$O_1 \, X \, O_2$

As you will note, there is only one line, so this design only has one group in the study. When you use this design, you can claim that clients gained on the target behavior during the treatment period, but you have no evidence that this gain was due to the intervention rather than something else.

Quasi-experimental designs
The quasi-experimental designs exercise some control over threats to internal validity, but do not do so at the optimal level of the experimental designs. One example is the *non-equivalent control group design*, sometimes referred to as simply the comparison group design. With this design, the growth of a group of clients, computed from pretest and posttest scores, is compared to the growth of a group of people who have not had the intervention. If the client group has a significantly greater gain than the comparison group there is evidence that the cause of the difference is the intervention rather than something like normal growth over time. If time is a potential cause of growth on this target behavior, the effect of it would

be seen in the comparison group, so maturation has been controlled in this study. Here is the graphic depiction of this design:

$$O_1 \; X \; O_2$$

$$O_1 O_2$$

You can see from this depiction that there are two groups that get measured at the pretest and posttest time but only the first group gets the treatment (depicted as X).

Another quasi-experimental design is the *time-series experiment.* There are several variations of the time-series experiment. In each variation, behavior is measured many times over a period of time both before the treatment begins and during the treatment period. In one variation, the clients are measured several times before the treatment is offered and several times during the treatment period. This design has also been labeled the AB single subject design in some intervention research textbooks. Another variation in the Campbell and Stanley classification calls for the behavior to be measured several times before the treatment is offered and several times after the treatment has been completed.

Experimental designs

The key distinction of the experimental design is that the groups of people in the study are assigned to their group on a random basis. The random assignment of people to their groups controls for a variety of threats to internal validity – maturation, history, and testing among others. The random assignment of people to groups logically assures equivalence between groups in regard to things other than the intervention that might be the cause of the measured client growth. If there are some people in the treatment group who will improve because of normal growth over time, there is likely to be an equivalent number of people in the control group who will do the same; thus, they will cancel each other out. But equivalence, of course, is not a certainty; it is merely a high likelihood. Thus, there are a variety of experimental designs that go to greater lengths to control for threats to internal validity. Only two experimental designs will be described in this chapter.

The most popular of these is the *pretest-posttest control group design*, sometimes referred to simply as the basic experimental design. This design compares the gain on target behavior of two groups of people who have been assigned to their group on a random basis. One of these groups gets the intervention and one group does not. Here is the graphic depiction of this design with the letter R indicating that the groups were assigned to their status on a random basis:

$$R: O_1 \; X \; O_2$$

$$R: O_1 \; O_2$$

As you can see, this design is the same as the comparison group design except that the people in the two groups are assigned to their group on a random basis.

A second experimental research design is the *posttest-only control group design*. With this design, the two groups (one with the treatment and one without) are not given a pretest, only a posttest. The posttest scores of the two groups are compared to see if the treatment group did better. Because the two groups of people have been assigned to their group on a random basis, it is logical to assume that the two groups were equivalent at the pretest time; thus, the pretest measurement of study subjects is not essential to the study's classification as an experimental design. Here is the graphic depiction of this design:

R: X O

R: O

With this design, the posttest scores of the two groups are compared to see if the treated group had better scores.

MIXED METHODS RESEARCH

Some research on mental health policy combines quantitative research methods and qualitative research methods. In other words, some of this research presents data on quantitative measures (e.g., quantitative characteristics of those in need) and qualitative measures (e.g., the statements that those in need might give to their most important concerns). According to Palinkas and others (2011), there has been a growing body of mixed methods research in mental health.

Quantitative research and qualitative research have different advantages. When you want to describe a population on concrete terms (e.g., the mean age), you will likely conduct quantitative research. When you examine the relationship between two variables to see if one explains the other, you are also likely to conduct quantitative research. The same is true for most evaluative research where quantitative data will be analyzed in regard to client outcomes. Thus, quantitative methods are most likely to be employed when you conduct descriptive research, explanatory research, or evaluative research.

But exploratory research tends to tackle themes where concrete data are not known, or are not adequate to find full understanding of social phenomena. If you wanted to better understand how people of different cultures perceive mental health in different terms, you would likely conduct a qualitative study where you either asked open-ended questions of people from different cultures or made observations of people in various life circumstances.

A review of the literature on mixed methods research in mental health by Palinkas and others (2011) revealed that such studies tended to be focused on existing services, implementation of services, innovations in services, developing new practices, or conducting need assessments. This review led to several conclusions. They found there to be a growing body of mixed methods research in recent decades but a lack of clarity on the rationale for using mixed methods. There was found to be a good diversity in the variety of measurement methods employed, and the reasons for the specific methods were well articulated.

STATISTICS FOR QUANTITATIVE RESEARCH

Research studies call for the collection of data. Statistics are used to analyze that data. There are two major types of statistics: descriptive and inferential. Descriptive statistics are used to characterize a study sample, with statistics such as the frequency, proportion, median, mean, and range. If you wanted to know the mean age of all clients who receive services from the children's division of your agency, you would be using a descriptive statistic. Inferential statistics are used to infer from a sample to a population. With inferential statistics, you analyze data from a sample and try to determine if these sample results would be similar to the entire population from which your sample was selected. A tool in this process is the study hypothesis. Inferential statistics are used to test the hypothesis in either explanatory research or evaluative research. The explanatory hypothesis might be "Scores for self-esteem are positively related to grades in school." This hypothesis is examining the relationship between two variables in order to examine whether one might be the cause of the other. An evaluative hypothesis might be "Scores for self-esteem will be higher at the end of strengths-based counseling service than the beginning." This hypothesis is evaluating the outcome for a treatment: strengths-based counseling.

When a study is testing a hypothesis, a statistic will be used to examine whether chance is a good explanation of the data that were collected. Chance refers to the possibility of something that is not explained by existing knowledge. In the analysis of data, the letter p (lower case) is used to represent the proportion of times a given set of data would occur by chance. If you see a p value of 0.05, you can say that these data would be expected to occur by chance 5 times in 100. And in social science research, we typically use this figure $p < .05$ as our standard to determine if the hypothesis has been confirmed. In other words, we conclude that our data have supported the hypothesis if it can be explained by chance less than 5 times in 100.

If you wanted to know if being left-handed is related to being creative, you could collect data on two variables: (i) being left- or right-handed, and (ii) a score on a scale of creativity. You might find that the creativity score for left-handed people is 23.4 while the creativity scores for right-handed people is 22.8. These scores are very close, so you may not be confident that a repeat of this study with a new sample of people would have the same result that favored left-handed people. In other words, it may be that you are not confident that you have truly found that left-handed people are more creative. Why are you in doubt? Perhaps it is because of the issue of chance – perhaps chance can explain the fact that left-handed people in your study sample had higher creativity scores. The likelihood that another study would favor right-handed people is too great for you to take a bet that favored the left-handed people.

Descriptive statistics are generally well known. The frequency is the incidence of something, such as the fact that there are 213 clients from your agency who have pre-school age children. The mean is the average of all scores, such as, for example, the fact the mean age of the clients in your tutoring program is 13.4. The median is the mid-point in an array of data arranged in numerical order. The median annual family income of a sample of families of a certain ethnic group may be $36,732. That means that if your family's annual income is $36,732 you will know that one-half of all people in this sample are above you in annual income and one-half are below you.

Inferential statistics is often used to test the hypothesis in either explanatory research or evaluative research. The correlation coefficient is one such statistic. It reveals the strength of the relationship between two variables and is indicated by the letter r (lower case). It can range from a low of r = 0, which means there is no relationship at all, to a high of r = 1.0, which means there is a perfect relationship between the two variables. It can be either positive or negative. A positive relationship would be expected in the correlation between scores on self-esteem and grades in school. This would indicate that those with higher self-esteem had higher grades. On the other hand, one would expect to find a negative relationship between scores for depression and grades in school (e.g., r = −0.43). This would mean that those who had higher grades had lower scores for depression. In addition to the correlation coefficient, you might find the results of a study being tested with one of the many t tests, regression analysis, analysis of variance, and this great number of additional options depending upon the structure of the data and the nature of the hypothesis. While you may not understand the intricacies of a given statistic used in a report, you normally will be given the value of p, which will tell you if the data were statistically significant.

The effect size is a quantitative measure of the magnitude of a relationship between variables in a research study. It is especially useful for intervention research because it represents the magnitude of the effect of the intervention upon client target behavior represented by the number of standard deviations. For example, if the effect size of the influence of cognitive-behavioral therapy upon depression in a study is 1.5, you would see that the intervention made a difference at the level of one and one-half standard deviations in scores on the depression scale employed. So, it does not matter if you are comparing several studies that used different scales for measuring the target behavior, because you will convert the data to the common statistic of the standard deviation.

The effect size is especially important in the meta-analysis, something that is important in evidence-based practice in intervention research. The meta-analysis entails the use of a specific protocol for the examination of existing research reports including the computation of an overall effect for the results of all studies included in the inquiry.

THE ADVANTAGES OF QUANTITATIVE RESEARCH FOR MENTAL HEALTH POLICY

There are a number of advantages of using the quantitative form of information. Among these are the advantages of quantitative research when the purpose of the study is either description, explanation, or evaluation. Descriptive research is advanced by precision, the hallmark of quantitative research. For example, a descriptive researcher might want to know the percent age of a population that has a certain characteristic, such as age, gender, race, or income. The percent age with a given mental health problem will help in social policy and planning. The explanatory research is also aided by the use of quantitative research because the examination of causation requires a certain type of precision where data can be examined in regard to correlations. Evaluative research is also helped by quantitative research partly because its precision in measurement is less vulnerable to the biases of people who are engaged in its design or interpretation.

Another advantage of quantitative research is that it is more efficient than qualitative research. It costs less to mail (or email) a survey to hundreds of people than to engage such people in personal interviews. The analysis of quantitative data is also more efficient because of the use of the computer where the computation of statistical significance can be done in seconds, while the qualitative analysis of answers to interview questions will take much more time.

A third advantage of quantitative research lies in the generalization of study findings. Generalization is aided by sampling procedures and sample size. You are more likely to bet your money that a repeat of your study will yield a similar result when you have a sample of 200 rather than a sample of 20. Betting your money on a repeat of your findings is an illustration of the concept of generalization of study findings. You are in a better position to wisely bet your money on a repeat to the extent that you feel safe in the generalization of your results.

In quantitative research, partly because of efficiency, you are more likely to have a larger sample than in a qualitative study.

A fourth advantage of quantitative research is that it is more objective. This means it is less likely than qualitative research to be influenced by the opinions of the researcher. In qualitative research, a lot of decisions are made about the meaning of various words that have been expressed by study subjects. Each of these decisions are vulnerable to the biases of the researcher.

A final advantage of quantitative research is social acceptability. This advantage is highly related to the advantage of objectivity. In our culture, objectivity is more highly valued and accepted than subjectivity. If someone says to you "That is just your opinion" you will know that they are questioning the usefulness of what you just said and are less likely to be influenced by it.

Quantitative research has been the focus of this chapter. It differs from qualitative research in the form of the information that will be analyzed. If you have conducted quantitative research, you have data that give numbers to study subjects that have numerical value, such as height measured in inches, or you have put study subjects into categories, such as *male* and *female* for the variable of gender. If you have qualitative data, you have words to analyze, such as the answers to an open-ended question on a questionnaire. Quantitative data, therefore, are more precise. It is less likely that different people will differ in their interpretations of the information they have seen. It is valuable for various types of mental health research, from the evaluation of mental health services to the estimation of the population parameters for a mental health behavior. Without quantitative research on mental health issues, we would be lacking in knowledge of how to improve the lives of our citizens.

REFERENCES

Alonso, J., & Lépine, J.-P. (2007). European Study of the Epidemiology of Mental Disorders/Mental Health Disability: A European Assessment in the Year 2000 Scientific Committee. Overview of key data from the European Study of the Epidemiology of Mental Disorders (ESEMeD). *The Journal of Clinical Psychiatry, 68*(Suppl. 2), 3–9.

American Psychological Association. (n.d.). Policy Statement on Evidence-based Practice in Psychology. Retrieved December 7, 2020 from https://www.apa.org/practice/guidelines/evidence-based-statement

Campbell, D.T., & Stanely, J.C. (1963). *Experimental and quasi-experimental designs for research.* Boston, MA: Houghton Mifflin.

Coren, E., Hossain, R., Pardo, J., & Bakker, B. (2016). Interventions for promoting reintegration and reducing harmful behaviour and lifestyles in street-connected children and young people. *Campbell Collaboration.* https://doi.org/10.4073/csr.2016.5

Costello, E.J., Burns, B.J., Angold, A., & Leaf, P.J. (1993). How can epidemiology improve mental health services for children and adolescents? *Journal of the American Academy of Child and Adolescent Psychiatry, 32*(6), 1114–7.

Definition of Epidemiology. (2020). Centers for Disease Control and Prevention. Retrieved September 4, 2020 from https://www.cdc.gov/csels/dsepd/ss1978/lesson1/section1.html

Frérot, M., Lefebvre, A., Aho, S., Callier, P., Astruc, K., & Aho Glélé, L.S. (2018). What is epidemiology? Changing definitions of epidemiology 1978–2017. *PLoS One, 13*(12), e0208442. https://doi.org/10.1371/journal.pone.0208442

Geddes, J., Reynolds, S., Steiner, D., Szatmari, P., & Maynes, B. (1998). Evidence-based practice in mental health. *British Psychological Journal, 1*(1), 4–5.

Hudson, C.G. (2020). Benchmarking psychiatric deinstitutionalization: Development, testing, and application of a model using predictive analytics. *Best Practices in Mental Health, 16*(1), 12–31.

Knapp, M., Beecham, J., & Anderson, J. (1990). The TAPS project 3: Predicting the community costs of closing psychiatric hospitals. *The British Journal of Psychiatry, 157*(5), 661–70.

Kessler, R.C., Rose, S.,Koenen, K.C. et al. (2014). How well can post-traumatic stress disorder be predicted from pre-trauma risk factors? An exploratory study in the WHO World Mental Health Surveys. *World Psychiatry, 13*(3).

Loeber, R., Farrington, D.P., Stroughhamer-Loeber, M., & Kammen, W.B. (1998). *Antisocial behavior in mental health problems.* Mahwah, NJ: Lawrence Erlbaum Associates.

MacDonald, G., Higgins, J., Ramchandani, P., Vaneltine, J. Bronger, L.P., Klein, P., O'Daniel, R., Pickering, M., Rademaker, B., Richardson, G., & Taylor M. (2012). Cognitive-behavioural interventions for children who have been sexually abused. *Campbell Collaboration.* https://doi.org/10.4073/csr.2012.14

McDaid, S., & Delaney, S. (2011). A social approach to decision making capacity. Exploratory research with people with experience of mental health treatment. *Disability & Society, 26*(6), 729–42.

Merikangas, K.R., Nakamura, E.F., & Kessler, R.C. (2009). Epidemiology of mental disorders in children and adolescents. *Dialogues in Clinical Neuroscience, 11*(1), 7–20.

Munnangi, S., & Boktor, S.W. (Updated May 4, 2020). Epidemiology of study design. In StatPearls [Internet]. Treasure Island, FL: StatPearls Publishing; 2020. Retrieved November 1, 2020 from https://www.ncbi.nlm.nih.gov/books/NBK470342/

Palinkas, L.A., Horwitz, S.M., Chamberlain, P., Hurlburt, M.S., & Landsverk, J. (2011). Mixed-methods designs in mental health services research: A review. *Psychiatric Services, 62*(3), 255–63.

Sevilla-Llewellyn-Jones, J. (2018). Web-based mindfulness interventions for mental health treatment: Systematic review and meta-analysis. *JMIR Mental Health, 5*(3), e10278.

York, R.O. (2020). *Social work research methods: Learning by doing.* Thousand Oaks, CA: Sage Publications.

5. Emerging research methods in mental health

Emily Ihara, JoAnn Lee, John Karavatas and Michael Wolf-Branigin

Mental health and substance use disorders are among the leading causes of disability (Whiteford et al., 2013) where substantial treatment gaps exist for more than 70 percent of those who need services but are unable to receive care (Kohn, Szena, Levav, & Sacraceno, 2004). Mental health systems in different countries continue to be characterized by siloed approaches to care, fragmentation of mental health services from other health and social services, and a lack of attention to the contexts that shape and perpetuate inequities among marginalized groups. Recent efforts to promote the interconnectedness of mental, physical, and social health and transform systems into collaborative, integrated networks have paved the way for care provider groupings such as primary care and mental health specialty care and providers of housing, employment services, and other support services (Braithwaite, 2015). Mental health policy research may be further enhanced by shifting the conceptual paradigm from segmented, linear models to non-linear, interactive subsystems to account for the patterns of relationships and adaptations that contribute to emergent behaviors and events. While traditional research methods that compare groups, determine group membership, identify trend lines, and identify underlying structures abound in mental health research (Tabachnick & Fidell, 2019), additional methods that take location and multiple iterations into account can further aid investigators in understanding these interactive subsystems, which in turn can inform mental health policy through a complex adaptive system lens. This chapter explores a few of these emerging methods focusing on separate but related research methods.

Our discussion of new methods and related statistics focuses on three approaches: *spatial and geographical information systems (GIS), computer simulation,* and *predictive analysis.* Concepts relating to social work's person-in-environment perspective and complexity theory underlie these three areas of methods with them sharing several foundational characteristics. These three methods are grounded in the third wave of systems thinking, complexity theory. Location and the influences from where phenomena occur had received limited attention until the use of spatial methods. Spatial methods that measure location provide a useful means of understanding how outcome variables may be sensitive to where a person lives. Spatial and social influences in relation to pattern recognition for mental health policy research are also key factors. The concept of cellular automata will provide a useful segue from the use of spatial methods to the more advanced computational methods. Finally, we relate the three approaches to mental health services and policy research through examples. Concepts underlying each method will be discussed along with the type of question each method addresses, specific methods applicable to each approach, the data required for each approach, and the form of answer each approach provides.

OVERVIEW OF THE THREE APPROACHES: SPATIAL, SIMULATION, PREDICTIVE ANALYSIS

In the last 20 years, the explosion of both available data and computational power have led to the application of spatial, computational, and predictive analytic approaches to the social sciences (Watts, 2013). This has generated interdisciplinary approaches that combine social sciences, computer science, and complexity science (Cioffi-Revilla, 2010). Computational methods crosscut these approaches and include five major areas: automated information extraction, social network analysis, geospatial analysis, complexity modeling, and social simulation models (Cioffi-Revilla, 2010).

Traditional statistical modeling approaches focus on aggregate patterns and seek to identify how separate entities are related to the aggregate (Rand, 2017). These approaches tend to assume a bell-shaped distribution, while complexity modeling allows for the examination of power-law distributions (Cioffi-Revilla, 2010). Usually, these traditional approaches do not take into account how individuals are interconnected and interactively affect each other. Thus, computational social science harnesses the power of computers and big data to examine social phenomenon through a complexity lens.

However, the field has evolved in isolation from other social sciences with studies published primarily in science, not social science literature (Lazer et al., 2009; Watts, 2013). An important challenge of computational approaches to making a significant impact includes the breadth of expertise necessary to effectively apply these computational methods and the lack of communication between computer scientists and social scientists (Lazer et al., 2009; Watts, 2013). There is tremendous potential for knowledge building for the public good in a variety of social science fields (Lazer et al., 2009), including social work (Ihara & Lee, 2019; Lee & Wolf-Branigin, 2020). Next, we explore the possibilities of spatial analysis, simulation, and predictive analytics.

Spatial Analysis and Statistics

Our discussion begins with methods and related statistics focusing on the importance of location. Although spatial statistics have been used for decades, their use in social work remains relatively limited (Hillier, 2007). Spatial methods – which use location in a two-dimensional space as their basis – provide much of the foundation for computational and predictive methods because location matters. For example, using different variables of residents such as level of disability by location may indicate the presence of segregation based on ableism. Spatial statistics and the related geographical information systems (GIS) aid in understanding the person-in-environment perspective and realizing the impacts of location on social phenomena through the use of census tracts (Freisthler, Levy, Gruenewald, & Chow, 2006) or through longitude and latitude coordinates (Wolf-Branigin, LeRoy, & Miller, 2001). Essential to using spatial statistics is that at least one variable represents location. In this section we will discuss a few common methods including point pattern analysis, cluster analysis, spatial autocorrelation and regression, and social network analysis.

Point pattern analysis (PPA) views spatial arrangements of points in a two-dimensional space. Using a simple scatterplot, it typically maps locations where the axes are equally scaled (Wolf-Branigin & Wolf-Branigin, 2008). Using PPA, researchers identify differing patterns within the scatterplots; they may be random or patterned. Spatial autocorrelation and regression build upon PPA with the purpose of quantifying the identified patterns. A common measure of spatial autocorrelation, Moran's I, functions similarly to a Pearson product coefficient. Moran's I has values that range from a −1.0 to 1.0, where a −1.0 appears when observations fall on a ring, whereas a 1.0 represents a very tight cluster. A coefficient of 0.0 appears when observations are completely random. Cluster analyses while being a highly used statistical method further builds on spatial correlation by having the capacity to identify and quantify numerous clusters derived from a PPA. This also occurs in a two-dimensional space.

In an examination of housing patterns for persons with intellectual and developmental disabilities (IDD), PPA and spatial autocorrelation methods identified several issues (Wolf-Branigin, LeRoy, & Miller, 2001). For example, those who were higher functioning tended to live along public transit lines and in more independent situations. Further building on this framework, the investigators applied a spatial regression model in order to measure the impacts of housing location on size of the home, access to public transportation, and strength of support for the person with IDD. This moved from simple pattern recognition to understanding and explaining influences. This example demonstrates the need to assure that workers and supporters of these individuals were available in order to support and advocate for persons with disabilities (Wolf-Branigin, Wolf-Branigin, & Israel, 2007).

Although social network analysis (SNA) is not technically a spatial method, we include it because of its focus on relationships. Many behavioral perspectives presume that the individual units of a study do not influence other units in that study; however, SNA uses this assumption as its foundation. Social network analysis examines the interdependency among individual units and the effects of that interdependency on outcomes (Wasserman & Faust, 1994). This perspective values relationships between its units rather than their characteristics or attributes. Wasserman and Faust (1994) offer an example of SNA to understand corporate philanthropy. Traditional social science and economic approaches would typically begin analysis by measuring characteristics of corporations such as size, profit, and other characteristics. However, the social network perspective argues that the relationship between different corporations is equally important to understand behavior. How one entity acts can change the behavior of another.

SNA involves several key concepts. Actors may be discrete individuals, corporations, or collective social units. SNA focuses its applications on actors of a similar type. Relational ties are links that connect actors. Some examples include association, behavioral interaction, physical connection, biological relation and affiliation (Wasserman & Faust, 1994). The final key concept is the dyad – the smallest relationship established between two actors or agents. Relationships are not restricted to dyads. SNA considers relationships of differing complexity. SNA allows researchers to characterize the relationships beyond the individual. For example, 90 percent of foster youth aging out of care report that they have a connection to a caring adult (Lee & Ballew, 2018), yet this fails to capture the resources and support the youth's social network actually provides. Thus, SNA has been promoted as an important method in the study of foster youth aging out of care (Blakeslee, 2012). On a more theoretical level of applying SNA to hierarchical analyses, the Girvan–Newman algorithm (2002) may identify communities by eliminating the edges from a network. The connected components of the remaining network represent communities. This algorithm focuses on edges that are most likely between communities. This result is a dendrogram, or tree diagram, produced in a top-down manner through an iterative process.

As we conclude this discussion of spatial analysis, a brief introduction of cellular automata will aid in understanding the link to computational methods (Hegselmann & Flache, 1998; Katerelos & Koulouris, 2004). Cellular automata models apply a single rule to all agents, which base their decisions on their own state and the state of their neighbors (Miller & Page, 2007). For example, the passage of the Civil Rights Act in 1964 outlawed discrimination of the basis of race, religion, sex, national origin, segregation practices, although individuals and communities often self-segregates themselves into homogeneous neighborhoods. If a member of a different race joined the neighborhood, this would disrupt that homogeneous makeup and create discontent among residents, prompting them to vacate their neighborhood. Thomas Schelling created a model that simulates members of two recognizable groups distributing themselves throughout a neighborhood. He sought to understand the mechanisms of unorganized individual behavior and its effects on group behavioral outcomes. Schelling hypothesized that his model would generate a greater understanding of unorganized individual behaviors that influenced a collective movement in or out of a neighborhood.

Schelling's design began as a linear model. In this Spatial Proximity Model, Schelling randomly distributed 35 zeros and 35 pluses in a line. The zeroes and plusses represented members of two distinguishable groups, forming a neighborhood. Each group was concerned with whether their neighbors were zeros or pluses.

Schelling hypothesized that each member of this neighborhood wanted their four closest neighbors on each side to belong to the same group. Simply stated, each member wanted to belong to a five to nine majority. All members not satisfied with their neighbors would move to a new position that meets their criteria. This movement would occur left to right, beginning with the first dissatisfied neighbor. Once the initial round of movement was complete, more rounds of movement continued until all members of a neighborhood were satisfied. After three rounds of movement, Schelling found that the members of his neighborhood model were most satisfied when separated into alternating groups of 12.

After further testing this model, Schelling concluded that individual movement in neighborhoods led to a "tipping" behavior that created discontent in members of that neighborhood, subsequently causing them to leave. This movement would have a domino effect. As member movement led to more discontent, it created further movement. This movement ultimately created homogeneous segregated neighborhoods. The implication of Schelling's findings in 1971 has a direct impact on modern emerging research methodologies in social science. While Schelling's original model was done by hand, greater computational advancements exist that accelerate the predictive power of his model. The dynamic nature of Schelling's Spatial Proximity Model has laid the foundation for the emergence of computational social science and spatial analysis.

As we move to simulation approaches, additional linkages arise, including cross applications (Crooks, Malleson, Manley, & Heppenstall, 2020) which link to agent-based modeling, discussed in the next section, and GIS with the intention of using big data to aid in predicting and identifying patterns. Additionally, new methods involving spatial computation (Anselin, Sridharan, & Gholston (2007) allow for the prediction of patterns of various outcomes of interest, such as child welfare needs in relation to social and mental health indicators.

Computer Simulation

Social simulation models are potentially useful to mental health research because of the ability to incorporate some of the other methods into a simulation model, particularly SNA, geospatial elements, and complexity theory. Simulation is neither exclusively deductive nor inductive, but rather, provides an alternative approach. Similar to a deductive approach, simulation requires the specification of a set of assumptions (Axelrod, 1997). Yet, rather than proving a set of theorems, simulation produces data that can be analyzed inductively, allowing the researcher to identify any new patterns in the empirical data (Axelrod, 1997). Simulation can be considered a third way of doing science and thus has the potential to contribute significantly to building new knowledge (Axelrod, 1997).

Computer simulation, which includes mathematical modeling to represent a reality in order to predict future behavior, promises to be particularly useful for studying complex systems such as phenomena related to mental health. Even knowing the correct basic assumptions, we may not fully understand the implications of those assumptions (Axelrod, 1997; Gilbert & Troitzsch, 2005; Simon, 1996). This idea of not understanding the implications of basic premises can be understood to reflect the concept of emergent phenomena in complexity theory, where understanding the behaviors of individuals (micro motives) does not necessarily lead to understanding collective actions (macro behaviors). As Schelling (1969) demonstrated in his classic residential segregation model, even when individual preferences were in favor of living in a neighborhood where they were a minority, segregated neighborhoods still emerged at the collective level. This disconnect between the individual motive and collective behavior is an emergent phenomenon.

In particular, simulation is useful for studying heterogeneous, adaptive agents. As Axelrod (1997) argues, "simulation is often the only viable way to study populations of agents who are adaptive rather than fully rational" (p. 18). Adaption is hard to anticipate if there are many interacting components. Computer simulation allows for individuals to adjust their strategies over time, which can produce new insights into human decision making.

Heterogeneous, adaptive agents contribute to non-linear outcomes, and often we cannot identify equations to predict these non-linear behaviors (Gilbert & Troitzsch, 2005). Simulation can be particularly useful for studying behaviors that reflect a power-law distribution rather than a normal distribution (Cioffi-Revilla, 2010). Examples of phenomena that reflect a power-law distribution include natural disasters and the size of organizations (Cioffi-Revilla, 2010), as well as the use of shelters and services among individuals who are homeless. Additionally, simulation can be useful for studying tipping point events. Examples of a tipping point event include the residential segregation model, where there may be a point where one person moving initiates a wave of unhappy residents seeking to move. Similarly, the classic standing ovation model reflects a tipping point event, whereby when enough people stand to applaud a performance, there is a tipping point where everyone will stand. Such a cascading phenomenon can best be studied through simulation, which can help generate new insights in a way that equations could not (Miller & Page, 2007).

Similarly, simulation can also be useful for developing new knowledge around "large events" – these are events that are often written off in other approaches (Miller & Page, 2007). These approaches often occur because there is positive feedback in the system, such as a stock market crash or riot (Miller & Page, 2007). In other words, if there is a change in the system and one or two people start selling off their stocks, this triggers a positive feedback process whereby these changes are amplified and more people continue to sell their stocks. Thus, the positive feedback process also reflects a cascading phenomenon and new insights can be generated through a simulation of such a process.

Simulation Techniques

Three common simulation models include system dynamics models, microsimulation, and agent-based models (Gilbert & Troitzsch, 2005). A *system dynamics model* seeks to capture a real-world system in terms of stocks (assets or resources), flows (movement of resources), and variables. A system dynamics model includes one level, does not allow for communication between agents, and agents are quite simple. Examples of system dynamics models in mental health research include studies on post-traumatic stress disorder (PTSD) and the military, which can model the stock and flow of individuals recruited and then deployed to locations with various exposure to trauma, with an outcome of a stock of individuals with and without a PTSD diagnosis (Langellier et al., 2019). In this model, the individuals are modeled in the aggregate, and thus do not have any individual characteristics, so there is no option for heterogeneity in the individual agents. In fact, individuals are not actually represented in this approach, and there is no opportunity to simulate interactions between individuals. Rather, interactions are based on the flow between stocks, which is an assumed variable in the model.

A *microsimulation model* is data and prediction oriented. With extensive data on a population, the researcher often also has a set of transition probabilities – the probability an individual will transition into a different state. There are either static or dynamic microsimulation models. A dynamic model moves the population through space and time (i.e., ages the population). In contrast to the system dynamics model, a microsimulation model includes two levels. Moreover, there can be many agents in a microsimulation, which allows for heterogeneity in the agents in contrast to the system dynamics model that does not actually represent individuals. However, there is no interaction between agents in this type of a model. A common use for a microsimulation model is estimating the impact of a change in tax rate (Gilbert & Troitzsch, 2005). Additionally, microsimulation can be used to generate synthetic populations.

Microsimulation has seen more limited uptake, probably because of the amount of data it requires. However, in the case of individuals involved in the criminal justice system, where risk assessments are often administered at intake and repeated, this may offer the opportunity to calculate transition properties based on various sanctions or treatment interventions. Then, microsimulation can examine how changing a transition property by changing a sanction or treatment intervention can generate changes in population-level outcomes such as recidivism.

Finally, *agent-based models (ABM)* create agents who can interact with each other and with their environment. Thus, in contrast to the system dynamics model and similar to the microsimulation model, more than one level is modeled in an ABM, and each agent can be programmed to be heterogeneous. Also, in contrast to the system dynamics model and similar to the microsimulation model, many agents can be included in the simulation. However, ABM differs from the other approaches in that, not only can agents interact with each other, but they also can interact with their environment.

An example of an ABM related to mental health is the simulation of the etiology of depression among those who are obese, where several dynamic processes are modeled, including social isolation based on comparisons with peers and ostracization by peers who "drop" the obese individual from their network (Langellier et al., 2019). This simulation incorporates features of SNA, where individuals are connected or disconnected from a network of peers.

Thus, because of the ability to create heterogeneous agents in an ABM, the system is not bound to be linear since it is not governed by equations and probabilities. In contrast, system dynamics models are governed by equations. Similarly, a microsimulation model is governed by the transition probabilities that an individual will transition into a different state. In contrast, ABM allows for the opportunity for positive or negative feedback to alter the dynamics of the system and allows the researcher to explore how introducing instability may impact the system. Additionally, ABM allows for the opportunity to identify potential factors that may contribute to a tipping point.

All three techniques provide opportunities to develop new knowledge, and the choice of technique depends on the available data and the purpose of the simulation. System dynamics models are useful when there may be little information on individual agents and there is an interest in the overall outcome of the system. Microsimulation is useful when there are lots of data on individuals, and prediction is of interest. ABM, however, offers the most versatility in allowing not only for the inclusion of heterogeneous agents, but also interaction between agents and the environment. At the same time, a system dynamics model requires fewer assumptions. Similarly, microsimulation would require fewer assumptions and is more rooted in empirical data and transition probabilities. In contrast, ABM may require more assumptions about individual behavior, and thus may require more upfront programming work.

Agent-Based Modeling

In order to demonstrate ABM and complex adaptive systems in social work research, we developed a basic ABM involving youth at-risk of juvenile justice involvement (Lee & Wolf-Branigin, 2020). The model was developed in NetLogo, free software with many online resources. The *Rebellion Model* (Wilensky, 2004) available in the *NetLogo 6.03* model library (Wilensky, 1999) was adapted. In the model, youth and cops were represented moving around a neighborhood, and youth could choose to engage in delinquency while nearby cops could choose whether to arrest the youth. We measured educational attainment of youth at-risk for juvenile justice involvement. Our assumption was that while in secure placement, youth were not progressing academically with their peers. Further, we assumed that after missing a certain amount of school, a youth falls so far behind that catching up with their peers is unlikely. The model demonstrates the usefulness of computer simulation in studying non-linear dynamics, and more specifically showed the results of systematically testing the impact of various maximum durations of secure placement (during which the youth's educational progress was disrupted) on the youth's eventual completion of high school.

Predictive Analytics

The final approach we will discuss is predictive analysis. Building upon computational methods, predictive analytics uses information that is extracted from data in order to predict *trends* and patterns. Predictive analytics apply statistical techniques including different regression models, *data modeling*, *data mining*, and machine learning. Unlike other approaches that seek to address simple description or explanation, predictive analysis specifically focuses on prediction and decision support.

In order to set the scene, imagine you are a corrections social worker concerned about your client's risk of recidivism. Traditionally, the client's case manager would recommend that the client receive a risk assessment. A clinician would administer the screening and then evaluate the client's risk accordingly. Once the screening has been administered, the clinician's result is static. If the client needs re-evaluation a week later for elevated risk, the same process mentioned previously would need to be repeated. This process is slow and costly; however, now imagine there was a method for evaluating client recidivism risk in real time with automatically collected data from a constantly growing database. Big data can offer a resolution to this question in real time.

Growing from the new technological revolution of the early 2000s, the burgeoning prevalence of big data has piqued interest in numerous scientific fields. Using data mining, machine learning, artificial intelligence, regression, and other tools, researchers developed methods of using massive amounts of data to predict the likelihood of certain outcomes. Predictive analytics is an emerging research methodology that leverages big data to generate real-time predictions of future events (Cohen et al., 2014). These predictive models use statistical and analytical algorithms to provide users with recommendations for actions by identifying trends within data sets (Russell, 2015). As the model aggregates additional data, it adjusts itself to produce more accurate predictions. Increased interest in the application of predictive analytics in social sciences prompted investigations into the efficacy of these models. Thus, pioneering researchers established standards for measuring any model's reliability.

Standards

As predictive analysis gains credibility and increased use as a result of real-time testing on new data in social service interventions, it is imperative that these models receive critical evaluation against clear standards that consider the wealth of human experience when generating predictions. For accurate predictions, a model must consider and demonstrate four standards: validity, equity, reliability, and usefulness (D'Andrade, Austin, & Benton, 2008).

Validity is based on whether a predictive model measures what is attempting to be measured (Russell, 2015). A valid model should produce outcomes that are characteristic of the input data. Providing an example of predictive model validity in child protection agencies, Russell writes, "if families classified as high risk do not actually have substantially higher rates of future maltreatment than do families classified as moderate risk, then the risk assessment is simply not producing accurate results" (2015, p. 184). Typically, validity is statistically determined by receiver operating characteristics (ROC) (Fogarty, Baker, & Hudson, 2005). ROC, graphically represented as a curve, measures the rate of true positives against the rate of false positives for a range of possible results, thus determining the accuracy of a measurement.

The second standard that predictive analytic models in social sciences must meet is equity. An equitable model considers the accuracy of its outcomes across subgroups. For example, a model that predicts risk must ensure risk is defined the same for males and females, ethnicity groups, and geographic location. Equity in predictive models is essential to preventing *crossover*. Models experience crossover when a higher-risk client from a group receives lower outcome rates than lower-risk clients from another subgroup (Russell, 2015). In order for predictive analytic models to function properly, one must ensure that models classify outcomes similarly across all populations. Failure to create equity in a predictive model discredits its role in social sciences.

Reliability is the third standard for predictive models. A reliable model must produce consistent outcomes despite any number of different users. If after multiple uses, a model creates different outcomes from the same data, it is unreliable.

The final standard is usefulness. The output of a useful predictive model must demonstrate value when practically applied to a client or situation. A useful model offers pertinent information and provides guidance for its users and their clients (Russell, 2015). Additionally, usefulness means that the model must be easy to operate. If a model provides excellent information but is difficult to use correctly, then that model's usefulness is diminished. The most useful models provide the most accurate information and greatest ease of use. With these clearly defined standards, one can begin exploring current uses of predictive analytics in social science.

Examples
The application of predictive analytics to social services – and in particular mental health research and related services – is a relatively new phenomenon. Despite its recent arrival, researchers have been successful in using predictive analysis as a framework for developing risk assessment tools such as future success of adolescents with disabilities (Ihara, Wolf-Branigin, & White, 2012) and persons who misuse substances (Greenfield & Wolf-Branigin, 2009). One such tool is the Risk-Need-Responsivity Simulation Tool (RNR Simulation Tool), developed by George Mason University's Center for Advancing Correctional Excellence (ACE), which provides valuable information on substance misuse and mental health. Moving beyond simple risk assessment, the RNR Simulation Tool assesses an individual's risk of recidivism and then matches the individual with appropriate services based on their risk level, strength, and needs (Taxman, 2020). The goal of the RNR Simulation Tool is to provide criminal justice staff with decision-support tools, aiming to provide superior client-specific services. Additionally, the RNR Simulation Tool features an online self-assessment, allowing providers to work closely with clients to ensure the decision-support services are evidence-informed (Taxman, n.d.). Currently, the RNR Simulation Tool has been implemented in over 200 corrections departments across the United States.

Recall the example of the corrections social worker. In that hypothetical situation, the RNR Simulation Tool represents significant advancement in the quality and speed of social services provided. As predictive models such as the RNR Simulation Tool aggregate additional data, the accuracy of its predictions will improve. Current predictive technologies operate as excellent risk assessment tools. However, potential developments make it possible for predictive analysis models to be used on an instantaneous real-time basis (Cohen et al., 2014).

Consider another application of predictive models in the field of mental health. Salem State University researcher Christopher Hudson sought to utilize predictive models as an effective method for estimating the needs of psychiatric beds against the current availability (2020). Hudson's research found actual hospitalization ranged from 0 to 200.3 beds per 100,000 (2020) across 166 nations. However, with his model, Hudson employed non-linear regression analysis that yielded results more representative of a variety of characteristics. The model produces an estimated need of beds that ranged between 10.6 to 117.7 (Hudson, 2020). These calculations revealed that need for psychiatric beds significantly exceeded the actual availability of them. Further exploration into more complex models is likely to reveal more accurate predictions that will aid mental health professionals in handling the allocation of psychiatric beds. In the field of mental health, predictive analytics is poised to increase quality and availability of care as technological as models improve. While the future implications for predictive models such as the RNR Simulation Tool and Hudson's psychiatric bed model are promising, several challenges need addressing before predictive analytics can advance in social science.

Challenges

Access to large sets of time-series data is a current major limitation to predictive analytics in social science. While private business organizations easily collect transaction histories and network traffic, social science researchers require more complex data sets. The intake of this data is slow and typically requires a human element. Without sufficiently sized data sets, the model's users risk inaccurate results.

An additional challenge in data collection is data quality. Was the client honest during the assessment? Did the clinician leave out any significant information? These are two concerns that could cause data quality to decline. As a consequence of poor data quality, inaccurate results may adversely affect client care. Poor data quality may also mean limited variables and can be corrected for identified gaps and biases in the data. Predictive models analyze interactions and combinatorial effects of variables (Russell, 2015). A model can produce higher-quality results when it has more factors to consider. Thus, the data given to predictive models should be thoroughly collected.

Along with the challenges of effective data collection, ethical concerns must be considered. The first factor to consider is the security of client data. In 1996, the Health Insurance Portability and Accountability Act (HIPAA) established a privacy rule that allows the use of de-identified client data. Applying this rule to predictive models would decrease the risk of client data breaches. However, the privacy rule significantly diminishes the amount of data a model can collect, thus decreasing its predictive ability (Cohen et al., 2014).

Researchers must also account for the clinician's role in predictive model use. Cohen et al. express concern for clinicians who may have their expertise questioned by the rise in predictive models. If a clinician's prior experience gives reason to provide a particular intervention, but the model provides a contradictory prediction, it creates tension for the clinician, complicating the administering of the intervention.

Additional concerns include clinician malpractice as a result of a model's prediction. If a model prescribes an intervention that causes the patient harm, how does one assign fault? Is it the clinician's fault for administering the intervention, or is it the fault of the company that produced the predictive model? These are serious ethical concerns that demand addressing before use of predictive models in social science and mental health becomes widespread. There is significant need to create a governing body that regulates the creation and implementation of predictive analytics in social science. Without such structure, professionals risk malpractice and ethics violations.

The benefits of predictive analytics in social science are clear. These emerging methodologies allow researchers to harness big data to provide accurate predictions about client risk and care. Examples such as the RNR Simulation Tool demonstrate the current applications of predictive models in social science. As the model's capability grows, researchers should ensure it continually demonstrates validity, equity, reliability and usefulness in its predictions. Christopher Hudson's model of measuring psychiatric beds demonstrates the applicability of predictive analytics in mental health as a multifaceted aid in the preparation for and care of clients and patients. Additionally, further action should be taken to establish governing bodies that guide the growth of predictive analytics in social science. These technologies represent significant advances in the speed and quality of social services.

Hudson's model and the RNR Simulation Tool are quintessential examples of the types of questions that predictive analytics can answer. Leveraging massive amounts of data empowers users to make informed decisions regarding patient and client health. With the

Table 5.1   Characteristics of emerging research methods

APPROACH	METHODS	USEFUL FOR:	REQUIRED DATA	FORM OF ANSWER
Spatial	Point pattern analysis Spatial autocorrelation & regression	Incorporating location into the analysis	2-dimension (longitude & latitude Frequency of observations by location	Patterns are identified with possible explanations
Computer Simulation	System Dynamics Microsimulation Agent-based Modeling (ABM)	Studying non-linear processes and/or complex adaptive systems/ complexity theory	Useful in calibrating and validating the models	Results of options presented
Predictive Analytics	Data mining, Machine learning, Artificial intelligence, Statistics	Making predictions	Big data sets	Prediction of categorical and scaled outcomes

RNR Simulation Tool, predictive models provide users with a recidivism rate and suggested treatment. Meanwhile, Hudson's model for need of psychiatric beds provides information that prepares hospitals to treat estimated numbers of patients. While predictive models are excellent at forecasting, additional uses include identifying outliers and clustering data.

For models to function effectively, a broad variety of classifiers and variables must be collected. Most importantly, these variables must reflect the desired outcome. The RNR Simulation Tool likely does not collect data like hair color because it does not reflect recidivism. However, phenotypic studies might consider collecting such a variable. The collection of superfluous data will disrupt the proper functioning of predictive models. Instead, data should be multifaceted. When collecting data, researchers must consider the level of specificity needed to create an effective model. Thus, the more predictors that a model can consider, the better data can be provided to its users. This provides valuable information similar to methods that predict group membership with the additional benefit of generating insights at the unit of analysis level.

CONCLUSIONS AND REVIEW

Pattern recognition, commonly through the framework of complex adaptive systems, aids in applying these emerging research methods to mental health. The relationship of complexity science to mental health policy research is that experiments can easily be run to simulate differing policy options and benefits to mental health policy research.

Complexity theory is increasingly being applied to different social work issues ranging from human trafficking (Wolf-Branigin, Garza, & Smith, 2010) to transportation for persons with disabilities (Wolf-Branigin & Wolf-Branigin, 2008) to grandparents caring for grandchildren (Ihara, Horio, & Tompkins, 2012) to caregiver stress (Kennedy et al., 2015). Further undergirding the application of these research methods in contemporary practice are concepts including big data and data mining. The growing availability and use of big data from social media and other platforms are increasingly applied to solving problem through GIS and predicting phenomena.

All three sets of methods are concerned with planning and predicting phenomena (Table 5.1). Spatial methods are often used for predicting concentrations of people and related services such as housing, transportation, schools, and related physical and behavioral health services (Wolf-Branigin & Wolf-Branigin, 2010). Computational methods likewise may run experiments in order to test different practice and policy options. Finally, predictive analysis provides estimates and trends for selected mental health and related phenomena.

REFERENCES

Anselin, L., Sridharan, S., & Gholston, S. (2007). Using exploratory spatial data analysis to leverage social indicator databases: The discovery of interesting patterns. *Social Indicator Research, 82,* 287–309. https://doi.org/10/1007/s11205-006-9034-x

Axelrod, R. (1997). Advancing the art of simulation in the social sciences. *Complexity, 3*(2), 16–22. https://doi.org/10.1002/(SICI)1099-0526(199711/12)3:2<16::AID-CPLX4>3.0.CO;2-K

Blakeslee, J. (2012). Expanding the scope of research with transition-age foster youth: Applications of the social network perspective. *Child & Family Social Work, 17*(3), 326–36. https://doi.org/10.1111/j.1365-2206.2011.00787.x

Braithwaite, J. (2015). Bridging gaps to promote networked care between teams and groups in health delivery systems: A systematic review of non-health literature. *BMJ Open, 5*(9), e006567. https://doi.org/10.1136/bmjopen-2014-006567

Cioffi-Revilla, C. (2010). Computational social science. *Wiley Interdisciplinary Reviews: Computational Statistics, 2*(3), 259–21. https://doi.org/10.1002/wics.95

Cohen, I.G., Amarasingham, R., Shah, A., Xie, B., & Lo, B. (2014). The legal and ethical concerns that arise from using complex predictive analytics in health care. *Health Affairs (Project Hope), 33*(7), 1139–47. https://doi.org/10.1377/hlthaff.2014.0048

Crooks, A., Malleson, N., Manley, E., & Heppenstall, A. (2020). *Agent-based modelling and geographical information systems: A practical primer (Spatial Analytics and GIS)*. Sage.

D'Andrade, A., Austin, M.J., & Benton, A. (2008). Risk and safety assessment in child welfare: Instrument comparisons. *Journal of Evidence-Based Social Work, 5*(1–2), 31–56. https://doi.org/10.1300/J394v05n01_03

Fogarty, J., Baker, R., & Hudson, S. (2005). Case studies in the use of ROC curve analysis for sensor-based estimates in human computer interaction. *Human Computer Interaction: Proceedings of Graphics Interface (GI 2005),* 129–36. https://doi.org/10.1145/1089508.1089530

Freisthler, B., Levy, B., Gruenewald, P., & Chow, J. (2006). Methods and challenges of analyzing spatial data for social work problems: The case of examining child maltreatment geographically. Social Work Research, 30(4), 198–210. https://doi.org/10.1093/swr/30.4.198

Gilbert, N., & Troitzsch, K.G. (2005). *Simulation for the social sciences*. 2nd ed. Open University Press.

Girvan M., & Newman, M.E.J. (2002). Community structure in social and biological networks, *Proceedings of the National Academy of Science, 99,* 7821–26.

Greenfield, L., & Wolf-Branigin, M. (2009). Mental health indicator interaction in predicting substance abuse treatment outcomes in Nevada. *American Journal of Drug and Alcohol Abuse, 35*(5), 350–7. https://doi.org/10.1080/00952990903108223

Hegselmann, R., & Flache, A. (1998). Understanding complex social dynamics: A plea for cellular automata based modelling. *Journal of Artificial Societies and Social Simulation, 1*(3). https://www.jasss.org/1/3/1.html

Hillier, A. (2007). Why social work needs mapping. *Journal of Social Work Education, 43*(2), 205–22.

Hudson, C. (2020). Benchmarking psychiatric deinstitutionalization: Development, testing, and application of a model using predictive analytics. *Best Practices in Mental Health.*

Ihara, E.S., & Lee, J.S. (2019). Agent-based modeling: Value added to social work research. *Families in Society: The Journal of Contemporary Social Services, 100*(3), 305–11. https://doi.org/10.1177/1044389419842764

Ihara, E.S., Horio, B.M., & Tompkins, C.J. (2012). Grandchildren caring for grandparents: Modeling the complexity of family caregiving. *Journal of Social Service Research, 38*, 619–36. https://doi.org/10.1080/01488376.2012.711684

Ihara., E.S., Wolf-Branigin, M., & White, P. (2012). Quality of life and life skill baseline measures of urban adolescents with disabilities. *Social Work in Public Health, 27*(7), 658–70. https://doi.org/10.1080/19371910903269596

Katerelos, I.D., & Koulouris, A.G. (2004). Is prediction possible? Chaotic behavior of multiple equilibria regulation model in cellular automata topology. *Complexity, 10*(1), 23–36. https://doi.org/10.1002/cplx.20052

Kennedy, W.G., Ihara, E.S., Tompkins, C.J., Inoue, M., & Wolf-Branigin, M.E. (2015). Computational modeling of caregiver stress. *Journal on Policy and Complex Systems, 2*(1), 31–43. https://doi.org/10.18278/jcps.2.1.5

Kohn, R., Saxena, S., Levav, I., & Saraceno, B. (2004). The treatment gap in mental health care. *Bulletin of the World Health Organization, 82*(11), 858–66.

Langellier, B.A., Yang, Y., Purtle, J., Nelson, K.L., Stankov, I., & Diez Roux, A.V. (2019). Complex systems approaches to understand drivers of mental health and inform mental health policy: A systematic review. *Administration and Policy in Mental Health and Mental Health Services Research, 46*, 128–44. https://doi.org/10.1007/s10488-018-0887-5

Lazer, D., Pentland, A., Adamic, L., Aral, S., Barabasi, A.-L., Brewer, D., Christakis, N., Contractor, N., Fowler, J., Gutmann, M., Jebara, T., King, G., Macy, M., Roy, D., & Alstyne, M.V. (2009). Computational social science. *Science, 323*, 721–3.

Lee, J.S., & Ballew, K.M. (2018). Independent living services, adjudication status, and the social exclusion of foster youth aging out of care in the United States. *Journal of Youth Studies, 21*(1), 940–57. https://doi.org/10.1080/13676261.2018.1435854

Lee, J.S., & Wolf-Branigin, M. (2020). Innovations in modeling social good: A demonstration with juvenile justice intervention. *Research on Social Work Practice, 30*(2), 174–85. https://doi.org/10.1177/1049731519852151

Miller, J.H., & Page, S.E. (2007). *Complex adaptive systems: An introduction to computational models of social life*. Princeton, NJ: Princeton University Press.

Rand, W. (2017). Introduction to agent-based modeling. Santa Fe Institute Complexity Explorer. Retrieved August 2022 from https://www.complexityexplorer.org/coures/90-introduction-to-agent-based-modeling

Russell, J. (2015). Predictive analytics and child protection: Constraints and opportunities. *Child Abuse and Neglect, 46*, 182–9. https://doi.org/10.1016/j.chiabu.2015.05.022

Schelling, T.C. (1969). Models of segregation. *The American Economic Review, 59*(2), 488–93.

Schelling, T. (1971). Dynamic models of segregation, *The Journal of Mathematical Sociology, 1*(2), 143–86. https://doi.org/10.1080/0022250X.1971.9989794

Simon, H.A. (1996). *The sciences of the artificial*. 3rd ed. MIT Press.

Tabachnick, B., & Fidell, L. (2019). *Multivariate statistics*. 7th ed. Pearson.

Taxman, F. S. (2020). Community Capacity-Building and Implementation Advances to Addressing the RNR Framework. In *Beyond Recidivism* (pp. 39-56). NYU Press. Wasserman, S., & Faust, K.L. (1994). *Social network analysis: Methods and applications*. Cambridge University Press.

Watts, D.J. (2013). Computational social science. *The Bridge on Frontiers of Engineering, 43*(4), 5–10.

Whiteford, H.A., Degenhardt, L., Rehm, J., Baxter, A.J., Ferrari, A.J., Erskine, H.E., Charlson, F.J., Norman, R.E., Flaxman, A.D., Johns, N., Burstein, R., Murray, C.L., & Vos, T. (2013). Global burden of disease attributable to mental and substance use disorders: Findings from the Global Burden of Disease Study 2010. *Lancet, 382*, 1575–86. http://dx.doi.org/10.1016/S0140-6736(13)61611-6

Wilensky, U. (1999). NetLogo. Evanston, IL: Center for Connected Learning and Computer-Based Modeling, Northwestern University. Retrieved August 2022 from http://ccl.northwestern.edu/netlogo/

Wilensky, U. (2004). NetLogo Rebellion model. Evanston, IL: Center for Connected Learning and Computer-Based Modeling, Northwestern University. Retrieved August 2022 from http://ccl.northwestern.edu/netlogo/models/Rebellion

Wolf-Branigin, M., & Wolf-Branigin, K. (2008). The emerging field of travel training services: A systems perspective. *Journal of Public Transportation, 11*(3), 105–19.

Wolf-Branigin, K., & Wolf-Branigin, M. (2010). A travel training cost benefit model for people with disabilities, public transportation agencies and communities. *TRANSED*. Washington, DC: US Transportation Research Board.

Wolf-Branigin, M., LeRoy, B., & Miller, J. (2001). Physical inclusion of people with developmental disabilities: An evaluation of the Macomb-Oakland Regional Center. *American Journal on Mental Retardation, 106*(4), 368–75.

Wolf-Branigin, M., Wolf-Branigin, K., & Israel, N. (2007). The complexity of attracting and retaining direct support professionals. *Journal of Social Work in Disability and Rehabilitation, 6*(4), 15–30. https://doi.org/10.1300/J198v06n04_02

Wolf-Branigin, M., Garza, S., & Smith, M. (2010). Reducing demand for human trafficking: A non-linear approach for developing capacity. *Social Work and Christianity: An International Journal, 37*(4), 424–36.

PART III

SELECTED RESEARCH RESULTS AND POLICY APPLICATIONS

6. Dissemination and implementation of mental health services: the problem, the response, the new science

Russell K. Schutt

What is true of individuals also holds true for organizations. Just as individuals do not often change established behaviors simply due to learning new facts or hearing rational arguments (Slovic, 1995), so too organizations do not readily change established practices after the evidence base shifts in new directions or recognized authorities change their recommendations (Erwin & Garman, 2010). Behavioral psychology's critique of simplistic rational choice explanations for individual behavior (Kahneman & Tversky, 1979) is thus paralleled at the organizational level by neo-institutional theory's emphasis on the power of organizational inertia and the constraints of operating in an organizational field (DiMaggio & Powell, 1983).

It is therefore not surprising that the scientific discovery of a better way to deliver healthcare – an "evidence-based practice" – is often not followed by widespread implementation: "the process of putting to use or integrating new practices within a setting" (Berwick, 2003; Institute of Medicine, 2001; Nilsen, 2015). As early as 1993, the American Medical Association had adopted 1,200 evidence-based practice guidelines – and was adding more than 300 each year – but evidence that the guidelines had a significant impact on medical practice was, at best, mixed (Lomas et al., 1993). It is also not surprising that, as one example in mental healthcare, interventions for children with psychiatric and developmental disorders are less effective in the community than in research settings, are not sustained over time, and take on average 20 years to integrate into routine practice (Dingfelder & Mandell, 2011). Neither diffusion – the unplanned spread of new practices – nor dissemination – the active, planned spread of new practices – ensures the implementation of new practices (Lomas et al., 1993; Nilsen, 2015).

What is surprising is that it took almost half a century for the healthcare research community that developed after World War II to identify dissemination and implementation as an important research focus and to begin to develop the theories, funding mechanisms, and systematic evidence that can improve the translation of research findings into more effective healthcare policies and programs. Surprising, not only because of the evident need to improve the translation process, but also because the history of mental health services is replete with efforts to implement new programs that have identified the challenges that must be overcome in the implementation process and that have generated hypotheses for systematic research about that process.

I will first discuss several historical examples of implementing new practices into mental health services that have identified key implementation challenges. I will also describe the institutional changes that have provided the foundation for the emergence of the science of implementation and have supported its rapid growth. I will then review this new science that has developed to better guide dissemination and implementation efforts, with attention to what has been learned in recent decades and where the field is headed (Bauer et al., 2015; Grimshaw

Table 6.1   Typology of mental health services

		Scope of Use	
		Extensive	Limited
Systemic	High	Deinstitutionalization	Assertive Community Treatment (ACT)
Complexity	Low	Psychotropic Medication	Cognitive Behavioral Therapy (CBT)

& Russell, 1993). Throughout the chapter, I will often use the term "implementation" to connote both the processes of dissemination and implementation, but my primary focus will be on implementation itself, as the process that is both a necessary condition for improving healthcare and the most difficult step in the research-to-practice pipeline.

IDENTIFYING THE PROBLEM

Deinstitutionalization, psychotropic medication, Assertive Community Treatment (ACT), and Cognitive Behavioral Therapy (CBT) each changed the experience of mental health services for millions. These interventions differed in both their complexity and their scope (Table 6.1), which in turn shaped the challenges faced during their implementation. Simply put, the two more complex interventions required more changes in the existing mental health service system, while the two interventions whose scope included a larger fraction of the client population had to cope with greater variability in effects. I conclude my review of these four interventions with a conceptual discussion of features that influence the success of implementation efforts.

Deinstitutionalization

The extraordinary depopulation of state psychiatric hospitals in the US from 1955 to 2010 is irrefutable proof that mental health services can be changed, even when they are deeply embedded in an established and supportive institutional matrix and when their scope is so broad as to affect millions of patients, family members, and employees. From a peak of 339 per 100,000 persons in 1955, the rate of hospitalization in state mental institutions plummeted by 96 percent to 14 per 100,000 persons in 2010 (Torrey et al., 2012). New laws redirected public funding; exposés in books, newspapers, and movies changed public sentiment; universities revised training programs; professional associations updated their standards (Schutt, 2016). The abandoned buildings and grounds that had once been objects of pride for an earlier era of reformers now bore mute testimony to "the shame of the states" that they had become (Deutsch, 1948).

Unfortunately, the history of deinstitutionalization also makes it clear that implementation of even a major change in mental health service organization – ostensibly even one motivated for many by good intentions and supportive research – will not necessarily improve service practice. Only one-third of the planned community mental health centers were built and many abjured treating the chronically ill discharged patients, while many of those needing services declined to accept what was offered (Grob, 1991). Compounding the problem, during the 1970s and 1980s, cheap lodging largely vanished from many cities (Schutt, 2011). As a result, for large numbers who became homeless or incarcerated, the effect of deinstitutionalization was a different form of maltreatment and neglect rather than improved services grounded in research discoveries.

There are three key reasons that the initially high hopes were not realized. First, the diverse groups of stakeholders that benefitted from depopulating state hospitals did not have a common stake in the success of services intended to replace them. Reducing state taxpayer burden, shifting fiscal responsibility from state to federal sources, enhancing the prestige of psychiatry, reducing the stigmatization of serious mentally ill persons, and increasing patient autonomy were benefits that did not increase even more with the development of effective community-based services for former inpatients. Any effort to translate research findings into new service practices must include careful identification of the costs and benefits for affected stakeholders and an implementation strategy that addresses them.

Further reducing effective implementation of deinstitutionalization was inadequate understanding of the problem institutional care had created. Belief that the disempowering effects of established hospital structures and processes were the only problem to be solved discounted the importance of building supportive social communities to aid functional recovery. Ongoing research both within and outside of state hospitals had yielded increasing evidence of the value of systematic programs to build social support (Grob, 1991; Moos, 1974; Talbott, 1978), but that research was largely ignored in the rush to reduce institutional funding. In this way, both the perceived efficacy of the intervention and the extent of understanding of the mechanism for its effects influenced the impact of research findings on service practice.

The context for deinstitutionalization beyond the mental health service system itself also shaped the way in which it was implemented. Constraints on state budgets made deinstitutionalization almost inevitable, while a broader cultural shift to greater respect for patient rights and greater attention to social issues in the profession of psychiatry were important contributing factors (Grob, 1994; Johnson, 1990; Mollica, 1983). Multiple contextual factors can be assumed to shape the success of any attempts to implement new mental health services.

Psychotropic Medication

The discovery in the 1950s of psychoactive drugs that could diminish symptoms of psychosis provided a key impetus for deinstitutionalization. Relieving the behavior resulting from psychotic delusions and paranoid thoughts made community-based services much more plausible, even though these new drugs did not improve the cognitive or social functioning that is so critical for community functioning (Grob, 1991; Schutt et al., 2015). With the introduction in the 1960s of benzodiazepines such as valium and Librium to treat symptoms of anxiety, followed by development of selective serotonin reuptake inhibitors (SSRIs) that could relieve depression, psychopharmacology became a dissemination and implementation success story. By 2015, about 70 percent of persons diagnosed with major depressive disorder in the US took one or more antidepressants, representing over one-tenth of persons 12 or over (Luo et al., 2020).

Unlike shifting stakeholder motivations during the process of deinstitutionalization, the widespread adoption of psychotropic medication provided sustained benefits for most stakeholders: extraordinary profits for pharmaceutical firms, more remunerative forms of practice for psychiatrists and other clinicians with prescribing privileges, easier treatment protocols for patients and their families – and some symptomatic relief for many patients. The apparent benefits of psychotropic medication – particularly the ability of the benzodiazepines and SSRIs to improve mood in the broader population – so far exceeded the costs that general practitioners became the primary providers of this form of mental health treatment and millions of persons who would not otherwise have received mental health services became patients (Kramer, 1987). It appeared that in this way implementation could become a self-fulfilling prophecy rather than a barrier to usage.

When the federally funded Schizophrenia Patient Outcomes Research Team (PORT) developed evidence-based treatment recommendations (see next section), 18 of its 30 recommendations concerned use of psychotropic medication (Lehman & Steinwachs, 1998). In fact, the first PORT recommendation was that antipsychotic medications should be the first treatment to reduce psychotic symptoms for persons experiencing an acute episode of schizophrenia, based on results of over 100 randomized double-blind trials indicating that 50–80 percent of persons treated in this way would improve significantly, compared with 5–45 percent of those in a placebo condition.

But there is more to the psychotropic medication implementation story. The initial hope that psychotropic medication would provide the necessary and sufficient cure for serious mental illness soon foundered on the shoals of side effects, the rocks of treatment resistance, and the diverse streams of human variability. Benzodiazepines could impair psychomotor and cognitive functioning, as well as disinhibit behavior and induce dependence (Lader, 2011). Early antipsychotic medication could induce tardive dyskinesia and impair cognition, while many of the second-generation antipsychotics introduced in the 1990s avoided these effects but led to severe weight gain or other medical risks (Barton et al., 2020). Efforts to find an efficacious drug protocol for each patient could seem like a series of hit-or-miss attempts rather than a scientifically guided process – although increasing hope for genome-based personalization (Corponi et al., 2018; Levchenko et al., 2020). The difficulty of identifying the neurobiological pathways that could restore healthy functioning thus created problems for consumers of psychotropic drugs that in turn generated resistance among some advocacy groups and other stakeholders. The widespread use of psychotropic medication thus exposed a lack of sufficient understanding of the causal mechanism of their effects that could guide prescribing practice.

Assertive Community Treatment

While implementation of deinstitutionalization and psychotropic medication affected many aspects of mental health services and millions of service consumers, the intended scope of Assertive Community Treatment was more limited. Developed at the Mendota Mental Health Institute in Madison, Wisconsin, to increase success in community living among persons with serious and persistent mental illness, ACT provides intensive, integrated interdisciplinary support teams that deliver and coordinate services across treatment settings (Stein & Santos, 1998). Its efficacy first established in a randomized controlled trial, ACT received a "Gold Achievement Award" from the Hospital and Community Psychiatry Service of the American Psychiatric Association in 1974 (Dixon, 2000). Since then, ACT's efficacy has been replicated in numerous randomized controlled trials, it has been adopted in more than 33 states, adapted to better serve persons dually diagnosed with a substance abuse disorder, persons who are homeless, and those on parole, and added to most recommendations of best practices (Lehman & Steinwachs, 1998; Phillips et al., 2001).

Two of the Schizophrenia PORT evidence-based treatment recommendations supported use of ACT, based on multiple randomized trials that demonstrated reduced inpatient use and some improvement in clinical and social outcomes (warranting a grade of A for the evidence), and some evidence supporting a recommendation to focus ACT on high-risk persons (with a grade of B) (Lehman & Steinwachs, 1998).

However, ACT is less general in its intended scope than deinstitutionalization and is a complex intervention to implement due to its multidisciplinary approach with 10–12 team members and need for ongoing support to maintain favorable outcomes. The ratio of benefits to costs for providing ACT is only favorable for mental health services if its use is limited to patients who tend otherwise to be frequently hospitalized (50 or more days annually) and if the cost of that hospitalization is included in the calculation (Dixon, 2000). As a result, maintaining support for full ACT services requires sufficient legislative support for the welfare of persons who are likely to otherwise be homeless, incarcerated, or institutionalized.

Cognitive Behavioral Therapy

CBT reflected a shift in psychotherapeutic practice from more psychoanalytic approaches focused on the origins of psychiatric maladies to a more present-oriented, problem-solving approach with attention to the cognitions associated with behaviors (Beck, 1976; Lorenzo-Luaces et al., 2016). CBT practitioners focus on patients' perceptions of situations and develop hypotheses with patients about the beliefs that shape their behavior and guide personalized tests of these hypotheses (Dattilio & Hanna, 2012). The widespread popularity of this approach in recent decades is reflected in hundreds of clinical trials and more than a dozen meta-analyses (Gaudiano, 2008). A recent systematic review and network meta-analysis of 91 studies of CBT found it effective in reducing depression, compared with treatment-as-usual, with little impact of variation in specific treatment components (López-López et al., 2019). Supportive findings have also been reported in systematic reviews and meta-analyses of the use of CBT for anxiety-related disorders (van Dis et al., 2020) and, to a lesser extent, for reducing symptoms of schizophrenia (Jauhar et al., 2014).

In general, however, effect sizes have been only small to moderate – and smaller when more rigorous research designs were used (Gaudiano, 2008; Lynch et al., 2010). What accounts for such success in implementation without demonstration of compelling benefits? Since providing CBT in mental health services primarily requires training therapists in this form of treatment, rather than hiring different types of practitioners or changing organizational structures, it is relatively easy to implement. The relative ease of its adoption may have had the effect of reducing the evidentiary requirements about CBT's efficacy.

These and many other variable results of efforts to change mental health services helped identify the potential for implementation, the need for systematic research on the implementation process, and some of the propositions about implementation that needed elaboration and testing. The probability of successful implementation seemed inversely related to the complexity of the changes required by the intervention in the mental health service system and by the scope of its intended application. Moreover, limited scope seemed able to compensate for more complexity (ACT), while limited complexity seemed able to compensate for extensive scope (psychotropic medication). The extent of implementation of new interventions could also be expected to vary with the strength of the evidence indicating effectiveness, costs and benefits for different groups of stakeholders, and the context in which implementation was to be attempted. Each of these influences could occur in many different forms and they could be expected to interact with each other. Systematic research was needed to develop and test the many possible hypotheses that could be generated by these and other experiences with implementation.

BUILDING THE FOUNDATION

The post-War World II emergence and expansion of the National Institutes of Health (NIH) in its current form fueled rapid growth of medical treatments supported by research and thus magnified the importance of effective dissemination and implementation. Increased political concern with the public benefit resulting from government spending also motivated more attention to the research-to-practice pipeline (Pew Research Center, 2015). Federally supported efforts to develop mental health research charted a different course for that pipeline than occurred in other areas of healthcare.

While the primary NIH focus was on basic research and clinical bioscience, the National Institute of Mental Health (NIMH) incorporated the former Division of Mental Hygiene in 1946 and supported training and service provision as well as research. The 1960s saw priorities shift toward service programs, but after several reorganizations during the Nixon years, NIMH was combined with the National Institute on Drug Abuse (NIDA) and National Institute on Alcohol Abuse and Alcoholism (NIAAA) in the new Alcohol, Drug Abuse, and Mental Health Administration (ADAMHA). The largest proportion of ADAMHA funds were used for services programs until 1982, when the Reagan administration shifted funding for most service activities to block grants to the states.

In 1988, as part of the Anti-Drug Abuse Act of 1988 (P.L. 100-690), Congress required the Secretary of Health and Human Services to have the National Academy of Sciences (NAS) review research at ADAMHA and NIH to determine, in part, "the appropriateness of administering health service programs in conjunction with the administration of biomedical and behavioral research" (Institute of Medicine, 1991, p. 4). Although the subsequent NAS report did not explicitly recommend a reallocation of responsibilities between agencies, it concluded that "co-administration of research and service programs can retard the productivity of both programs" (Institute of Medicine, 1991, p. 6). Acknowledging the difficulty of creating a research-to-practice pipeline, the report's authors also concluded that

> Many of the reform efforts of the past have rested on the assumption that change can be devised and implemented at the administrative level, which will provoke change at the point of service delivery. The experience of these years, however, suggests that such a relationship may be an act of faith rather than demonstrated by evidence. (p. 12)

In 1992, the ADAMHA Reorganization Act attempted to resolve these difficulties by abolishing ADAMHA, moving NIMH, NIAAA, and NIDA back into NIH with a mandate to support research, and creating the Substance Abuse and Mental Health Services Administration (SAMHSA) with a mandate to reduce the impact of substance abuse and mental illness on American communities (About Us | SAMHSA).

After the reorganization, efforts continued to improve NIH's ability to translate research findings into more effective practice. In 1993, Congress established the NIH Office of Behavioral and Social Science Research (OBSSR) to, in part, identify and encourage research "to develop viable pathways to improve individual and population health" and to encourage "behavioral intervention research in the context in which these interventions are intended to be delivered."[1]

The National Academy of Sciences' Institute of Medicine convened a committee to develop a report reflecting a similar change in 2000 (Smedley & Syme, 2000). One of the most important NIMH initiatives in response to "much concern that this knowledge [about effective treatment for schizophrenia] is not being disseminated so that all persons may benefit from it" was the Schizophrenia PORT developed in collaboration with the Agency for Health Care Policy and Research (AHCPR) (Lehman et al., 1995). The PORT was charged with a comprehensive review of the outcomes literature as the foundation for developing and disseminating recommendations for treatment of schizophrenia based on scientific evidence. The result was 30 recommendations in seven categories: (1) antipsychotic medications; (2) adjunctive pharmacotherapies for anxiety, depression, aggression/hostility; (3) electroconvulsive therapy; (4) psychological interventions; (5) family psychoeducation; (6) vocational rehabilitation; (7) assertive community treatment/assertive case management (Lehman and Steinwachs, 1998). Based on a review of between 427 (family interventions) and 5,129 (medications – including adjunctive) citations found between 1965 and 1993 in the different areas, the level of evidence for each of the resulting recommendations was graded as A (good research-based evidence with some expert opinion) – 8 recommendations; B (fair research-based evidence with substantial expert opinion) – 16 recommendations; or C (minimal research-based evidence but significant clinical experience, primarily expert opinion) – 6 recommendations.

Recognizing that the dissemination of PORT's recommendations did not result in widespread adoption in mental health services, the Robert Wood Johnson Foundation then funded the Implementing Evidence-Based Practices Project in 1998 to improve implementation of evidence-based practices – interventions "for which there is strong research demonstrating effectiveness in assisting consumers to achieve outcomes" (Mueser et al., 2003, p. 389). The project developed intensive implementation packages for each of five psychosocial practices recommended by PORT in a process involving extensive consultation with stakeholders and then field-testing and refining implementation packages at a limited number of sites in eight states, before implementing the practices within 53 community mental health centers across the eight states. Implementation packages included procedures for developing administrative support structures with each participating program, engaging clinicians, families, and consumers, and two days of intensive training of the practitioners who would deliver each evidence-based practice, followed by regular visits and weekly telephone supervision (Torrey et al., 2005). Complete implementation "toolkits" for each practice included a user's guide, implementation tips, videos and PowerPoint presentations and brochures, as well as practitioner workbooks and the scales to be used to measure implementation fidelity (McHugo et al., 2007).

Processes and outcomes of implementation were then studied for two years at each site using a mixed-methods design (McHugo et al., 2017). The success of implementation varied across the five psychosocial practices. ACT, supported employment, and family psychoeducation each received fidelity scores in the acceptable range, with three-quarters of the sites reaching the goal of high-fidelity implementation. However, fidelity scores attained in illness management and recovery practices and in integrated dual disorders treatment received average scores below the fidelity threshold, with fewer than half of the sites achieving high-fidelity implementation. McHugo et al. (2007) suggest the differences in implementation success could be due to the faster pace of implementation possible with practices such as ACT and supported employment that involve structural changes, as compared with the slower pace required with practices that are more dependent on extensive clinical training and supervision.

In 2005, NIH established a new Institutional Clinical and Translational Science Awards program and in the same year sponsored a meeting of biomedical researchers who reached agreement on the need to enhance clinical and translational science. An NIH Roadmap outlined steps to both accelerate the pace of scientific discovery and improve the translation of these discoveries into clinical practice (Zerhouni, 2006). Reflecting the "growing concern with implementation and dissemination within health services," NIMH developed a center in collaboration with UCLA and RAND to lessen the gap between research and practice (Mendel et al., 2008). In 2009, NIH hosted a Research Week on community engagement to improve research impact. In 2012, Congress funded a new NIH National Center for Advancing Translational Sciences (NCATS).

Apart from NIH, The Cochrane Collaboration developed in 1993 a structure for soliciting systematic reviews to evaluate research on medical treatments and improve dissemination of evidence-based practices, including now more than 8,600 reviews (about 2,300 referencing mental health) and more than 1.7 million records of controlled trials (about 3,800 pertaining to mental health interventions).[2] The Veterans Health Administration launched in 1998 the Quality Enhancement Research Initiative (QUERI) to "systematically [implement] … clinical research findings and evidence-based recommendations into routine clinical practice" (Damschroder, 2009). SAMSHA (nd) developed Evidence-Based Practices Kits to support implementation of efficacious interventions for serious mental illnesses.[3] The 2010 Patient Protection and Affordable Care Act (Obamacare) included funding for a new Patient-Centered Outcomes Research Institute (PCORI) with a mandate "to improve the quality and relevance of evidence available to help patients, caregivers, clinicians, employers, insurers, and policy makers make better-informed health decisions" based on a foundation of comparative effectiveness research.[4]

These institutional developments have transformed the foundation for building scientific evidence about implementation efforts. The result has been substantial progress in that evidentiary base, but as the next section indicates, much more work must be completed before implementation science provides sufficient guidance for successful implementation of new mental health interventions in diverse settings.

DEVELOPING THE SCIENCE

Difficulties in implementing new approaches in public and mental health services and increased institutional attention to improving the research-to-practice pipeline fueled development of Implementation Science: "the scientific study of methods to promote the systematic uptake of research findings and other EBPs (evidence-based practices) into routine practice, and hence, to improve the quality and effectiveness of health services" (Bauer et al., 2015). Early implementation science projects relied on a linear model of the research-services continuum, in which basic research was to be followed by applied and clinical research, that would in turn lead to the process of implementing the new practices (Institute of Medicine, 1991, p. 76). More specifically, randomized clinical trials would first establish an intervention's efficacy, followed by evaluation studies to establish the intervention's effectiveness in real-world settings before the resulting "evidence-based practices" would be implemented in community settings and then examined through implementation research projects.

In 1999, Glasgow et al. established the importance of guiding implementation research with a multi-dimensional conceptual model. His RE-AIM framework had five dimensions:

1. **Reach**: number and characteristics of participants compared with intended population.
2. **Efficacy:** (subsequently "effectiveness"): impact on positive and negative outcomes, including behavior and quality-of-life.
3. **Adoption**: proportion and representativeness of settings that adopt the intervention.
4. **Implementation**: extent to which intervention delivered as intended.
5. **Maintenance**: extent to which intervention becomes stable, enduring behavior (for individual and/or organization/community).

Yet efforts to use Glasgow's model to study the implementation process revealed new challenges (Glasgow et al., 2019). Harden et al.'s (2015) subsequent systematic review of 107 articles representing 82 unique intervention studies that had used the RE-AIM framework (53 percent being randomized controlled trials) found little evidence that it had stimulated more holistic implementation research. About half of these articles reported on the intervention's effectiveness in influencing individual behavioral outcomes – outcomes were positive for 89 percent – but most studies did not report on all five of the RE-AIM outcomes and few sought to improve any outcome other than effectiveness.

The Robert Wood Johnson Foundation's Implementing Evidence-Based Practices Project (IEBPP) also "had not uncovered any simple, generally applicable recipe for enabling practice change" during its Phase II effort to implement EBPs in eight states (Torrey et al., 2005, p. 304). Instead, IEBPP researchers learned that implementing evidence-based practices was often not a top priority and that the implementation process was complex and required highly skilled leaders and trainers. EBPs that solved clear problems, such as using ACT to lessen repeated hospitalizations, tended to attract more interest. In a joint 2009 report, the National Research Council and Institute of Medicine highlighted "growing concerns that evidence-based interventions (EBIs) have yet to deliver on the promise of population-level impact."

New approaches intended to improve implementation efforts include hybrid research designs that blur the distinction between effectiveness trials and implementation efforts, iterative approaches that engage stakeholders in decision-making about implementation, systematic analysis of and adaptation to the context surrounding the program being implemented, and increased attention to intervention sustainability over time – as well as the need to "de-implement" unsuccessful programs. Comprehensive frameworks for implementation that include many of these new approaches have also been proposed and tested.

Hybrid Designs

Landes et al. (2019) proposed accelerating implementation with one of three types of hybrid designs in which testing effectiveness could occur simultaneously with evaluating implementation:

1. **Type 1 hybrid**: focuses primarily on effectiveness outcomes while exploring implementability of intervention.

2. **Type 2 hybrid**: dual focus on effectiveness and implementation outcomes, allowing simultaneous testing or piloting of implementation strategies during effectiveness trial.
3. **Type 3 hybrid**: focuses primarily on implementation outcomes while also collecting effectiveness outcomes related to uptake or fidelity. Usually works best with easily accessible outcomes from patient records.

The rationale for the Type 2 hybrid design illustrates the appeal of this approach. A new government policy may mandate use of an intervention whose efficacy has not yet been adequately tested or in a setting where it has not previously been implemented. A research team adopting the Type 2 design would continue to test the intervention's effectiveness, while also collecting data on the implementation process in that setting. The result should be more data on effectiveness and enriched understanding of implementation challenges.

Stakeholder Input

Many researchers have sought to obtain stakeholder feedback before, during, and after the implementation (McHugo et al., 2007). The goal is to learn from insiders in the community involved in implementation about the organizational context that may affect interest in and implementation of the intervention, as well as to improve the communication of findings to populations of concern (Mazzucca et al., 2021). Powell and Beidas note that "Failing to account for different types of stakeholders may be a recipe for failure" (2016, p. 830).

Potential clients can have in-depth knowledge of circumstances that will affect reactions to the intervention, stakeholders in positions ranging from clinical staff to community health workers and social workers may play key roles in delivering the intervention, and community leaders can play a key role in developing trust among potential clients of the intervention and in communicating study findings (Frank et al., 2014). Social pressure for implementation of early intervention in psychosis programs was increased by alliances with users, family members, non-governmental organizations, and community organizations (Csillag et al., 2018). The importance of stakeholder involvement is magnified for interventions implemented with socially disadvantaged populations that are separated from researchers by social class, power, race, and ethnicity (Frank et al., 2014).

Context

Implementation experience also highlights the importance of taking context into account. Defined as "social, organizational, and external factors that influence the success of implementation," the context for an implementation effort can include organizational culture, financial constraints, and political influences (Mazzucca et al., 2021, p. 137). Moullin et al. (2019) and others distinguish the "outer context" from the "inner context" for implementation:

1. Outer context: leadership, service environment/publics, funding/contracting, inter-organizational environment and networks, physicians/client characteristics, patient/client advocacy.
2. Inner context: leadership, organizational characteristics, quality and fidelity monitoring/support, organizational staffing process, individual characteristics.

Mazzucca et al. (2021, pp. 140–1) emphasize that the organizational context should directly inform implementation efforts and that partnerships should be built with community organizations on the basis of mutual trust and benefit, rather than just the needs of the academic institution.

Sustainability

Implementing interventions in community settings also requires attention to the extent to which they are sustained over time. As R. Saunders et al. (2020) document for the Psychology of Parenting Project, the extent to which an intervention is delivered with high fidelity can be increased with such techniques as standardized training, manualizing materials, ongoing supervision after training, developing an accreditation system, and creating support networks of trained practitioners. However, there is an inherent tension between maximizing fidelity and adapting an intervention to changing contexts and other circumstances. Powell and Beidas (2016) recommend considering the entire system of care and delivery during the adaptation process. Gonzales (2017, p. 690) concludes that adaptations during adoption and implementation of an intervention are inevitable because of this tension, and so challenge the assumption that

> Fidelity to a static intervention model should be the end goal and that cultural adaptation will occur primarily through a sequence of planned adaptations that are conducted by program designers prior to adoption and implementation.

Gonzales (2017) also urges that the adaptation process be managed to maintain fidelity and conceptual consistency with the original intervention model rather than allowing haphazard changes.

After reviewing 24 definitions used in over 200 studies, Moore et al. (2017, p. 2) developed an expansive definition of sustainability that recognizes the likelihood of adaptation to sustain an intervention:

> After a defined period of time, the program, clinical intervention, and/or implementation strategies continue to be delivered and/or individual behavior change (i.e., clinician, patient) is maintained; the program and individual behavior change may evolve or adapt while continuing to produce benefits for individuals/systems.

Powell and Beidas (2016) recommend "flexible give and take" with local communities to improve sustainability. Glasgow et al. (2020) suggest mid-course corrections based on rapid assessment and feedback. In five different Veterans Administration projects, they found that team meetings of participants allowed such corrections and so iteratively improved implementation.

De-implementation

The other side of the insight that adaptation can improve the sustainability of interventions is the recognition that interventions may outlive, or even never achieve, their potential for positive impact. Helfrich (2020) estimates that between 10 percent and 46 percent of health-care delivered in the US is without demonstrable benefit or actually incurs identifiable harm, representing an expenditure of $75.7–101.2 billion annually on overtreatment and low-value practice. As a result, "de-implementation" may be the appropriate strategy, even in the face of practitioner and patient resistance.

Comprehensive Frameworks

Increasing recognition of the multiple factors that affect the success of program implementation have led to the development of more holistic conceptual frameworks to guide implementation research. A comprehensive framework for implementing evidence-based practices can have five basic steps:

> Needs assessment; (2) partnership engagement; (3) selecting the appropriate intervention or suite of interventions, including tailoring the intervention to the local setting; (4) actual program implementation; (5) continual monitoring and feedback to ensure the process is achieving the intended outcome. (J. Saunders et al., 2020, p. 1326)

One of the most widely used comprehensive frameworks is Damschroder et al.'s (2009) Consolidated Framework for Implementation Research (CFIR). The CFIR is a meta-theoretical framework that was constructed after a comprehensive review of implementation theories that in turn identified important constructs related to influences on the implementation process. Five domains encompass the constructs: intervention characteristics, outer setting, inner setting, characteristics of the individuals involved, and the implementation process. Identifying 39 specific constructs across these five domains, the CFIR provides

> A road-map for the journey of accumulating an ever more rich understanding of the complexities of implementation, and a more predictable means by which to ensure effective implementations. (Damschroder et al., 2009, p. 50)

Six years after the introduction of the CFIR, Kirk et al.'s (2016) systematic review found that the framework had been used meaningfully in a wide range of studies (n = 26), but mostly just to guide data analysis rather than the design of the implementation research itself. Most studies (15) focused on describing barriers and facilitators of implementation, rather than investigating implementation outcomes (Kirk et al., 2016).

Another popular framework for implementation research developed from a review of the literature on implementation (in social and health service systems) is EPIS: Exploration, Preparation, Implementation, Sustainment (Aarons et al., 2011). Its four defining phases focus attention on the process of developing and implementing sustainable interventions, while multiple aspects of three factors focus on the context for implementation – the outer context, the inner context, and the bridging factors that link inner and outer context. An additional set of factors highlight the characteristics of the intervention itself, of its developers, and of its fit to the surrounding system context.

In 2019, Moullin et al.'s systematic review identified 67 articles that represented the use of EPIS in 49 unique research projects in 11 countries. Almost all examined inner context factors in the implementation process, but the average project examined only about half of the five EPIS factors.

Comprehensive conceptual frameworks such as CFIR and EPIS have helped to advance implementation research by identifying key factors that measure implementation processes and outcomes. They represent a major advance in this century over previous, less comprehensive and linear conceptualizations of the implementation process. However, this research is still at an early stage and so the full potential benefit of using these frameworks has yet to be realized.

CONCLUSIONS

Recognition of the many difficulties encountered in implementing new treatments, creating a robust institutional foundation for studying and improving the implementation process, and developing a new body of scientific evidence to guide this process represent major advances for mental health services research and practice. The insights about the implementation process that can be gleaned from the historical record can now be tested with and complemented by the concepts and methods of implementation science. Although the body of findings adduced by implementation science has not yet led to an overarching paradigm nor guidelines that ensure success, the discipline already provides a wealth of information that can improve every implementation project.

Implementation science will continue to advance as progress is made in recognizing the importance of early attention to implementation issues during the research-to-practice pipeline: taking stakeholder interests and knowledge into account; adapting processes to the particulars of different contexts; and acknowledging implementation as an ongoing process requiring both active efforts to sustain some interventions and difficult decisions to eliminate others (and see Powell & Beidas, 2016). The COVID-19 pandemic interrupted the progress of much implementation research as it challenged the work of practitioners throughout the healthcare system, but it has also magnified the historical lesson with which this chapter began: the gap between what we know about effective interventions and our ability to implement them when they are needed. Never has the need for advancing the science of implementation been so clear.

NOTES

1. https://obssr.od.nih.gov/about/strategic-plan/ (retrieved August 14, 2022).
2. https://www.cochranelibrary.com (retrieved August 14, 2022).
3. https://www.samhsa.gov/resource-search/ebp (retrieved August 14, 2022).
4. https://www.pcori.org/ (retrieved August 14, 2022).

REFERENCES

Aarons, G.A., Hurlburt, M., & Horwitz, D.M. (2011). Advancing a conceptual model of evidence-based practice implementation in public service sectors. *Administration and Policy in Mental Health, 38,* 4–23.

Bauer, M.S., Damschroder, L., Hagedorn, H., Smith, J., & Kilbourne, A.M. (2015). An introduction to implementation science for the non-specialist. *BMC Psychology, 3*(1). https://doi.org/10.1186/S40359 -015-0089-9

Barton, B.B., Segger, F., Fischer, K., Obermeier, M., & Musil, R. (2020). Update on weight-gain caused by antipsychotics: A systematic review and meta-analysis. *Expert Opinion on Drug Safety, 19*(3), 295–314.

Beck, A.T. (1976). *Cognitive therapy and the emotional disorders*. New York: International Universities Press.

Berwick, D.T. (2003). Disseminating innovations in health care. *JAMA, 289*, 1969–75.

Corponi, F., Fabbri, C., & Serretti, A. (2018). Pharmacogenetics in psychiatry. *Advances in Pharmacology, 83*, 297–331.

Csillag, C., Nordentoft, M., Mizuno, M., McDaid, D., Arango, C., Smith, J., Lora, A., Verma, S., di Fiandra, T., & Jones, P.B. (2018). Early intervention in psychosis: From clinical intervention to health system implementation. *Early Intervention in Psychiatry, 12*(4), 757–64. https://doi.org/10.1111/eip.12514

Damschroder, L.J., Aron, D.C., Keith, R.E., Kirsh, S.R., Alexander, J.A., & Lowery, J.C. (2009). Fostering implementation of health services research findings into practice: A consolidated framework for advancing implementation science. *Implementation Science, 4*(1). https://doi.org/10.1186/1748-5908-4-50

Dattilio, F.M., & Hanna, M. A. (2012). Collaboration in Cognitive-Behavioral Therapy. *Journal of Clinical Psychology, 68*(2), 146–58. https://doi.org/10.1002/jclp.21831

Deutsch, A. (1948). *The shame of the states*. New York: Harcourt, Brace.

DiMaggio, P.J., & Powell, W.W (1983). The iron cage revisited: Institutional isomorphism and collective rationality in organizational fields. *American Sociological Review, 48*, 147–60.

Dingfelder, H.E., & Mandell, D.S. (2011). Bridging the research-to-practice gap in autism intervention: An application of diffusion of innovation theory.n *Journal of Autism and Developmental Disorders, 41*(5), 597–609. https://doi.org/10.1007/s10803-010-1081-0

Dixon, L. (2000). Assertive community treatment: Twenty-five years of gold. *Psychiatric Services, 51*, 759–65.

Erwin, D.G., & Garman, A.N. (2010). Resistance to organizational change: Linking research and practice. *Leadership and Organization Development Journal, 31*(1), 39–56. https://doi.org/10.1108/01437731011010371

Frank, L., Basch, E., & Selby, J.V. (2014). The PCORI perspective on patient-centered outcomes research. *JAMA, 312*(15), 1513–14.

Gaudiano, B.A. (2008). Cognitive-behavioural therapies: Achievements and challenges. *EBMH Notebook, 11*(1), 5–7.

Glasgow, RE., Vogt, T.M., Boles, S.M., & Glasgow, E. (1999). *Evaluating the public health impact of health promotion interventions: The RE-AIM framework* (Vol. 89, Issue 9). Retrieved from http://www.ori

Glasgow, R.E., Harden, S.M., Gaglio, B., Rabin, B., Smith, M.L., Porter, G.C., Ory, M.G., & Estabrooks, P.A. (2019). RE-AIM planning and evaluation framework: Adapting to new science and practice with a 20-year review. *Frontiers in Public Health, 7*, March. Frontiers Media S.A. https://doi.org/10.3389/fpubh.2019.00064

Glasgow, RE., Battaglia, C., McCreight, M., Ayele, R.A., & Rabin, B.A. (2020). Making implementation science more rapid: Use of the RE-AIM framework for mid-course adaptations across five health services research projects in the Veterans Health Administration. *Frontiers in Public Health, 8*. https://doi.org/10.3389/fpubh.2020.00194

Gonzales, N.A. (2017). Expanding the cultural adaptation framework for population-level impact. *Prevention Science, 18*(6), 689–93. https://doi.org/10.1007/s11121-017-0808-y

Grimshaw, J.M., & Russell, I.T. (1993). Effect of clinical guidelines on medical practice: A systematic review of rigorous evaluations. *The Lancet, 342*, 1317–22.

Grob, G.N. (1991). *From asylum to community: Mental health policy in modern America*. Princeton, NJ: Princeton University Press.

Grob, G.N. (1994). *The mad among us: A history of the care of America's mentally ill*. New York: The Free Press.

Harden, S.M., Gaglio, B., Shoup, J.A., Kinney, K.A., Johnson, S.B., Brito, F., Blackman, K.C.A., Zoellner, J.M., Hill, J.L., Almeida, F.A., Glasgow, R.E., & Estabrooks, P.A. (2015). Fidelity to and comparative results across behavioral interventions evaluated through the RE-AIM framework: A systematic review. *Systematic Reviews, 4*(1). https://doi.org/10.1186/s13643-015-0141-0

Helfrich, C. (2020). What potentially makes de-implementation different than implementation and why does it matter? Thoughts on theory, outcomes and patient experience. Cyberseminar Transcript, 10/22. Retrieved August 14, 2022 from http://www.hsrd.research.va.gov/cyberseminars/catalog-archive.cfm

Institute of Medicine. (1991). *Research and service program in the PHS: Challenges in organization.* Washington, DC: The National Academies Press. https://doi.org/10.17226/1871

Institute of Medicine. (2001). *Crossing the quality chasm: A new health system for the 21st century.* Washington, DC: The National Academies Press.

Jauhar, S., McKenna, P.J., Radua, J., Fung, E., Salvador, R., & Laws, K.R. (2014). Cognitive-behavioural therapy for the symptoms of schizophrenia: Systematic review and meta-analysis with examination of potential bias. *British Journal of Psychiatry, 204*(1), 20–9. Royal College of Psychiatrists. https://doi.org/10.1192/bjp.bp.112.116285

Johnson, A.B. (1990). *Out of Bedlam: The truth about deinstitutionalization.* New York: Basic Books.

Kahneman, D., & Tversky, A. (1979). Prospect theory: An analysis of decision under risk. *Econometrica, 47*(2), 263–91.

Kirk, M.A., Kelley, C., Yankey, N., Birken, S.A., Abadie, B., & Damschroder, L. (2016). A systematic review of the use of the Consolidated Framework for implementation research. *Implementation Science, 11*(1). BioMed Central. https://doi.org/10.1186/s13012-016-0

Kramer, M. (1987). Psychiatric services and the changing institutional scene, 1950–1985. DHEW Publication No. (ADM)77-433. Washington, DC: National Institute of Mental Health.

Lader, M. (2011). Benzodiazepines revisited – will we ever learn? *Addiction, 106*(12), 2086–109. https://doi.org/10.1111/j.1360-0443.2011.03563.x

Landes, S.J., McBain, S.A., & Curran, G.M. (2019). An introduction to effectiveness-implementation hybrid designs. *Psychiatry Research, 280.* https://doi.org/10.1016/j.psychres.2019.112513

Lehman, A.F., Steinwachs, D.M., & the Co-Investigators of the PORT Project. (1998). Translating research into practice: The Schizophrenia Patient Outcomes Research Team (PORT) treatment recommendations. Schizophrenia Bulletin, 24(1), 1–10.

Lehman, A.F., Thompson, J.W., Dixon, L.B., & Scott, J.E. (1995). *Schizophrenia: Treatment outcomes research – editors' introduction, 21*(4) 561–6.

Levchenko, A., Vyalova, N.M., Nurgaliev, T., Pozhidaev, I.V., Simutkin, G.G., Bokhan, N.A., & Ivanova, S.A. (2020). NRG1, PIP4K2A, and HTR2C as potential candidate biomarker genes for several clinical subphenotypes of depression and bipolar disorder. *Frontiers in Genetics, 11.* Retrieved August 2014, 2022 from https://www.frontiersin.org/articles/10.3389/fgene.2020.00936/full

Lomas, J., Sisk, J.E., & Stocking, B. (1993). From evidence to practice in the United States, the United Kingdom, and Canada. *The Milbank Quarterly, 71*(3).

López-López, J.A., Davies, S.R., Caldwell, D.M., Churchill, R., Peters, T.J., Tallon, D., Dawson, S., Wu, Q., Li, J., Taylor, A., Lewis, G., Kessler, D.S., Wiles, N., & Welton, N.J. (2019). The process and delivery of CBT for depression in adults: A systematic review and network meta-Analysis. *Psychological Medicine, 49*(12), 1937–477. Cambridge University Press. https://doi.org/10.1017/S003329171900120X

Lorenzo-Luaces, J., Keefe, R.J., & DeRubeis, L.R. (2016). *Cognitive-behavioral therapy: Nature and relation to non-cognitive behavioral therapy.* Retrieved August 2014, 2022 from http://www.elsevier.com/locate/bt

Luo, Y., Kataoka, Y., Ostinelli, E.G., Cipriani, A., & Furukawa, T.A. (2020). National prescription patterns of antidepressants in the treatment of adults with major depression in the US between 1996 and 2015: A population representative survey based analysis. *Frontiers in Psychiatry, 11.* https://doi.org/10.3389/fpsyt.2020.00035

Lynch, D., Laws, K.R., & McKenna, P.J. (2010). Cognitive behavioural therapy for major psychiatric disorder: Does it really work? A meta-analytical review of well-controlled trials. *Psychological Medicine, 40*, 9–24.

Mazzucca, S., Arredondo, E.M., Hoelscher, D.M., Haire-Joshu, D., Tabak, R.G., Kumanyika, S. K., & Brownson, R.C. (2021). Expanding implementation research to prevent chronic diseases in community settings. *Annual Review of Public Health, 42*, 135–58. https://doi.org/10.1146/annurev-publhealth

McHugo, G.J., Drake, R.E., Whitley, R., Bond, G.R., Campbell, K., Rapp, C.A., Goldman, H.H., Lutz, W.J., & Finnerty, M.T. (2007). Fidelity outcomes in the National Implementing Evidence-Based Practices Project. *Psychological Services, 58*(10), 1279–84.

Mendel, P., Meredith, L.S., Schoenbaum, M., Sherbourne, C.D., & Wells, K.B. (2008). Interventions in organizational and community context: A framework for building evidence on dissemination and implementation in health services research. *Administration and Policy in Mental Health and Mental Health Services Research, 35*(1–2), 21–37. https://doi.org/10.1007/s10488-007-0

Mollica, R.F. (1983). From asylum to community: The threatened disintegration of public psychiatry. *The New England Journal of Medicine, 308,* 367–73.

Moore, J.E., Mascarenhas, A., Bain, J., & Straus, S.E. (2017). Developing a comprehensive definition of sustainability. *Implementation Science, 12*(1). https://doi.org/10.1186/s13012-017-063

Moos, R.H. (1974). *Evaluating treatment environments: A social ecological approach.* New York: Wiley.

Moullin, J.C., Dickson, K.S., Stadnick, N.A., Rabin, B., & Aarons, G.A. (2019). Systematic review of the Exploration, Preparation, Implementation, Sustainment (EPIS) framework. *Implementation Science, 14*(1). BioMed Central. https://doi.org/10.1186/s13012-018-0842-6

Mueser, K.T., Torrey, W.C., Lynde, D., Singer, P., & Drake, R.E. (2003). Implementing evidence-based practices for people with severe mental illness. *Behavior Modification, 27*(3), 387–411. https://doi.org/10.1177/0145445503253834

Nilsen, P. (2015). Making sense of implementation theories, models and frameworks. *Implementation Science, 10*(1). https://doi.org/10.1186/s13012-015-0242-0

Pew Research Center. (2015). Americans, politics and science issues. July 1. Retrieved August 2014, 2022 from https://www.pewresearch.org/science/2015/07/01/americans-politics-and-science-issues/

Phillips, S.D., Burns, B.J., Edgar, E.R., Mueser, K.T., Linkins, K.W., Rosenheck, R.A., Drake, R.E., & McDonel Herr, E.C. (2001). Moving assertive community treatment into standard practice. *Psychiatric Services, 52*(6), 771–9.

Powell, B.J., & Beidas, R.S. (2016). Advancing implementation research and practice in behavioral health systems. *Administration and Policy in Mental Health and Mental Health Services Research, 43*(6), 825–33). Springer New York. https://doi.org/10.1007/s10488-016-0762-1

Saunders, J., Hipple, N.E., Allison, K., & Peterson, J. (2020). Estimating the impact of research practitioner partnerships on evidence-based program implementation. Justice Quarterly, 37(8), 1322-42. https://doi.org/10.1080/07418825.2020.1831578

Saunders, R., Brack, M., Renz, B., Thomson, J., & Pilling, S. (2020). An evaluation of parent training interventions in Scotland: The Psychology of Parenting Project (PoPP). *Journal of Child and Family Studies, 29*(12), 3369–80. https://doi.org/10.1007/s10826-020-01817-y

Schutt, R.K. (2011). *Homelessness, housing, and mental illness.* Cambridge, MA: Harvard University Press.

Schutt, R.K. (2016). Social environment and mental illness: The progress and paradox of deinstitutionalization. *Advances in Medical Sociology, 17.* https://doi.org/10.1108/S1057-629020160000017004

Schutt, R.K., Seidman, L.J., & Keshavan, M.S., Eds. (2015). *Social neuroscience: Brain, mind, and society.* Cambridge, MA: Harvard University Press.

Slovic, P. (1995). The construction of preference. *American Psychologist, 50*(5), 364–71.

Smedley, B.D., Syme, S.L. (Sherman L., & Institute of Medicine (US). Committee on Capitalizing on Social Science and Behavioral Research to Improve the Public's Health). (2000). *Promoting health: Intervention strategies from social and behavioral research.* Washington, DC: National Academies Press.

Stein, L.I., & Santos, A.B. (1998). *Assertive community treatment of persons with severe mental illness.* New York: Norton.

Substance Abuse and Mental Health Services Administration (SAMSHA), (nd). Evidence-Based Practices Resource Center. Rockville MD: SAMSHA. https://www.samhsa.gov/resource-search/ebp (Downloaded 9/27/2022).

Talbott, J.A. (1978). *The death of the asylum: A critical study of state hospital management, services, and care.* New York: Grune & Stratton.

Torrey, W.C., Lynde, D.W., & Gorman, P. (2005). Promoting the implementation of practices that are supported by research: The national implementing evidence-based practice project. *Child and Adolescent Psychiatric Clinics of North America, 14*(2), 297–306. W.B. Saunders. https://doi.org/10.1016/j.chc.2004.05.004

Torrey, E.F., Fuller, D.A., Geller, J., Jacobs, C., & Ragosta, K. (2012). *No room at the inn: Trends and consequences of closing public psychiatric hospitals, 2005–2010.* Arlington, VA: Treatment Advocacy Center.

Van Dis, E.A., van Veen, S.C., Hagenaars, M.A., Batelaan, N.M., Bockting, D.L.H., van den Heuvel, R.M., Cuijpers, P., & Engelhard, I.M. (2020). Long-term outcomes of cognitive behavioral, therapy for anxiety-related disorders: A systematic review and meta-analysis. *JAMA Psychiatry, 77*(3), 265–73.

Zerhouni, E.A. (2006). Clinical research at a crossroads: The NIH roadmap. *Journal of Investigative Medicine, 54*(4), 171–3. https://doi.org/10.2310/6650.2006.X0016

7. National, state, and local mental health policy: meeting the needs for research pluralism and application of knowledge

David A. Rochefort and Jared M. Hirschfield

Recent assessment of the field of mental health research highlights deficiencies in its scope, focus, quality, and level of financial support. Reacting to Woelbert et al.'s (2020) global analysis of mental health research between 2015 and 2019, Patel (2020, p. 171) unsparingly observed in *The Lancet* that the level of resources devoted to mental health versus total health research was "pathetic." Such mental health research as did take place was biased geographically, "with less than 10% of funding being spent in countries that have 90% of global health problems," and inordinately concerned with questions of etiology and biology as opposed to "health services research, clinical research, and prevention" (Patel, 2020, p. 171). In 2010–11, the US National Institute of Mental Health (NIMH) had spearheaded an international exercise to spotlight the most pressing mental health research needs based on input from hundreds of leading researchers, clinicians, advocates, and program administrators (Collins et al., 2011). Comparing data from the NIMH project with this latest empirical report, Patel decried the ongoing misalignment of resources including the neglect of Implementation Science for applying the insights of research-based knowledge.

In the same year that the above commentary was published, another mental health research critique appeared, this one by a distinguished specialist in children and adolescent services. Based on a career spanning five decades of research and teaching, Bickman (2020) arrived at several conclusions: few clients receive evidence-based mental health services; few evidence-based mental health services are implemented with fidelity to their therapeutic content; many existing mental health services and programs are of unknown efficacy; and scant research exists on how generic interventions might be optimized through individualization across clients and care settings. While acknowledging the potential rigor and clarity of information collected by randomized clinical trials (RCTs), Bickman also questioned the predominance of this research design, characterizing its rigid requirements and capabilities as often at odds with the complexity of disorders, clients, and services encountered in the mental health environment.

The process of mental health policymaking serves as a critical link in the translation of basic mental health research into operating mental health programs and services (Jenkins, 2003). Policy formulation is the governmental mechanism for allocating resources to societal needs, resolving demands from competing political stakeholders, and determining the design of the service system. And when the government opts to delegate functions to professionals and organizations in the private market – a prominent feature of mental health care in a country like the United States – it is public policy that supports the administrative infrastructure for sustaining and regulating these responsibilities.

Mental health policy research has its own strengths and weaknesses as an area of study with some academic fields (e.g., sociology, social work, psychology, economics) exhibiting robust interest in the topic, and others (e.g., political science, public administration) lagging behind despite a manifest concern with public policy in these disciplines (Rochefort, 1994). Further, it has been common even for excellent books about the political dynamics and policy choices involved in health reform to omit significant discussion of mental health care (see, e.g., Cohn, 2020; Emanuel & Gluck, 2020; McDonough, 2011). Given the latter's relevance for problems experienced by many patient groups today – arbitrary treatment by insurance companies, mismanagement of severe illness, and limited community integration of people with chronic illness and disability – this omission counts as a loss not just for those in the mental health community, but those interested in the general health care scene as well. To be sure, no sector in which the prevalence of disease approximates 20 percent of the adult population (SAMHSA, 2020), and where treatment services account for an estimated $200+ billion in spending annually (SAMHSA, 2014), should be neglected within either government policymaking or the province of policy research and analysis.

The purpose of this chapter is to trace the contemporary evidence-based movement for mental health policy, underscoring the opportunities as well as the pitfalls that exist for an enhanced empirical orientation within this domain. The importance of randomized experimental designs for evaluating program outcomes will be addressed. At the same time, a pluralistic, or eclectic, perspective will be advanced that goes beyond RCTs in identifying alternate forms of research better suited for mental health planning, administration and implementation, regulation, and policy learning. Finally, we discuss the difficulty of making use of the evidence gained from policy research.

FROM EVIDENCE-BASED PRACTICE TO EVIDENCE-BASED POLICY

The call for mental health policies that are firmly supported by research evidence can be traced to two distinct, but analogous, campaigns within medical practice and the field of applied public policy (Figure 7.1).

According to Eddy (2005, p. 16), evidence-based medicine (EBM) is "a set of principles and methods intended to ensure that to the greatest extent possible, medical decisions, guidelines, and other types of policies are based on and consistent with good evidence of effectiveness and benefit." Key to this focus was a recognition by the 1970s that much of what took place in patient care was characterized by inconsistency, use of questionable procedures, and an unsystematic approach to clinical decision making. At this point in time, the chasm separating medical practice and medical research was wide. Only a small minority of treatments in active use had been validated by RCTs.

Increasingly over subsequent decades, an agenda emerged among leaders in the medical profession – researchers, educators, and major professional associations – to compile guidelines rooting the daily practice of medicine in reliable scientific evidence. Insurers and government authorities added their own weight to the initiative, motivated by concerns about efficacy and quality as well as cost savings. The effort advanced with the speed of a brush fire. Based on one tabulation, within five years of first appearance of the term "evidence-based medicine"

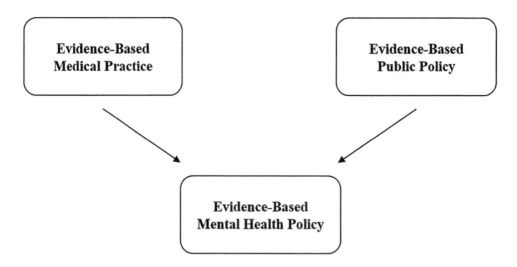

Figure 7.1   *Origins of the evidence-based mental health policy movement*

in the *Journal of the American Medical Association* in 1992, more than 1,000 articles employing the new phrase dotted the medical literature (Zimerman, 2013, p. 71).

The EBM movement has been described as "one of modern medicine's greatest intellectual achievements" (Smith & Rennie, 2014), a "paradigm shift" (Guyatt et al., 1992, p. 2420), and a "milestone" among other top breakthroughs in the history of medicine (Thoma & Eaves, 2015, p. NP261). With the passage of time, however, EBM has raised as many questions as it has answered, a fact well delineated in a special issue of the journal *Health Affairs* on the status of EBM in January/February of 2005. What kinds of information deserve consideration in evidence-based practice? How much evidence is sufficient to trigger a recommendation for, or against, an established pattern of care? What are the barriers that impede dissemination of clinical practice guidelines, and how should they be addressed? What linkage should exist between medical research evidence, on the one hand, and the application of health policy instruments such as subsidy and regulation, on the other? None of these issues is simple to resolve even when the underlying research itself satisfies high standards of reliability and validity.

The collection of data as a prerequisite guide for public policymaking is nothing new. Fittingly enough, one distant precursor of today's focus on evidence-based policy comes to us from the mental health field. Disturbed by the neglected and mistreated individuals with mental illness whom she encountered when visiting a local jail in her home state of Massachusetts in March of 1841, Dorothea Dix resolved to bring the attention of state officials to the matter. After traveling around the state documenting the ghastly conditions in jails, poor houses, and other unsuitable circumstances where those with mental illness were confined, Dix wrote up her findings in painstaking detail as a memorial for delivery to the Massachusetts legislature (Michel, 1995). Informed and moved by this evidence of glaring need, lawmakers agreed to fund the expansion of Worcester State Hospital, the state's only mental institution at the time (Grob, 1994). For Dix, the episode launched a career of research and advocacy on behalf of the mental hospitalization movement in the United States and other countries that would last some 40 years.

Other early roots of the evidence-based policy (EBP) movement can be traced to the formalization and empiricization of the social sciences during the late 1800s and early 1900s, a period when academic researchers, "muckraking" journalists, and settlement house reformers all became committed to new forms of fact-driven investigation of social problems, sometimes in close collaboration with each other (Bulmer, 2001). With the help of funding from East Coast philanthropy – the Carnegie Corporation and the Rockefeller Foundation, in particular – social scientists undertook major studies of urban crime and poverty, immigration, and other issues (Featherman & Vinovskis, 2001a). The New Deal's arrival in the 1930s spurred on the union between government and social science as a wave of academics from economics, public administration, social work, and other fields entered the bureaucracy, bringing their knowledge of society and their training as researchers to the planning and implementation of new federal programs (Jennings & Callahan, 1983). As one scholar states, "Although the social sciences were relative newcomers both as scientific disciplines and as members of and/or advisors to government, by 1937 their methodologies and insights had already made considerable inroads" (Blanpied, 2010, Social Science and Government section).

The birth of the community mental health program in the post-World War II era shows how applied research helped to steer the national government as it entered a new policy realm, first, in the National Mental Health Act of 1946, second, in the Mental Health Study Act of 1955, and, third, in the Community Mental Health Centers Act of 1963. Supporting this legislative trifecta were studies of mental illness in the military during wartime, the emerging concept of mental health services as a continuum of care, and the documented clinical performance of early community care programs (Bloom, 1977). Also in this period, many administrative and treatment advances were occurring within state mental hospitals, providing another focal point for evaluation research. Collectively, such information helped galvanize a new federal role in the country's mental health system, an active push for deinstitutionalization on the state level, and a program of research to chart the progress of the community mental health endeavor (Grob, 1991, chapters 3, 8–10).

The Great Society has been deemed a "golden age of relevance" for the social sciences with data, theories, and methodologies from a variety of disciplines contributing to large-scale social projects (Featherman & Vinovskis, 2001b, p. 3; Jennings & Callahan, 1983). RCTs and related designs, used in evaluations of the New Jersey Negative Income Tax Experiment (Kershaw, 1969) and the early childhood education program Head Start (Westinghouse Learning Corporation & Ohio University, 1969), came into their own as tools for applied social science, coupling the notion of "sound evidence" with highly structured quantitative and experimental methodologies (Featherman & Vinovskis, 2001b).

Building on the tradition associated with such iconic figures as political scientist Harold Lasswell and sociologist Paul Lazarsfeld, whose use of applied research to improve the knowledge base for public policy dated back to the 1940s, the policy sciences constituted an estimable force within, but not entrapped by, the academy by the 1980s (Puppis & Van den Bulck, 2019, p. 14). Multidisciplinarity was the hallmark of this growing vein of research, together with an orientation to problems and solutions that had the objective of "simultaneously saying something to the real world while avoiding the sterility of academic parlor games" (Ascher, 1986, p. 365). Writing about the role of policy research in government some two decades later, Richard Nathan (2000, pp. 12-13), a noteworthy figure in this movement, emphasized the need for rigor in three categories: (1) demonstration studies to test new policies and program approaches; (2) evaluation research to assess ongoing public programs; and (3) studies to document social conditions and trends. Knowledge generation in these areas remains paramount among evidence-based policy specialists today no matter whether the work takes place inside government, universities, "think tanks," or service-providing organizations.

Attempting to refine, and to "center," the use of empirical evidence for social intervention, the Obama administration issued a series of evidence-based policy initiatives aimed at "replac[ing] program evaluation by anecdote and flawed comparison group analysis with rigorous evaluation featuring random group assignment" (Haskins, 2015, p. 20). While this stance did not rule out alternative strategies for certain research questions, it identified "RCTs as the best method to establish causality" in the larger means-ends equation of social action (p. 20). In March of 2016, Congress unanimously approved the Commission on Evidence-Based Policymaking. While lacking any binding guidance, the group's final report on "The Promise of Evidence-Based Policymaking" held that "[g]enerating and using evidence to inform government policymaking and program administration is not a partisan issue" (p. 3), and it outlined recommendations to more fully incorporate scientific evidence within the policymaking process (Commission on Evidence-Based Policymaking, 2017). Interestingly, during this same period in the United Kingdom, RCTs similarly gained privileged standing in the call for a knowledge-driven form of governance (Pearce & Raman, 2014).

Upon becoming president in January of 2021, Joseph Biden sent a memorandum to all heads of executive departments and agencies on "restoring trust in government through scientific integrity and evidence-based policymaking" (The White House, 2021). Reacting to a period in which the credibility and influence of scientific knowledge had fallen to a low water mark in national affairs during the Trump administration, most profoundly in the latter's mishandling of the coronavirus (Tollefson, 2020), the memorandum underscored the need to insulate the generation of scientific guidance from political interference.

THE CHALLENGE OF EVIDENCE-BASED POLICY FOR MENTAL HEALTH CARE

As early as the mid-1990s, the case for evidence-based medical practice was being advanced with increased frequency. The consequence was not merely prioritization of controlled experiments for existing and proposed treatments, but also initiation of a new field of Implementation Science that adopted a mixed-methods approach for studying the spread of beneficial practices (Bauer & Kirchner, 2020). The logical connection between evidence-based medical practice and evidence-based health policy became obvious as well, if society was to reap the dividends of this growing program of research (Bauer & Kirchner, 2020). An editorial in the *British Medical Journal* made the leap to mental health policy explicit, if unexplained: "The impact of policies that are poorly designed and untested may be disastrous – witness the recent failures in mental health services" (Ham et al., 1995, p. 71). At this time, meta-reviews of outcome studies rarely focused on mental health service interventions per se (Cooper, 2003). However, as Goldman and Azrin (2003) pointed out, the overlap between treatments and policies was plain given research demonstrating that administrative and financing policies could either obstruct or facilitate access to evidence-based practices as well as shape the organization of the mental health service system. Meanwhile, sophisticated research programs were underway in areas such as the development of community support systems for people with severe mental illness and the reduction of homelessness among this population (Anthony & Blanch, 1989; Goldman et al., 1992).

Still, the pursuit of evidence-based policy for an area such as mental health care raised distinctive issues concerning the context in which government action took place. Coming to the fore were two cardinal questions: What is meant by the concept of "mental health policy" and What special challenges does the mental health policy domain present for the EBP movement?

A well-known political scientist has defined public policy as "whatever governments choose to do or not to do" (Dye, 2008, p. 1). The weakness of such a statement is that, while nothing relevant is excluded, it casts a net that lacks precision, especially when the aim is distinguishing a field such as mental health care from other matters of government, domestic and foreign. More suitable for present purposes, then, is a definition of mental health policy as that element of government action specifically concerned with mental health issues and problems, including the provision of support for the large ecosystem of services, bureaucracies, programs, laws, regulations, and financial mechanisms that contribute to the functioning of the mental health sector. In considering how this dense swirl of activity manifests in practice, the multilayered and boundary-spanning properties of mental health policy become evident.

The United States is not a unitary system of government but a federal state in which authority and responsibility are shared across national, state, and local jurisdictions. It is, as well, a political system with three branches, a form of government meant to broaden involvement in public policy development while offering myriad institutional venues for issue advancement. Certain policy areas are more easily intelligible than others because decision making and administration are dominated by a single level of government and the terrain is free of fundamental legal disputes about questions of state power and individual rights. However, mental health care – marked by a history of both shared and independent action at different levels of government and by the important role of the courts in the modern era of community care – is surely not one of those straightforward cases.

As a program area, mental health also exhibits exceptional complexity in the services it provides. Not only does this activity encompass an extensive array of preventive, acute, and chronic care interventions in both public and private facilities, for some consumers mental health care requires the assiduous arrangement of resources from other social welfare sectors like housing, income maintenance, and job training and employment. Unsurprisingly, fragmentation is one of the enduring problems of mental health care in a society like the United States where harmonious coordination is neither central to the mission of large bureaucracies nor routinized in their operations.

Should our concept of mental health policy be confined to the formal laws, regulations, programs, and judicial decisions that are produced with the objective of improving, or expanding, the mental health sector? If so, much government activity that is relevant to people with mental health problems would escape notice. Kiesler and Sibulkin (1987, p. 17) emphasized a definition of mental health policy that includes its *de jure* and *de facto* dimensions: *de jure* policy refers to activity that "is intentional in nature and usually legislated into law," while *de facto* policy refers to "the net outcome of overall practices, whether the outcome is intended or not." According to these researchers, although *de jure* mental health policy in the United States during the 1960s, 1970s, and 1980s was marked by discourse and policy decisions centering on deinstitutionalization and community services, *de facto* mental health policy resulting from the practices of public and private health insurance plans had the effect of incentivizing, and channeling the bulk of resources to, hospitalization. This discrepancy, coupled with ambiguity surrounding the constitutive activities of the nation's so-called "mental health system," distorted the lens for viewing questions of mental health reform in this period. It is a misdirection that continues, to some extent, today even as criticism persists concerning the performance of both hospital and community care sectors of the mental health system.

Policy domains are defined not simply by substantive focus and organizational involvement, but also by cultural constructs (Burstein, 1991). As an essential characteristic of the general cultural environment in which mental health policy is formulated and implemented, the social stigma associated with mental illness has great relevance for evidence-based research in this area (Knaak et al., 2017). Tanenbaum (2005) also discusses intra-domain cultural values in her analysis of the resistance to evidence-based practice and policy within the mental health sector. Reflecting expectations that have no exact counterpart in the practice of general medicine, some mental health consumers and providers alike object to the proposed scientific standardization of care; the application of inflexible research methodologies to interventions with varying philosophies and forms of client engagement; and the neglect of consumer preference as part of the very technology of healing for a service such as psychotherapy.

RECOGNIZING THE VALUE OF RESEARCH PLURALISM

As discussed, RCTs have long been the "gold standard" of empirical research within medical practice and public policy. The methodological reason for this enthusiasm should be appreciated, along with awareness of the gains in knowledge that RCT studies have provided for the mental health sector. Elevating RCTs to a unique status, however, some researchers have turned a blind eye to other forms of research and the important policy questions they, too, can be instrumental in answering (Commission on Evidence-Based Policymaking, 2017; Peters et al., 2018, p. 12; Shlonsky & Mildon, 2014).

Outcome Evaluation

The steps of RCT research are: first, identifying a group of subjects appropriate for the purposes of a given study; second, randomizing the subjects into control and experimental groups; third, exposing the latter to a treatment (X) whose impact is under examination; and, fourth, making a before-after statistical comparison to gauge the size and significance of outcome differences between the two groups. A study in which participants, researchers, and data analysts all are "blind" with respect to which group has undergone X provides an additional safeguard against biases that could affect results for one or both groups. Assuming a sufficiently large sample size and appropriate outcome measures, RCTs can be relied on to accurately gauge the impact of X (Sharoon & Khandhar, 2020). This documentation of causal effect is what accounts for the great appeal of RCT research for questions of treatment efficacy and program evaluation.

Although numerous clinical practices still await evaluation with RCT research, many mental health treatments have, in fact, undergone the RCT process. Some of the most well-known program innovations in the mental health field have been repeatedly evaluated by RCTs. By 2001, more than 25 such studies had been published about Assertive Community Treatment (ACT), a program for supporting individuals with severe and chronic mental illness in the community setting. This corpus of research went far in advancing the diffusion of ACT programs across the United States and internationally (Rochefort, 2019). Recent years have seen the growth of evidence-based program website registers meant "to assist policy makers and practitioners in selecting interventions with the greatest potential benefit to individuals and society" (Burkhardt et al., 2015, p. 92). Such registers exist in the United States and other countries, some of them backed by government funding. While criteria and standards vary for the identification of listed services and programs, RCT evaluation is the most important criterion for inclusion in the highest tier of practices, that is, those considered to have the greatest degree of scientific support. For some registers, a candidate entry cannot be listed unless it has undergone study by RCT methodology.

A classic RCT relevant to mental health care is the RAND Health Insurance Experiment that took place between 1974 and 1982 in six sites across the United States (Manning et al., 1989). A group of nearly 7,000 insured individuals were randomly assigned into health plans with varying coinsurance provisions. Results showed not only that use of outpatient mental health services declined somewhat in response to cost-sharing increases, but that sensitivity to cost was greater for mental health care than for other types of medical treatment. According to a retrospective by the RAND Corporation in 2016, this research "remains the largest, most comprehensive, evidence-based health policy study in U.S. history" (RAND Corporation, 2016). For mental health policy analysts, it sparked a long-term interest in the impact of cost-sharing provisions in different types of insurance plans, including those with managed care controls, and the possible effect of financial barriers on consumers' utilization of mental health care (Frank & McGuire, 2000). This debate would prove to be germane in the battle for parity insurance for mental health and substance use treatment services, a fight still being waged on state and federal levels more than 25 years after the nation's first federal parity legislation in 1996.

RCTs have proven unquestionably valuable in generating the kind of evidence necessary for challenging entrenched patterns of mental health treatment and programming. The irony is, however, that the findings of RCT research can function as the imprimatur for an alternative kind of consensus, one whose claims also overreach the generalizability of evidence collected (Pearce & Raman, 2014).

Critical literature on the use of RCTs for decision making in mental health care and other fields of medicine, as well as for public policy generally, has grown in recent years. For the most part, this literature does not seek to discredit what RCTs have to offer, only to gauge where the bounds of their application appropriately lie. The following are some of the most significant reservations expressed by commentators on the subject (see, e.g., Cowen et al., 2017; Deaton & Cartwright, 2018; Essock et al., 2003; Faulkner, 2015; Haskins, 2015; Pearce & Raman, 2014):

1. RCTs are often impractical to plan and carry out for reasons of cost, the long timeframe of research, and, in the context of government action, ethical objections to framing public policy in experimental terms.
2. Findings of efficacy from RCT research do not necessarily indicate that a service should supplant current treatment regimens. Hesitation to alter the status quo may exist due to considerations of cost-effectiveness, or when there is lack of comparability between RCT research design and the actual mix of treatments and patient populations in real-world settings.

3. Even after RCT research has validated that a treatment, or program, is effective in achiev-
    ing stated goals, the question of *how* "X" works may remain unanswered because of the
    issue of "causal density" and the multifactorial character of many interventions.
4. Disagreement will often exist among clinical researchers, program administrators, and
    consumers regarding the outcome variables most relevant for measurement in RCT
    research.

Many suggestions have been made for addressing the difficulties that can arise when using
RCT research as a tool for guiding mental health practice. These include such remedies as
broadening the group involved in designing the research to gather more diverse input on
appropriate outcome measures, expanding sample sizes to create more heterogeneous study
populations, and combining RCT and non-RCT research in mixed-methods designs to leverage
the advantages of each approach. Randomized sampling of clusters, rather than individuals,
can be employed in situations where there is heightened possibility of contamination between
experimental and control groups, or where the focus is not on individual patients but groups
of patients subject to the same policies or treatment environments (Heagerty & DeLong, n.d.).
Specific research designs also are available to help disentangle complex causal mechanisms by
manipulating the variables that mediate between treatments and outcomes (Imai et al., 2013).
With respect to research implementation, Hudson (2009) proposed the utility of structured
methods for marrying RCT results with professional judgment through such means as "if,
then" heuristics and decision trees.

The remainder of this section will identify alternatives to RCT research that are relevant for
tasks in the policy process beyond program outcome measurement (Table 7.1). The orientation of this discussion is not only that different kinds of research questions call for different
research methods, but also that the choice of method must be influenced by a multitude of
factors, including audience, existing evidence on a topic, requirements for policy legitimation,
and the opportunities that present themselves for policy refinement versus transformation
(Stoker & Evans, 2016a).

Planning

According to the World Health Organization, the planning process is intrinsic to realizing
the "vision and objectives" of a nation's mental health policy (WHO, n.d.). To the extent that
a true "system" of care is in place, or under development, it is the planning mechanism that
defines the scope of that system (geographically and socially), the distribution of responsibilities, levels of current and projected need, the composition and capacity of service-providing
entities, and a feasible timeframe for filling identified gaps in services and other resources.
While mental health planning is not a purely data-driven enterprise – stakeholder consultation
and intra- and inter-departmental organizational analysis must also be undertaken – the preparation of a meaningful plan is impossible without rigorous needs assessment.

In practice, formalized mental health policies are found in a variety of institutional and
organizational contexts. Within the United States, states have long played the lead role in
delivering public mental health services, and it is primarily at this level that "mental health
system" planning takes place as mental health administrators respond to accountability
demands from elsewhere within state government (e.g., the legislature) and from the federal
agencies that channel program funding into state hands. Beginning in FY1988, the federal

Table 7.1   *Aligning mental health policy tasks and research methodologies*

POLICY TASK	INFORMATION NEEDED	METHODS & DATA MOST COMMONLY USED
Outcome Evaluation	Rigorous measurement of the impact of specific programs and policies with respect to pre-established goals	Randomized controlled trials Qualitative research is typically secondary but can help to generate hypotheses on how/why a complex program or policy has achieved its results or encountered obstacles
Planning	Collection and analysis of numerical data for assessing aggregate future need for services and documenting disparities of need and services utilization across sub-groups of the population	Social Indicators Analysis Historical tracking of service utilization, resource capacity, and other descriptive data on the operation of the mental health system and related sectors Determination of consumer satisfaction and preferences
Administration and Implementation	Quantitative and qualitative evidence pertaining to mental health administration, particularly the process of program implementation as a complex inter-organizational task of assembly and coordination	Eclectic use of quantitative, qualitative, and mixed-methods research that can synthesize a broad variety of information from both primary and secondary sources
Regulation	Determination of organizational adherence to established legal rules and standards for program operation and service delivery	Analysis of reporting data submitted to the regulating agency by regulated parties as a legal requirement, with the possibility of more detailed audits of selected organizations Convening of public hearings to collect reports of consumer experiences and to categorize, and estimate the frequency of, different types of complaints Possible consideration of supplementary information generated from other government sources/private researchers that may be derived from ongoing data monitoring activity or new data collection by means of surveys and other methods
Policy Learning	Information about the design, operation, and outcomes of mental health policies and laws already in existence in other settings – both domestic and international – that is needed to inform consideration of their adoption in new geographic or institutional contexts	Heavy reliance on literature reviews of published and unpublished policy analysis and program evaluation reports concerning the identified area of interest

government mandated that states produce comprehensive mental health services plans or face fiscal penalties for non-performance (P.L. 99-660). Currently, states must submit an extensive set of data that includes an inventory of services directly provided or contracted for, different types of expenditures, estimates of the size of target populations in the categories of Adults with Severe Mental Illness and Children with Serious Emotional Disturbance, consumer profiles, and more.

For researchers focused on experimental studies or advanced statistical analysis, the tabulation of descriptive information of this kind might seem rudimentary. For many states, however, it is not a given. Even more ambitiously, designing, maintaining, and continuously improving reliable systems of data collection that can accurately track all activity relevant to mental health care and determine resource allocation decisions remains a work-in-progress. In 2009, the National Alliance on Mental Illness reported that "[t]he gaps in states' collection, compilation, and monitoring of data regarding mental illness and mental health services are both wide and deep" (Aron et al., 2009, p. 16). From state to state, limitations and inconsistencies are evident across multiple dimensions: integration of planning for kindred areas such as mental illness and substance use; formulation of standard definitions of services and resources; capacity to follow individuals as they move from mental health facilities and providers to other systems of service, support, and custody; and linkages across the databases of different public bureaucracies (Hoagwood et al., 2016; Teich, 2016). Although mental health policymakers and advocates increasingly emphasize evidence-based treatments and programs, the data arm of the mental health system is not well prepared to monitor this priority.

To a great extent, mental health planning focuses on the use of social indicators for calculating population need for services and for distributing funds to organizations well situated to respond. As Cagle and Banks (1986, p. 127) have observed, "The plethora of accessible social indicators may be as much a curse as a blessing for the mental health planner." Researchers must be selective in their choice of data, considering conventional criteria such as validity and reliability as well as verified correlation between the indicators and core conceptualizations of need within the planning process. While it may be easy, and therefore inviting, to insert such indicators into complex models, "it is not clear that the statistically most sophisticated technique necessarily is the best one for identifying need" (p. 128). Bearing in mind that the goal of evidence-based policy is to improve systemic quality and effectiveness, it is important that social indicators research be used to collect information that does more than replicate the status quo when service gaps and consumer dissatisfaction are present.

Administration and Implementation

The position of state mental health commissioner has been described as an "impossible job in public management" based on such factors as the diverse, sometimes intractable, needs of the client population, warring constituencies that vie for control of the department's mission and targeting of resources, and limitations on the authority of the commissioner, a position embedded within the dense matrix of government administrative bureaucracy (Miller & Iscoe, 1990, p. 109). Demands may not be as intense or ubiquitous for administrators lower down the ladder, but many of the same organizational tensions, resource scarcity problems, service delivery issues, and conflicting ideologies manifest themselves throughout the mental health system.

The responsibility of mental health administrators to plan and lead implementation efforts creates an important focal point for policy-oriented research. In his classic study of the Lanterman-Petris-Short Act that spearheaded the movement from institutional to community mental health care in California, Bardach (1977, p. 10) analyzed the process of policy implementation as a myriad of substantive and relational tasks involving "elements of intergovernmental relations, interagency relations, relations between government and private contractors, professional participation as providers and overseers, interprofessional rivalries, regulatory as well as service delivery activities, intra-bureaucratic politicking, important interface problems with other policy areas, and continuing legislative oversight and intervention." Characterized in this way, the programmatic terrain takes on a kaleidoscopic quality that renders the job of implementation one of "program assembly" within and across levels. This observation is a mere abstraction, of course. Identifying the specific pieces for any building block of activity, and the necessary coordinating linkages among them, yields an endless variety of scenarios, each requiring their own administrative response. Critical to this strategic process is the collection and analysis of information.

Many questions animate the study of implementation and, so, many kinds of research are deemed relevant for this component of the policy process. A recent issue of the journal *Administration and Policy in Mental Health and Mental Health Services Research* (Vol. 48, Issue 1) published 13 research articles on the subject of program implementation, or program implementation and outcome. Significantly, little consistency marks the methodological approaches in these papers, which include quantitative studies, qualitative studies, and mixed-methods research. Types of data and research designs also vary a great deal: semi-structured and in-depth interviews with program participants/program staff/key stakeholders; focus groups; survey data; analysis of existing administrative data; analysis of Medicaid spending records; and crowd-sourcing information. No controlled experiments or quasi-experimental investigations can be found within the collection, unless one were to count an article using therapists versus independent lay observers to assess the delivery of evidence-based treatment in a sample of psychotherapy sessions (Brookman-Frazee et al., 2021).

As noted earlier, with the birth of the Implementation Science field (Boulton et al., 2020) a distinct branch of research took form focusing on the "barriers and facilitators" that impact the spread of "evidence-based clinical innovations" (Bauer & Kirchner, 2020, p. 3). Building on prior work in political science, psychology, management, sociology, and other disciplines, the effect was to accelerate the sophistication of inquiry and enhance attention to the role played by a multitude of variables at different levels of analysis (structural, organizational, individual, etc.) (see, e.g., Chaudoir et al., 2013). The agenda is a far-reaching one that embraces the knowledge available from quantitative and qualitative research alike (Palinkas, 2014). In a recent paper on the importance of qualitative methods in implementation research, Hamilton and Finley (2019) cite the example of a collaborative mental health treatment program for depression among female veterans. Despite demonstrable effectiveness of the model of care, questions arose about *why* there was a lack of engagement with the program on the part of some women and some providers, and *how* this reluctance might be overcome within the context of this organization. These are the kinds of concerns for which the Implementation Science framework was fashioned.

Regulation

Regulation is a policy activity concerned with the compliance of individuals, corporations, and units of government with specific standards of required behavior under threat of fines and other sanctions (Kraft & Furlong, 2013, p. 104). Field (2007, p. 3) states that "[h]ealth care is among the most heavily regulated industries in America." Effective health care regulation involves the "perpetual juggling" of three objectives of a well-functioning system: high quality, widespread access, and affordable costs (p. 4). Like the scattered organization of the system itself, the regulatory landscape in health care is "disjointed" with federal, state, and local agencies sharing in the responsibilities.

In part, regulation within the mental health sector focuses on many of the same issues and processes found in other areas of health care; in part, it focuses on issues and processes particular to mental health organizations and activities. The former includes items such as privacy protection, professional certification, fair billing practices, anti-fraud measures, ethical considerations in the conduct of medical research, and insurance products and practices. The latter includes requirements for the operation of mental health facilities (e.g., community mental health centers), qualifications for mental health funding programs (e.g., Substance Abuse and Mental Health Block Grants), legal procedures such as inpatient and outpatient commitment, and special legislation like that governing the parity of insurance practices for patients with behavioral health and other types of conditions. In areas of overlapping activity, federal regulations often seek to establish a "floor" upon which regulatory bodies on state and local levels can build. While this duality may facilitate constructive policy experimentation, it also results in substantial variation of standards across different geographic jurisdictions. Documenting and assessing this diversity is just one of many current research topics in mental health regulation.

To a great extent, the regulatory function depends on regular submission of required reporting data to the government by the entities being regulated. Yet existing data collection systems may not keep pace adequately with emerging regulatory issues. Regulated parties may also have reason to conceal activities within their organization. The following pair of current controversies speaks to how the regulatory policy process compiles evidence-based data from varied sources and methods over time.

The case of antipsychotic prescribing practices in skilled nursing facilities (SNFs) illustrates the difficulty of mental health care regulation in a context of oscillating political agendas. The Food and Drug Administration (FDA) has issued black box warnings stating that off-label use of antipsychotic drugs in elderly patients with dementia can result in serious injury or death (CMS, 2015). In 2016, in the wake of a report by the US Department of Health and Human Services Office of the Inspector General (2011) documenting inappropriate use of antipsychotic medications, the Centers for Medicare and Medicaid Services adopted stricter regulations for this drug class and imposed heftier fines on SNFs in violation of federal standards. A recent report on this issue by the majority staff of the US House of Representatives Ways and Means Committee (2020) arrived at two main conclusions: (i) approximately 20 percent of SNF residents in 2019 received antipsychotic drugs, while only 2 percent had qualifying conditions; and (ii) a 200 percent increase in citations for antipsychotic drug misuse from 2015 to 2017 was followed by a 22 percent decrease from 2017 to 2018, the result of regulatory rollbacks under the Trump administration. The purpose of these summary statistics, calculated using administrative and publicly available datasets, was to gauge the current state of affairs: How is policy shaping practices on the ground? Are current regulations being enforced? Other evidence undergirding the Committee's approach to the antipsychotic medication issue drew from literature reviews (Brooks & Hoblyn, 2007; Chiu et al., 2015; Introcaso, 2018; Mattingly, 2015), advanced statistical analyses (Fraser et al., 2015; Maust et al., 2015; Phillips et al., 2018), survey and descriptive studies (Long Term Care Community Coalition, 2018; Urick et al., 2016), and mixed-methods reports (Flamm, 2018).

Despite the adoption of national and state laws to eliminate restrictions on mental health and substance use coverage that are absent from other areas of health care, information from legal cases, journalistic investigations, and mental health advocacy groups has continued to point to regulatory violations by insurers (Elejalde-Ruiz, 2018; Gold, 2015). In October 2016, the Obama administration charged the Mental Health & Substance Use Disorder Parity Task Force (2016) with reviewing progress to date on parity, addressing shortcomings in parity implementation, and issuing recommendations for future action. The Task Force compiled academic research, administrative data, and public input to generate a holistic assessment, with the group's review of literature on parity legislation revealing positive impacts across several empirical measures, including increased mental and behavioral health treatment rates, improved mental health outcomes, and reduced out-of-pocket costs. At the same time, analysis of Department of Labor enforcement actions provided insight into the most prevalent types of parity violations. In seeking to capture "real-world" feedback from a diverse set of stakeholders, the Task Force also conducted a qualitative analysis of written comments and listening sessions with consumer groups and advocates. From all this evidence came a set of recommendations that included, among other steps, expanding consumer education, improving parity in government health plans, and enhancing compliance/enforcement requirements under existing law.

Policy Learning

According to Kingdon (1995), three conditions are necessary for major public policy change to occur. First, the tenor of the times must be favorable based on election outcomes, public mood, effective issue leadership, and other political variables. Second, there must be widespread agreement, based on factual documentation as well as normative argument, about the reality of a social problem and the need for public intervention. Third, a suitable policy remedy, or combination of remedies, must be at hand. Our discussion of planning, administration/implementation, regulation, and evaluation reviewed the kinds of social science data that are called upon for the purpose of identifying mental health problems in society and for appraising the performance of existing service programs. Here we consider information relevant for innovation on a grander scale, including the possible transfer of policy frameworks and laws that are reportedly effective in one environment to another that is markedly different culturally, politically, economically, administratively, and so on.

When a shift from one policy agenda to another is under consideration, careful attention must be given to the design of alternative approaches, their acceptability among important stakeholder groups, and their likely capacity for satisfying unmet needs in the adopting jurisdiction. For its most significant policy resets, the mental health community has often turned to national commissions as an instrument for surveying the state of clinical knowledge and for weighing the accumulated findings of applied policy research (Thompson, 2012). Even in the absence of such high-profile political ventures, however, intelligence gathering is ongoing about mental health policy developments inside the country and abroad. Description, analysis, and informed prognostication all are involved. "Lesson-drawing is contingent. One cannot borrow blindly or condemn blindly, for the success of a programme is affected by the specifics of context as well as generic attributes," explains Rose (1991, p. 4). "The critical analytic question is: Under what circumstances and to what extent would a programme now in effect elsewhere also work here?"

The conduct of controlled experiments in program evaluation is a form of primary research carried out directly by the researcher (Gough & Tripney, 2016). For the activities of planning, administration/implementation, and regulation, a greater variety of methods is valuable, including not only certain kinds of primary research but also secondary research that synthesizes data collected by others. When it comes to transferring policy across differing environments, or dramatic changes in the scale at which a policy will be expected to operate, the researcher will need to consult sources of information about the larger context and history of programmatic activity as well as its organizational scaffolding. While such materials may be quite disparate in format and content, it is possible, to a great extent, to standardize the process of curation in how items are selected for review and in spotlighting fundamental questions of interest. As Gough and Tripney (2016, p. 47) describe it, a "systematic review" of this kind is a methodology for "interrogating existing research studies" that can be shaped according to the purposes of different audiences, including officials and their advisors who seek a rigorous empirical grounding for making policy choices. Currently, a topic featured in numerous published reviews by government and private researchers is the increase of mental health needs and service interventions related to the COVID-19 pandemic. One illustration of the popular tool "Preferred Reporting Items for Systematic Reviews and Meta-Analysis" (PRISMA) can be found in Soklaridis et al. (2020).

THE GAP BETWEEN AVAILABLE RESEARCH KNOWLEDGE AND ITS APPLICATION

As demonstrated in the applied mental health examples above, evidence can – and often does – play a key role in the policymaking process. However, the role of evidence in policymaking should not be confused with the role of evidence in the scientific process. In fact, many of the barriers to translating evidence into policy lie in the fact that policymaking "follows a logic that is different from that of the scientific enterprise" (Jewell & Bero, 2008, p. 178). When analyzed through the lens of policy theory, rather than through a scientific lens, the distinctively *political* side of evidence-based policy comes into view. Aside from "supply-side" concerns related to the quantity, quality, accessibility, and usability of the evidence itself (Jewell & Bero, 2008, pp. 187–90), the challenges facing the integration of research and policy stem from tensions inherent in political decision making for mental health care just as for other public issues (Williams, 2010). Evidence-based practice is in no way immune to the "cognitive and institutional features of the political process," a dynamic venue whose competing interests and limited resources can present notable difficulties (Jewell & Bero, 2008, p. 178).

For one, policymaking does not occur in a sterile laboratory but within an "interactive, discursive and negotiation arena" in which research competes as just one of many "valid meaning-frames" (Williams, 2010, p. 197). In the political arena, even the most ardent supporters of evidence-based practice must balance the use of evidence with what Jewell and Bero (2008) call "competing sources of influence": personal political values, prior commitments, interest group demands, and the pressure felt among elected representatives to remain in office. In attempting to produce "good" policy, policymakers are often building agreement, weighing public opinion, and engaging across different levels of government (Cairney, 2019). Competing against the "politics" of the policymaking process, evidence can easily be overshadowed or consciously deprioritized.

The unpredictable timing of the policymaking process places another hurdle before the consistent use of evidence (Oliver et al., 2014). Policymakers use evidence in environments over which they have limited control, where policy is being made more or less continuously and "decisions to solve problems intersect" (Cairney, 2019, p. 5). A crisis or rapid shift in public opinion can derail "a carefully evidenced and prepared policy process" – or, thrust it to the top of the political agenda (Stoker & Evans, 2016b, p. 22). For evidence to be successfully translated into policy, it must not merely be available, but available "at a certain time and in a particular form, to solve a very specific problem" (Cairney, 2016, p. 60). Evidence not disseminated during such a window may easily escape policymakers' attention.

Policymakers also generally operate in a "time-poor environment," without sufficient opportunity to read or reflect on research findings (Lewig et al., 2010; Stoker & Evans, 2016b, p. 21). Facing limited time and practically unlimited demands, policymakers are forced to take shortcuts that make it easier to gather and process information (Cairney, 2019; Jewell & Bero, 2008). Realistically, this bounded rationality means that policymakers "have to ignore the majority of the information 'signals' that they receive because they can only process a small proportion" (Cairney, 2016, p. 65).

Even with ample time, other barriers may persist. While some policymakers have expertise in specific issue areas, most are not trained research professionals and have limited experience assessing research designs or analyzing research results for policy relevance (Jewell & Bero, 2008; Oliver et al., 2014). This situation is exacerbated for mental health care due to the many points of intersection with adjacent policy areas that have their own arcane knowledge, delivery systems, and research literatures. There is also a high turnover rate among policymakers and public officials, which inhibits development of the expertise that can only be acquired organically from years of work in a policy arena (Cairney, 2016; Jewell & Bero, 2008).

A compelling case has been made for public policy as a potentially powerful agent in the dissemination of evidence-based practices throughout the mental health sector when bolstered by strong national leadership, a coordinated program of knowledge development linking science with service development, and financing mechanisms that strategically target support for treatments of proven efficacy (Goldman & Azrin, 2003). The fact is that, as studies of policy innovation and agenda setting across a host of issue areas indicate, reforms of large social systems occur through a combination of ongoing small improvements and periodic "big bang" advances (Klein, 1995). The existence of policymaking cycles in the mental health sector is well documented, with widely varying levels of political engagement, mission clarity, and openness to institutional change at different historical moments (Rochefort, 1997). An interlocking movement for evidence-based practice and evidence-based policy in mental health care could help modulate this cyclical pattern by providing a touchstone of consensus about desirable change that is tethered to quality information. However, nothing is straightforward in the policy world, not the pathways by which information is diffused through the decision-making environment, nor the import of information for actors in different roles. Researchers need to be accepting of these realities even as they patiently work toward better outcomes from the process.

CONCLUSION

Although this chapter focuses on activity at the national, state, and local levels, and primarily on developments in the United States, the challenges of mental health and mental health care are universal and increasingly framed as such today. With broad engagement from international organizations, governments, universities, funders, humanitarian groups, and professional associations, the field of "global mental health" has arrived. Its purpose is collaborative action to reduce the disparity between rich and poor countries in mental health treatments and outcomes relying heavily on the information gained from research investigations and implementation of the guidance they provide (Collins, 2020; Patel & Prince, 2010). As noted at the start of this chapter, the perspective on mental health research priorities and funding must truly be a global one if movement away from long-standing imbalances across different kinds of services and societies is to be possible.

Evidence-based practice and evidence-based mental health policy lie at the heart of this undertaking, along with an overriding commitment to the principle of access to health and mental health care as a universal human right. A new frontier of opportunities beckons for "research pluralism and application of knowledge," although not in any simplistic sense where the distilled experience of one group of advantaged countries is meant to serve inflexibly as a template for another group striving "to catch up." Rather, as the research enterprise expands, and as systemic reforms are launched in a host of varied settings, a more comprehensive and more nuanced body of practical learning inevitably will evolve for all to absorb. And as fact gathering proceeds, supported by the animus of a moral imperative, it is encouraging to imagine a mental health policy process that could itself become self-renewing, one in which no social stratum or nation of people will be left behind.

REFERENCES

Anthony, W.A., & Blanch, A. (1989). Research on community support services: What have we learned. *Psychosocial Rehabilitation Journal*, 12(3), 55–81. https://doi.org/10.1037/h0099533

Aron, L., Honberg, R., Duckworth, K., Kimball, A., Edgar, E., Carolla, B., Meltzer, K., Usher, L., Gay, K., Giliberti, M., Carrasco, M.J., Pandya, A., & Fitzpatrick, M. (2009). *Grading the states 2009: A report on America's health care system for adults with serious mental illness*. National Alliance on Mental Illness. Retrieved July 15, 2021, from https://www.nami.org/Support-Education/Publications-Reports/Public-Policy-Reports/Grading-the-States-2009

Ascher, W. (1986). The evolution of the policy sciences: Understanding the rise and avoiding the fall. *Journal of Policy Analysis and Management*, 5(2), 365–73. https://doi.org/10.2307/3323551

Bardach, E. (1977). *The implementation game: What happens after a bill becomes a law*. MIT Press.

Bauer, M.S., & Kirchner, J. (2020). Implementation science: What is it and why should I care? *Psychiatry Research*, 283, Article 112376. https://doi.org/10.1016/j.psychres.2019.04.025

Bickman, L. (2020). Improving mental health services: A 50-year journey from randomized experiments to artificial intelligence and precision mental health. *Administration and Policy in Mental Health and Mental Health Services Research*, 47, 795–843. https://doi.org/10.1007/s10488-020-01065-8

Blanpied, W. (2010). *A history of federal science policy from the New Deal to the present*. Connexions. Retrieved July 15, 2021, from https://cnx.org/contents/tl65wQku@2.2:HQufyFdP@2/Knowledge-for-Governance-Social-Science-Perspectives-on-Science-Policy-through-1940

Bloom, B.L. (1977). *Community mental health: A general introduction*. Brooks/Cole Publishing.

Boulton, R., Sandall, J., & Sevdalis, N. (2020). The cultural politics of "Implementation Science". *Journal of Medical Humanities*, 41, 379–94. https://doi.org/10.1007/s10912-020-09607-9

Brookman-Frazee, L., Stadnick, N.A., Lind, T., Roesch, S., Terrones, L., Barnett, M.L., Regan, J., Kennedy, C.A., Garland, A.F., & Lau, A.S. (2021). Therapist-observer concordance in ratings of EBP strategy delivery: Challenges and targeted directions in pursuing pragmatic measurement in children's mental health services. *Administration and Policy in Mental Health and Mental Health Services Research*, 48, 155–70. https://doi.org/10.1007/s10488-020-01054-x

Brooks, J.O., & Hoblyn J.C. (2007). Neurocognitive costs and benefits of psychotropic medications in older adults. *Journal of Geriatric Psychiatry and Neurology*, 20(4), 199–214. https://doi.org/10.1177/0891988707308803

Bulmer, M. (2001). Knowledge for the public good: The emergence of social sciences and social reform in late-nineteenth-and early-twentieth-century America, 1880–1940. In D.L. Featherman & M.A. Vinovskis (Eds.), *Social science and policy-making: A search for relevance in the twentieth century* (pp. 16–39). University of Michigan Press.

Burkhardt, J.T., Schröter, D.C., Magura, S., Means, S.N., & Coryn, C.L.S. (2015). An overview of evidence-based program registers (EBPRs) for behavioral health. *Evaluation and Program Planning*, 48, 92–9. https://doi.org/10.1016/j.evalprogplan.2014.09.006

Burstein, P. (1991). Policy domains: Organization, culture, and policy outcomes. *Annual Review of Sociology*, 17, 327–50. https://doi.org/10.1146/annurev.so.17.080191.001551

Cagle, L.T., & Banks, S.M. (1986). The validity of assessing mental health needs with social indicators. *Evaluation and Program Planning*, 9(2), 127–42. https://doi.org/10.1016/0149-7189(86)90033-9

Cairney, P. (2016). *The politics of evidence-based policy making*. Palgrave Macmillan.

Cairney, P. (2019). The UK government's imaginative use of evidence to make policy. *British Politics*, 14, 1–22. https://doi.org/10.1057/s41293-017-0068-2

Chaudoir, S.R., Dugan, A.G., & Barr, C.H. (2013). Measuring factors affecting implementation of health innovations: A systematic review of structural, organizational, provider, patient, and innovation level measures. *Implementation Science*, 8, Article 22. https://doi.org/10.1186/1748-5908-8-22

Chiu, Y., Bero, L., Hessol, N.A., Lexchin J., & Harrington, C. (2015). A literature review of clinical outcomes associated with antipsychotic medication use in North American nursing home residents. *Health Policy*, 119(6), 802–13. https://doi.org/10.1016/j.healthpol.2015.02.014

CMS. (2015). *Atypical antipsychotic medications: Use in adults*. US Department of Health and Human Services. Retrieved July 15, 2021, from https://www.cms.gov/Medicare-Medicaid-Coordination/Fraud-Prevention/Medicaid-Integrity-Education/Pharmacy-Education-Materials/Downloads/atyp-antipsych-adult-factsheet11-14.pdf

Cohn, J. (2020). *The Ten Year war: Obamacare and the unfinished crusade for universal coverage*. St. Martin's Press.

Collins, P.Y. (2020). What is global mental health? *World Psychiatry*, 19(3), 265–6. https://doi.org/10.1002/wps.20728

Collins, P.Y., Patel, V., Joestl, S.S., March, D., Insel, T.R., Daar, A.S., Bordin, I.A., Costello, E.J., Durkin, M., Fairburn, C., Glass, R.I., Hall, W., Huang, Y., Hyman, S.E., Jamison, K., Kaaya, S., Kapur, S., Kleinman, A., Ogunniyi, A., . . . & Walport, M. (2011). Grand challenges in global mental health. *Nature*, 475, 27–30. https://doi.org/10.1038/475027a

Commission on Evidence-Based Policymaking. (2017). *The promise of evidence-based policymaking: Report of the Commission on Evidence-Based Policymaking*. Retrieved July 15, 2021, from https://bipartisanpolicy.org/wp-content/uploads/2019/03/Full-Report-The-Promise-of-Evidence-Based-Policymaking-Report-of-the-Comission-on-Evidence-based-Policymaking.pdf

Cooper, B. (2003). Evidence-based mental health policy: A critical appraisal. *The British Journal of Psychiatry*, 183(2), 105–13. https://doi.org/10.1192/bjp.183.2.105

Cowen, N., Virk, B., Mascarenhas-Keyes, S., & Cartwright, N. (2017). Randomized controlled trials: How can we know "what works"? *Critical Review*, 29(3), 265–92. https://doi.org/10.1080/08913811.2017.1395223

Deaton, A., & Cartwright, N. (2018). Understanding and misunderstanding randomized controlled trials. *Social Science & Medicine*, 210, 2–21. https://doi.org/10.1016/j.socscimed.2017.12.005

Dye, T.R. (2008). *Understanding public policy*, 12th ed. Pearson/Prentice Hall.

Eddy, D.M. (2005). Evidence-based medicine: A unified approach. *Health Affairs*, 24(1), 9–17. https://doi.org/10.1377/hlthaff.24.1.9

Elejalde-Ruiz, A. (2018, April 8). Holes in federal law to protect insurance coverage put mentally ill at risk, advocates say. *Chicago Tribune*. Retrieved July 15, 2021, from https://www.chicagotribune.com/business/ct-biz-illinois-mental-health-parity-20180327-story.html

Emanuel, E.J., & Gluck, A.R. (2020). The trillion dollar revolution: How the Affordable Care Act transformed politics, law, and health care in America. PublicAffairs.

Essock, S.M., Drake, R.E., Frank, R.G., & McGuire, T.G. (2003). Randomized controlled trials in evidence-based mental health care: Getting the right answer to the right question. *Schizophrenia Bulletin*, 29(1), 115–23. https://doi.org/10.1093/oxfordjournals.schbul.a006981

Faulkner, A. (2015). *Randomised controlled trials: The straitjacket of mental health research?* The McPin Foundation. Retrieved July 15, 2021, from https://mcpin.org/wp-content/uploads/talking-point -paper-1.pdf

Featherman, D.L., & Vinovksis, M.A. (2001a). Growth and use of social and behavioral science in the federal government since World War II. In D.L. Featherman & M.A. Vinovskis (Eds.), *Social science and policy-making: A search for relevance in the twentieth century* (pp. 40–82). University of Michigan Press.

Featherman, D.L., & Vinovksis, M.A. (2001b). In search of relevance to social reform and policy-making. In D.L. Featherman & M.A. Vinovskis (Eds.), *Social science and policy-making: A search for relevance in the twentieth century* (pp. 1–15). University of Michigan Press.

Field, R.I. (2007). *Health care regulation in America: Complexity, confrontation, and compromise.* Oxford University Press.

Flamm, H. (2018). *"They want docile": How nursing homes in the United States overmedicate people with dementia.* Human Rights Watch. Retrieved July 15, 2021, from https://www.hrw.org/sites/ default/files/report_pdf/us_nursinghomes0218_web.pdf

Frank, R.G., & McGuire, T.G. (2000). Economics and mental health. In A.J. Culyer & J.P. Newhouse (Eds.), *Handbook of health economics* (Vol. 1B, pp. 893–954). Elsevier. https://doi.org/10.1016/ S1574-0064(00)80029-3

Fraser, L.A., Liu, K., Naylor, K.L., Hwang, Y.J., Dixon, S.N., Shariff, S.Z., & Garg, A.X. (2015). Falls and fractures with atypical antipsychotic medication use: A population-based cohort study. *JAMA Internal Medicine*, 175(3), 450–2. https://doi.org/10.1001/jamainternmed.2014.6930

Gold, J. (2015, August 3). Advocates say mental health "parity" law is not fulfilling its promise. *Kaiser Health News*. Retrieved July 15, 2021, from https://khn.org/news/advocates-say-mental-health-parity -law-is-not-fulfilling-its-promise/

Goldman, H.H., & Azrin, S.T. (2003). Public policy and evidence-based practice. *Psychiatric Clinics*, 26(4), 899–917. https://doi.org/10.1016/S0193-953X(03)00068-6

Goldman, H.H., Morrissey, J.P., Ridgely, M.S., Frank, R.G., Newman, S.J., & Kennedy, C. (1992). Lessons from the Program on Chronic Mental Illness. *Health Affairs*, 11(3), 51–68. https://doi.org/10 .1377/hlthaff.11.3.51

Gough, D., & Tripney, J. (2016). Systematic reviews for policy. In G. Stoker & M. Evans (Eds.), *Evidence-based policy making in the social sciences: Methods that matter* (pp. 43–68). Policy Press. https://doi.org/10.2307/j.ctt1t89d4k.10

Grob, G.N. (1991). *From asylum to community: Mental health policy in modern America.* Princeton University Press.

Grob, G.N. (1994). *The mad among us: A history of the care of America's mentally ill.* Free Press.

Guyatt, G., Cairns, J., Churchill, D., Cook, D., Haynes, B., Hirsh, J., Irvine, J., Levine, M., Nishikawa, J., Sackett, D., Brill-Edwards, P., Gerstein, H., Gibson, J., Jaeschke, R., Kerigan, A., Neville, A., Panju, A., Detsky, A., Enkin, M., . . . Tugwell, P. (1992). Evidence-based medicine: A new approach to teaching the practice of medicine. *JAMA*, 268(17), 2420–5. https://doi.org/10.1001/jama.1992 .03490170092032

Ham, C., Hunter, D.J., & Robinson, R. (1995). Evidence based policymaking. *BMJ*, 310, 71. https://doi .org/10.1136/bmj.310.6972.71

Hamilton, A.B., & Finley, E.P. (2019). Qualitative methods in implementation research: An introduction. *Psychiatry Research*, 280, Article 112516. https://doi.org/10.1016/j.psychres.2019.112516

Haskins, R. (2015). Introduction: The Obama strategy for attacking social problems. In R. Haskins & G. Margolis (Eds.), *Show me the evidence: Obama's fight for rigor and results in social policy* (pp. 1–30). Brookings Institution Press.

Heagerty, P.J., & DeLong, E.R. (n.d.). Experimental design and randomization schemes: Cluster randomized trials. In *Rethinking clinical trials: A living textbook of pragmatic clinical trials* (Section 3). NIH Health Care Systems Research Collaboratory. https://doi.org/10.28929/004

Hoagwood, K.E., Essock, S., Morrissey, J., Libby, A., Donahue, S., Druss, B., Finnerty, M., Frisman, L., Narasimhan, M., Stein, B.D., Wisdom, J., & Zerzan, J. (2016). Use of pooled state administrative data for mental health services research. *Administration and Policy in Mental Health and Mental Health Services Research*, 43, 67–78. https://doi.org/10.1007/s10488-014-0620-y

Hudson, C.G. (2009). Decision making in evidence-based practice: Science and art. *Smith College Studies in Social Work*, 79(2), 155–74. https://doi.org/10.1080/00377310902832334

Imai, K., Tingley, D., & Yamamoto, T. (2013). Experimental designs for identifying causal mechanisms. *Journal of the Royal Statistical Society*, 176, Part 1, 5–51. https://doi.org/10.1111/j.1467-985x.2012.01032.x

Introcaso, D. (2018, April 27). The never-ending misuse of antipsychotics in nursing homes. *Health Affairs Blog*. https://doi.org/10.1377/hblog20180424.962541

Jenkins, R. (2003). Supporting governments to adopt mental health policies. *World Psychiatry*, 2(1), 14–19. https://doi.org/10.1108/13619322200500008

Jennings, B., & Callahan, D. (1983). Social science and the policy-making process. *The Hastings Center Report*, 13(1), 3–8. https://doi.org/10.2307/3561557

Jewell, C.J., & Bero, L.A. (2008). "Developing good taste in evidence": Facilitators of and hindrances to evidence-informed health policymaking in state government. *The Milbank Quarterly*, 86(2), 177–208. https://doi.org/10.1111/j.1468-0009.2008.00519.x

Kershaw, D. (1969). *The negative income tax experiment in New Jersey: General discussion.* Mathematica Policy Research. Retrieved July 15, 2021, from https://www.mathematica.org/download-media?MediaItemId=%7B4658BD23-0E7A-4F39-8384-5072F0188CE3%7D

Kiesler, C.A., & Sibulkin, A.E. (1987). *Mental hospitalization: Myths and facts about a national crisis.* SAGE Publications.

Kingdon, J.W. (1995). *Agendas, alternatives, and public policies.* 2nd ed. Longman.

Klein, R. (1995). Big bang health care reform – does it work?: The case of Britain's 1991 National Health Service reforms. *The Milbank Quarterly*, 73(3), 299–337. https://doi.org/10.2307/3350370

Knaak, S., Mantler, E., & Szeto, A. (2017). Mental illness-related stigma in healthcare: Barriers to access and care and evidence-based solutions. *Healthcare Management Forum*, 30(2), 111–16. https://doi.org/10.1177/0840470416679413

Kraft, M.E., & Furlong, S.R. (2013). *Public policy: Politics, analysis, and alternatives.* 4th ed. CQ Press.

Lewig, K., Scott, D., Holzer, P., Arney, F., Humphreys, C., & Bromfield, L. (2010). The role of research in child protection policy reform: A case study of South Australia. *Evidence & Policy: A Journal of Research, Debate and Practice*, 6(4), 461–82. https://doi.org/10.1332/174426410X535855

Long Term Care Community Coalition. (2018). *LTCCC alert: Despite promised crackdown, citations for inappropriate drugging remain rare.* NursingHome411. Retrieved July 15, 2021, from https://nursinghome411.org/wp-content/uploads/2018/11/LTCCC-Advisory-Nursing-Home-Drugging-Citations-November-2018.pdf

Manning, W.G., Wells, K.B., Buchanan, J.L., Keeler, E.B., Burciaga Valdez, R., & Newhouse, J.P. (1989). *Effects of mental health insurance: Evidence from the Health Insurance Experiment.* RAND Corporation. Retrieved July 15, 2021, from https://www.rand.org/pubs/reports/R3815.html

Mattingly, T.J., II. (2015). A review exploring the relationship between nursing home staffing and antipsychotic medication use. *Neurology and Therapy*, 4, 169–75. https://doi.org/10.1007/s40120-015-0032-2

Maust, D.T., Kim, H.M., Seyfried, L.S., Chiang, C., Kavanagh, J., Schneider, L.S., & Kales, H.C. (2015). Antipsychotics, other psychotropics, and the risk of death in patients with dementia: Number needed to harm. *JAMA Psychiatry*, 72(5), 438–45. https://doi.org/10.1001/jamapsychiatry.2014.3018

McDonough, J.E. (2011). *Inside national health reform.* University of California Press.

The Mental Health & Substance Use Disorder Parity Task Force. (2016). *Final report.* Executive Office of the President of the United States. Retrieved July 15, 2021, from https://www.hhs.gov/sites/default/files/mental-health-substance-use-disorder-parity-task-force-final-report.PDF

Michel, S. (1995). Dorothea Dix; or, the voice of the maniac. *Discourse*, 17(2), 48–66. Retrieved July 15, 2021, from https://www.jstor.org/stable/41389368

Miller, G.E., & Iscoe, I. (1990). A state mental health commissioner and the politics of mental illness. In E.C. Hargrove & J.C. Glidewell (Eds.), *Impossible jobs in public management* (pp. 103–32). University Press of Kansas.

Nathan, R.P. (2000). *Social science in government: The role of policy researchers.* The Rockefeller Institute Press.

Oliver, K., Innvar, S., Lorenc, T., Woodman, J., & Thomas, J. (2014). A systematic review of barriers to and facilitators of the use of evidence by policymakers. *BMC Health Services Research*, 14, Article 2. https://doi.org/10.1186/1472-6963-14-2

Palinkas, L.A. (2014). Qualitative methods in mental health services research. *Journal of Clinical Child & Adolescent Psychology*, 43(6), 851–61. https://doi.org/10.1080/15374416.2014.910791

Patel, V. (2020). Mental health research funding: Too little, too inequitable, too skewed. *The Lancet Psychiatry*, 8(3), 171–2. https://doi.org/10.1016/S2215-0366(20)30471-5

Patel, V., & Prince, M. (2010). Global mental health: A new global health field comes of age. *JAMA*, 303(19), 1976–77. https://doi.org/10.1001/jama.2010.616

Pearce, W., & Raman, S. (2014). The new randomised controlled trials (RCT) movement in public policy: Challenges of epistemic governance. *Policy Sciences*, 47, 387–402. https://doi.org/10.1007/s11077-014-9208-3

Peters, S., Hossain, F., & Bissell, M. (2018). *Bridging the gap between public policy and evidence to improve social outcomes*. Project Evident. Retrieved July 15, 2021, from https://static1.squarespace.com/static/58d9ba1f20099e0a03a3891d/t/5c87d21c9b747a32bdd0bede/1552405022356/Brief+PE+Policy+and+Evidence+FINAL.pdf

Phillips, L.J., Birtley, N.M., Petroski, G.F., Siem, C., & Rantz, M. (2018). An observational study of antipsychotic medication use among long-stay nursing home residents without qualifying diagnoses. *Journal of Psychiatric and Mental Health Nursing*, 25(8), 463–74. https://doi.org/10.1111/jpm.12488

Puppis, M., & Van den Bulck, H. (2019). Introduction: Media policy and media policy research. In H. Van den Bulck, M. Puppis, K. Donders, & L. Van Audenhove (Eds.), *The Palgrave handbook of methods for media policy research* (pp. 3–21). Palgrave Macmillan. https://doi.org/10.1007/978-3-030-16065-4

RAND Corporation. (2016). *40 years of the RAND Health Insurance Experiment*. Retrieved July 15, 2021, from https://www.rand.org/health-care/projects/HIE-40.html#:~:text=Forty%20years%20later%2C%20RAND's%20Health,researchers%20and%20the%20news%20media.

Rochefort, D.A. (1994). Mental health policy inquiry, its importance, and its rewards. *Policy Studies Journal*, 22(4), 653–60. https://doi.org/10.1111/j.1541-0072.1994.tb01495.x

Rochefort, D.A. (1997). *From poorhouses to homelessness: Policy analysis and mental health care*. 2nd ed. Auburn House.

Rochefort, D.A. (2019). Innovation and its discontents: Pathways and barriers in the diffusion of Assertive Community Treatment. *The Milbank Quarterly*, 97(4), 1151–99. https://doi.org/10.1111/1468-0009.12429

Rose, R. (1991). What is lesson-drawing? *Journal of Public Policy*, 11(1), 3–30. https://doi.org/10.1017/S0143814X00004918

SAMHSA. (2014). *Projections of national expenditures for treatment of mental and substance use disorders, 2010–2020*. US Department of Health and Human Services. Retrieved July 15, 2021, from https://www.store.samhsa.gov/sites/default/files/d7/priv/sma14-4883.pdf

SAMHSA. (2020). *Key substance use and mental health indicators in the United States: Results from the 2019 National Survey on Drug Use and Health*. US Department of Health and Human Services. Retrieved July 15, 2021, from https://www.samhsa.gov/data/sites/default/files/reports/rpt29393/2019NSDUHFFRPDFWHTML/2019NSDUHFFR1PDFW090120.pdf

Sharoon, D., & Khandhar, P.B. (2020, September 20). *Double-blind study*. StatPearls Publishing. Retrieved July 15, 2021, from https://www.ncbi.nlm.nih.gov/books/NBK546641/

Shlonsky, A., & Mildon, R. (2014). Methodological pluralism in the age of evidence-informed practice and policy. *Scandinavian Journal of Public Health*, 42(Suppl. 13), 18–27. https://doi.org/10.1177/1403494813516716

Smith, R., & Rennie, D. (2014). Evidence based medicine – an oral history. *BMJ*, 348, g371. https://doi.org/10.1136/bmj.g371

Soklaridis, S., Lin, E., Lalani, Y., Rodak, T., & Sockalingam, S. (2020). Mental health interventions and supports during COVID-19 and other medical pandemics: A rapid systematic review of the evidence. *General Hospital Psychiatry*, 66, 133–46. https://doi.org/10.1016/j.genhosppsych.2020.08.007

Stoker, G., & Evans, M. (2016a). Crafting public policy: Choosing the right social science method. In G. Stoker & M. Evans (Eds.), *Evidence-based policy making in the social sciences: Methods that matter* (pp. 29–40). Policy Press. https://doi.org/10.2307/j.ctt1t89d4k.9

Stoker, G., & Evans, M. (2016b). Evidence-based policy making and social science. In G. Stoker & M. Evans (Eds.), *Evidence-based policy making in the social sciences: Methods that matter* (pp. 15–28). Policy Press. https://doi.org/10.2307/j.ctt1t89d4k.8

Tanenbaum, S.J. (2005). Evidence-based practice as mental health policy: Three controversies and a caveat. *Health Affairs*, 24(1), 163–73. https://doi.org/10.1377/hlthaff.24.1.163

Teich, J. (2016). Better data for better mental health services. *Issues in Science and Technology*, 32(2). Retrieved from https://issues.org/better-data-for-better-mental-health-services/

The White House. (2021, January 27). *Memorandum on restoring trust in government through scientific integrity and evidence-based policymaking*. Retrieved July 15, 2021, from https://www.whitehouse .gov/briefing-room/presidential-actions/2021/01/27/memorandum-on-restoring-trust-in-government -through-scientific-integrity-and-evidence-based-policymaking/

Thoma, A., & Eaves, F.F. (2015). A brief history of evidence-based medicine (EBM) and the contributions of Dr David Sackett. *Aesthetic Surgery Journal*, 35(8), NP261–NP263. https://doi.org/10.1093/ asj/sjv130

Thompson, K.S. (2012). National commissions on mental health in the United States: How many tries to get it right? *Mental Health Review Journal*, 17(4), 260–6. https://doi.org/10.1108/13619321211289335

Tollefson, J. (2020, October 7). How Trump damaged science – and why it could take decades to recover. *Nature*, 586, 190–4. https://doi.org/10.1038/d41586-020-02800-9

US Department of Health and Human Services Office of the Inspector General. (2011). *Medicare atypical antipsychotic drug claims for elderly nursing home residents* (OEI-07-08-00150). Retrieved July 15, 2021, from https://oig.hhs.gov/oei/reports/oei-07-08-00150.pdf

US House of Representatives Ways and Means Committee (majority staff). (2020). *Under-enforced and over-prescribed: The antipsychotic drug epidemic ravaging America's nursing homes*. Retrieved July 15, 2021, from https://waysandmeans.house.gov/sites/democrats.waysandmeans.house.gov/files/ documents/WMD%20Nursing%20Home%20Report_Final.pdf

Urick, B.Y., Kaskie, B.P., & Carnahan, R.M. (2016). Improving antipsychotic prescribing practices in nursing facilities: The role of surveyor methods and surveying agencies in upholding the Nursing Home Reform Act. *Research in Social & Administrative Pharmacy*, 12(1), 91–103. https://doi.org/10 .1016/j.sapharm.2015.04.006

Westinghouse Learning Corporation, & Ohio University. (1969). *The impact of Head Start: An evaluation of the effects of Head Start on children's cognitive and affective development*. Retrieved July 15, 2021, from https://files.eric.ed.gov/fulltext/ED036321.pdf

WHO. (n.d.). *Mental health policy, planning & service development*. Retrieved July 15, 2021, from https://www.who.int/mental_health/policy/services/en/

Williams, A. (2010). Is evidence-based policy making really possible? Reflections for policymakers and academics on making use of research in the work of policy. In H.K. Colebatch, R. Hoppe, & M. Noordegraaf (Eds.), *Working for Policy* (pp. 195–209). Amsterdam University Press.

Woelbert, E., Lundell-Smith, K., White, R., & Kemmer, D. (2020). Accounting for mental health research funding: Developing a quantitative baseline of global investments. *The Lancet Psychiatry*, 8(3), P250–P258. https://doi.org/10.1016/S2215-0366(20)30469-7

Zimerman, A.L. (2013). Evidence-based medicine: A short history of a modern medical movement. *AMA Journal of Ethics*, 15(1), 71–6. https://doi.org/10.1001/virtualmentor.2013.15.1.mhst1-1301

8. A critique of children's mental health research
Yvonne Vissing

When I was a graduate student during the early 1980s, I coded data for a professor's project seeking to understand how children's diagnosis of "hyperactivity" was made. The trend showing up in the dataset was clear and grabbed my attention – the most common way parents got the diagnosis of hyperactivity came not from a physician but from a teacher or well-intended acquaintance who "had experience with kids like that." The trajectory was simple – parents were concerned that their children had "ants in their pants" so went to the doctor who put the children on a medication such as Ritalin. Rarely was the diagnosis made through official tests or from a referral to specialists. As a medical sociologist, I saw how easy it was to label a child with a diagnosis and put them on brain and body-altering medication without ever getting a complete work-up by a doctor to make sure that the child actually had the labeled condition (Bhandari, 2020).

This finding hadn't surprised me. I had been a B.A.-level counselor in a community mental health center in the Midwest and worked with families who had "challenging children." I was also responsible for coding tests like the Minnesota Multiphasic Personality Inventory (MMPI). A physician came into the center for a few hours once a week to write prescriptions that we counselors then handed over to their clients; in most cases the physician never met the client, especially if they were young. In my role as a clinician and coder of the MMPI, I was the one who picked what diagnosis the clients had. With hindsight, I did not remotely have the qualifications to make such diagnoses. I chose the condition by perusing through the *Diagnostic Statistical Manual* (DSM) and put it on the forms to be sent to the MD, who sent them on to the insurance company for reimbursement.

My occupation as a mental health counselor lasted about four years. My power to make decisions over what kinds of mental illnesses people would be officially labeled with made me feel very uncomfortable. I knew I did not have the depth of professional expertise to make the kinds of determinations that I was making. My client load was primarily young people, and I held the power to assign labels and make decisions that could alter the course of their lives. I quit, went to graduate school and focused on children and social organizations. There I learned that my prior observations were systemic.

Fast forward a decade-and-a-half. While going through a horrid divorce, I thought my children would benefit from receiving counseling. At the end of the second visit, the therapist (who was not a psychiatrist) gave my child a label and prescription for a brain-altering medication. The assigned label didn't fit. My child's emotional distress was logical, normal, expectable, and my experience as a National Institute of Mental Health Post-Doctoral Research Fellow helped me to know that the treatment was not appropriate. An adjustment counselor who used talk-therapy instead was located.

These personal experiences shape my understanding of how children get diagnosed by the mental health community. Since those days I have conducted decades of research on mental health, mental illness, and children's emotional distress. My work as an international scholar in the field of human rights has shaped my ability to look at how children are treated within social institutions. This includes my research leading to the development of this chapter.

I have utilized a human rights framework to examine how children's mental health is researched. To provide the reader with a context, know that I am a believer in mental health services. The field has matured significantly and I view mental health counseling as essential as physical health care. I see my own therapist when in crisis and periodically otherwise to preserve good mental health maintenance. I am a Family-to-Family trainer with NAMI, the National Alliance on Mental Illness. and am an ardent supporter of the field of mental health.

But as a professional in the field, I know mental health clinicians today who have a bachelor's degree, just like I did many years ago, who are making diagnoses and working with clients. I listen to well-intended psychologists, social workers, and "counselors" espouse positions that I know from my analysis of the field are subjective. I observe them providing care that is not necessarily indicative of best practices or a goodness-of-fit of what the client needs and what they receive. It's this gap that pushes me to study how the field of mental health research can do due-diligence to find the best services for children in distress. Given the high rates of substance abuse, suicidal ideation, and emotional distress in young people (Child Welfare Information Gateway, 2020; Miller, 2020; SAMHSA, 2020; Wu et al., 2004), ensuring they get the right help at the right time in the right way can be life-saving. This chapter considers the trajectory of mental health research regarding children and youth within a child rights framework and provides concrete recommendations for its future development.

THE CONUNDRUM

Mental health is predicted to become the next pandemic (Parrish, 2020) and is already at epidemic proportions in children, according to the World Health Organization (2021). Existing research identifies demographic characteristics of children with mental illness, how many there are, causes of their mental illness, and their diagnoses. While this is helpful, researchers know that in any type of study there is always some amount of "missing data." As this pertains to mental illness in children, it is reasonable to question whether the numbers that exist reflect over- or under-counting, how the children and their diagnoses get identified, what kinds of treatment they get (if any), and the outcomes.

Study of children under age 18 has been problematic for many reasons (Ashan, 2009; Cree et al., 2018; James, 2007; Qvortrup, Corsaro, & Honig, 2013). One, children are not generally allowed to receive clinical care or participate in mental health research projects without parental consent. Trying to obtain parental consent has logistical challenges, including inconvenience, suspicion, and parents not wanting their children to participate in research. Two, there are ethical principles that must be followed to ensure that children are safe during the research process. Sometimes in order to overcome administrative and ethical obstacles, investigators have opted to research people over age 18 and generalize those findings to younger persons. But children have a right to be properly researched and have their voices heard and respected (Beazley et al., 2009; Bradwell et al., 2011; Foucault, 1988). Three, parents, teachers, and other adults have often chosen to speak for their children instead of allowing them to speak for themselves. Their insights may, or not, be accurate reflections of children's realities. Four, children have seldom been involved in the entire research process from idea development, variable selection, survey design, data collection, analysis or interpretation of findings. Children participating in studies often aren't given the opportunity to learn the findings of the projects in which they participated (Christensen, 2004; Christensen & James, 2008). Five, adults have interpreted children's intentions, understandings, and behaviors without asking the children if their interpretations were accurate from the children's point of view. While this may be understandably convenient and appropriate for some levels of analysis, it omits the voice of young people. Six, children are often studied in the context of the family system, rather than as independent agents. Seven, young people have been assumed not to have the ability to comprehend research questions or were deemed not good informants, so often aren't even asked. But if they are not asked, they are denied the opportunity to give input about their emotions, experiences, or needs (Jabeen, 2009; Mason & Danby, 2011; Morrow, 2001; September & Savahl, 2009), information that could be quite informative for developing policies, practices, and interventions. Eight, research is expensive to conduct so studies tend to have many variables that can be analyzed for future reports. This means that a singular research project can yield dozens or hundreds of reports that would imply that there are different studies conducted when in actuality all the data came from the same sample/respondents in the same study. There are, in short, significant methodological and ethical obstacles that have curtailed stellar research about children (Fraser et al., 2004).

Mental health remains a touchy subject with people being afraid of disclosing problems for fear of stigmatization (Auslander & Penny, 1998; Larson, 2018; Shorter, 1997). People may assume certain behaviors or emotions are "normal" and do not identify when they, or others, are having mental disorders. Young people learn not to show certain emotions for fear of being seen as "crazy" or being penalized by parents or police. As a result, while depression and anxiety are common responses to stress, children may learn it is wiser for them to mask emotions that adults could find disturbing. What adults see and know about children's emotions and perceptions may be limited as a result. This means that children may not be divulging their true emotional landscape. It also means that when adults are in the driver's seat in charge of giving authorities feedback on their children's wellbeing, they may not always be providing the most accurate information. They may not know or they may simply choose not to report family dynamics.

It is easy to miss markers of mental disorder. We know that growing up can be hard. Children are regularly exposed to emotional challenges and forms of trauma. Some parents may be unaware of what children think and feel, they may over-react, or they may strategically deny their children's mental distress if they feel they will be blamed for it, if interventions may be forced upon them, or if their child might be removed from their care. Additionally, there are developmental issues in childhood that make it hard to know when there is a true mental disorder occurring or if distress is related to a peer situation, hormonal response, physical ailment, insufficient sleep, or need of a snack. They may be external in origin and adults assume that children may have sufficient coping mechanisms to deal with them. There are often not trained mental health providers available and accessible for children to receive care. Because there are few expert caregivers readily available, treatment may be postponed, hoping problems will go away. What is known about the emotional and mental health/illness of youth comes from adult informants who perceive children's behaviors to be disturbing, troublesome. If a child's behavior hasn't risen to the level of being identified as abnormal, it is likely that the child can fly under-the-radar for years without being identified as needing mental health services.

Mix these two problems together – the challenges of conducting good research on mental distress in children and the lack of direct research protocols with children – and the result is that good research on mental health experiences of children has been grossly inadequate. In recent years there have been significant attempts to address this paucity, but as we will see in this chapter, we still have a long way to go.

HOW IS DATA ON CHILDREN'S MENTAL HEALTH COLLECTED?

Since the days of COVID-19 there has been a greater awareness of children's depression, anxiety, stress, and other mental illness responses (Wagner, 2020). Mental illness has become a more commonly discussed topic in homes, schools, community, and professional arenas. Children, like adults, have not been immune from emotional distress associated with the coronavirus. Reports indicate greater depression, anxiety, stress, and grief in children due to COVID-19 (Rodriguez, 2021). On a positive note, the distress generated from the pandemic has opened the door for more open public discussion about mental health in general and mental health for young people in particular.

Even without the stressors resulting from COVID-19, childhood is fraught with many challenges that youth negotiate. They experience social, psychological, biological and developmental challenges, school pressures, peer and intimate relationships, family pressures, identity, self-esteem, and figuring out their place in the world. Given school shootings, suicide attempts, and mental distress, the American School Counselor Association (ASCA) finds there has never been a more critical time to make sure students have access to mental health professionals (Bray, 2019). Schools provide a logical location for youth to access mental health services (Jacobson, 2019). The ASCA recommends a ratio of 250 students or fewer per counselor but the American School Counselor Association (2019) has found that the actual average student-to-school-counselor ratio is 464 to 1 and studies indicate it could be as high as 905 students for every counselor, as in Arizona (Bray, 2019). One in five students (8 million) don't have access to a school counselor and 3 million have no access to other school support staff (Barshay, 2020). Janine Menard, chair of the Arizona School Counselors Association, has a caseload of 1,100 students (Quinn, 2019). Even with a "low" rate of 250 students per counselor, most distressed students will likely never access one. Moreover, many school counselors don't have time to do actual therapy with students, rather, their time is orchestrated to focus on testing or college preparation (Jacobson, 2019). This means that while children benefit from mental health counseling, during the pandemic, it has been even harder to access mental health services they may need.

School counselors have contact with children and first-hand information about their emotional needs. But during remote learning this direct line of communication may be less available (Tate, 2020; Verlenden, 2021; Wood, 2021). Much of what is officially known about children's mental health and emotional issues comes from indirect sources such as parent or teacher observations. Adults operate as a filter-bubble when it comes to assessing children's mental health. They may not identify when children are having mental health problems (Schwartz, 2016). Adults may report children's mental disorders that they interpret from their own emotions, concerns, experiences and backgrounds and become gatekeepers to link children to services. Studies have found that both over- and under-reporting of a child's actual mental status may be colored by the parent's interpretation that comes from their own history. Najman et al. (2001) found that the more emotionally impaired the mother, the greater the degree to which she imputes the child to have behavior problems. As the mother's current emotional impairment increased, so her reports of the child's behavior problems increased, when compared with the child's own reports. Maternal depressive symptoms were associated with mother-child reporting discrepancies, with depressed mothers reporting more problems than their child reported (van der Toorn et al., 2010). In fairness, it is relevant to note that some researchers indicate that maternal bias does not impact the diagnosis of a child's mental illness and that parental report of a child's mental illness may be a valid indicator of its existence (Olino et al., 2020).

Adult attitudes and bias have been found to impact their perception of children's mental health status (Edge, 2020). This may occur even in infants (Arnold, McWilliams, & Arnold, 1998) or preschool-age children (Banashewski, 2010). It is also possible that through adult filters they may miss, misinterpret, or strategically fail to report when children are in actual need of mental health services (Gold, 2016; Lambert, 2020; Mostafavi, 2019; National Center for Learning Disabilities, 2017; Providence Health, 2020; Yourman, 1932).

For those children who do have contact with mental health professionals or those who diagnose them to have a mental illness, misdiagnosis of mental illness in children is not uncommon (Spiro, 2020). Often children's misbehavior may be ignored when there is mental illness, or when it is misinterpreted, or exaggerated (Gartrell, 1995). Common misdiagnoses occur when children have attention issues, intrusive distressing thoughts, speech problems, sadness, fatigue, and difficulties thinking clearly, disruptive behavior, and learning difficulties (Spiro, 2020).

It is important to be able to understand children's emotional distress and treatment needs from their point of view in order to be of maximum benefit to them. But children may have problems accessing mental health care for a variety of reasons. These include embarrassment, not realizing they have an emotional problem for which there could be treatment, not knowing who to ask for help, getting parental approval, insurance or ways to pay for care, transportation, and accessibility and availability of appointments. Seeking care is complicated when children are experiencing problems that they are afraid will get them in trouble if they tell adults, or when it is their parents who are causing problems. The result is if there is no contact between children and mental health providers, data comes from adult, not child informants. While some may be accurate informants of children's actual mental health situation, some adult-delivered information may not be accurate or provide complete understandings of the causal and outcome factors. Because mental illness in children is challenging to identify, parents and teachers are encouraged to look for warning signs, such as mood or behavior changes, eating or sleeping changes, headaches, persistent sadness, isolation and withdrawal, self-harm, irritability or behavioral outbursts that are extreme or out of control, changes in school performance, or talking about death or suicide (Mayo Clinic, 2021).

Research about children's mental health is skewed because it relies so heavily upon parent and adult perceptions of the children's experiences. The result is that often what we know about children's mental health doesn't come directly from young people themselves. It comes from parents, teachers, or other adults who are in a position where they can identify when something in the children's life is amiss and they are knowledgeable about how to use the caregiving system to access help.

HOW ACCURATE IS THE DATA ON WHAT WE KNOW ABOUT CHILDREN'S MENTAL HEALTH?

The Centers for Disease Control (2021) reports that close to 50 percent of all Americans will be diagnosed with a mental illness or disorder at some point in their lifetime. If we assume that many people will have mental disorders which are not addressed, this would indicate that most people will have a diagnosable mental illness at some point. It would also indicate that any number that we have is likely an underestimate of actual prevalence.

Mental illness in children is hard to identify (Mayo Clinic, 2021). This is because, as children develop, they go through physical, hormonal, emotional, cognitive, and social changes that fluctuate over time. Internal and external situational factors may be time-limited and create behaviors that are quite normal. However, mental distress and behavioral abnormalities could be signs of a more serious condition. What is considered normal may vary depending on a child's age, biology, culture, and family experience.

As a general overview, research indicates that over 7.7 million children and teens in the US, or one in seven, have at least one treatable mental health disorder, including depression, anxiety, or attention deficit hyperactivity disorder (ADHD) according to a 2016 National Survey of Children's Health. Almost 47 million children were included in the study and almost 17 percent had at least one mental health disorder (Whitney & Peterson, 2019). Over 45 percent of children have experienced at least one traumatic life experience (Robert Wood Johnson Foundation, 2017; Sacks & Murphey, 2018); the more adverse life experiences (ACES) a child has, the greater the likelihood of toxic stress and mental illnesses. Black and Hispanic children experience more ACES than White or Asian children, associated with higher rates of poverty. Poverty is associated with children's mental illness (Dallas, 2017; Jakovljevic, Miller, & Fitzgerald, 2016). So is exposure to violence in general (Rueve & Welton, 2008) and child abuse and domestic violence in particular (Child Welfare, 2021; Straus & Donnelly, 1994).

According to the National Alliance on Mental Illness (2021), one in five children have, or will have, a serious mental illness such as depression, anxiety, mood disorders, or other mental health conditions. Half of all mental illnesses have started by the age of 14, and 75 percent of these illnesses are apparent by age 24. NAMI reports that 37 percent of students with mental health conditions drop out of school, and this is the highest dropout rate of any disability group. About 70 percent of youth in the juvenile justice system have a mental illness. Suicide is the third leading cause of death in children aged 10–24; 90 percent of youth who die from suicide have underlying mental illnesses. Therefore, studies paint a clear picture that mental health is a significant concern in children and youth.

Research from a variety of studies find that the most common mental disorders among children include anxiety, depression, attention deficit or hyperactivity disorders, autism spectrum disorders, eating disorders, stress or post-traumatic stress disorders (Danielson et al., 2018; Ghandour et al., 2018; Kessler, Berglund, & Demler, 2005; Mayo Clinic, 2021; National Institute of Mental Health, 2021; Perou et al., 2013; Whitney & Peterson, 2019). The impact of traumatic brain injuries in children, through accidents, sports or play, may yield long-term mental health problems as well and has become a more recent area of study (Schachar, Park, & Dennis, 2015). Mental illness-related problems associated with human-made disasters are also found to be significant in children (SAMHSA, 2019).

Data on children's mental health is better than it has ever been, which is a benefit of scientific principles shown in Wallace's (1971) Great Wheel of Science approach where what we learned yesterday in studies influences today's research designs. There are a variety of governmental and national organizations, such as the National Institute of Mental Illness, National Center for Maternal and Child Health, US Department of Health and Human Services, Administration for Children and Families or the National Alliance on Mental Illness, as well as university research centers and non-profit organizations dedicated to understanding and promoting children's mental health. We can therefore anticipate that research methods will continually improve in the future in the way research is undertaken on mental health in young people.

But it must be said that the field of child mental health research still has a way to go if is going to utilize a child rights framework. The need for the use of better methodologies has been reinforced by major mental health leaders. Kollins (2021) writes in his editorial,

> This editorial considers whether our traditional approaches to child mental health research – and specifically the papers that are published in the *Journal of Child Psychology and Psychiatry* (JCPP) – may inadvertently introduce structural barriers for advancing knowledge and improving mental health for children of all racial and ethnic backgrounds. (Kollins, 2021)

In 2015, the American Academy of Pediatrics published a comprehensive summary of the role of racial, ethnic, and SES factors on children's physical and mental health and strongly recommended a number of steps that the field of pediatric health research could take to better understand and address inequalities (Cheng, Goodman, & Committee on Pediatric Research 2015). However, Kollins (2021) observes that it is not clear the degree to which such recommendations have been followed in contemporary research on children's wellbeing.

Snowden (2003, p. 241) argues that

> It is likely that clinicians' interpretations of client behavior, both causes and effect, may be impacted by their bias and assumptions, some of which they may be unaware they hold. More research is recommended that directly evaluates the contribution of bias, especially as it may impact one's interpretation of mental illness in children and youth.

The importance of implicit bias of which even professionals may be unaware, impacts the way we see others and the decisions that we make about them (Harvard University, 2021). Diagnostic evaluation of psychiatric disorders in children and adolescents relies in part on adult subjective interpretations of what they think is going on for the young people. Clinicians interpret and contextualize information obtained from family, caregivers, and educators in order to assign a diagnosis. Environmental, biological, and sociocultural influences can make the diagnosis of psychiatric disorders in youth particularly challenging. Although the cause of diagnostic disparities is multifactorial, there is concern that unconscious biases may play a role in diagnostic decision-making. As a result of these biases, mental health practitioners may judge and interpret behaviors differently based on age, race or ethnicity, putting vulnerable populations (especially non-white children) at risk. Even though the current standard of practice is to routinely consider a broad range of differential of comorbid disorders, when youth exhibit disruptive symptoms, clinician and adult biases may inadvertently result in them being less likely to explore alternative potential explanations for behavior (Fadus et al., 2020). Behavioral and emotional problems in infants and young children have posed significant challenges of clinical assessment and intervention (Drotar, 2002).

A simple example of this is to assume that school or mass shootings are caused by mental illness (Duwe & Rocque, 2018; Qui & Bank, 2018). "A mass shooting is so disturbing, so irrational, and horrifying, people want to know why it happened, and mental illness is the perfect master explanation" (Liorente, 2018). How valid is this argument, from a research perspective? Not very, according to experts (Ducharme, 2018). The vast majority of people with mental illness are likely to be victims of violence, not perpetrators of it (Canadian Mental Health Association 2022; Ghiasi, Azhar, & Singh 2022).

How often are the underlying assumptions of a research project seriously evaluated by the public or practitioners? Often people are looking for sound-bites, quick take-aways that give them a snap-shot image of a phenomenon instead of a detailed understanding and analysis. This is true when it comes to assessing mental health and youth. It's important for scholars to be attentive to underlying assumptions and rigorous methodological considerations when they enter into research projects. It's important, as consumers of information, that we use a critical eye to assess to what degree what we are reading is valid and representative of good science, not rhetoric.

While there is a lot of information available about mental health available, how accurate is it for understanding children's mental illness? In a simple Google search, I found over one billion hits using the term "mental health research" – but when I added the term "about children" it reduced to 861 million, with 151 million results for the term "children's mental health articles," or about 7 percent of all mental health research articles. Most of these articles appear to rely upon parent or adult data about children, not data from young people themselves. As pointed out earlier, we have learned much from adult-informant studies of children's mental health. But there is also understanding to be gained when we are surveying children's mental health from children's point of view. To what extent does dominant child mental health research involve children directly?

As a simple example, entries in the Centers for Disease Control's (CDC) Key Findings and Recent Scientific Articles section of their website were reviewed to determine the methodologies employed (Table 8.1). There were seven Key Findings articles and 17 scientific articles showcased on their website. All of their key findings and nine of the scientific studies were selected for inclusion in this analysis, for a total of 16 studies posted on the CDC's website devoted to providing information about children's mental health. There were duplications between Key Findings and Scientific Articles so duplicates were eliminated in the table below. Five of the articles were not included in the table because they focused on organizational policies and practices and not about children's mental health per se.

The majority of articles posted (12 of 16) drew upon the National Survey of Children's Health (NSCH), which is a nationally representative, cross-sectional survey of parents and guardians (Table 8.1). The NSCH is funded and directed by the Health Resources and Services Administration's Maternal and Child Health Bureau (HRSA, MCHB) and conducted by the U.S. Census Bureau. Only one of the studies included direct youth input, as gained from the CDC's Youth Risk Behavior Survey (2019).

The CDC data in Table 8.1 does not rely upon direct information from young people under age 18. It does rely primarily upon parent data. Many of the reports are generated from the same dataset – the NSCH. The information is focused on enumerating different types and amounts of mental disorders in young people that were obtained from adults. As pointed out earlier in this chapter, there are pragmatic challenges with obtaining information about children's mental health and the strategies used were undoubtedly selected for cost, convenience,

Table 8.1   *Centers for Disease Control and Prevention children's mental health posted studies*

Methodology	Title	Web link
2-stage data collection. In Stage 1 teachers determined student risk status; in Stage 2 parents interviewed to identify child disorders	Mental health symptoms in school-aged children in four communities	https://www.cdc.gov/childrensmentalhealth/features/school-aged-mental-health-in-communities.html
NSCH parent survey	Gaps in helping adolescents with mental, behavioral, and developmental disorders	https://www.cdc.gov/childrensmentalhealth/features/health-care-transition-gaps.html
4146 Nurse managers completed 55-item survey	Characteristics Related to Having Pediatric Mental Healthcare Policies	https://www.cdc.gov/childrensmentalhealth/features/policies-in-emergency-departments.html
NSCH parent survey	US Children with Diagnosed Anxiety and Depression	https://www.cdc.gov/childrensmentalhealth/features/anxiety-and-depression.html
Meta-analysis of 64 articles	Treatment of Disruptive Behavior Problems	https://www.cdc.gov/childrensmentalhealth/features/kf-disruptive-behavior.html
NSCH parent survey	Health care, Family, and Community Factors Associated with Mental, Behavioral, and Developmental Disorders in Early Childhood	https://www.cdc.gov/ncbddd/childdevelopment/features/key-finding-factors-mental-behavioral-developmental-early-childhood.html
CDC Mental Health Surveillance among Children report describes federal monitoring mental disorders & estimates of number of children with specific mental disorders	Children's Mental Health Report	https://www.cdc.gov/childrensmentalhealth/features/kf-childrens-mental-health-report.html
NSCH parent survey	Factors Associated with Self-regulation in a Nationally Representative Sample of Children Ages 3–5 Years	https://link.springer.com/article/10.1007/s10995-020-03039-6
NSCH parent survey	Support for Transition from Adolescent to Adult Health Care among Adolescents with and without Mental, Behavioral, and Developmental Disorders	https://www.cdc.gov/mmwr/volumes/69/wr/mm6934a2.htm?s_cid=mm6934a2_w
NSCH parent survey	Health Care, Family, and Community Factors Associated with Mental, Behavioral, and Developmental Disorders and Poverty among Children Aged 2–8 Years	https://www.cdc.gov/mmwr/volumes/67/wr/mm6750a1.htm
Organization policy lever analysis	Policy Levers to Promote Access to and Utilization of Children's Mental Health Services	https://link.springer.com/article/10.1007/s10488-018-00916-9
NSCH parent survey	Prevalence and Treatment of Depression, Anxiety, and Conduct Problems in US Children	https://www.jpeds.com/article/S0022-3476(18)31292-7/fulltext

Methodology	Title	Web link
Parent report	Prevalence of Parent-Reported Traumatic Brain Injury in Children and Associated Health Conditions	https://jamanetwork.com/journals/ jamapediatrics/fullarticle/2703481 ?utm_source=silverchair&utm_medium =email&utm_campaign=article_alert -jamapediatrics&utm_content=olf&utm _term=092418
NSCH parent survey	Epidemiology and Impact of Health Care Provider-Diagnosed Anxiety and Depression among US Children	https://www.ncbi.nlm.nih.gov/pmc/ articles/PMC6003874/
Triangulated analysis of national surveys, administrative data & community studies	Interpreting the Prevalence of Mental Disorders in Children	https://journals.sagepub.com/doi/full/10 .1177/1524839916677730
9 major national surveys pertaining to children's health including Youth Risk Behavior Survey	Mental Health Surveillance among Children – United States, 2005–2011	https://www.cdc.gov/mmwr/preview/ mmwrhtml/su6202a1.htm?s_cid= su6202a1_w

Source: CDC, Articles and key findings about children's mental health. Retrieved July 17, 2022 from https://www .cdc.gov/childrensmentalhealth/articles.html

and accessibility purposes. Research is a complicated and expensive process. The information is largely focused on improving parental or institutional delivery of services or developing interventions, which surely would be of benefit to children. The point is that most existing studies do not incorporate children directly into the research process or feedback loop. As the field of children's mental health research grows forward, these are fruitful considerations to be pondered.

HOW COULD DATA GATHERING ON CHILDREN'S MENTAL HEALTH BECOME MORE ACCURATE?

There is a hearty literature on how to conduct research utilizing a children's human rights perspective to guide us (Alderson, 2008; Alderson & Morrow 2011; Boyden & Ennew, 1997; Punch, 2002; Tisdall, Davis, & Gallagher, 2009). In the past, research on children has seldom been designed or implemented by young people, even as consultants (De Winter, 2002; Stafford et al., 2003). Most had little input into studies, their premise, questions, sampling strategies, or implementation plans. They're seldom involved with data gathering or analysis. When studies are completed young people usually never get to learn the findings, even for school-based studies. Excluding children as research partners may limit the quality and utility of well-intended research on children's mental health (Smith, Monaghan, & Broad, 2002). "Gerontocentism" is the process by which adults fail to accurately interpret children's words and their explanations of their social experiences (Jenks, 1996). "Like the white researcher in black society, the male researcher studying women, the adult researcher is obviously different from children that are in the study and try as they might, their interpretations of the 'other's' experience will not be totally accurate" (Fine & Sandstrom, 2010, p. 151).

There has been an increased attempt to involve young people in different aspects of research (Corsaro, 2010; James & Prout 2015; Tisdall, Davis, & Gallagher, 2009). Scott's (2000) review of research studies found that even young children are good respondents when asked in ways that they can understand about events that are meaningful in their lives. She agrees that children have been systematically neglected from participating in survey research or providing researchers with data about their lives. Alderson (2008) found young people are an underestimated and underused resource in conducting research. Young people can effectively help refine questions to be studied, the design, assist with research instruments, data collection, analysis, report writing, and dissemination of findings.

While adult-provided information may be valuable, such input must be contextualized, child voice must be included, and gaps of nonrepresentation of children (especially or traditionally excluded or marginalized groups) must be filled (Kollins, 2021; Mascendaro, Herman, & Webster-Stratton, 2012; Vidair et al., 2011). Implicit bias must be confronted (Weber, 1949) in how we design projects, collect data, and interpret findings. Some questions that child rights research scholars ask to be considered include those raised in the following subsections.

Who is the Research for?

The position of the child rights field is that much of what we know *about* children comes from information written *by* adults, *for* adults, using *adultified* theoretical assumptions and *adult-based* methodologies. What we know about how children think, act, and feel often comes from adults – not from young people themselves (Qvortrup, 2009). As researchers, are we conducting research *with* children, *for* children, or research *about* children? Child-participatory research is encouraged (Tisdall, Davis, & Gallagher, 2009). Howard Becker (1967) asked the question "Whose side are we on?" Our answer becomes apparent in our theories and methodologies. Lack of children as research subjects reflects children not being a priority, their general invisibility, and the social lack of recognition of their personhood (Wyness, 2012). Children can be studied directly and indirectly. They can also help throughout the entire research process as valuable collaborators. Even young children have opinions, ideas, feelings, and can give information, provide data in well-designed projects. But often, research on children continues to regard them as objects rather than participants.

The trend in child and youth studies has been to move away from research on or about children to research with or for children (Mason & Watson, 2014). This change isn't merely linguistic – it repositions children to be subjects, rather than objects of research (Christensen & James, 2012). Employing methods that give voice to children's concerns and provide detailed descriptions and interpretations as children live their childhoods have great potential "because they do not focus so much on how children become adults (which is the goal of most traditional research on socialization), but rather on what children can teach and tell us about their shared experiences and their struggles to gain some control over more powerful adults and adult rules" (Corsaro, 2005, p. 49).

Incorporating young people in research has been actively pursued by children's human rights scholars around the world. As examples of these initiatives, Magenta Simmons (2020) at the Centre for Youth Mental Health at The University of Melbourne, Australia, studies how young people are important contributors in mental health research. Their unique contributions throughout all stages of the research process can help improve the quality and value of research activities, from setting research priorities through translating findings into practice and policy. Her research showcases the importance of empowering youth as collaborators in research projects, in clinical decision-making regarding their own mental health care, and as peer workers supporting other young people. The Anna Freud Center (2021) in London, in conjunction with Kings College, conducts a variety of research with secondary-age students as collaborators regarding mental health issues that youth confront. In Sweden, greater interest is shown in youth participatory approaches in mental health research.

Although participatory approaches have user involvement in common, they differ in terms of the explicit guidance on how to actually involve and engage children and young people in health research. An interpretative scoping literature review showed that participatory approaches were most often used in the development of interventions in school settings and in community and health care settings, and on issues concerning support in lifestyle or in managing illness or disease. The level of participation varied from children and young people taking part just as active informants, through stages of greater participation both in quantitative and qualitative terms, to children and young people becoming an active agent involved as a co-researchers where the research process was shaped by views of a higher level of mutuality. Participatory approaches aiming for a higher level of participation where children and young people work together with the researchers in partnerships are thus warranted (Larsson et al., 2018). Additionally, digital mental health interventions and online mental health resources are regularly used by youth to address their own mental health concerns. Their participation in conducting research on their own conditions and possible treatments is an important way that young people engage with mental health, and is a fruitful area for further inquiry (Liverpool et al., 2020). In the UK, by regulation, all research bids to the National Institute of Health Research have to be looked at by representatives of the public and patients (titled PPI: Public and Patients Involvement). This has led to establishing in some places young people teams who are trained to look specifically at research proposals about young people and children and to express their views concerning the suitability of the research proposal. They are paid for this type of involvement (Bagley et al., 2016).

Research Designs

It is important to consider what type of research designs and methodologies to employ when studying children and youth. Because of their developmental stages and need for ethical considerations, different types of methodologies may be necessary, as compared with studying adults (Greene & Hogan, 2005). Children as research subjects can be risky unless done well and with appropriate safeguards (Hood, Kelley, & Mayall, 1996). Use of a triangulated, multifaceted research design may yield results that give a broader picture of children's mental health (Denzin, 1970).

Funders

Research is expensive to conduct and funding is necessary. Funders give money because they are interested in a topic or perhaps a certain outcome to be documented. Researchers may feel pressured to select certain populations, subjects or methodologies, thus observing who has funded the research is an important consideration in assessing its findings.

Units of Analysis and Samples

Who is it that we want to learn about – who are our units of analysis? If we are interested in how schools handle student mental distress, that requires a different type of study than looking at how families address mental disorders, which are different from understanding how young people identify emotional distress causes, experiences, and coping strategies. Sometimes information is collected about one group and assumptions are applied to another group without really having focused upon them. For instance, Immigration and Customs Enforcement (ICE) officials are not the best informants about the emotional impact of children being separated from their parents at the US-Mexico border – talking to the children themselves provides a different picture of their experience (Vissing, 2021).

We want to make sure that our sample is representative of all the people that we're interested in studying, not just a group that's convenient or available. If we want to study children's experiences, we must talk with children to accurately report what they think and feel. Using a sample of rural students may not be accurate reflectors of what school is like for urban dwellers. Issues of inclusion and discrimination may be more accurate when talking with students who have actually had those experiences. Relying on parent or teacher feedback on such topics may be valuable, but it does not replace the importance of knowing what young people think.

Bias

Bias, whether unconscious or known, may lead to misleading or false conclusions (Šimundić, 2013). The acronym GIGO means "garbage-in, garbage-out"; if we start with flawed assumptions we're going to get questionable results. When we're biased, we're going to get biased results.

Ecological Fallacy

We must beware of the ecological fallacy (Hsieh, 2017; Lavrakas, 2008), or tendency to take data at one level and apply it to people at another level. Aggregated research tells us about what is true for the majority of people the majority of the time, but it doesn't necessarily predict an individual's experience. An ecological fallacy in research like this occurs when people make conclusions about individuals based on their interpretation of group-level data, or vice versa. Research needs to have a goodness-of-fit to be relevant, especially since groups of children may have different experiences.

Who's Conducting the Research?

Research is an art and good artists are well trained. Just as a Picasso differs from finger-painting, there is a wide variation between expert researchers and everyday researchers. Expert researchers have extensive training, experience, and insights that novice researchers don't. When assessing quality of research, it's wise to consider the background of the researcher. For convenience or financial considerations, sometimes organizations use their own staff to conduct research. There are pros and cons to this. Pros are that staff know the organization, cons are that they may not have the expertise and could have unintentional biases that influence their research methods or findings. Adults who have a pre-existing relationship with children may be recruited to provide data about children. The most common are teachers and parents. Much existing research on children has relied upon "Parents as Researchers" (PAR) (Adler & Adler, 1998). The notion behind this strategy is that children who are comfortable with parents (or teachers) are more likely to act naturally. These adults have an ongoing contextual familiarity with the children's routines, experiences, and networks and can provide convenient observations at home, school, playgrounds, or with peers. Having a pre-established relationship between the researcher and respondents, employing multiple methodologies that include "natural" conversations, and engaging in reciprocity have been found to be helpful in obtaining more accurate data (Elder & Fingerson, 2002; Mayall, 2000). But adults must be careful not to take advantage of their positions of authority when acting as researchers with children (Mandell, 1991; Punch, 2002). There is the chance of role conflict. Adults are older and larger than children which make them intimidating; they have more formal education and may speak or behave in ways conveying authority, which children may find off-putting. Parents have the power to decide what to report and how to report it. When adults report what they think children think, feel, or experience, it denies youth voice; it may also result in inaccurate data because adults may not perceive things the same way as young people. Adults have the power to decide what to disclose in the role of a "researcher" and what information to keep confidential in the role of a "parent" (Sternheimer, 2010, p. 139). As convenient as it may be, it is challenging for researchers to rely upon information provided by adults in close relationship with youth (Corsaro, 2005; Finkelhor, 2000).

Ethical Considerations

Collecting data from or about children, especially concerning their mental health issues, requires extensive safeguards. Children have not always had the rights of minors protected in the research process (Christiansen & Prout, 2002). They've been done-to, talked about, asked to do things, misunderstood, and had decisions made for them over which they were never given information or provided consent. When studying young people today we must ensure that children's right to be properly researched is enforced, along with the basic human rights principles of dignity and respect to involve children's partnership in research. Ethical strategies should be an integral part of all research designs.

Young people are entitled to special protections to ensure that they aren't exploited because of their age and status. This is required in Article 5 of the United Nations Convention on the Rights of the Child (UNCRC) about protecting the evolving capacities of the child, their age, personal experiences and circumstances (Ennew, 2005; Lansdown, 2005). Researchers must take special measures to make sure that in the process of studying minors their rights are protected. The international Ethical Research Involving Children project, or ERIC, assists researchers to plan and conduct ethical research involving children and young people in different geographical, social, cultural, and methodological contexts. Oversight organizations seek to ensure research on children and youth meets ethical standards. These standards share common themes: children are persons in their own right and worthy of recognition and respect; children have agency to consent and have voice in research; research with young people should adhere to high quality standards; children's competencies, and perceptions may differ from those of adults. Also, the age of children may require that information be asked in specific ways and that adult research partners should be skilled, caring and provide appropriate support to help them participate in a safe and meaningful way so the research has meaningful consequences to the wellbeing of children, their families, and communities (Lundy & McEvoy, 2012).

Ethical concern in young people's research include (Dahlberg & Moss, 2005; Graham et al., 2013; Greene & Hill, 2005; Tisdall, Davis, & Gallagher, 2009):

1. Benefit of the research: Research should improve the status, rights and wellbeing of children. Who is the research for and why is it important)?
2. Maleficence: Do no harm! Benefit must always outweigh risks. What is the potential harm to the individual child, as well as to aggregate groups?
3. Informed consent: Children and their families have the right to full information about the research process and must give consent.
4. Privacy and confidentiality: Information obtained while conducting research with children should remain confidential. Researchers must tell young subjects that while they will try to keep what they say confidential, there may be information that they might have to disclose in order to keep them safe. If a child conveys they're at risk of harm or neglect, or if there is criminal behavior in the home, the line of researcher and mandated reporter become blurred. Child wellbeing must always take priority. Researchers cannot guarantee child respondents absolute confidentiality because they have a duty to act on any information given to them by the child relating to abuse, irrespective of the effects this has on the integrity of the research (Wyness, 2012).
5. Respect: Treating children's personhood with dignity over their cultural, physical, emotional, verbal, and social dimensions is essential.
6. Justice: Children's lives are situated in unequal relationships. The principle of justice requires researchers be attentive to power differences inherent in the adult/child research relationship, consistent with Article 12 of the UNCRC.

CONCLUSIONS

This chapter has explored the necessity for a new child-focused paradigm when it comes to researching the mental health of children and youth (Kellett, 2005). As Thomas Kuhn (1977) theorized, revolutions in scientific knowledge always point to the necessity of revolution or changing the paradigms we use so that we can continue to do better and more appropriate research. Paradigm change is often slow to come and is frequently met with both institutional and professional resistance. But just because we have done things a certain way in the past does not mean that we should continue those habitual normative operations in the future when better options may be available.

Indeed, research on children's mental health is better than it has been in the past. Given research protocols, funding, access challenges, and ethical considerations, studies reflect honorable attempts to understand mental illness and emotional challenges in young people. A concern is that the information may not adequately express the realities that youth face. Without understanding children's realities from their points of view, the policies and practices created to address their mental health may be ill-placed (Fattore, Mason, & Watson, 2009; Fernandez, 2011).

Representativeness of mental illness in young people is worthy of further exploration. There are gender, race, ethnic, and cross-cultural variations that have not been adequately teased out or tested in the data (Carpenter-Song et al., 2010; Marrast, Himmelstein, & Woolhandler, 2016). Mental illness of children is a global problem (Bartlett & Stratford, 2021; Brenner,

2019; Chen, 2017; Rice-Oxley, 2019). It is estimated that one in four people worldwide has a mental illness; 300 million people suffer from depression; 70–85 percent of the world's population lack access to mental health services; undiagnosed mental disorders in children and youth are enormous, and cost over a trillion dollars annually (Project Hope, 2020). Reports indicate that there are over 17 million children in the US with a mental illness, that anxiety and depression have increased by 40 percent in recent years, and that suicide is the second highest cause of youth death (Morgan Stanley Alliance on Children's Mental Health, 2019). These are likely conservative numbers, since we know that those suffering from mental illnesses are afraid of being stigmatized and thus more reticent to report. Numbers of mental distress have likely increased during the days of COVID. We know that most data is generated from adults so the figures may be an under-representation or give an incomplete analysis of mental health in young people.

Existing information clearly conveys the necessity to design better mental health promotion and mental illness prevention and treatment programs for children and youth. This could be catapulted by bringing in young people into the mix of the entire research process from A to Z. As researchers, it is our responsibility to push forward the Great Wheel of Science to incorporate the experiences, perceptions, needs, and lifestyles of young people if we are going to protect their future wellbeing, as well as that of society as a whole. It is long past time, as child rights expert Michael Freeman (1987) argues, to take children seriously in every aspect of our work.

REFERENCES

Adler, P., & Adler, P. (1998). *Peer power: Preadolescent culture and identity.* Brunswick, NJ: Rutgers University Press.

Alderson, P. (2008). *Children as researchers: Participation rights and research methods.* New York: Routledge.

Alderson, P., & Morrow, V. (2011). *The ethics of research with children and young people.* London: Sage.

American School Counselor Association. (2019). School Counselors Matter. https://www.schoolcounselor .org/Publications-Research/Research/ASCA-Research-Reports Data Source: US Department of Education, National Center For Education Statistics, Common Core of Data (CCD), State Nonfiscal Public Elementary/Secondary Education Survey, 2018–19 V.1a.

Anna Freud Center. (2021). Research and Policy Center. https://www.annafreud.org/research-and -policy/research-policy/

Arnold, D., McWilliams, L., & Arnold, E. (1998). Teacher discipline and child misbehavior in day care: Untangling causality with correlational data. *Developmental Psychology, 34*(2), 276–87.

Ashan, M. (2009). The potential and challenges of rights-based research with children and young people: Experiences from Bangladesh. Children's Geographies, 7(4), 391–403.

Auslander, M., & Penny, D. (1998). *The prevalence of abuse history in the mental health system. NASMHPD.* Retrieved from https://www.nasmhpd.org/content/prevalence-abuse-histories-mental -health-system

Bagley, H.J., Short, H., Harman, N.L., et al. (2016). A patient and public involvement (PPI) toolkit for meaningful and flexible involvement in clinical trials – a work in progress. *Research Involvement and Engagement, 2,* 15. https://doi.org/10.1186/s40900-016-0029-8

Banashewski, T. (2010). Editorial: Preschool behavior problems – over-pathologized or under identified? A developmental psychopathology perspective is needed. *The Journal of Child Psychology and Psychiatry, 51*(1), 1–2.

Bartlett, J., & Stratford, B. (2021). A national agenda for children's mental health. *Child Trends.* Retrieved from https://www.childtrends.org/publications/a-national-agenda-for-childrens-mental -health

Barshay, J. (2020, April 27). *Lowest student to school counselor rate since 1986.* The Hechinger Report. https://hechingerreport.org/lowest-student-to-school-counselor-ratio-since-1986/

Beazley, H., Bessell, S., Ennew, J., & Waterson, R. (2009). Editorial: The right to be properly researched: Research with children in a messy, real world. Children's Geographies, 7(4).

Becker, H. (1967). Whose side are we on? Social Problems, *14*(3), Winter, 239–47. https://doi.org/10 .2307/799147

Bhandari, Smitha. (2020). A brief history of ADHD. Retrieved from https://www.webmd.com/add-adhd/ adhd-history#:~:text=Today%2C%20methylphenidate%20is%20the%20stimulant,to%20improve %20symptoms%20of%20ADHD

Boyden, J., & Ennew, J. (1997). *Children in focus: A manual for participatory research with children.* Stockholm: Radda Barnen.

Bradwell, J., Crawford, D., Crawford, et al. (2011). How looked after children are involved in their review process. Child Indicators Research, 4, 221–9

Bray, B. (2019, May 10). One school counselor per 455 students: Nationwide average improves. *Counseling Today*. Retrieved from https://ct.counseling.org/2019/05/one-school-counselor-per-455 -students-nationwide-average-improves/

Brenner, E. (2019). The crisis of youth mental health. *Stanford Social Innovation Review*. Retrieved from https://ssir.org/articles/entry/the_crisis_of_youth_mental_healthEliot

Canadian Mental Health Association. (2022). The myth of mental illness and violence. Retrieved from https://cmhadurham.ca/finding-help/the-myth-of-violence-and-mental-illness/

Carpenter-Song, E., Chu, E., Drake, R.E., Ritsema, M., Smith, B., & Alverson, H. (2010). Ethno-cultural variations in the experience and meaning of mental illness and treatment: implications for access and utilization. Transcultural Psychiatry, *47*(2), 224–51.

Centers for Disease Control. (2021). Data and publications. Retrieved from https://www.cdc.gov/ mentalhealth/data_publications/index.htm

Chen, M. (2017). Mental illness is a global crisis. *The Nation.* Retrieved from https://www.thenation .com/article/archive/mental-illness-is-a-global-crisis/

Cheng, T., Goodman, E., & Committee on Pediatric Research. (2015). Race, ethnicity and socioeco-nomic status in research on child health. *Pediatrics, 135*, e225–e237.

Child Welfare. (2021). Long term consequences of child abuse and neglect. Retrieved from https://www .childwelfare.gov/topics/can/impact/long-term-consequences-of-child-abuse-and-neglect/health/#: ~:text=The%20immediate%20emotional%   20effects%20of,addiction%20to%20drugs%20and%20 alcohol

Child Welfare Information Gateway. (2020). Retrieved from https://www.childwelfare.gov/organizations/ ?CWIGFunctionsaction=rols:main.dspList&rolType=Custom&RS_ID=118

Christensen, P.H. (2004). Children's participation in ethnographic research: Issues of power and rep-resentation. Children & Society, 18(2), 165–76.

Christensen, P.H., & James, A. (Eds.). (2008). *(2nd ed.). Routledge/Taylor & Francis Group.*

Christensen, P.H., & James, A. (2012). *Research with children: Perspectives and practices.* London: Falmer.

Christensen, P.H., & Prout, A. (2002). Working with ethical symmetry in social research with children. Childhood, 9(4), 477–97.

Corsaro, W. (2005). *Sociology of childhood.* Thousand Oaks, CA: Sage.

Corsaro, W. (2010). *The Sociology of Childhood.* Sage.

Cree R.A., Bitsko, R.H., Robinson, L.R., et al. (2018, December 21). Health care, family, and com-munity factors associated with mental, behavioral, and developmental disorders and poverty among children aged 2–8 years – United States, 2016. *MMWR Morbidity and Mortalality Weekly Report, 67*(50):1377–83. doi: 10.15585/mmwr.mm6750a1

Dahlberg, G., & Moss, P. (2005). *Ethics and politics in early childhood education.* New York: Routledge.

Dallas, M. (2017). The toll poverty takes on children's mental health. *CBS.* Retrieved from https://www .cbsnews.com/news/poverty-children-mental-health/

Danielson, M.L., Bitsko, R.H., Ghandour, R.M., Holbrook, J.R., & Blumberg, S.J. (2018, January 24). Prevalence of parent-reported ADHD diagnosis and associated treatment among U.S. children and adolescents. Journal of Clinical Child and Adolescent Psychology. doi: 10.1080/15374416.2017.1417860

De Winter, M. (2002). The century of the participating child. In E. Knorth, P. Van Den Berg, & F. Verheij (Eds.), Professionalisation and participation in child and youth care (pp. 62–78). Hampshire, UK: Ashgate.

Denzin, N. (1970). *The research act.* New Brunswick, NJ: Aldine Press.

Drotar, D. (2002). Behavioral and emotional problems in infants and young children: Challenges of clinical assessment and intervention. *Infants and Young Children, 14*(4), 1–5.

Ducharme, J. (2018). Stop blaming school shootings on mental illness. *Time.* Retrieved from http://time.com/5162927/mass-shootings-mental-health-apa/

Duwe, G., & Rocque, M. (2018). Actually there is a clear link between mass shootings and mental illness. Retrieved from http://www.latimes.com/opinion/op-ed/la-oe-duwe-rocque-mass-shootings-mental-illness-20180223-story.html

Edge, E. (2020). Teacher bias, teacher interactions and child behavioral health. *University of Massachusetts.* Retrieved from https://scholarworks.umass.edu/cgi/viewcontent.cgi?article=3083&context=dissertations_2

Elder, D., & Fingerson, L. (2002). Interviewing children and adolescents. In J.K. Gubrium & J.A. Holstein (Eds.), *Handbook of interview research* (pp. 57–71). London: Sage.

Ennew, J. (2005). How can we define citizenship in childhood? *Harvard Center for Population and Development Studies Working paper series, 10*(12), Cambridge, MA: Harvard School of Public Health.

Fadus, M.C., Ginsburg, K.R., Sobowale, K., et al. (2020). Unconscious bias and the diagnosis of disruptive behavior disorders and ADHD in African American and Hispanic youth. *Academic Psychiatry, 44*, 95–102. https://doi.org/10.1007/s40596-019-01127-6

Fattore, T., Mason, J., & Watson, E. (2009). When children are asked about their well-being: Towards a framework for guiding policy. Child Indicators Research, 2(1), 57–77.

Fernandez, E. (2011). Child inclusive research, policy and practice. Children and Youth Services Review, 33(4), 487–9.

Fine, G., & Sandstrom, K. (2010). Researchers and kids. In K. Sternheimer (Ed.), *Childhood in American society* (pp. 23–52). Boston, MA: Allyn and Bacon.

Finkelhor, D. (2000). Crimes against children. Retrieved from http://www.unh.edu/ccrc/factsheet.html

Foucault, M. (1988). Madness and civilization: A history of insanity in the age of reason. New York: Vintage Books.

Fraser, S., Lewis, V., Ding, S., Kellett, M., & Robinson, C. (2004). Doing research with children and young people. London: Sage.

Freeman, M. (1987). Taking children's rights seriously. Children & Society, 1(4), 299–319.

Gartrell, D. (1995). Misbehavior or mistaken behavior? *Young Children, 50*(5), 27–34.

Ghandour, R.M., Jones, J.R., Lebrun-Harris, L.A. *et al.* The Design and Implementation of the 2016 National Survey of Children's Health. *Maternal Child Health J* **22**, 1093–1102 (2018). https://doi.org/10.1007/s10995-018-2526-x

Ghiasi N, Azhar Y, Singh J. (2022, January). *Psychiatric illness and criminality.* In StatPearls [Internet]. Treasure Island, FL: StatPearls Publishing. Retrieved from https://www.ncbi.nlm.nih.gov/books/NBK537064/

Gold, J. (2016). One in five children have mental illnesses and often schools don't help. *PBS.* Retrieved from https://www.pbs.org/newshour/health/one-five-children-mental-illness-schools-often-dont-help

Graham, A., Powell, M., Taylor, N., Anderson, D., & Fitzgerald, R. (2013). *Ethical research involving children.* Florence: UNICEF Office of Research – Innocenti Ethical Research Involving Children.

Greene, S., & Hill, M. (2005). Researching children's experience: Methods and methodological issues. In Greene, S. & Hogan, D. (Eds.), Researching children's experience: Approaches and methods. London: Sage.

Greene, S., & Hogan, D., Eds. (2005). Researching children's experience: Approaches and methods. London: Sage.

Harvard University. (2021). Implicit bias. Retrieved from https://implicit.harvard.edu/implicit//user/pimh/bibliochrono.html

Hood, S., Kelley, P., & Mayall, B. (1996). Children as research subjects: A risky enterprise. Children & Society, 10(2), 117–12.

Hsieh, J. (2017). Ecological fallacy. In *Encyclopedia Britannica.* Retrieved from https://www.britannica .com/science/ecological-fallacy

Jabeen, T. (2009). "But I've never been asked!": Research with children in Pakistan. Children's Geographies, 7(4), 405–19.

Jacobson, L. (2019, June 6). With growing calls for mental health services states tackle school counselor caseloads. *K-12 Dive.* https://www.k12dive.com/news/with-growing-calls-for-more-mental-health -services-states-tackle-school-co/556169/

Jakovljevic, I., Miller, A., & Fitzgerald, B. (2016). Children's mental health: Is poverty the diagnosis? Retrieved from https://bcmj.org/sites/default/files/public/BCMJ_Vol58_No8_Children-mental-health -poverty%20%28ID%20106172%29.pdf

James, A. (2007). Giving voice to children's voices: Practices and problems, pitfalls and potentials. American Anthropologist, 109(2), 261–72.

James, A., & Prout, A. (2015). *Constructing and reconstructing childhood.* London: Routledge.

Jenks, C. (1996). *Childhood.* New York: Routledge.

Kellett, M. (2005). Children as active researchers: A new research paradigm for the 21st century. London: ESRC National Centre for Research Method.

Kessler, R.C., Berglund, P., & Demler, O. (2005). Lifetime prevalence and age-of-onset distributions of DSM-IV disorders in the national comorbidity survey replication. *Archives of General Psychiatry, 62*(6), 593–602.

Kollins, S. (2021, January). Is child mental health research structurally racist? *Journal of Child Psychology and Psychiatry.* Retrieved from https://acamh.onlinelibrary.wiley.com/doi/full/10.1111/ jcpp.13376

Kuhn, T.S. (1977). *The essential tension: Selected studies in scientific tradition and change.* Chicago, IL: University of Chicago Press.

Lambert, L. (2020). Why parents are silent about mental illness. *Child Mind.* Retrieved from https:// childmind.org/article/why-parents-are-silent-about-mental-illness/

Lansdown, G. (2005). Can you hear me? The right of young children to participate in decisions affect- ing them. Retrieved from http://lst-iiep.iiep-unesco.org/cgi-bin/wwwi32.exe/[in=epidoc1.in]/?t2000= 023480/(100)

Larson, Z. (2018). America's long suffering mental health system. *Origins.* Retrieved from https:// origins.osu.edu/article/americas-long-suffering-mental-health-system

Larsson, I., Staland-Nyman, C., Svedberg, P., et al. (2018). Children and young people's participation in developing interventions in health and well-being: A scoping review. *BMC Health Services Research, 18,* 507. https://doi.org/10.1186/s12913-018-3219-2

Lavrakas, P. (2008). Ecological fallacy. In *Encyclopedia of survey research methods.* London: Routledge. https://dx.doi.org/10.4135/9781412963947.n151

Liorente, E. (2018, March 4). How prevalent is mental illness in mass shootings? Fox News. Retrieved from https://www.foxnews.com/us/how-prevalent-is-mental-illness-in-mass-shootings

Liverpool S., Pinheiro Mota, C., Sales, C.M.D., et al. (2020, June 23). Engaging children and young people in digital mental health interventions: Systematic review of modes of delivery, facilitators, and barriers. *Journal of Medical Internet Re*search, 22(6), e16317. doi: 10.2196/16317

Lundy, L., & McEvoy, L. (2012). Children's rights and research processes: Assisting children to (in) formed views. *Childhood, 19*(1), 1–16. https://doi.org/10.1177/0907568211409078

Mandell, N. (1991). The least adult role in studying children. In F. Waksler (Ed.), *Studying the social worlds of children: Sociological readings.* London: The Falmer Press.

Marrast, L., Himmelstein, D.U., & Woolhandler, S. (2016). Racial and ethnic disparities in mental health care for children and young adults: A national study. International Journal of Health Services, *46*(4).

Mascendaro, P.M., Herman, K.C., & Webster-Stratton, C. (2012). Parent discrepancies in ratings of young children's co-occurring internalizing symptoms. *School Psychology Quarterly, 27*(3), 134–43. doi: 10.1037/a0029320

Mason, J., & Danby, S. (2011). Children as experts in their lives: Child inclusive research. Child Indicators Research, 4, 185–9.

Mason, J., & Watson, E. (2014). Researching children: Research on, with, and by children. A. Ben-Arieh, F. Casas, I. Frønes, & J. Korbin (Eds.), *Handbook of child well-Being.*, pp. 212–31. Dordrecht: Springer. https://doi.org/10.1007/978-90-481-9063-8_109 & https://link.springer.com/referenceworkentry/10.1007%2F978-90-481-9063-8_109

Mayall, B. (2000). The sociology of childhood in relation to children's rights. *International Journal of Children's Rights, 8,* 243–59. Retrieved from http://citeseerx.ist.psu.edu/viewdoc/download?doi=10.1.1.536.2916&rep=rep1&type=pdf

Mayo Clinic. (2021). Mental illness in children. Retrieved from https://www.mayoclinic.org/healthy-lifestyle/childrens-health/in-depth/mental-illness-in-children/art-20046577

Miller, C. (2020). Mental health disorders and teen substance use. *Child Mind.* Retrieved from https://childmind.org/article/mental-health-disorders-and-substance-use/

Morgan Stanley Alliance on Children's Mental Health. (2019). The global crisis in children's mental health. Retrieved from https://www.morganstanley.com/pub/content/dam/msdotcom/about-us/giving-back/mental_health_alliance/Mental_Health_Alliance_Paper.pdf

Morrow, V. (2001). Using qualitative methods to elicit young people's perspectives on their environments: Some ideas for community health initiatives. Health Education Research, 16(3), 255–68.

Mostafavi, Beata. (2019). Half of US children's mental health disorders are not treated. Retrieved from https://labblog.uofmhealth.org/rounds/half-of-us-children-mental-health-disorders-are-not-treated

Najman, J.M., Williams, G.M., Nikles, J., et al. (2001, April). Bias influencing maternal reports of child behaviour and emotional state. *Social Psychiatry and Psychiatric Epidemiology, 36*(4), 186–94. doi: 10.1007/s001270170062

National Alliance on Mental Illness. (2021). Mental health by the numbers. Retrieved from https://www.nami.org/mhstats

National Center for Learning Disabilities. (2017). Identifying struggling students. Retrieved from https://www.ncld.org/research/state-of-learning-disabilities/identifying-struggling-students/

National Institute of Mental Health. (2021). Child and adolescent mental health. Retrieved from https://www.nimh.nih.gov/health/topics/child-and-adolescent-mental-health/index.shtml

Olino, T.M., Guerra-Guzman, K., Hayden, E.P., & Klein, D.N. (2020). Evaluating maternal psychopathology biases in reports of child temperament: An investigation of measurement invariance. Psychological Assessment, 32(11), 1037–46. https://doi.org/10.1037/pas0000945

Parrish, E. (2020, July). The next pandemic: COVID-19 mental health pandemic. *Perspectives in Psychiatric Care, 56*(3), 485. doi: 10.1111/ppc.12571

Perou R, Bitsko RH, Blumberg SJ, Pastor P, Ghandour RM, Gfroerer JC, Hedden SL, Crosby AE, Visser SN, Schieve LA, Parks SE, Hall JE, Brody D, Simile CM, Thompson WW, Baio J, Avenevoli S, Kogan MD, Huang LN; Centers for Disease Control and Prevention (CDC). Mental health surveillance among children--United States, 2005-2011. MMWR Suppl. 2013 May 17;62(2):1-35. PMID: 23677130.

Project Hope. (2020). Global mental health crisis. Retrieved from https://www.projecthope.org/the-global-mental-health-crisis-10-numbers-to-note/10/2020/

Providence Health. (2020). Is mental health neglected in our children's school? Retrieved from https://blog.providence.org/archive/is-mental-health-neglected-in-our-children-s-schools

Punch. (2002). Research with children: The same or different from that of adults? *Childhood, 9*(3), 322–3.

Qui, L., & Bank, J. (2018). Checking facts and falsehoods about gun violence and mental illness. *New York Times.* Retrieved from https://www.nytimes.com/2018/02/16/us/politics/fact-check-parkland-gun-violence-mental-illness.html

Quinn, M. (2019, July). Many students are in crisis: So is America's school counseling system. *Governing.com.* Retrieved from https://www.governing.com/archive/gov-school-counselor-crisis.html

Qvortrup, J. (2009). Are children human beings or human becomings? A critical assessment of outcome thinking. *Rivista Internazionale Di Scienze Sociali, 117*(3/4), 631–53. Retrieved from http://www.jstor.org/stable/41625246

Qvortrup, J., Corsaro, W., & Honig, M.S. (2013). Researching children's experience: Approaches and methods. London: Sage.

Rice-Oxley, M. (2019). Mental illness: Is there really a global epidemic? *Guardian.* Retrieved from https://www.theguardian.com/society/2019/jun/03/mental-illness-is-there-really-a-global-epidemic

Robert Wood Johnson Foundation. (2017). Traumatic experiences widespread in US youth. Retrieved from https://www.rwjf.org/en/library/articles-and-news/2017/10/traumatic-experiences-widespread -among-u-s--youth--new-data-show.html

Rodriguez, T. (2021). Impact of the COVID-19 pandemic on adolescent mental health. *Psychiatry Advisor.* Retrieved from https://www.psychiatryadvisor.com/home/topics/child-adolescent -psychiatry/adolescent-mental-health-issues-are-further-exacerbated-by-the-covid-19-pandemic/

Rueve, M.E., & Welton, R.S. (2008). Violence and mental illness. *Psychiatry (Edgmont (PA: Township), 5*(5), 34–48.

Sacks, V., & Murphey, D. (2018). The prevalence of adverse childhood experiences. Retrieved from https://www.childtrends.org/publications/prevalence-adverse-childhood-experiences-nationally-state -race-ethnicity

SAMHSA. (2019). Mental health issues and conditions in children and youth exposed to human caused disasters. Retrieved from https://www.samhsa.gov/sites/default/files/mental-health-substance-use -issues-exposed-youth.pdf

SAMHSA. (2020). Warning signs and risk factors of emotional distress. Retrieved from https://www .samhsa.gov/find-help/disaster-distress-helpline/warning-signs-risk-factors

Schachar, R.J., Park, L.S., & Dennis, M. (2015). Mental health implications of traumatic brain injury (TBI) in children and youth. Journal of the Canadian Academy of Child and Adolescent Psychiatry/ Journal de l'Académie Canadienne de Psychiatrie de L'enfant et de L'adolescent, 24(2), 100–8.

Schwartz, K. (2016). Why don't teachers get training on mental health disorders? Retrieved from https:// www.kqed.org/mindshift/46729/why-dont-teachers-get-training-on-mental-health-disorders

Scott, J. (2000). Children as respondents: The challenge for quantitative methods. In Christensen, P. & James, A. (Eds.), *Research with children: Perspectives and practices* (Chapter 5). London: Falmer Press.

September, R. & Savahl, S. (2009). Children's perspective on child wellbeing. The Social Work Practitioner-Researcher, 21(1), 23–40.

Shorter, E. (1997). A history of psychiatry: From the era of the asylum to the age of prozac. Hoboken, NJ: John Wiley & Sons.

Simmons, M. (2020). Involving young people as partners in mental health research. Retrieved from https://socialequity.unimelb.edu.au/news/events/involving-young-people-as-partners-in-mental -health-research

Šimundić A.M. (2013). Bias in research. *Biochemia Medica (Zagreb), 23*(1), 12–15. doi: 10.11613/ bm.2013.003

Smith, R., Monaghan, M., & Broad, B. (2002). Involving young people as co-researchers: Facing up to the methodological issues. Qualitative Social Work, 1(2), 191–207.

Snowden, L.R. (2003). Bias in mental health assessment and intervention: Theory and evidence. *American Journal of Public Health, 93*(2), 239–43. https://doi.org/10.2105/ajph.93.2.239

Spiro, L. (2020). The most common misdiagnoses in children. *Child Mind.* Retrieved from https:// childmind.org/article/the-most-common-misdiagnoses-in-children/

Stafford, A., Laybourn, A., Walker, M., & Hill, M. (2003). "Having a say": Children and young people talk about consultation. Children & Society, 17(5), 361–73.

Sternheimer, K. (2010). *Childhood in American society.* New York: Allyn and Bacon.

Straus, M.A., & Donnelly, D.A. (1994). *Beating the devil out of them: Corporal punishment in American families.* New York: Lexington Books.

Tate, E. (2020). Child abuse is harder to spot during the pandemic. *Edsurge.* Retrieved from https:// www.edsurge.com/news/2020-11-10-child-abuse-is-harder-to-spot-during-the-pandemic-what-can -educators-do

Tisdall, K., Davis, J., & Gallagher, M. (2009). *Researching with children and young people: Research design, methods and analysis.* London: Sage.

Van der Toorn, S.L., Huizin, A,C., Utens, E.M.W.J., Verhulst, F.C., Ormel, J., & Ferdinand, R.F. (2010, April). Maternal depressive symptoms, and not anxiety symptoms, are associated with pos-itive mother-child reporting discrepancies of internalizing problems in children. *European Child & Adolescent Psychiatry, 19*(4), 379–88. doi: 10.1007/s00787-009-0062-3

Verlenden, J. (2021). Association of children's mode of school instruction with child and parent experiences and well-being during the COVID pandemic. *MMWR Morbidity and Mortality Weekly Reports, 70,* 369–76. Retrieved from https://www.cdc.gov/mmwr/volumes/70/wr/mm7011a1.htm?s_cid=mm7011a1_w

Vidair, H.B., Reyes, J.A., Shen, S., et al. (2011, May). Screening parents during child evaluations: Exploring parent and child psychopathology in the same clinic. *Journal of the American Academy of Child Adolescent Psychiatry, 50*(5), 441–50. doi: 10.1016/j.jaac.2011.02.002

Vissing, Y. (2021). Unaccompanied children at the United States-Mexico border. In Vissing, Y. & Leitao, S. (Eds.), *The rights of unaccompanied minors: Perspectives and case studies.* New York: Springer.

Wagner, K. (2020). New findings about children's mental health during COVID-19. *Psychiatric Times.*

Wallace, W. (1971). *The logic of science in sociology.* Chicago, IL: Aldine-Atherton.

Weber, M. (1949). *The methodology of the social sciences.* New York: Free Press.

Whitney, D.G., & Peterson, M.D. (2019). US national and state-level prevalence of mental health disorders and disparities of mental health care use in children. JAMA Pediatrics, *173*(4), 389–91. doi:10.1001/jamapediatrics.2018.5399

Wood, A. (2021). Virtual school can be damaging to children's mental health. Retrieved from https://www.wbaltv.com/article/virtual-school-can-be-damaging-to-childrens-mental-health-cdc-study-says/35955469#

World Health Organization. (2021). *Adolescent mental health.* Retrieved from https://www.who.int/news-room/fact-sheets/detail/adolescent-mental-health

Wu, P., Hoven, C.W., Liu, X., Cohen, P., Fuller, C.J., & Shaffer, D. (2004). Substance use, suicidal ideation and attempts in children and adolescents. *Suicide & Life-Threatening Behavior, 34*(4), 408–20. https://doi.org/10.1521/suli.34.4.408.53733

Wyness, M. (2012). Childhood and society*: An introduction to the sociology of childhood.* New York: Palgrave Macmillan.

Yourman, J. (1932). Children identified by their teachers as problems. *The Journal of Educational Sociology, 5*(6), 334–43. doi:10.2307/2960660

Youth Risk Behavior Survey. (2019). Retrieved from https://www.cdc.gov/healthyyouth/data/yrbs/index.htm

9.   The sociology of stigma and pathways to care
Carla D. Kundert and Patrick W. Corrigan

The pernicious effects of stigma toward people with mental illness can be just as debilitating as, if not more than, symptoms of mental illness themselves. Namely, stigma serves as a barrier to recovery in that it can impede social inclusion, empowerment, education, employment, self-esteem, self-efficacy, and often serves as a roadblock on the path to appropriate, sufficient care (Corrigan, 2004; Corrigan et al., 1999, 2009; Rüsch et al., 2013; Xu et al., 2016). This chapter aims to unpack the sociology of stigma toward people with mental illness, the various pathways to mental healthcare, and how stigma impacts those pathways. In addition, the text explores approaches for addressing various types of stigma.

COMPONENTS OF STIGMA EXPERIENCED BY PEOPLE WITH MENTAL ILLNESS

Stigma, as described by Erving Goffman (1963), can apply to a number of conditions including tribal identities such as race/ethnicity, physical abnormalities, and blemishes of individual character which includes mental illness (MI) and addiction. The social cognitive model of stigma expounds further on its three components: stereotypes, prejudice, and discrimination.

Stereotypes

Stereotypes are the negative beliefs or attitudes about the stigmatized group – the cognitive component of the social cognitive model. For people with MI, stereotypes often include perceptions of incompetence ("People with bipolar disorder can't work"); dangerousness ("Molly's schizophrenia makes her unpredictable and violent"); laziness ("If Malik would just get moving, he wouldn't feel depressed"); and permanence ("People never recover from mental illness"). These often-harmful perceptions then influence emotions and behavior toward people with MI.

Prejudice

Prejudice is the emotional reaction that results from endorsing stereotypes (Link & Phelan, 2001). Stereotypes of dangerousness and unpredictability of people with MI may elicit feelings of fear. Assumptions of being disruptive or burdensome may evoke feelings of disgust and anger. Perceived incompetence may lead to pity. Prejudice is the feeling that connects cognitions (stereotypes) to actions (discrimination).

Table 9.1   *Components of stigma across types*

	Public Stigma	Self-Stigma	Structural Stigma	Courtesy Stigma
Stereotypes (cognitive)	"People with mental illness are dangerous."	"Mental illness is permanent."	"People with mental illness are incompetent and can't live on their own."	"People with depression are just plain lazy."
Prejudice (affective)	The store clerk is fearful when Annie, who appears to be experiencing symptoms of mental illness, walks into his store.	Ricardo thinks to himself, "I don't think I will ever live in recovery from my bipolar disorder."	Policy makers feel pity for people with mental illness because they believe they cannot live independently.	Parents at Matt's school blame his family for his mental illness. They think "he wouldn't be so depressed if his parents, Kim and Mickey, instilled in him a stronger work ethic."
Discrimination (behavioral)	The store clerk asks Annie to leave and does not allow her to purchase the groceries.	"Why bother going to treatment if I will never get better?"	Programs for independent living are underfunded in favor of segregated living facilities like group homes and nursing homes	Kim and Mickey are ignored by the other parents from Matt's school and are not invited to join the Parent Teacher Association

Discrimination

Discrimination is the behavioral component of stigma that stems from stereotypes and prejudice (Link & Phelan, 2001). These behaviors may take the form of avoidance, segregation, coercion, and interpersonal discrimination. *Avoidance* behaviors aim to minimize interaction with people with MI, such as ignoring them in social situations or denying them opportunities to housing, healthcare, or employment (Corrigan et al., 2006; Harangozo et al., 2014; Newman & Goldman, 2009). *Segregation* aims to separate where people with MI live, work, and recreate from the rest of society. For example, because of housing discrimination, people with MI are more likely to live in residential facilities, nursing homes, or low-income neighborhoods (Draine et al., 2002; Topor et al., 2014). *Coercion* includes compulsory treatment such as mandated medication and restriction of autonomy and liberty by way of confinement or guardianship (Strauss et al., 2013). *Interactional discrimination* is often more nuanced slights in interpersonal exchanges, such as using a dismissive, patronizing tone or speaking slowly and loudly (Link & Phelan, 2014). Often referred to as microaggressions in racial discrimination research (Wong et al., 2014), this subtle type of discrimination may be embedded even in supportive relationships. For example, a professor interacting with a student who has disclosed her experience of mental illness might say, "Lara, you did so well in this class – you're really smart for someone with bipolar disorder!" While the intent may have been to express their genuine admiration, the comments reveal a belief that people with bipolar disorder are not academically capable.

TYPES OF STIGMA

Public stigma refers to the stereotypes, prejudice, and discrimination endorsed by the "public" toward the stigmatized group. *Courtesy stigma* refers to the stigma applied to those associated with stigmatized others (e.g., family members and friends of people with MI). *Structural stigma* occurs when discrimination occurs at larger systemic levels that restrict the rights and opportunities of the stigmatized group (Angermeyer et al., 2014; Corrigan et al., 2004). *Self-stigma* occurs when people belonging to the stigmatized group apply the public's negative beliefs or stereotypes to themselves – this will be explored in more detail later (Goffman, 1963; Muñoz et al., 2011). Table 9.1 demonstrates examples of the three components of stigma at each of these levels. *Implicit* or *automatic stigma* is, as the name implies, a more concealed form of public or self-stigma that is outside of conscious awareness (Brener et al., 2013).

FACTORS THAT INFLUENCE STIGMA DEVELOPMENT

Several factors influence the stigma endorsed and expressed by others. *Controllability and responsibility* refer to the extent to which one is perceived to control their membership to a stigmatized group. When people believe that individuals are responsible for the development of or recovery from a condition, they are more likely to endorse stigmatizing beliefs (Jorm & Griffiths, 2008; Malterud & Ulriksen, 2011). Fearful affective responses to people with MI, often elicited by stereotypes of dangerousness, are associated with higher levels of stigma and greater desire for social distance than other affective responses (Corrigan, et al., 2002; Janulis et al., 2013). *Familiarity* is the spectrum of knowledge and experiences one has with MI, ranging from seeing a television depiction of someone with MI to one's own personal or familial experiences with mental health. Increased levels of familiarity with MI are associated with lower desire for social distance and more positive perceptions (Broussard et al., 2012; Corrigan et al., 2001).

A DEEPER DIVE INTO SELF-STIGMA

Self-stigma can be understood with a four-stage model of development: (1) *awareness* of stereotypes; (2) *agreement* with those stereotypes; (3) *application* of stereotypes to oneself; and (4) the subsequent *harm* done (Figure 9.1). Specifically, the harm done by self-stigma includes feelings of shame or embarrassment and damage to one's self-esteem, self-concept, and self-efficacy (Boyd et al., 2014; Drapalski et al., 2013; Rüsch & Thornicroft, 2014). Higher self-stigma is associated with lower levels of empowerment in decision-making and taking action (Rüsch et al., 2010; Thornicroft, 2013). These contribute to the Why Try effect – "Why apply for a job? People with bipolar disorder like me are too unstable" (Corrigan et al., 2009). The Why Try effect has been demonstrated to mediate the relationship between self-stigma and increased symptoms of depression (Corrigan et al., 2019).

While the responsibility of eliminating stigma of mental illness should lie on society, interventions that encourage empowerment may help alleviate harms already wrought by self-stigma (Corrigan & Rao, 2012). Cognitive behavioral interventions counter negative stereotypes and prejudice about oneself with evidence to the contrary (Lucksted et al., 2011).

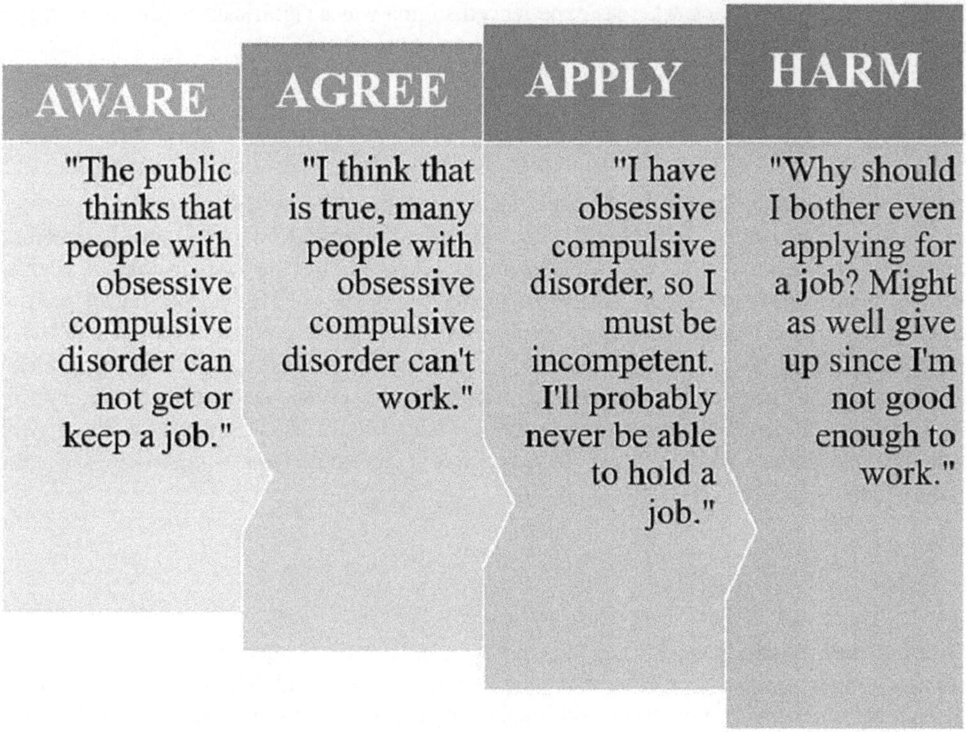

AWARE	AGREE	APPLY	HARM
"The public thinks that people with obsessive compulsive disorder can not get or keep a job."	"I think that is true, many people with obsessive compulsive disorder can't work."	"I have obsessive compulsive disorder, so I must be incompetent. I'll probably never be able to hold a job."	"Why should I bother even applying for a job? Might as well give up since I'm not good enough to work."

Figure 9.1   An example of the development of self-stigma

Engagement with peers in recovery can diminish self-stigma and improve quality of life (Corrigan et al., 2013; Lloyd-Evans et al., 2014). Peer-led interventions such as Honest, Open, Proud that empower disclosure decision-making help reduce self-stigma and stigma stress while increasing care-seeking attitudes (Corrigan et al., 2015; Mulfinger et al., 2018; Rüsch et al., 2014).

STIGMA ACROSS MENTAL HEALTH CONDITIONS

Experiences of public and self-stigma vary across mental health diagnoses, as stereotypes differ with symptom presentation, prognosis, prevalence, and level of perceived responsibility (Feldman & Crandall, 2007). Individuals with personality disorders tend to experience increased levels of provider stigma based on stereotypes that they are manipulative and untreatable (Fairfax, 2011). Those with comorbid depression and anxiety are more likely to report experiencing stigma than those with either condition alone (Alonso et al., 2008). People with schizophrenia report higher levels of self-stigma and diminished self-esteem and relationship satisfaction than those with mood disorders (Oliveira et al., 2015). Individuals with schizophrenia also report higher levels of stigma impact than those with mood disorders, even when holding sociodemographic factors, symptom intensity, and illness duration constant (Świtaj et al., 2016). Among those with schizophrenia, self-stigma was the only significant predictor of stigma impact, whereas experienced stigma was a significant predictor of stigma impact among those with affective disorders (Świtaj et al., 2016).

STIGMA'S PERVASIVE INFLUENCE ON PATHWAYS TO CARE

Pathways to care for people with MI vary widely by gender, race and ethnicity, culture, region, and healthcare structures. First contact with care after the onset of a mental health challenge can vary from weeks to over two years depending on region, but the average delay in accessing treatment worldwide sits at around 16 weeks (Volpe et al., 2015). The role of general practitioner (GP) as a gatekeeper to psychiatric services is often required in Europe and North America (Phillips et al., 2011). Worldwide, self-referral to psychiatric treatment sits at about 30 percent. While self-referral can reduce referral delays, service users may lose out on provider insights in identifying appropriate services (Volpe et al., 2015). Gender stereotypes for both men and women, while different, have reportedly contributed to treatment delays (Ferrari et al., 2018).

LABEL AVOIDANCE

At every turn, stigma can serve as a roadblock, or at least a speedbump, on the path to accessing evidence-based, collaborative care. Namely, people with MI who are aware of the stigma that comes with a mental health diagnosis may avoid treatment settings to elude the stigmatizing label – called *label avoidance*. Engaging in label avoidance may mean failure to seek out treatment from the start, engaging only partially, or withdrawing from services early (Ben-Zeev et al., 2012; Clemente et al., 2014; Corrigan et al., 2014). When service users were asked about barriers to treatment, the top five barriers identified were stigma-related (Dockery et al., 2015). Service users with higher levels of education reported more stigma-related barriers, while those who had longer contact with treatment endorsed lower levels of such barriers (Dockery et al., 2015). Higher levels of perceived stigma can negatively impact help-seeking attitudes and sustained engagement with care (Sirey et al., 2001; Xu et al., 2016). In fact, lower levels of stigma stress have been associated with positive attitudes toward treatment (Rüsch et al., 2013).

COURTESY STIGMA AND CARE-SEEKING

People with mental health challenges may also engage in label avoidance to protect their loved ones from courtesy stigma, the stigma that comes with being associated with a person with MI. Parents have long shouldered society's blame for mental illness onset, a since-dispelled myth that is still reported as a reason for delaying engagement in care (Corrigan & Miller, 2004; Rose et al., 2011; Shefer et al., 2013). Responsibility for managing illness and preventing relapse of MI is often projected onto spouses and siblings (Corrigan & Miller, 2004). Greenberg and colleagues noted that siblings of people with MI have internalized these stereotypes, reporting concerns about treatment adherence and beliefs that they are to blame for increases in symptoms (1997). Courtesy stigma as a barrier to care varies between cultural and ethnic groups (Shefer et al., 2013).

NEGATIVE PATHWAYS TO CARE

When care-seeking is delayed, because of label avoidance or barriers such as cost or accessibility, acute crises may arise, leading to the increased likelihood of access via *negative pathways to care*. Negative pathways are often coercive and/or adversarial, including intervention by law enforcement or emergency services, emergency room use, and access within the justice system. Research indicates that people of color with MI are more likely to enter care through these negative pathways than their White counterparts (Halvorsrud et al., 2018; Merritt-Davis & Keshavan, 2006; Rotenberg et al., 2017). Engagement with primary care and supportive relationships may be protective factors against entering treatment through adversarial routes and can decrease treatment delays (Anderson et al., 2013; Cole et al., 1995).

Accessing care through these negative pathways can be rather difficult, as stigma is pervasive throughout these systems. Risk of involuntary admission, mandated medication, punitive measures, loss of liberty and autonomy, and even violence are associated with these various pathways.

Emergency Department Use

Hospital emergency departments (EDs), given their ease of access and visibility, are often a first point of contact to mental healthcare, especially where standalone mental health providers are lacking (McLoughlin et al., 2020). Hospital EDs are rarely equipped to appropriately screen and serve people with MI in the long or short term. Use of EDs for mental healthcare is associated with increased inpatient admissions, utilization of more restrictive clinical interventions such as restraints, and increases in medication errors (Al-Khafaji et al., 2014; Bakhsh et al., 2014; Gibbons et al., 2012; Knott et al., 2007). Continuity of care after discharge is difficult as services are often disjointed and ED staff may not have the time or resources to support transition to longer-term services (Waring et al., 2015).

Law Enforcement Intervention

Calls regarding mental health and substance use make up about 1 percent of all calls to law enforcement in North America, with many officers responding to crises and transport calls regularly (Lamanna et al., 2018). The frequent contact with police increases risk for police violence, arrest, ED use, and involuntary admission (Lamanna et al., 2018). A recent push to include mental health specialists in crisis calls would ideally increase referral to services, decrease ED use, decrease escalation, and reduce adverse events. However, the research on these interventions is limited and models studied have been inconsistent (McKenna et al., 2015; Puntis et al., 2018).

Care in Correctional Facilities

Research indicates that prevalence of MI among incarcerated individuals may be as high as 48 percent (Al-Rousan et al., 2017). Care within correctional facilities often falls short due to improper screening, lack of prioritization by staff, and underfunding of primary mental health services (Forrester et al., 2018). Acute crises during incarceration should ideally prompt a transfer to a care facility but wait times can range from weeks to months (Hopkin et al., 2016). Correctional systems may utilize solitary units when acute care is unavailable, though this raises serious ethical and wellness concerns (Edgar & Rickford 2009). Diversion programs and mental health courts have gained traction in recent years, promoting care rather than punishment of people with MI. While research on these programs is limited, initial outcomes appear promising for improving functioning and reducing recidivism (Cosden et al., 2005; Landess & Holoyda, 2017). Continuity of care after incarceration remains challenging given community providers' stigma toward justice-involved individuals and relative transience of this population (Brooker & Gojkovic, 2009). Pre-release case management to address gaps in insurance, housing, and financial support is associated with increased engagement in mental healthcare post-incarceration (Hamilton & Belenko, 2016).

PROVIDER STIGMA IMPEDES CONTINUED ENGAGEMENT

Stigma endorsed by mental health providers can impact the quality of care, and its harms to self-efficacy and empowerment may hinder continued engagement. Provider stigma includes the use of restrictive treatment approaches for people with MI, greater desire for social distance, or interactional transgressions such as using a patronizing tone. Lower quality care is associated with higher levels of stigma among providers (Dell et al., 2020). Even among providers who outwardly endorse positive attitudes toward service users, those with more implicit bias were more likely to over-diagnose patients and favored controlling clinical approaches (Stull et al., 2013). Furthermore, service users who perceive stigma from their providers are more likely to report self-stigma and feel disempowered in treatment (Wang et al., 2018).

This disempowerment may impact engagement in continued care, particularly when moving between service systems, such as the transition from intensive or inpatient care to more community-based services. While still under-researched, a few key ingredients may help improve the transition between providers. Providers should utilize shared decision-making and provide comprehensive information about treatment options to service users from intake to discharge (Sather et al., 2019). Collaborative individual plans of care improve engagement and continuity of care (Stiggelbout et al., 2012; Wright et al., 2016). Such as increasing collaboration with external providers (e.g., outpatient counselors, physical health providers, psychiatrists) before and during discharge is beneficial to service users' transition outcomes (Sather et al., 2019; Waring et al., 2015).

Central to these is deference to the service user. Their lived experience, goals, and needs are central to the care planning and transition process to improve engagement and, more importantly, support life in recovery. While treatment adherence and stages of change were once the focus of research and practice, discussion has moved largely to *self-determination* (SD) of service users. Self-determination for people with MI involves self-empowerment to envision choices and make decisions, including but not limited to care decisions (Corrigan,

Angell, Davidson et al., 2012). Efforts to reduce self-stigma are crucial to enhancing SD, as self-stigma can undermine self-empowerment and competence (e.g., the Why Try effect). As a society, we must question (and move to change) how our policies, systems, and providers contribute to coercive, patronizing, and restrictive practices that undermine agency and autonomy.

STRUCTURAL STIGMA

Structural stigma might prove the most pervasive barrier as its presence in institutions, policies, and practices make evidence-based treatment less accessible. Overt structural stigma includes legislation that allows for more coercive, segregated care, decreases protections for people with MI, and restricts liberties and choices (Corrigan et al., 2005). Underfunding of mental health treatment and research have left gaps in care and knowledge (Livingston, 2013). Stigma in employment, housing, the justice system, and education is unfortunately quite common among people with MI (Corrigan et al., 2003). Structural stigma can be complex and interwoven with issues of public stigma, racism, classism, and ableism as well. For example, housing and employment discrimination (public stigma) can lead to segregation of people with MI into low-income neighborhoods, areas often deprived of resources (e.g., access to public transportation, affordable treatment options, healthy food, and areas for recreation) by government budgets and private enterprises.

REDUCING STIGMA AS A BARRIER TO CARE

Education, protest, and contact-based interventions can reduce the stigma of MI. *Education* interventions counter negative stereotypes and attitudes with facts, which are useful in disseminating information about MI, but evidence indicating significant behavioral change is limited (Corrigan, 2016). *Protest* admonishes the public for endorsing stigmatizing attitudes. While protest may encourage stigma suppression, it is likely ineffective at reducing actual stigma endorsement (Corrigan & Penn, 1999). *Contact* strategies, where people with MI interact with others and share stories of recovery, have demonstrated significantly greater, sustained effects in stigma reduction than education interventions (Corrigan, Morris, Michaels et al., 2012).

Policy change that considers research on stigma reduction and values self-determination will be critical in addressing stigma as a barrier to care. Education interventions have been valuable in targeting public stigma in both specific groups (e.g., healthcare providers or police officers) and the general public via educational campaigns such as Beyondblue in Australia and Mental Health First Aid (Corrigan, 2016; Rüsch et al., 2005). Training and experience mandates for providers may be useful in mitigating the harmful effects of stigma in healthcare. For example, in the Anti-Stigma Project, people with lived experience of MI facilitated discussions with service providers about stigma, its impacts, and how to address it; the program resulted in increased stigma awareness and endorsement of service user self-determination while prejudice was diminished (Michaels et al., 2014). Structural stigma, which is often deeply entrenched in systems and legislation, may be most directly addressed with policy change, such as mandates to include service users in treatment decision-making, implementation of psychiatric advance directives, and changes to involuntary admission requirements (Corrigan, Morris, Michaels et al., 2012). Policy reform within law enforcement and problem-solving courts is crucial in addressing increased risk of negative pathways of care, particularly for people of color. Finally, policies that focus on mental health treatment parity, universal and comprehensive insurance, and increased pathways of entry into treatment may begin addressing the structural stigmas that makes evidence-based, person-centered care inaccessible for many.

CHAPTER SUMMARY AND CONCLUSION

Stigma's deleterious effects have long acted as a barrier to accessing care and living in recovery for people with mental illness. Stereotypes, prejudice, and discrimination are pervasive at many levels, including along the pathways to care. Research indicates that centering and elevating the lived experience voice can help reduce self-stigma through empowered decision-making about disclosure; improve engagement with care through self-determination; and address stigma via contact-based interventions and policy efforts focused on empowerment of people with mental illness.

REFERENCES

Al-Khafaji, K., Loy, J., & Kelly, A.M. (2014). Characteristics and outcomes of patients brought to an emergency department by police under the provisions (Section 10) of the Mental Health Act in Victoria, Australia. *International Journal of Law and Psychiatry, 37*, 415–19. https://doi.org/10.1016/j.ijlp.2014.02.013

Al-Rousan, T., Rubenstein, L., Sieleni, B., Deol, H., & Wallace, R.B. (2017). Inside the nation's largest mental health institution: A prevalence study in a state prison system. *BMC Public Health, 17*(1), 342. https://doi.org/10.1186/s12889-017-4257-0

Alonso, J., Buron, A., Bruffaerts, R., He, Y., Posada-Villa, J., Lepine, J.P., Angermeyer, M.C., Levison, D., de Girolamo, G., Tachimori, H., Mneimneh, Z.N., Medina-Mora, M.E., Ormel, J., Scott, K.M., Guereje, O., Haro, J.M., Gluzman, S., Lee, S., Vilagut, G., ... Von Korff, M. (2008). Association of perceived stigma and mood and anxiety disorders: Results from the world mental health surveys. *Acta Psychiatrica Scandinavica, 118*, 305–14. https://doi.org/10.1111/j.1600-0447.2008.01241.x

Anderson, K.K., Fuhrer, R., Schmitz, N., & Malla, A.K. (2013). Determinants of negative pathways to care and their impact on service disengagement in first-episode psychosis. *Social Psychiatry and Psychiatric Epidemiology, 48*(1), 125–36.

Angermeyer, M.C., Matschinger, H., Link, B.G., & Schomerus, G. (2014). Public attitudes regarding individual and structural discrimination: Two sides of the same coin? *Social Science and Medicine, 103*, 60–6. https://doi.org/10.1016/j.socscimed.2013.11.014

Bakhsh, H., Perona, S., Shields, W., Salek, S., Sanders, A., & Patanwala, A. (2014). Medication errors in psychiatric patients boarded in the emergency department. *International Journal of Risk & Safety in Medicine, 26*(4), 191–8. https://doi.org/10.3233/jrs-140634

Ben-Zeev, D., Corrigan, P.W., Britt, T.W., & Langford, L. (2012). Stigma of mental illness and service use in the military. *Journal of Mental Health, 21*(3), 264–73. doi:10.3109/09638237.2011.621468

Boyd, J.E., Otilingam, P.G., & Deforge, B.R. (2014). Brief version of the Internalized Stigma of Mental Illness (ISMI) scale: Psychometric properties and relationship to depression, self esteem, recovery orientation, empowerment, and perceived devaluation and discrimination. *Psychiatric Rehabilitation Journal, 37*(1), 17–23. https://doi.org/10.1037/prj0000035

Brener, L., Grenville, R., von Hippel, C., & Wilson, H. (2013). Implicit attitudes, emotions, and helping intentions of mental health workers toward their clients. *Journal of Nervous and Mental Disease, 201*, 460–3. doi: 10.1097/NMD.0b013e318294744a

Brooker, C., & Gojkovic, D. (2009) The second national survey of mental health in-reach services in prisons. *Journal of Forensic Psychiatry & Psychology, 20,* 11–28.

Broussard, B., Goulding, S.M., Talley, C.L., & Compton, M.T. (2012). Social distance and stigma toward individuals with schizophrenia: Findings in an urban, African-American community sample. *Journal of Nervous and Mental Disease, 200*(11), 935–40. https://doi.org/10.1097/nmd.0b013e3182718c1b

Clemente, S., Schauman, O., Graham, T., Maggioni, F., Evans-Lacko, S., Bezborodovs, N., Morgan, C., Rüsch, N., Brown, J.S., & Thornicroft, G. (2014). What is the impact of mental health-related stigma on help-seeking? A systematic review of quantitative and qualitative studies. *Psychological Medicine,* 1–17. https://doi.org/10.1017/s0033291714000129

Cole, E., Leavey, G., King, M., Johnson-Sabine, E., & Hoar, A. (1995). Pathways to care for patients with a first episode of psychosis: A comparison of ethnic groups. *The British Journal of Psychiatry, 167*(6), 770–6. https://doi.org/10.1192/bjp.167.6.770

Corrigan, P.W. (2004). How stigma interferes with mental health care. *American Psychologist, 59*(7), 614–25. https://doi.org/10.1037/0003-066X.59.7.614

Corrigan, P.W. (2016). Lessons learned from unintended consequences about erasing the stigma of mental illness. *World Psychiatry, 15*(1), 67–73. https://doi.org/10.1002/wps.20295

Corrigan, P.W., & Miller, F.E. (2004). Shame, blame, and contamination: A review of the impact of mental illness stigma on family members. *Journal of Mental Health, 13*(6), 537–48. https://doi.org/10.1080/09638230400017004

Corrigan, P.W., & Penn, D. (1999). Lessons from social psychology on discrediting psychiatric stigma. *American Psychologist, 54,* 765–76. https://doi.org/10.1037//0003-066x.54.9.765

Corrigan, P.W., & Rao, D. (2012). On the self-stigma of mental illness: Stages, disclosure, and strategies for change. *The Canadian Journal of Psychiatry, 57*(8), 464–9. https://dx.doi.org/10.1177%2F070674371205700804

Corrigan, P.W., Giffort, D., Rashid, F., Leary, M., & Okeke, I. (1999). Recovery as a psychological construct. *Community Mental Health Journal, 35*(3), 231–9. https://doi.org/10.1023/A:1018741302682

Corrigan, P.W., Green, A., Lundin, R., Kubiak, M.A., & Penn, D.L. (2001). Familiarity with and social distance from people who have serious mental illness. *Psychiatric Services, 52*(7), 953–8. https://doi.org/10.1176/appi.ps.52.7.953

Corrigan, P.W., Rowan, D., Green, A., Lundin, R., River, P., Uphoff-Wasowski, K., White, K., & Kubiak, M.A. (2002). Challenging two mental illness stigmas: Personal responsibility and dangerousness. *Schizophrenia Bulletin, 28,* 293–309. https://doi.org/10.1093/oxfordjournals.schbul.a006939

Corrigan P.W., Thompson, V., Lambert D., Sangster Y., Noel J.G., & Campbell J. (2003). Perceptions of discrimination among persons with serious mental illness. *Psychiatric Services, 54*(8), 1105–10. https://doi.org/10.1176/appi.ps.54.8.1105

Corrigan, P.W., Markowitz, F.E., & Watson, A.C. (2004). Structural levels of mental illness stigma and discrimination. *Schizophrenia Bulletin, 30*(3), 481–91. https://doi.org/10.1093/oxfordjournals.schbul.a007096

Corrigan, P.W., Watson, A.C., Heyrman, M.L., Warpinski, A., Gracia, G., Slopen, N., & Hall, L.L. (2005). Structural stigma in state legislation. *Psychiatric Services, 56*(5), 557–63. https://doi.org/10.1176/appi.ps.56.5.557

Corrigan, P.W., Larson, J.E., Watson, A.C., Boyle, M., & Barr, L. (2006). Solutions to discrimination in work and housing identified by people with mental illness. *Journal of Nervous and Mental Disease, 194*(9), 716–18. https://doi.org/10.1097/01.nmd.0000235782.18977.de

Corrigan, P.W., Larson, J.E., & Rüsch, N. (2009). Self-stigma and the "why try" effect: Impact on life goals and evidence-based practices. *World Psychiatry, 8*(2), 75–81. https://doi.org/10.1002/j.2051-5545.2009.tb00218.x

Corrigan, P.W., Angell, B., Davidson, L., Marcus, S.C., Salzer, M.S., Kottsieper, P., Larson, J.E., Mahoney, C.A., O'Connell, M.J., & Stanhope, V. (2012). From adherence to self-determination: Evolution of a treatment paradigm for people with serious mental illnesses. *Psychiatric Services, 63*(2), 169–73. https://doi.org/10.1176/appi.ps.201100065

Corrigan, P.W., Morris, S., Michaels, P., Rafacz, J.D., & Rüsch, N. (2012). Challenging the public stigma of mental illness: A meta analysis of outcome studies. *Psychiatric Services, 63,* 963–73. https://doi.org/10.1176/appi.ps.201100529

Corrigan, P.W., Sokol, K.A., & Rüsch, N. (2013). The impact of self-stigma and mutual help programs on the quality of life of people with serious mental illnesses. *Community Mental Health Journal, 49*(1), 1–6. https://doi.org/10.1007/s10597-011-9445-2

Corrigan, P.W., Druss, B.G. & Perlick, D.A. (2014). The impact of mental illness stigma on seeking and participating in mental health care. *Psychological Science in the Public Interest, 15*(2), 37–70. https://doi.org/10.1177/1529100614531398

Corrigan, P.W., Larson, J.E., Michaels, P.J., Buchholz, B.A., Rossi, R. Del, Fontecchio, M.J., Castro, D., Gause, M., Krzyzanowski, R., & Rüsch, N. (2015). Diminishing the self-stigma of mental illness by coming out proud. *Psychiatry Research, 229*(1–2), 148–54. https://doi.org/10.1016/j.psychres.2015.07.053

Corrigan, P.W., Nieweglowski, K., & Sayer, J. (2019). Self-stigma and the mediating impact of the "why try" effect on depression. *Journal of Community Psychology, 47*(3), 698–705. https://doi.org/10.1002/jcop.22144

Cosden, M., Ellens, J., Schnell, J., & Yamini Diouf, Y. (2005). Efficacy of a mental health treatment court with assertive community treatment. *Behavioral Sciences and the Law, 23*, 199–214. https://doi.org/10.1002/bsl.638

Dell, N.A., Vidovic, K.R., Vaughn, M.G., & Sasaki, N. (2020). Mental health provider stigma, expectations for recovery, and perceived quality of care provided to persons with mental illness. *Stigma and Health.* https://doi.org/10.1037/sah0000227

Dockery, L., Jeffery, D., Schauman, O., Williams, P., Farrelly, S., Bonnington, O., Gabbidon, J., Lassman, F., Szmukler, G., Thornicroft, G., & Clement, S. (2015). Stigma- and non-stigma-related treatment barriers to mental healthcare reported by service users and caregivers. *Psychiatry Research, 228*(3), 612–19. https://doi.org/10.1016/j.psychres.2015.05.044

Draine, J., Salzer, M.S., Culhane, D.P., & Hadley, T.R. (2002). Role of social disadvantage in crime, joblessness, and homelessness among persons with serious mental illness. *Psychiatric Services, 53*(5), 565–73. https://doi.org/10.1176/appi.ps.53.5.565

Drapalski, A.L., Lucksted, A., Perrin, P.B., Aakre, J.M., Brown, C.H., DeForge, B.R., & Boyd, J.E. (2013). A model of internalized stigma and its effects on people with mental illness. *Psychiatric Services, 64*(3), 264–9. https://doi.org/10.1176/appi.ps.001322012

Edgar, K., & Rickford, D. (2009). *Too little, too late: An independent review of unmet mental health need in prison.* London: Prison Reform Trust.

Fairfax, H. (2011). Re-conceiving personality disorders: Adaptations on a dimension? *Counseling Psychology Quarterly, 24*, 313–22. doi:10.1080/09515070.2011.6305

Feldman, D.B., & Crandall, C.S. (2007). Dimensions of mental illness stigma: What about mental illness causes social rejection? *Journal of Social and Clinical Psychology, 26*(2), 137–54. https://doi.org/10.1521/jscp.2007.26.2.137

Ferrari, M., Flora, N., Anderson, K.K., Haughton, A., Tuck, A., Archie, S., Kidd, S., McKenzie, K., & ACE Project Team. (2018). Gender differences in pathways to care for early psychosis. *Early Intervention in Psychiatry, 12*(3), 355–61. https://doi.org/10.1111/eip.12324

Forrester, A., Till, A., Simpson, A., & Shaw, J. (2018) Mental illness and the provision of mental health services in prisons. *British Medical Bulletin, 127*(1), 101–9. https://doi.org/10.1093/bmb/ldy027

Gibbons, P., Lee, A., Parkes, J., & Meaney, E. (2012). Value for money: A comparison of cost and quality in two models of adult mental health service provision. Health Service Executive, Dublin.

Goffman, E. (1963). *Stigma: Notes on the management of spoiled identity.* Englewood Cliffs, NJ: Prentice Hall. https://doi.org/10.2307/2575995

Greenberg, J.S., Kim, H.W., & Greenley, J.R. (1997). Factors associated with subjective burden in siblings of adults with severe mental illness. *American Journal of Orthopsychiatry, 67*, 231–41. https://doi-org.ezproxy.gl.iit.edu/10.1037/h0080226

Halvorsrud, K., Nazroo, J., Otis, M., Hajdukova, E.B., & Bhui, K. (2018). Ethnic inequalities and pathways to care in psychosis in England: A systematic review and meta-analysis. *BMC Medicine, 16*(1), 1–17. https://doi.org/10.1186/s12916-018-1201-9

Hamilton, L., & Belenko, S. (2016). Effects of pre-release services on access to behavioral health treatment after release from prison. *Justice Quarterly, 33*(6), 1080–102. https://doi.org/10.1080/07418825.2015.1073771

Harangozo, J., Reneses, B., Brohan, E., Sebes, J., Csukly, G., López-Ibor, J.J., Sartorius, N., Rose, D., & Thornicroft, G. (2014). Stigma and discrimination against people with schizophrenia related to medical services. *International Journal of Social Psychiatry, 60*(4), 359–66. https://doi.org/10.1177/0020764013490263

Hopkin, G., Samele, C., Singh, K., & Forrester, A. (2016). Letter to the editor: Transferring London's acutely mentally ill prisoners to hospital. *Criminal Behaviour and Mental Health, 26*, 76. https://doi.org/10.1002/cbm.1992

Janulis, P., Ferrari, J.R., & Fowler, P. (2013). Understanding public stigma toward substance dependence. *Journal of Applied Social Psychology, 43*(5), 1065–72. https://doi.org/10.1111/jasp.12070

Jorm, A.F., & Griffiths, K.M. (2008). The public's stigmatizing attitudes towards people with mental disorders: How important are biomedical conceptualizations? *Acta Psychiatrica Scandinavica, 18*, 315–21. doi:10.1111/j.1600-0447.2008.01251.x

Knott, J., Pleban, A., Taylor, D., & Castle, D. (2007). Management of mental health patients attending Victorian emergency department. *Australian and New Zealand Journal of Psychiatry, 41*, 759–67. https://doi.org/10.1080/00048670701517934

Lamanna, D., Shapiro, G.K., Kirst, M., Matheson, F.I., Nakhost, A., & Stergiopoulos, V. (2018). Coresponding police–mental health programmes: Service user experiences and outcomes in a large urban centre. *International Journal of Mental Health Nursing, 27*(2), 891–900. https://doi.org/10.1111/inm.12384

Landess, J., & Holoyda, B. (2017). Mental health courts and forensic assertive community treatment teams as correctional diversion programs. *Behavioral Sciences & the Law, 35*(5–6), 501–11. https://doi.org/10.1002/bsl.2307

Link, B.G., & Phelan, J.C. (2001). Conceptualizing stigma. *Annual Review of Sociology, 27*(1), 363–85. https://doi.org/10.1146/annurev.soc.27.1.363

Link, B.G., & Phelan, J. (2014). Stigma power. *Social Science and Medicine, 103*, 24–32. https://doi.org/10.1016/j.socscimed.2013.07.035

Livingston, J.D. (2013). Mental illness-related structural stigma: The downward spiral of systemic exclusion. Calgary, Alberta: Mental Health Commission of Canada. Retrieved 2021 from http://www.mentalhealthcommission.ca

Lloyd-Evans, B., Mayo-Wilson, E., Harrison, B., Istead, H., Brown, E., Pilling, S., Johnson, S., & Kendall, T. (2014). A systematic review and meta-analysis of randomised controlled trials of peer support for people with severe mental illness. *BMC Psychiatry, 14*, 39. https://doi.org/10.1186/1471-244X-14-39

Lucksted, A., Drapalski, A., Calmes, C., Forbes, C., DeForge, B., & Boyd, J. (2011). Ending self-stigma: Pilot evaluation of a new intervention to reduce internalized stigma among people with mental illnesses. *Psychiatric Rehabilitation Journal, 35*(1), 51–4. https://doi.org/10.2975/35.1.2011.51.54

Malterud, K., & Ulriksen, K. (2011). Obesity, stigma, and responsibility in health care: A synthesis of qualitative studies. *International Journal of Qualitative Studies on Health & Well-Being, 6*(4), 1–11. https://doi.org/10.3402/qhw.v6i4.8404

McKenna, B., Furness, T., Oakes, J., & Brown, S. (2015). Police and mental health clinician partnership in response to mental health crisis: A qualitative study. *International Journal of Mental Health Nursing, 24*(5), 386–93. https://doi.org/10.1111/inm.12140

McLoughlin, C., Abdalla, A., MacHale, S., & Barry, H. (2020). Impact of changes in community psychiatric service provision on mental health presentations to the emergency department. *Irish Journal of Medical Science,* 1–6. https://doi.org/10.1007/s11845-020-02442-w

Merritt-Davis, O.B., & Keshavan, M.S. (2006). Pathways to care for African Americans with early psychosis. *Psychiatric Services, 57*(7), 1043–4. https://doi.org/10.1176/ps.2006.57.7.1043

Michaels, P.J., Corrigan, P.W., Buchholz, B., Brown, J., Arthur, T., Netter, C., & MacDonald-Wilson, K.L. (2014). Changing stigma through a consumer-based stigma reduction program. *Community Mental Health Journal, 50*(4), 395–401. https://doi.org/10.1007/s10597-013-9628-0

Muñoz, M., Sanz, M., Pérez-Santos, E., & Quiroga, M. de los Á. (2011). Proposal of a socio-cognitive-behavioral structural equation model of internalized stigma in people with severe and persistent mental illness. *Psychiatry Research, 186*(2–3), 402–8. https://doi.org/10.1016/j.psychres.2010.06.019

Mulfinger, N., Müller, S., Böge, I., Sakar, V., Corrigan, P.W., Evans-Lacko, S., Nehf, L., Djamali, J., Samarelli, A., Kempter, M., Ruckes, C., Libal, G., Oexle, N., Noterdaeme, M., & Rüsch, N. (2018). Honest, Open, Proud for adolescents with mental illness: Pilot randomized controlled trial. *Journal of Child Psychology and Psychiatry, 59*(6), 684–91. https://doi.org/10.1111/jcpp.12853

Newman, S., & Goldman, H. (2009). Housing policy for persons with severe mental illness. *Policy Studies Journal, 37*(2), 299–324. https://doi.org/10.1111/j.1541-0072.2009.00315.x

Oliveira, S.E., Esteves, F., & Carvalho, H. (2015). Clinical profiles of stigma experiences, self-esteem and social relationships among people with schizophrenia, depressive, and bipolar disorders. *Psychiatry Research, 229*(1–2), 167–73. https://doi.org/10.1016/j.psychres.2015.07.047

Phillips, R.L., Miller, B.F., Petterson, S.M., & Teevan, B. (2011). Better integration of mental health care improves depression screening and treatment in primary care. *American Family Physician, 84*(9), 980.

Puntis, S., Perfect, D., Kirubarajan, A., Bolton, S., Davies, F., Hayes, A., Harriss, E., & Molodynski, A. (2018). A systematic review of co-responder models of police mental health "street" triage. *BMC Psychiatry, 18*(1), 256. https://doi.org/10.1186/s12888-018-1836-2

Rose, D., Willis, R., Brohan, E., Sartorius, N., Villares, C., Wahlbeck, K., & Thornicroft, G. (2011). Reported stigma and discrimination by people with a diagnosis of schizophrenia. *Epidemiology and Psychiatric Sciences, 20*, 193–204. https://doi.org/10.1017/s2045796011000254

Rotenberg, M., Tuck, A., Ptashny, R., & McKenzie, K. (2017). The role of ethnicity in pathways to emergency psychiatric services for clients with psychosis. *BMC Psychiatry, 17*(1), 1–11. https://doi.org/10.1186/s12888-017-1285-3

Rüsch, N., & Thornicroft, G. (2014). Does stigma impair prevention of mental disorders? *British Journal of Psychiatry, 204*(4), 249–51. https://doi.org/10.1192/bjp.bp.113.131961

Rüsch, N., Angermeyer, M.C., & Corrigan, P.W. (2005). Mental illness stigma: Concepts, consequences, and initiatives to reduce stigma. *European Psychiatry, 20*(8), 529–39. https://doi.org/10.1016/j.eurpsy.2005.04.004

Rüsch, N., Corrigan, P.W., Todd, A.R., & Bodenhausen, G.V. (2010). Implicit self-stigma in people with mental illness. *Journal of Nervous and Mental Disease, 198*(2), 150–3. https://doi.org/10.1097/nmd.0b013e3181cc43b5

Rüsch, N., Heekeren, K., Theodoridou, A., Dvorsky, D., Müller, M., Paust, T., Corrigan, P.W., Walitza, S., & Rössler, W. (2013). Attitudes towards help-seeking and stigma among young people at risk for psychosis. *Psychiatry Research, 210*(3), 1313–15. https://doi.org/10.1016/j.psychres.2013.08.028

Rüsch, N., Abbruzzese, E., Hagedorn, E., Hartenhauer, D., Kaufmann, I., Curschellas, J., Ventling, S., Zuaboni, G., Bridler, R., Olschewski, M., Kawohl, W., Rössler, W., Kleim, B., & Corrigan, P.W. (2014). Efficacy of coming out proud to reduce stigma's impact among people with mental illness: Pilot randomised controlled trial. *British Journal of Psychiatry, 204*(5), 391–7. https://doi.org/10.1192/bjp.bp.113.135772

Sather, E.W., Iversen, V.C., Svindseth, M.F., Crawford, P., & Vasset, F. (2019). Patients' perspectives on care pathways and informed shared decision making in the transition between psychiatric hospitalization and the community. *Journal of Evaluation in Clinical Practice, 25*(6), 1131–41.

Shefer, G., Rose, D., Nellums, L., Thornicroft, G., Henderson, C., & Evans-Lacko, S. (2013). "Our community is the worst": The influence of cultural beliefs on stigma, relationships with family and help-seeking in three ethnic communities in London. *International Journal of Social Psychiatry, 59*(6), 535–44.

Sirey, J.A., Bruce, M.L., Alexopoulos, G.S., Perlick, D.A., Raue, P., Friedman, S.J., & Meyers, B.S. (2001). Perceived stigma as a predictor of treatment discontinuation in young and older outpatients with depression. *American Journal of Psychiatry, 158*(3), 479–81. https://doi.org/10.1176/appi.ajp.158.3.479

Stiggelbout, A.M., Van der Weijden, T., De Wit, M.P., Frosch, D., Légaré, F., Montori, V.M., Trevena, L., & Elwyn, G. (2012). Shared decision making: Really putting patients at the centre of healthcare. *BMJ, 344*, e256. https://doi.org/10.1136/bmj.e256

Strauss, J.L., Zervakis, J.B., Stechuchak, K.M., Olsen, M.K., Swanson, J., Swartz, M.S., Weinberger, M., Marx, C.E., Calhoun, P.S., Bradford, D.W., Butterfield, M.I., & Oddone, E.Z. (2013). Adverse impact of coercive treatments on psychiatric inpatients' satisfaction with care. *Community Mental Health Journal, 49*(4), 457–65. https://doi.org/10.1007/s10597-012-9539-5

Stull, L.G., McGrew, J.H., Salyers, M.P., & Ashburn-Nardo, L. (2013). Implicit and explicit stigma of mental illness: Attitudes in an evidence-based practice. *The Journal of Nervous and Mental Disease, 201*(12), 1072–9. https://doi.org/10.1097/NMD.0000000000000056

Świtaj, P., Chrostek, A., Grygiel, P., Wciórka, J., & Anczewska, M. (2016). Exploring factors associated with the psychosocial impact of stigma among people with schizophrenia or affective disorders. *Community Mental Health Journal, 52*(3), 370–8. https://doi.org/10.1007/s10597-014-9800-1

Thornicroft, G. (2013). Premature death among people with mental illness. *British Medical Journal, 346*, Article F2969. https://doi.org/10.1136/bmj.f2969

Topor, A., Andersson, G., Denhov, A., Holmqvist, S., Mattsson, M., Stefansson, C.G., & Bülow, P. (2014). Psychosis and poverty: Coping with poverty and severe mental illness in everyday life. *Psychosis, 6*(2), 117–27. https://doi.org/10.1080/17522439.2013.790070

Volpe, U., Mihai, A., Jordanova, V., & Sartorius, N. (2015). The pathways to mental healthcare world-wide: A systematic review. *Current Opinion in Psychiatry, 28*(4), 299–306. https://doi.org/10.1097/YCO.0000000000000164

Wang, K., Link, B.G., Corrigan, P.W., Davidson, L., & Flanagan, E. (2018). Perceived provider stigma as a predictor of mental health service users' internalized stigma and disempowerment. *Psychiatry Research, 259*, 526–31. https://doi.org/10.1016/j.psychres.2017.11.036

Waring, J., Marshall, F., & Bishop, S. (2015). Understanding the occupational and organizational boundaries to safe hospital discharge. *Journal of Health Services Research & Policy, 20*(1 Suppl.), 35–44. https://doi.org/10.1177/1355819614552512

Wong, G., Derthick, A.O., David, E.J.R., Saw, A., & Okazaki, S. (2014). The what, the why, and the how: A review of racial microaggressions research in psychology. *Race and Social Problems, 6*(2), 181–200. https://dx.doi.org/10.1007%2Fs12552-013-9107-9

Wright, N., Rowley, E., Chopra, A., Gregoriou, K., & Waring, J. (2016). From admission to discharge in mental health services: A qualitative analysis of service user involvement. *Health Expectations, 19*(2), 367–76. https://doi.org/10.1111/hex.12361

Xu, Z., Müller, M., Heekeren, K., Theodoridou, A., Dvorsky, D., Metzler, S., Brabban, A., Corrigan, P.W., Walitza, S., Rössler, W., & Rüsch, N. (2016). Self-labelling and stigma as predictors of attitudes towards help-seeking among people at risk of psychosis: 1-year follow-up. *European Archives of Psychiatry and Clinical Neuroscience, 266*(1), 79–82. https://doi.org/10.1007/s00406-015-0576-2

10. Involuntary civil commitment for persons with mental illness

Jonathan Lukens and Phyllis Solomon

Involuntary psychiatric commitment is the process of detaining or monitoring individuals in inpatient or outpatient settings and/or treating without consent. It is seen by some practitioners as a necessary tool to keep persons with mental illnesses safe from harming themselves or harming others. However, patient rights advocates view the process as overly coercive and paternalistic. While medical paternalism is not unique to the history of care for persons with mental illness, mental health is an area of practice where it has pronounced ethical implications. Ensconced in the long tradition of English and American common law, persons who have been deemed a threat to themselves may be held or treated against their will under the legal principle of *parens patriae*. Individuals may also be involuntarily committed by the states' utilization of police power to protect the community or other individuals from persons with mental illness who have indicated an intention to harm others (Fulop, 1995). Despite this long legal heritage, civil commitment remains controversial, perceived by treatment providers as a necessary tool for client safety and treatment adherence, while decried by patient rights advocates as an instrument of coercion, social control, and an affront to patient autonomy and dignity.

Over the past half century, there has been a marked shift in fundamental understandings of patients' rights and the proper use of and limits on involuntary commitment and coercive treatment (Mulvey, Geller, & Roth, 1987). Key federal court decisions have established narrower criteria for civil commitment, thus limiting the power of states to treat clients against their will, and by extension, forcing providers to approach treatment less paternalistically. But despite the more narrowly defined criteria, the controversy over involuntary treatment persists. As mental health consumers and advocates push for even greater control over treatment decision making and curtailment of coercive treatments, treatment advocates and providers lament the problem of the revolving door of hospital admissions and the plight of persons with mental illness living in prisons, homeless shelters, or on the streets (Appelbaum, 2001). This ethical and legal conundrum is not solved once and for all, as the pendulum swings between the limits of patient rights and medical paternalism. As one hospital superintendent pronounced in the wake of several federal court decisions that restricted involuntary treatment, patients were now "dying with their rights on," and that the pendulum had swung from "frank paternalism to frank abandonment" (Treffert, 1973, p. 1041). More than 40 years after this opine, as mental health advocates have seen patient self-determination ensconced in federal regulation, some bioethicists have pushed back and argued that to improve psychiatric care we must "bring back the asylum" (Sisti, Segal, & Emanuel, 2015). To a lesser extreme, other treatment advocates have supported policies they regard as less coercive (such as outpatient commitment), but which confer to providers greater power to ensure treatment adherence. Consumers continue to resist such policies as being little more than coercive practices and mechanisms of social control. Prior to exploring policy specifics, it is worth understanding the historical development of consumer rights and the curtailment of involuntary treatment.

PSYCHIATRIC SURVIVORS AND THE DISABILITY RIGHTS MOVEMENTS

In the United States, the 1950s and 1960s was the civil rights era, a time in which Black and Brown Americans were fighting for social justice and equal rights under the law. This movement inspired other marginalized groups whose basic human dignity was also being denied to take action to gain their rights as well. By the 1970s, one of the prominent groups battling to overcome centuries of fears, negative stereotypes and biases of being perceived as incapable of fully participating in or contributing to society was those with disabilities, specifically those with psychiatric disabilities. The consequences of such stigma left Americans with disabilities marginalized and greatly impoverished. Judi Chamberlin, one of the leaders of what was called the mental patients' liberation movement, proclaimed that people with psychiatric illnesses were an oppressed group – "oppressed by laws and public attitudes, relegated to legalized second-class citizenship" (Chamberlin, 1995, p. 39). For example, although federal laws granted persons with severe mental illnesses the right to vote, there were/are state laws with specific eligibility requirements that did/do not allow them to do so. Court cases in 2000–01 in the states of New Jersey and Maine are cause for optimism, as the courts found these laws unconstitutional and violated the Americans with Disability Act (UPENN Collaborative for Community Integration, n.d.). Similarly, based on the presumption of incapacity, a recent review found that 37 percent of countries worldwide "explicitly prohibit marriage by persons with mental health problems" (Bhugra et al., 2016, p. 386).

In the 1970s, a small group of psychiatric survivors banded together to voice their concerns regarding a mental health system "that had taken away their power and their control over their own lives" (Chamberlin, 1995, p. 39). This was an unfunded political movement of ex-patients who shared common experiences and developed self-help/mutual support services as alternatives to the traditional mental health system that had disrespected them, did not listen to or believe them, and deprived them of their rights to control their own financial resources and living environments. People diagnosed with a mental illness were frequently perceived as being incompetent and incapable of making good decisions and lacking insight into their illness, therefore, requiring a mental health professional to do so on their behalf, justifying this on the basis of being in their best interest (Chamberlin, 1995). While mental health professionals believed beneficence was the principled approach to treating persons with psychiatric disabilities, the clients themselves argued that autonomy should be the guiding value. Many of the leaders were ex-patients who had experienced abuses by psychiatric providers and institutions, been forced to take treatments that had unbearable side effects, and endure restraints and seclusion, and consequently losing their dignity and personhood (Solomon & Petros, 2020). This movement was thus often labeled as an anti-psychiatry movement and members saw themselves as psychiatric survivors (Kaufman, 1999).

This advocacy effort did make some headway. There emerged patient alternative programs and services that were funded on a small scale by state mental health authorities, private foundations, and local governments. These client-run programs demonstrated that they could be effective in breaking the cycle of frequent hospitalizations and enabling patients to live on their own in the community (Chamberlin, 1995). By the mid-1980s there was new research that for the first time talked about the recovery of patients with severe mental illness, particularly those diagnosed with schizophrenia. A cohort of patients hospitalized for years that were part of a comprehensive rehabilitation program in a long-term psychiatric institution were followed-up ten years after their discharge. These investigators found what other studies such as those by the World Health Organization (Bland, Parker, & Orn, 1976; Ciompi, 1980) had determined – that such a diagnosis did not inevitably follow a chronic long-term downward course, but rather from half to two-thirds of participants had improved and many had recovered (Harding et al., 1987).

In the 1980s a new generation of mental health advocates emerged who referred to themselves as mental health consumers. Many of these consumers entered the mental health service system under a period of deinstitutionalization and therefore spent shorter time, if any, in hospitals and were less likely to have been subjected to the abuses of an earlier era (Solomon & Petros, 2020). They were a more moderate group as opposed to the radical reformists who wanted to annihilate the system but rather desired to reform the system. This new movement wanted choices and respect from the system of care, as well as "the dignity of risk and the right to failure" (Deagan, 1992, p. 13). This movement was also more accepted by the mental health establishment. The Community Support Program (CSP) at the National Institute of Mental Health (began in 1997 and ended in the early 2000s at Substance Abuse Mental Health Services Administration (SAMHSA)) began funding peer-run mental health services as did state mental health authorities which also established Offices of Consumer Affairs that were staffed by mental health consumers (Solomon & Petros, 2020). In the late 1970s CSP began funding annual consumer conferences (Frese & Davis, 1997). Writings by consumers began to appear in scholarly journals about their experiences with the system and their recoveries, whereas in the past radical advocates had published their own newspapers such as *Madness Network News*.

In the late 1980s and early 1990s we saw the beginning of consumer provided services in which consumers were offering traditional mental health services, such as case management. But these programs were offered infrequently and on an experimental basis. Research found that these services were equally as effective as those provided by mental health providers and that there were no detrimental effects to consumers themselves or others (Solomon & Draine, 2001). A more recent review indicated that evidence was moderate with consumers having greater improvement in recovery outcomes and reduction in hospital use, but did not achieve a high level of recovery (Chinman et al., 2014). Other research reviews noted that while internationally the uptake of the promotion of peer support services had occurred, the evidence does not support their effectiveness, even though there are some positive outcomes such as reduced hospitalizations, reduction in overall symptoms, and increased service satisfaction (Chien et al., 2019; Lloyd-Evans et al., 2014). With the issuance of the President's New Freedom Commission Report in 2003, which promoted the transformation of the mental health system of care into a recovery-oriented one, the federal government agency, SAMHSA, issued policies and guidelines for achieving such a system. Subsequently, nationwide behavioral health agencies hired mental health consumers, who in this new recovery orientation were called peer providers/specialists, to realize this policy. In 1999, the state of Georgia used Medicaid reimbursement for peer delivered services and by 2007 Centers for Medicaid and Medicare (CMS) issued guidance for states to use certain waivers and rehabilitation options to pay for these services. In the letter of issuance, CMS declared peer provided services as "an evidence-based mental health model of care." For billing, peers had to be certified by the states and in 2016, 44 states, the District of Columbia, and the Veterans Administration provided certification and over 25,000 peers were certified at the time of the survey (Wolf, 2018). Peer specialists are currently accepted and established members of behavioral health care teams.

The persistence of peer specialists and consumer advocates has had a significant impact on systems of care. As autonomy has supplanted beneficence as the core value in treatment, clients play a more significant role in treatment planning, while the use of coercion as a means of gaining treatment compliance and exercising social control has ebbed over the past half century. However, these efforts are not without their critics who see significant medical, social, and fiscal implications to reducing the use of involuntary treatment. Diving deeper into the ethical and legal challenges to civil commitment, we see that treatment advocates pivot toward new strategies.

THE ETHICAL AND LEGAL BACKGROUND

Concurrent with the civil rights movement and changes in service provision were a series of revelations about the ethically questionable (if not unconscionable) activities of doctors and researchers prompting an explosion of interest in biomedical ethics. This rights revolution has placed the medical profession as a whole, and psychiatry in particular, under a greater level of ethical scrutiny than had previously been the case. This turns out to have been merely a prelude to several notable court cases which affirmed and reaffirmed the right of patients to live free of medical coercion outside of a specifically proscribed circumstance. The Lessard v. Schmidt (1972) decision established that involuntary psychiatric commitment constituted a substantive curtailment of individual liberty, similar to that experienced by defendants in criminal cases. As such, patients held against their will are entitled to many, if not most, of the same due process protections (including right to a hearing, counsel) accorded to those accused of crimes. Furthermore, the courts established that judges may only order involuntary treatment "based upon finding of recent overt act, attempt or threat to do substantial harm to oneself or another" (Lessard v. Schmidt, 1972). In the related case of O'Connor v. Donaldson (1975), the courts determined that

> A finding of "mental illness" alone cannot justify a State's locking a person up against his/her will and keeping him/her indefinitely in simple custodial confinement. In short, a state cannot constitutionally confine a non-dangerous individual who is capable of surviving safely in freedom by him/herself or with the help of willing and responsible family members or friends. (O'Connor v. Donaldson, 422 U.S. 563, 1975)

Imminent dangerousness remains the primary legal standard for civil commitment (Miller, 1988). This is often interpreted as meaning an act likely to occur within a matter of days. However, providers became increasingly concerned that this strict standard made it significantly more difficult to get their clients the treatment they needed, prompting some treatment advocates to lobby for a lesser standard of "need for treatment" and an expanded use of involuntary outpatient treatment. Presently, some states (Massachusetts, California, Illinois, and others) do allow for an exception to the standard of imminent dangerousness in circumstances of "grave disability," a standard invoked, for instance, in cases of anorexia nervosa (Applebaum & Rumpf, 1998).

The other ethico-legal trend worth noting is the separation between commitment and the ability to consent to (or refuse) treatment. Historically, the concept of civil commitment contained an implicit assumption that committed patients lacked the capacity to consent to or refuse treatment. As Meisel (1983) points out, this conflation was likely reinforced by the concept of the "right to treatment" which some courts took to mean that the obligation to provide treatment necessarily implied an obligation by patients to accept it. In 1975, patients who had been civilly committed in Massachusetts petitioned the courts arguing the right to refuse treatment despite being committed. Courts found in favor of the petitioners, and in the subsequent decades, numerous other cases have further divorced commitment from consent to or refusal of treatment, except under special circumstances (Stransky, 1996).

Inpatient Commitment/Outpatient Commitment/Assisted Outpatient Treatment

In the United States, involuntary civil commitment is a legal intervention by which a person displaying symptoms of a psychiatric disorder and who meets a state's other statutory requirements as determined by the court can be committed for psychiatric treatment in an inpatient or community outpatient psychiatric setting (SAMHSA, 2019) or face "sanctions for noncompliance" (Torrey & Zdanowicz, 2001, p. 337). In the 1960s, with the deinstitu-tionalization movement, eligibility for commitment became more circumscribed admission criteria, length of stay for those who were committed was shortened, and the number of beds available was greatly reduced as state psychiatric institutions closed, making it more difficult to commit individuals who in a prior period would have been hospitalized (Lamb & Bachrach, 2001). At the same time, the availability and accessibility of community-based mental health resources were extremely limited, resulting in a new generation of persons with severe mental illness revolving in and out of hospitals. Furthermore, some were going untreated, which was believed to have resulted in homelessness, criminal justice involvement, illegal substance use, and engagement in self-harm and harm to others (Lamb & Bachrach, 2001). These phenomena coupled with the increasing concerns of policy-makers and the public regarding growing fears of the potential for violent behavior among this population provoked the development of out-patient commitment laws (Torrey & Zdanowicz, 2001).

There are three approaches to involuntary outpatient treatment: conditional release, dispo-sitional alternative, or preventative commitment (McCafferty & Dooley, 1990). Conditional release allows a patient who has been committed to inpatient care to be conditionally released to outpatient care as the patient's symptoms improve. In this case, the patient may be returned to inpatient care should there be a worsening of symptoms or problems with treatment adher-ence. Dispositional alternative to inpatient care is commitment to outpatient services when the legal standard for inpatient commitment has been met, that is, dangerousness, but the patient is determined to be more likely to benefit from care in an outpatient setting. For years, outpatient commitment had been available in many states under existing involuntary commitment laws, but had been used mainly as provisional or conditional release from long-term psychiatric hos-pitals and was seen as the least restrictive alternative to hospitalization, which was a pervasive policy of the 1970s (Stefan, 1987).

The third alternative has gained some traction in recent decades, despite clinical and legal controversy: preventative commitment. Preventative commitment involves commitment to outpatient treatment under a less stringent legal standard such as "need for treatment" than is utilized in the other two alternatives. Preventative outpatient commitment remains the most controversial from clinical and civil rights perspectives, but despite this, it is also widely promoted by treatment advocates within the medical community. Media accounts of such incidents, such as the one in 1999 when Andrew Goldstein pushed Kendra Webdale in front of an oncoming subway in New York, fueled concerns for public safety. Consequently, there was a belief that individuals needed to be coerced into treatment for their own safety and that of the community (Torrey & Zdanowicz, 2001). Preventative commitment appeared to many to be a viable option. However, it was unclear if Goldstein would have met criteria for this commitment, as he had sought treatment on numerous occasions from the mental health system.

By the early 2000s, states began establishing Assisted Outpatient Treatment (AOT) laws which were frequently named for the victims, such as Kendra's Law in New York State and Laura's Law in California. E. Fuller Torrey, a psychiatrist, advocated for such laws and euphemistically rebranded them as assisted treatment under the assumption that they would assist people who lacked awareness of their illness and, therefore, would not seek needed treatment on their own, leaving them vulnerable to possible violent acts. According to SAMHSA (2019), as of 2016, 47 states have some form of outpatient commitment with 32 states having preventative type commitment intended to prevent future dangerousness to self or others or deterioration that likely would lead to future dangerousness. Further, 20 states have active AOT programs. These commitment laws are justified as a means to obtain essential services in lieu of inpatient psychiatric care. Today, hospitalization remains infrequent and when it does occur, it averages between 7–10 days. Unlike the past, hospital environments tend to be clean, safe, in urban rather than distant locations, and are often psychiatric units of general medical facilities (SAMHSA, 2019).

Despite the widespread use of AOT or community treatment orders, labeled as such in a number of western countries including the United Kingdom, Canada, and Australia, it has created a great deal of controversy. While there are those who see them as a means to receiving needed treatment and prevention of possible negative consequences of untreated illness, such as homelessness, incarceration, suicide, and violence, others view these orders as an unwarranted loss of liberty that harkens back to psychiatric paternalism and mechanism of social control of an earlier era. These are coercive interventions that force individuals who are not dangerous, do not meet standards for involuntary inpatient commitment, and are legally competent into complying with treatment against their wishes (Allen & Smith, 2001). Therefore, opponents find no legal or ethical justifications for taking away an individual's freedom and autonomy when competent to make their own treatment decisions. These laws do not require nor make provision for decisional capacity (Goldman, 2014).

On a rights-based ethical approach, the rights of an individual are paramount such that interference by the state or otherwise is unacceptable unless the risk is so great, in which case inpatient commitment is an available option (Lally, 2013). It is also difficult to make an argument for beneficence when all that these laws do in practicality is imply forced receipt of available community mental health services. Court cases have made determinations that competent individuals cannot legally be forced to take psychiatric medications against their will, barring an emergency (Allen & Smith, 2001). Providers often do not want to be enforcers and monitors. These laws are not treatment per se, but a strategy for mandating service providers to leverage force over non-compliant individuals to accept mental health treatment, particularly prescribed psychiatric medications. However, with difficulties in implementation, many view these laws as having no teeth (Solomon, 2017).

Preventative outpatient commitment's lack of meaningful sanctions threatens to fatally undermine any ethical or legal justifications for such policies. There are several states where outpatient commitment statutes allow for the apprehension of non-treatment adherent clients by law enforcement, after which they can be forcibly returned to the designated provider. The question remains though, to what end? Under such circumstances (non-adherence) providers are not authorized to forcibly medicate clients. The ability to coerce compliance is reliant on the clients' perception that failure to acquiesce will result in involuntary treatment, perhaps committed into an inpatient setting. However, such involuntary treatment would again require the individual to meet the state's higher commitment standard criterion of dangerousness; not just the "need for treatment." Thus, the real power of preventative involuntary outpatient treatment is illusory and its effectiveness may in time wane as clients become increasingly aware of the illusion and push back against providers (Applebaum, 2001; Fulop, 1995). In cases where a client is disabled to the point where they are unable to exercise the kind of judgement necessary for making medical or financial decisions, there are already procedures in place in all states to address this situation. If a client is deemed to lack capacity, the courts may appoint a guardian to make decisions on their behalf. This, however, is not the case with AOT, wherein there is no legal process that establishes capacity or lack of capacity, at least in the United States, whereas elsewhere, such as Canada, this is not the case. Persons on AOT do not generally meet the legal criteria of dangerousness, or else they would be civilly committed through existing provisions for inpatient care. Rather, persons receiving AOT are subjected to surveillance and threat of coercion based on a dubious legal status.

It is also worth noting that while involuntary outpatient commitment is lauded as a "least restrictive alternative" to inpatient care, this justification only holds for conditional release or when used as a dispositional alternative to hospitalization. When applied to preventative involuntary outpatient commitment, the standard of "least restrictive" no longer applies. The concept of least restrictive is usually interpreted in physical terms; for instance, treatment in a locked inpatient unit as being more restrictive than treatment in an outpatient setting. Under such a definition it seems reasonable to infer that commitment to outpatient treatment is less restrictive. However, restrictiveness may also be interpreted in terms of voluntariness, but in so doing, preventative outpatient commitment is not the least restrictive alternative. In fact, *voluntary inpatient* treatment would be less restrictive because it at least is somewhat time limited with a clear understanding of what needs to be accomplished for it to end compared with long-term surveillance associated with AOT. For instance, under New York's Kendra's Law (1999), a client may be mandated for up to a year of supervision under an initial order, which can be renewed for successive years. Thus, contrary to the perception of a least restrictive alternative, some legal scholars have argued that it may be more restrictive than inpatient care (Fulop, 1995; Schwartz & Costanzo, 1987)

These assisted outpatient treatment orders continue to be promoted internationally, regardless of the fact that the evidence to date has not supported their effectiveness. The results of three randomized controlled trials show no effect on hospital admission, length of hospital stay, and use of community services; thus, offering no clinical advantage to warrant the denial of personal liberty than would be obtained from voluntary services (Burns et al., 2013; Dawson, 2016; Rugkasa, 2016; Rugkasa, Dawson, & Burns, 2014; Steadman et al., 2001; Swartz et al., 1999). Non-randomized studies provide more conflictual results, but do not offer convincing evidence of advantages of these orders. A recent population-based study did find that, while on treatment orders, individuals did increase their receipt of community care and hospital admissions were delayed, but the researchers recognized the lack of clarity regarding what happens when orders are no longer in effect (Harris et al., 2019). Research has shown that orders may be effective for individuals who believe that sanctions can be applied should they not comply. Providers frequently do not correct these misconceptions fearing that then the effectiveness would be undercut (Stroud, Banks, & Dougherty, 2015). As stated earlier, non-compliance is not a criterion for hospital admission, consequently, the individual must still meet the standards for hospitalization. But all too often, the individual is not made aware of this.

With the effectiveness of the intervention in question, the ethical foundation begins to crumble. The Wyatt v. Stickney decision (1974) establishes that committed clients have a "constitutional right to receive such individual treatment as will give each of them a realistic opportunity to be cured or to improve his or her mental condition." Furthermore, "To deprive any citizen of his or her liberty upon the altruistic theory that the confinement is for humane therapeutic reasons and then fail to provide adequate treatment violates the very fundamentals of due process" (Wyatt v. Stickney, 1971). One could argue that this standard does not apply to involuntary outpatient treatment, as it does not utilize the level of "confinement" present in the Wyatt v. Stickney case. Such a conclusion though misses the deeper ethical issues. Again, restrictiveness need not be considered as solely physical confines, but also voluntariness. As such, outpatient treatment through its coercion and open-ended surveillance still represents a substantive taking away of one's individual liberty and autonomous choice. Given the centrality of autonomy to medical ethics in general, and social work ethics in particular, we must follow a similar injunction, if not in a legal sense, then at least in an ethical one. The ethical justification for curtailing client autonomy via outpatient commitment is predicated upon the client receiving the kind of treatment and services that could be reasonably expected to return the patient to a state wherein he/she may again exercise autonomous choice and be free of coercion and surveillance. Therefore, the ethical justification for involuntary outpatient treatment hinges not only on issues of right and wrong, but also the practical considerations of treatment access and effectiveness.

PSYCHIATRIC ADVANCE DIRECTIVES

Psychiatric advance directives (PADS) are viewed as an antidote to coercive interventions such as psychiatric hospital commitment and AOT. PADS are legal documents, usually written, that enable a competent person to make known their wishes regarding either to refuse or consent to specific psychiatric treatments in an event of a crisis situation and at points in which the person's decisional capacity is compromised (Appelbaum, 1991; Zelle, Kemp, & Bonnie, 2015). Generally, these documents also provide for designated proxy decision maker to make informed choices on their behalf (Zelle et al., 2015). The underlying frameworks of this complex multifaceted process are to enhance autonomy, improve therapeutic alliance of the individual and treatment provider, and integrate care through a working partnership between the individual and provider (Nicaise et al., 2013; Zelle, Kemp, & Bonnie, 2015). This mechanism, which goes by various names such as psychiatric wills, advance statements, advance agreements, advance instructions, and crisis cards (Nicaise et al., 2013), was developed during the anti-psychiatric movement to protect patients from psychiatrists (Scholten et al., 2019). It was first introduced in California in 1976 for mental health clients to retain choice and control over their psychiatric treatment during times of decisional incapacity (Swanson, McCrary, Swartz, et al., 2006). The Patient Self Determination Act of 1990 provided the momentum for recovery-oriented care which precipitated the enactment of legislation in about two-thirds of US states for the development of PADs (Zelle, Kemp, & Bonnie, 2015). But PADS are not limited to the United States, many other countries have provisions for PADs including Australia, Belgium, Canada, Germany, Ireland, India, Scotland, the Netherlands, and the United Kingdom. All of these countries have ratified the United Nations Convention on the Rights of Persons with Disabilities, with the exception of the United States and PADs are consistent with the aims of this document (Scholten et al., 2019).

Despite survey data from the United States and elsewhere that from about 40 percent to over 80 percent of mental health users would like to write a PAD, the rates of actually writing them are extremely low (Scholten et al., 2019; Van Dorn et al., 2010). For example, in one survey of five US cities only from 4 percent to 13 percent had a PAD (Swanson, Swartz, Ferron, et al., 2006). Providers conceptually endorse these tools to enhance consumer involvement in treatment, but frequently did not perceive PADs as beneficial. They feared that users would refuse all treatment and that they, as providers, would be legally bound liable for a decision that they did not have the right to make (Nicaise et al., 2013). A survey of clinicians found that just under half believed them beneficial to people with severe mental illness (Elbogen et al., 2006), however, those who would most benefit from PADs are least likely to write one (Nicaise et al., 2013). But research reviewing written PADs did not find that users refused all treatment and did justify reasons for refusing specific treatments (Nicaise et al., 2013; Van Dorn et al., 2010). Families tend to take a more middle position of seeing them as empowering users in treatment decisions, but are concerned for the liability of providers. They also favor compulsory treatment and surrogate decision makers more so than providers, as they expect that this would give them more control in making treatment decisions (Nicaise et al., 2013).

These multi-stage, complex interventions have numerous challenges to both developing them and executing them. Nicaise and colleagues' (2013) recent "realist systematic review" assessed PADs in terms of the three-stage process: (1) Types and functions of PADs; (2) Completion and content of PADs and (3) Accessing and honoring PADs. These documents usually specify preferences for medications and hospitals, relapse symptoms, persons to notify, and other clinical information. Some individuals add non-treatment information such as care of dependents, pets, and finances, others to notify and people to bar from visiting (Nicaise et al., 2013). The classic PADs are to be completed by the individual on their own. There are a number of barriers to completion of these: cognitive impairment and question of capacity without support, inability to find proxies and witnesses, difficulty notarizing and filing or registering the documents (Scheyett et al., 2007). Due to the fact that uptake has been extremely limited, attempts have been made to assist individuals in their completion through training, structured booklets, and computer-assisted directives (Nicaise et al., 2013). In addition, there are facilitated PADs completed with the assistance of a peer, but not a clinician. The United Kingdom has experimented with a Joint Crisis Plan (JCP) where a clinician assists in a negotiated process and may also include third parties such as family members, friends, or a case manager (Nicaise et al., 2013). The evidence does not indicate that a particular type is more effective in enhancing autonomy, but JCP does seem to improve the therapeutic alliance more than the classic PAD. PADs are often used to include Durable Powers of Attorney, but can also designate a surrogate decision maker, which raises concerns. Given that proxies tend to use a "best interest" standard as opposed to a substitute judgement standard, they do not necessarily decide on what they think the user's preference would be. This decision process could result in legal conflict between user's instructions and proxy's decisions, which may include litigation against the provider (Nicaise et al., 2013). However, there is a lot of legal room to override PADs (Scholten et al., 2019). Physicians may override PADs if they believe they do not meet the current standard of care. Further, PADs may be overturned when the individual meets requirements for civil commitment orders. It is rather ironic that this is the situation given that PADs were created to "avoid or decrease the incidence of involuntary treatment" (Swanson, McCrary, Swartz, et al, 2006, p. 389). However, policies and laws largely favor physicians' decision making in cases where patients desire to evade standard treatment. Clinicians are concerned about their legal risk and would rather be sued by a "disenfranchised psychiatric patient than by their family members (or, in the worst case, by the victims of the patients)" (Swanson, McCrary, Swartz, et al, 2006, p. 393).

Other barriers to utilizing PADs include providers not being particularly knowledgeable regarding PADs, not being able to easily access them, particularly during a crisis, and lack of coordination among providers (Scheyett et al., 2007; Zelle, Kemp, & Bonnie, 2015). Research has not been able to determine the extent to which PADs have been honored (Nicaise et al., 2013). A systematic review of PADs included only two randomized control trials (RCTs) and found no significant differences in hospital admissions, number of outpatient services received, compliance with treatment, self-harm, arrests, but did determine less use of social workers, fewer violent acts, and fewer involuntary admissions than usual care. These were small RCTs, and therefore more research is needed. However, greater intensive interventions do show promise, but practice can't rely on evidence from RCTs. These researchers recommended using these as an alternative to compulsory treatment orders (CTOs) or AOT (Campbell & Kisely, 2009).

CONCLUSION

Despite narrowing criteria for the use of involuntary civil commitment, it remains controversial. Once a widely used tool for treating persons with mental illness, the civil rights movements of the 1950s and 1960s in general, and the consumer rights movement in particular, brought attention to the abuses of involuntary treatment, while federal courts limited the criteria under which individuals could be civilly committed. In response to these limitations and concerns about revolving door admissions and community and client safety, states enacted laws that expanded the use of involuntary outpatient or assisted outpatient treatment to compensate for this lack of confinement. However, these new laws are not without controversy, stemming from ongoing questions regarding effectiveness, legality, and ethical propriety. Proponents argue that AOT laws are a vital tool for treating persons with mental illness, while critics argue they are just another instrument of social control, which may even be *more* restrictive than inpatient commitment. In an attempt to bridge the divide between treatment advocates and client rights, psychiatric advance directives emerged as a means of ensuring a client's treatment choices are known and respected in times of psychiatric exacerbation and subsequent psychiatric crisis/emergency. However, there are legal issues and implementation challenges that have limited their utility.

REFERENCES

Allen, M., & Smith, V.F. (2001). Opening Pandora's Box: The practical and legal dangers of involuntary outpatient commitment. *Psychiatric Services, 52*(3), 342–6.

Appelbaum, P. (1991). Advance directives in mental health treatment. *Hospital and Community Psychiatry, 42,* 983–4.

Applebaum, P. (2001). Thinking carefully about outpatient commitment. *Psychiatric Services, 52*(3), 347–50.

Applebaun, P., & Rumpf, T. (1998). Civil commitment of the anorexic patient. *General Hospital Psychiatry, 20*(4), 225–30.

Bhugra, D., Pathare, S., Nardodke, R., Gosavi, C., Ng, R., Torales, J., & Ventriglio, A. (2016). Legislative provisions related to marriage and divorce of persons with mental health problems: A global review. *International Review of Psychiatry, 28*(4), 386–92.

Bland, R.C., Parker, J.H., & Orn, H. (1976). Prognosis in schizophrenia: A ten-year follow-up of first admissions. *Archives of General Psychiatry, 33*(8), 949–54.

Burns, T., Rugkasa, J., Molodynski, A., Dawson, J., Yeeles, K., Vazquez-Montese, M., Voysey, M., Sinclair, J., & Priebe, S. (2013). Community treatment orders for patients with psychosis (OCTET): A randomized controlled trial. *Lancet. 381,* 1627–33.

Campbell, L., & Kisely, S. (2009). Advance treatment directives for people with severe mental Illness (Review). *Cochrane Database of Systematic Reviews,* Issue 1, Article No. CD005963.

Chamberlin, J. (1995). Rehabilitation ourselves: The psychiatric survivor movement. *International Journal of Mental Health, 24*(1), 39–46.

Chien, W., Clifton, A., Zhao, S., & Lui, S. (2019). Peer support for people with schizophrenia or other serious mental illness. *Cochrane Database of Systematic Reviews,* Issue 4, Article No. CD010880.

Chinman, M., Dougherty, G., Daniels, A., Ghose, S., Swift, A., & Delphin-Rittman, M. (2014). Peer support services for individuals with serious mental illnesses: Assessing the evidence. *Psychiatric Services, 65*(4), 429–41.

Ciompi, L. (1980). Catamnestic long-term study on the course of life and aging of schizophrenics. *Schizophrenia Bulletin, 6*(4), 606–18.

Dawson, J. (2016). Doubts about the clinical effectiveness of community treatment orders. *The Canadian Journal of Psychiatry, 61*(1), 4–6.

Deagan, P. (1992). The independent living movement and people with psychiatric disabilities: Taking back control over our own lives. *Psychosocial Rehabilitation Journal, 15*(3), 3–19.

Elbogen, E., Swartz, M., Van Dorn, R., Swanson, J., Ferron, J., Kim, M., & Scheyett, A. (2006). Clinician decision-making and views about psychiatric advance directives, *Psychiatric Services, 57,* 350–5.

Frese, F., & Davis, W. (1997). The consumer-survivor movement, recovery, and consumer professionals. *Professional Psychology, Research and Practice, 28*(3), 243–5.

Fulop, N.J. (1995). Involuntary outpatient civil commitment: What can Britain learn from the U.S. experience? A civil liberties perspective. *International Journal of Law and Psychiatry, 18*(3), 291–303.

Goldman, H. (2014). Outpatient commitment reexamined: A third way. *Psychiatric Services, 65*(6). 816–17.

Harding, C., Brooks, G., Ashikaga, T., Strauss, J., & Breier, A. (1987). The Vermont Longitudinal Study of Persons with Severe Mental Illness, I: Methodology, study sample, and overall status 32 years later. *American Journal of Psychiatry, 144*(6), 718–26.

Harris, A., Chen, W., Jones, S., Hulme, M., Burgess, P, & Grant, S. (2019). Community treatment orders increase community care and delay readmission while in force: Results from a large population-based study. *Australian and New Zealand Journal of Psychiatry, 53,* 228–35.

Kaufman, C. (1999). An introduction to the mental health consumer movement. In A. Horwitz & T. Scheid (Eds.), *A handbook for the study of mental health* (pp. 493–507). New York: Cambridge University Press.

Lally, J. (2013). Liberty or dignity: Community treatment orders and rights. *Irish Journal of Psychological Medicine, 30,* 141–9.

Lamb, R., & Bachrach, L. (2001). Some perspectives on deinstitutionalization. *Psychiatric Services, 52,* 1039–45.

Laws of New York (1999). Chap 408.

Lessard v. Schmidt, 349 F. Supp 1078 (E.D. Wis. 1972).

Llyod-Evans, B., Mayo-Wilson, E., Harrison, B., Istead, H., Brown, E., Pilling, S., Johnson, S., & Kendall, T. (2014). A systematic review and mete-analysis of randomized controlled trials of peer support for peer with severe mental illness. *BMC Psychiatry,* 14, 39.

McCafferty, G., & Dooley, J. (1990). Involuntary outpatient commitment: An update. *Mental and Physical Disability Law Reporter,* 14(3), 277–87.

Meisel, A. (1983). Making mental health care decisions: Informed consent and involuntary civil commitment. *Behavioral Sciences & the Law,* 1(4), 73–88.

Miller, R. D. (1988). Outpatient Civil Commitment of the Mentally Ill: An Overview and an Update. Behavioral Sciences & the Law, 6(1), 99–118. https://doi.org/10.1002/bsl.2370060108

Mulvey, E.P, Geller, J.L., & Roth, L.H. (1987). The promise and peril of involuntary outpatient commitment. *American Psychologist,* 42(6), 571–84.

Nicaise, P., Lorant, V., & Dubois, V. (2013). Psychiatric Advance Directives as a complex and multi-stage intervention: A realistic systematic review. *Health and Social Care in the Communitym, 21*(1), 1–14. doi:10.1111/j.1365-2524.2012.01062.x

O'Connor v. Donaldson, 422 U.S. 563 (1975).

Rugkasa, J. (2016). Effectiveness of community treatment orders: The international evidence. *The Canadian Journal of Psychiatry,* 61(1), 15–24.

Rugkasa, J., Dawson, J., & Burns, T. (2014). CTOS: What is the state of the evidence? *Social Psychiatry and Psychiatric Epidemiology,* 49, 1861–71.

Scheyett, A., Kim, M., Swanson, J., & Swartz, M. (2007). Psychiatric advance directives. A tool for consumer empowerment and recovery. *Psychiatric Rehabilitation Journal,* 31(1), 70–5.

Scholten, M., Gieselmann, A., Gather, J., & Vollman, J. (2019). Psychiatric advance directives under the Convention on the Rights of Persons with Disabilities: Why advance instructions should be able to override current preferences. *Frontiers in Psychiatry,* Article 631.

Schwartz, S., & Costanzo, C. (1987). Compelling treatment in the community: Distorted doctrines and violated values. *Loyola of Los Angeles Law Review, 20*(4), 1329–429.

Sisti, D.A., Segal, A.D., & Emmanuel, E.J. (2015). Improving long term psychiatric care: Bring back the asylum. *Journal of the American Medical Association,* 313(3), 243–4.

Solomon, P. (2017). Forced mental health treatment will not prevent violent tragedies. In Jackson, J. (ed.), *Social policy and social justice* (pp. 97–110). Pennsylvania, PA: University of Pennsylvania Press.

Solomon, P., & Draine, J. (2001). The state of knowledge of the effectiveness of consumer provided services. *Psychiatric Rehabilitation Journal,* 25, 20–7.

Solomon, P., & Petros, R. (2020). Finding common ground for diverging policies for persons with severe mental illness. *Psychiatric Quarterly,* 91, 1193–208.

Steadman, H., Gounis, K., Dennis, D., Hopper, K., Roche, B., Swartz, M., & Robbins, P. (2001). Assessing the New York City involuntary outpatient commitment pilot program. *Psychiatric Services,* 52, 330–6.

Stefan, S. (1987). Preventive commitment: The concept and its pitfalls. *Mental and Physical Disability Law Reporter,* 11(4), 288–302.

Stransky, D.S. (1996). Civil commitment and the right to refuse treatment: Resolving disputes from due process perspective. *University of Miami Law Review,* 50(2), 413–44.

Stroud, J., Banks, L., & Dougherty, K. (2015). Community treatment orders: Learning from experience of service users, practitioners and nearest relatives. *Journal of Mental Health, 24*(2), 88–92. doi: 10.3109/09638237.2014.998809

Substance Abuse and Mental Health Services Administration (SAMHSA). (2019). *Civil commitment and the mental health care continuum: Historical trends and principles for law and practice.* Office of the Chief Medical Office of Communication, SAMHSA, HHS.

Swanson, J., McCrary, V., Swartz, M., Elbogen, E., & Van Dorn, R. (2006). Superseding psychiatric advance directives: Ethical and legal considerations. *Journal of the American Academy of Psychiatry and Law,* 34, 385–94.

Swanson, J., Swartz, M., Ferron, J., Elbogen, E., & Van Dorn, R. (2006) Psychiatric advance directives among public mental health consumers in five cities: Prevalence, demand and correlates. *Journal of the American Academy of Law & Psychiatry,* 34(1), 143–57.

Swartz, M., Swanson, J., Wagner, H., Burns, B., Hiday, V., & Borum, R. (1999). Can involuntary outpatient commitment reduce hospital recidivism? Findings from a randomized trial with severely mentally ill individuals. *American Journal of Psychiatry,* 156, 1968–75.

Torrey, E.F., & Zdanowicz, M. (2001). Outpatient commitment: What, why, and for whom. *Psychiatric services,* 52(3), 331–41.

Treffert, D. (1973). Dying with their rights on. *American Journal of Psychiatry,* 130(9), 1041.

UPENN Collaborative for Community Integration. (n.d). *Exercising the right to vote.* Author, Philadelphia.

Van Dorn, R., Scheyett, A., Swanson, J., & Swartz, M. (2010). Psychiatric advance directives and social workers: An integrative review. *Social Work,* 55(2), 157–67.

Wolf, J. (2018). National trends in peer specialist certification. *Psychiatric Services,* 69(10), 1049.

Wyatt v. Stickney, 325 F.Supp. 781 (M.D. Ala. 1971).

Zelle, H., Kemp, K., & Bonnie, R. (2015). Advanced directives in mental health care: Evidence, challenges and promise. *World Psychiatry,* 14(3), 278–80.

11. Deinstitutionalization and the development of community mental health

John R. Belcher

Deinstitutionalization began in the 1930s as "depression-poor public mental hospitals" moved to downsize "patient populations in an effort to save resources" (Goldman & Morrissey, 1985, p. 727). Goldman and Morrissey point out that the "Process did not gain momentum … until psychiatrists returning from World War II introduced rapid treatment techniques and an attitude of therapeutic optimism" (p. 727). Community mental health legislation introduced by the Kennedy-Johnson administration "blossomed in a unique, optimistic social climate holding the belief that most, if not all, mentally ill people could adapt successfully to living in their communities" (Belcher & Toomey, 1988, p. 145). Thus, deinstitutionalization became a public policy as states quickly moved to close state mental health beds and move patients to the community. This chapter critically reviews this process and shows where this policy led to homelessness and criminalization for many people with severe mental illness (SMI) (such as schizophrenia).

CONTEXT

Deinstitutionalization in the United States began in the 1950s and 1960s, but in other nations, "it did not emerge until the 1990s or later" (Hudson, 2016, p. 135). In fact, inpatient care continues to be dominant "in many parts of the world" (Hudson, 2016. p.136). Community mental health resources were slow to develop in much of Europe (Haug & Rossler, 1999). It would appear that some of the forces behind deinstitutionalization were not present in other parts of the world. Hudson (2016) makes the point that as compared with the United States, other countries did not engage in "the development of highly institutional systems of mental health care," which proved to be "predictive of deinstitutionalization" (p. 149). A major force that led to deinstitutionalization in the United States was the anti-psychiatric movement (Novella, 2008).

It is also important to note that the United States as well as Europe experienced a gradual shift towards civil libertarianism and the civil rights movement. Moreover, there was an expansion of disability rights. State hospitals were viewed as "Snakepits." In addition, there was a gradual shift towards bioethics and the importance of patient rights.

Many of the actors behind the deinstitutionalization movement were not clinicians; instead, they were often patients, advocates, community advocates and radicals. It is also important to note that many ex-patients provided mutual aid to former patients. The self-help movement also played an important role.

The 1960s and early 1970s were times of great change in the United States; the anti-psychiatry movement flourished in these times of change and a move to the political left (Nasser, 1995). (Some scholars note that the anti-psychiatry movement began in the United States in the 1950s.) Rissmiller and Rissmiller (2006) note,

> Deinstitutionalization in Europe occurred over a decade later … Despite such notable successes and after nearly two decades of prominence, the international anti-psychiatry movement began to dramatically diminish in the early 1980s. Organized psychiatry, by addressing some of the movement's key grievances, was able to defuse it to some degree. (p. 864)

Thus, deinstitutionalization was driven in part by the anti-psychiatry movement and the movement took place earlier in the United States than in Europe. The advent of Thorazine in the 1950s provided policy makers with alleged evidence that people with schizophrenia could be "cured." This assertion proved to be false, but nevertheless, many policy makers seized on it.

EARLY YEARS

An examination of state mental hospitals in the late 1940s showed that many of them were overcrowded and in significant disrepair (Burnham, 2006). Patients were often neglected. While this was true, there was no psychotropic medication and no known treatment for people with SMI. What many policy makers and supporters of deinstitutionalization failed to acknowledge is summed up by Passamanic, Scarpitti, and Dinitz (1967):

> One of the reasons for the 1960s rebellion against the state hospital system as a treatment center derives from the fact that the state hospital system was starved (of financial resources) for so long that it could not innovate very much, attract many capable professionals, or provide much in the way of therapy. (p. 263)

Thus, rather than invest in state hospitals and secure the best mental health professionals that could be found, state governments preferred to close them and save money.

Sutherland (2015) notes that

> This particular wave of deinstitutionalization (referring to the 1960s) occurred during the disillusionment with quality of care in light of increasing awareness for human rights in the 1960s and resulting in changing perceptions of quality of life, patient autonomy and changing government policy. (p. 35)

Sutherland points out further that "Mental patients were viewed as 'guiltless patient-prisoners' trapped within the institutions and separated from broader society" (p. 35). It was with this naive view of mental illness that deinstitutionalization began; the fact that mental illness, particularly SMI with its many challenges and limitations, was overlooked in favor of the notion that simply "freeing" these patients would achieve success. These reformers "Believed that the chronicity of the inflictions plaguing institutionalized patients could simply be prevented earlier, and therefore hospitals would be rendered obsolete" (p. 37).

There was no research analysis to support this; instead, it was simply a belief that the philosophy of deinstitutionalization was true. This naivety was viewed as an "opportunity (by states) to divest themselves of the financial burden of public hospitals" (Chafetz, Goldman, & Taube, 1982–83; Sutherland, 2015, p. 39).

There is no doubt that states did the math and realized that the federal government was going to enable them to achieve significant cost savings (Warner, 1989). Hudson (2019) notes that

> expansion in inpatient psychiatric beds took place between 1840 and 1955, from one per 100,000 population to 338.9 per 100,000. (Calculated from Stroup and Manderscheid, 1988, p. 70)

Hudson (2016) notes further,

> Overall, there has been a median decline of close to one-half percent (0.41%) per year in the availability of psychiatric hospitalizations across the world during the 2000–2014 period. The United States saw an average annual decline of 3.92% continuing the already dramatic declines from 1955 to 2001. (p. 146)

Slate (2017) commenting more about the reduction, points out that "it is estimated that 35,000 people with mental illness are housed in state hospitals in America" (p. 341). This reduction represents a 94 percent reduction in "state hospital patients since the heyday of institutionalization in 1955" (p. 341).

In the United States, the Kennedy-Johnson administrations created Supplemental Social Income (SSI) and accompanying Medicaid. These two programs enabled states to close their state mental hospitals, discharge patients to the community, where they would be provided living expenses through SSI and their medical bills would be paid for by Medicaid. At the time of its development, state government paid 50 percent of the cost of Medicaid and the federal government paid the other 50 percent. Thus, states at first realized significant costs savings by transferring patients to SSI and Medicaid (Bachrach & Lamb, 1989).

Goldman and Morrissey (1985) point out the dramatic reduction in state hospital beds,

> Between 1950 and 1980 for example, the resident population of state mental hospitals was reduced from approximately 560,00 to less than 140,000; admissions to psychiatric inpatient facilities increased dramatically; and outpatient services expanded twelve-fold. (p. 728)

This dramatic reduction in state hospital beds was unfortunately accompanied by what some authors referred to as "transinstitutionalization" in which patients left psychiatric hospitals and went to nursing homes and criminal justice institutions (Primeau et al., 2013).

Oftentimes, the patients sent to nursing homes suffered from dementia (aka, organic brain syndrome). These transfers were made possible because Medicaid paid the bill.

Bachrach (1983) points out that deinstitutionalization is a process in which "It may be understood as a dynamic and continuing series of adjustments involving constant accommodation of all the components of the mental health system" (p. 11). Furthermore, Bachrach observes that

> The philosophy of deinstitutionalization proceeds from at least three fundamental – and largely untested assumptions concerning community care. First, there is an assumption that community mental health is a good thing – that community based care is preferable to institutional care for most, if not all, mental patients. A second underlying assumption is that communities not only can but, are also willing to assume responsibility and leadership in the care of the most seriously ill. And a third assumption regarding deinstitutionalization is that the functions performed by mental hospitals can be equally, if not better performed by community based facilities. (p. 13)

As we look at these assumptions, we need to remember that they were only assumptions. They had not been tested. One of the most important points about these assumptions is that they did not come about through a consensus of policy makers at the federal, state and local level. In fact, policy makers at various levels of government disagreed. For example, there was never agreement about "a social reform ideology" (Bachrach, 1983, p. 14). Many of the people behind the deinstitutionalization movement were committed ideologues who believed that by emptying state hospitals, they had accomplished a "grand idea." They forgot to realize that not everyone was an ideologue and did not view the emptying of state hospitals as achieving a "grand idea." Instead, some policy makers simply wanted to empty state hospitals and close them down to save money. For example, state policy makers, fiscal conservatives, were attempting to save dollars by emptying patients to the community where their care and services could be provided by the federal government through SSI and Medicaid. They did not agree to replace state hospitals with expensive community care.

Primeau et al. (2013) note, "When a community is unable or unwilling to support the mentally ill, the ideals and purpose of deinstitutionalization collapse" (p. 2). While the state hospitals represented a large cost for states, it is important to note that the patient rights movement was also important.

The struggle between the federal government and the states provided a backdrop for the deinstitutionalization movement. The federal government appeared to assume that states would willingly provide funding for comprehensive community care. Unfortunately, states did not see it this way and failed to financially support, for example, community mental health centers.

Lawyers countered the lack of treatment for the mentally ill, which the struggle between the federal government and the states created with a series of court cases. Perlin (2011) argues that Wyatt *v.* Stickney "was the most important institutional rights case in the history of domestic mental disability law" (p. 121). Perlin that this case "spawned copycat litigation in multiple district courts and state superior courts" (p. 121). The case also led to the "creation of a Patient's Bill of Rights in most states" (p. 121). It also led to the Development Disabilities Assistance and Bill of Rights Act and the Mental Health Systems Act Bill of Rights which was not funded and vetoed.

There is no doubt that Wyatt *v.* Stickney did lead to significant changes in mental health law and services in Alabama. However, the "U.S. Supreme Court eventually failed to constitutionalize some of these holdings" (Perlin, 2011, p. 125). Often legal cases are either found unconstitutional or they are not funded or vetoed. Perlin argues that Wyatt "remains powerful to this day" (p. 126). Yes, Wyatt definitely had an impact on many later laws; however, did it force states to fully fund community mental health systems? Unfortunately, the promise of Wyatt was never fully realized and many former patients continued to go without care.

Not everyone agreed with its ideals and purpose. It was a very appealing idea to state legislatures that community care could be cheaper than state hospital care. Both Cramer (1978) and Talbott (1980) observed that the fiscal superiority of deinstitutionalization, in which community programs were thought to be cheaper than state hospitals, was never "firmly established" (Bachrach, 1983, p. 15).

In the early years of the deinstitutionalization, policy makers on the federal level became convinced that the overwhelming majority of people with SMI could live successfully in the community. No experimental research was done showing that this was possible. Instead, policy makers viewed state mental hospitals as warehouses where people with SMI rotted away.

As patient populations were significantly reduced, important elements of caring for people with SMI, such as discharge planning, were overlooked (Belcher, 1999). The appropriate and necessary role of the state hospital was ignored and instead simplistic optimism and cost savings became more important (Belcher & DeForge, 2005). Goldman and Morrissey (1985) note that by "late 1950s and 1960s, institutions and institutional care had become anathema to be avoided at all costs" (p. 728). They note further, "Exposes, sociological treatises, public commissions, and even organized psychiatry deplored asylum conditions and advocated change" (p.728). Slowly, research was beginning to show that this dumping of the SMI resulted in the transfer of patients to other institutional facilities (nursing homes) or the street and jails (Mowbray, Grazier, & Holter, 2002).

It is asserted that deinstitutionalization is controversial. On one hand, some researchers did point out that deinstitutionalization was linked to criminalization (Belcher, 1988; Stelovich, 2006). On the other hand, some researchers pointed out that it was hard to document the link between deinstitutionalization and criminalization (Lamb & Bachrach, 2001). One of the challenges in making the link is that there were very few studies done in which patients from state hospitals were followed into the community. If these patients ended up in jail; the question is, did other intervening factors lead to their incarceration? There were some studies done on individual jails and prisons. A study done in San Mateo County, California, after passage of the Lanterman-Petris-Short Act found "that the arrests of persons with mental illness during this period increased four and one half times" (Slate, 2017, p. 347; Sosowsky, 1980). Scholars, such as Slate and others, based on these studies, made the assertion that "State hospitals downsized or closed, resulting in more persons with mental illness gravitating to the streets and encountering a society and a criminal justice system not equipped to deal with their needs" (p. 347). Again, no direct link was established, but a negative environment was created by deinstitutionalization, which led to criminalization.

A study done in South America examined the link between deinstitutionalization and criminalization. The study examined ten South American countries which had adapted "a Western model of deinstitutionalization" (Mundt et al., 2015). The study found that the majority of patients benefited from deinstitutionalization; however, "the most difficult to treat patients remain inadequately supported and eventually present to other, often inappropriate, institutions (e.g. Acute hospitals or prisons) or end up homeless" (Mundt et al., 2015, p. 116). This finding was called the Penrose hypothesis.

One of the major challenges with deinstitutionalization was that the movement never fully realized the stark difference between chronic versus acute illness. Gruenberg and Archer (1983) noted,

> There are going to be patients who are going to be dependent on psychiatric care for many years; today [this was written in 1983] we cannot predict with confidence whether an individual patient in crisis will restitute quickly or slowly, whether he will restitute almost completely or only partially. And for the restituted patient, we cannot predict whether or when he will relapse. (pp. 30–1)

In part, the deinstitutionalization movement assumed that most, if not all, people with SMI would get better quickly after release from the state hospital and there would be no need for ongoing care. Thus, the deinstitutionalization movement failed to realize the need for long-term care. Research by Gruenberg and Archer showed the importance of a "hospital-based community care service"; they also showed the fact that many communities were resistant to people with SMI.

Gruenberg and Archer (1983) argue that the "crisis of abandonment was paved with good intentions"; however, the fact that the movement failed to recognize the need for the provision of hospital care for many people with chronic SMI borders on neglect. One of the unwritten assumptions underlying deinstitutionalization was that released patients would continue to take their medication. Yet, research began to slowly cast doubt on this assumption as more and more patients' experience in the community showed they were not medication adherent (Barofsky & Connelly, 1983, p. 84). Thus, the rush to deinstitutionalize failed to acknowledge some major challenges. Belcher and Toomey (1988) note,

> First, psychotropic medication does not effectively cure the loss of set and disordered thinking that often results from psychiatric illnesses such as schizophrenia. Second, and this is still true; some mentally ill people need extensive periods in structured environments that facilitate recompensation recovery from acute-flare ups. Third, and this is still true; some mentally ill people decompensate despite regular medication and experience cycles of recompensation and decompensation. Fourth, and this is still true, aftercare in deinstitiutionalization programming is inadequate to meet the overall needs of chronically mentally ill persons. Fifth and this is still true; not all patients can leave the hospital and maintain a level of success in the community and sixth; admission to state mental hospitals for recompensation is impossible in many jurisdictions unless the individual is deemed dangerous to self or others. (p. 146)

These criticisms demonstrate the fact that the majority of the people behind the deinstitutionalization movement were not clinicians, but were often people with no real knowledge of SMI. One of the most obvious challenges is that many non-clinicians did not fully understand the clinical ramifications of schizophrenia. For example, the disordered thinking that often accompanies the illness and leaves the patient in a state of confusion and unable to fend for themselves. The notion that these individuals could live on their own was almost farcical and an oxymoron.

The notion of recompensation is important to examine. When a person with schizophrenia decompensates, which frequently happens (Lang, 2004), they often need some time in a structured and supportive environment to recover (Mojtabai et al., 2009). Moreover, despite medication, many people with SMI will decompensate (Schiffman et al., 2002). Many of these challenges along with premature discharge and poor aftercare planning often led to disaster. Pandiani, Banks, and Schatt (1997) examined data from eight states and found that short community tenure (less than five years) was associated with re-hospitalization. Unfortunately, Belcher and DeForge (2005) note that "poor treatment outcomes were often blamed on people with severe mental illness who were non-compliant and did not follow through with treatment" (p. 19). One result of the need for re-hospitalization was shown by the fact that hospital emergency rooms became overcrowded by people with SMI (Belcher et al., 1995).

The assumption in deinstitutionalization is that these many challenges could be solved by aftercare models. But, as early as the 1970s, aftercare models were proving that they were inadequate (DeForge & Belcher, 2005; Susnick & Belcher, 1995). To be fair, many clients with SMI do not have the ability or capacity to be successful in aftercare programs (Donlon & Becker, 1973).

One of the guiding principles in deinstitutionalization is that of the "least restrictive alternative," which led to commitment laws that were very narrow. While some activists celebrated this narrowness; it proved to be difficult for people with SMI who were unable to care for themselves, but were not dangerous to self or others (Belcher, 1988; Belcher & Blank, 1989).

The past and present failures of deinstitutionalization are summed up by Hudson (2020) who notes,

> Thus, it is clear that increasing community mental health services will not necessarily have an immediate impact in diminishing the need for hospitalization. In fact, such services (particularly the introduction of emergency services) may serve to increase required psychiatric beds. (p. 19)

DEINSTITUTIONALIZATION TODAY

Interestingly, despite the studies and research showing the dramatic failures of deinstitutionalization,

> In 2009 President Obama launched the "Year of Community Living," renewing the commitment to the process of deinstitutionalization and commemorating the 10th anniversary of the Supreme Court decision in Olmstead v. L. C. (1999), which originally codified into the law the process. (U.S. Department of Health and Human Services (USDHHS), 2012. (Segal & Jacobs, 2013, p. 2)

Study after study began to point out that jails and prisons had become new psychiatric institutions for many people with SMI (Kim, 2016; Torrey et al., 2010; White & Whiteford, 2006). Raphel and Stoll (2013) estimate that, between 1950 and 1980, 4 to 7 percent of incarceration rates were due to deinstitutionalization. Police encounters with the SMI began to increase as deinstitutionalization continued to accelerate (Barker, 2013). Homelessness also grew as deinstitutionalization continued (Dear & Wolch, 2014).

Mental health policy seems to be at a crossroads regarding deinstitutionalization; there has been some discussion about bringing back the asylum in response to the criminalization and homelessness of people with SMI (Sisti et al., 2015; Thornicroft et al., 2016). States continue to "downsize" or close state hospital beds with none of these savings being transferred to the community (Lamb & Bachrach, 2001; Thornicroft et al., 2016). States are transferring patients from state hospitals to either general hospitals or public health hospitals which are not subject to the IMD (institute on mental disorder) rule that Medicaid and Medicare can only be paid if the percentage of mentally ill patients is less than 50 percent. When states do this, it represents a kind of cost shifting to Medicare or Medicaid which pay for care in these facilities (general hospitals, public hospitals).

It is important to meet the needs of people with SMI. The debate about deinstitutionalization continues. However, re-hospitalization should not be viewed as an indictment. Instead, state hospitals should continue to provide for short-term hospitalizations.

Not all studies have supported the idea that deinstitutionalization should be stopped; instead, many of the studies that support deinstitutionalization have been done in Europe where governments have transferred monies from hospital closures to the community (Salisbury & Thornicroft, 2016; Taylor et al., 2009).

Certainly, physical environments do make a difference in patient outcome (Dijkstra, Pieterse, & Pruyn, 2006). Moreover, supported employment is also very helpful in the rehabilitation of people with schizophrenia (Lehman et al., 2004). There is a great deal of research that supports community care (Taylor et al., 2009). The real debate, which is often overlooked, is do hospitals have a place in the treatment of people with SMI? There is research supporting the need for hospitals in the treatment of people with schizophrenia (Law et al., 2008).

Thus, it appears that many people with SMI can be successfully treated in the community; however, some people with SMI, particularly with schizophrenia, may need hospitalization at times because of their tendency to not be medication adherent. There is some debate about the ability of people with schizophrenia to be able to live in the community. E. Fuller Torrey would agree that it is often difficult for people with schizophrenia to fully live in the community without some hospitalization. Pat Deegan would disagree. Also, the Vermont longitudinal study shows that people with schizophrenia are able to successfully live in the community. People with SMI need a comprehensive community system as well as a well-functioning hospital. Otherwise, many people with SMI will be neglected and end up becoming homeless and/or criminalized.

Unfortunately, historically and currently, few states in the United states transfer dollars saved from the closing of state hospital beds to the community. Instead, the saved monies are put to use elsewhere in state budgets. Prins (2011) asked a very important question, "Does deinstitutionalization explain the overrepresentation of people with serious mental illness in the criminal justice system?" (p. 716). The answer to this question depends on how one views the deinstitutionalization movement. Again, the movement never sought "consensus" among policy makers and different policy makers at different levels of government came to different opinions on what it meant. Federal policy makers had a "grand vision" to treat people with SMI in the community. However, many state policy makers saw deinstitutionalization as an opportunity to save money. At the time of this writing, there is still no consensus that would agree on the need for a comprehensive community care system.

Under the Constitution of the United States, federal policy makers cannot force state policy makers to fully fund community care. Moreover, it is unlikely that states will decide now, decades after the advent of deinstitutionalization, to fund community care. Thus, while we know clinically that greater community care would be in the best interest of people with SMI, policy makers are not in such agreement. In the final analysis, it comes down to money, which the federal government and state governments continue to debate.

Thus, should we as a nation continue deinstitutionalization? I am not sure because its continuation will most likely result in more criminalization and homelessness for people with SMI. Historically, we have seen that an attempt to move the states in a particular direction has rarely been successful.

CONCLUSION

This chapter has examined deinstitutionalization. Research has shown that the policy of deinstitutionalization has often resulted in negative outcomes for people with SMI, such as homelessness and criminalization. Unfortunately, state policy makers in the United States often saw the opportunity to save money by closing state hospitals and transferring patients to the community. However, states did not often take the savings from the closure of state hospital beds and transfer them to community programs.

Clinically, we know that many people with SMI would be treated better in the community than in the hospital; however, other people with SMI will at times need hospitalization. Thus, it makes little sense to close state hospitals, instead they should be integrated into community care.

REFERENCES

Bachrach, L.L. (1983). Concept and issues in deinstitutionalization. In Ivan Barofsky & Richard D. Budson (Eds.), *The chronic psychiatric patient in the community: Principles of treatment*. New York: SP Medical & Scientific Books, A division of Spectrum Publications, pp. 5–28.
Bachrach, L.L., & Lamb, H.R. (1989). What we have learned from deinstitutionalization. *Psychiatric Annuals, 52*(8), 12–21.

Barker, J. (2013). Police encounters with the mentally ill after deinstitutionalization. *Psychiatric Times,* *30*(1), 1–12.

Barofsky, I., & Connelly, C.E. (1983). Problems in providing effective care for the chronic psychiatric patient. In Ivan Barofsky & Richard D. Budson (Eds.), *The chronic psychiatric patient in the community: Principles of treatment.* New York: SP Medical & Scientific Books, A division of Spectrum Publications, pp. 83–129.

Belcher, J.R. (1988). Are jails replacing the mental health system for the homeless mentally ill. *Community Mental Health Journal, 24,* 185–95.

Belcher, J.R. (1999). *Discharge planning. The working conference on discharge planning.* Presented at the Interagency Work Group on Discharge Planning Coordinated by the Center for Mental Health Services for the Interagency Council on Homeless, Washington, DC.

Belcher, J.R., & Blank, H. (1989). Protecting the right to involuntary commitment. *The Journal of Applied Social Sciences, 14,* 74–88.

Belcher, J.R., & DeForge, B.R. (2005). The longitudinal discharge planning and treatment model (LDPTM) part I. *Social Work in Mental Health, 3*(4), 17–31.

Belcher, J.R., & Toomey, B.G. (1988). Relationship between the deinstitutionalization model, psychiatric disability and homelessness. *Health and Social Work,* 145–53.

Belcher, J.R., DeForge, B.R., Thompson, J.W., & Myers, C.P. (1995). Psychiatric hospital care and changes in insurance strategies: A national study. *Journal of Mental Health Administration, 22,* 377–87.

Burnham, J.C. (2006). A clinical alternative to the public health approach to mental illness: A forgotten social experiment. *Perspectives in Biology & Medicine, 49*(2), 220–37.

Chafetz, L., Godman, H.H., & Taube, C. (1982–83). Deinstitutionalization in the United States. *International Journal of Mental Health, 11*(4), 48–63.

Cramer, P.K. (1978). Report on the current state of deinstitutionalization: Period of retrenchment. *Commentaries on Human Service Issues,* Health and Welfare Council, Philadelphia.

Dear, M.J., & Wolch, R. (2014). *Landscapes of despair: From deinstitutionalization to homelessness.* Princeton Legacy Library.

DeForge, B.R., & Belcher, J.R. (2005). The longtitudinal discharge planning and treatment model (LDPTM): Part 2. *Social Work in Mental Health, 3*(4), 33–61.

Djikstra, K., Pieterse, M., & Pruyn, A. (2006). Physical environmental stimuli that turn healthcare facilities into healing environments through psychological effects: Systematic review. *Journal of Advanced Nursing, 56,* 166–81.

Donlon, P.T., & Becker, K.H. (1973). Stage of schizophrenic decompensation and reintegration. *Journal of Nervous and Mental Disease, 157*(3), 200–9.

Goldman, H.H., & Morrissey, J.P. (1985). The alchemy of mental health policy: Homelessness and the fourth cycle of reform. *American Journal of Public Health, 75*(7), 727–31.

Gruenberg, E.M. & Archer, J. (1983). Preserving chronic patients assets for self-care. In Ivan van Barofsky & Richard D. Budson (Eds.), *The chronic psychiatric patient in the community: Principles of treatment.* New York: SP Medical & Scientific Books, A division of Spectrum Publications (pp. 29–48).

Haug, H., & Rossler, W. (1999). Deinstitutionalization of psychiatric patients in central Europe. *European Archives of Psychiatry and Clinical Neuroscience, 249*(3), 115–22.

Hudson, C.G. (2016). A model of deinstitutionalization of psychiatric care across 161 nations: 2001–2014. *International Journal of Mental Health, 45,* 135–53.

Hudson, C.G. (2019). Deinstitutionalization of mental hospitals and rates of psychiatric disability: An international study. *Health and Place, 56,* 70–9.

Hudson, C.G. (2020). Benchmarking psychiatric deinstitutionalization: Development, testing, and application of a model using predictive analytics. *Best Practices in Mental Health. 2,* 30–45.

Kim, D.Y. (2016). Psychiatric deinstitutionalization and prison population growth: A critical literature review and its implications. *Criminal Justice Policy Review, 27*(1), 3–21.

Lamb, R.H., & Bachrach, L.L. (2001). Some perspectives on deinstitutionalization. *Psychiatric Services,* *52*(8), 1039–45.

Lang, M.V. (2004). *Trends in schizophrenia research.* New York: Nova Science Publisher.

Law, M.R., Soumerai, S.B., Ross-Degnan, D., & Adams, A.S. (2008). A longitudinal study of medication adherence and hospitalization risk in schizophrenia. *Journal of Clinical Psychiatry, 69*(1), 47–53.

Lehman, A. F., Kreybenbuhl, J., Buchann, R.W., et al. (2004). The schizophrenia patient outcomes research team (PORT): Updated treatment recommendations. *Schizophrenia Bulletin, 30*, 193–217.

Mojtabai, R., Fochtmann, L., Chang, S-W., Kotov, R., Craig, T.J., & Bromet, E. (2009). Unmet need for mental health care in schizophrenia: An overview of literature and new data from a first-admission study. *Schizophrenia Bulletin, 35*(4), 679–95.

Mowbray, C.T., Grazier, K.L., & Holter, M. (2002). Managed behavioral health in the public sector: Will it become the third shame of the states? *Psychiatric Services, 26*(3), 157–70.

Mundt, A.P., Chow, W.S., Ardoino, M., et al. (2015). Psychiatric beds and prison populations in South America since 1990. Does the Penrose hypothesis apply? *JAMA Psychiatry, 72*, 112–18.

Nasser, M. (1995). The rise and fall of anti-psychiatry. *Psychiatric Bulletin, 19*, 743–6.

Novella, E.J. (2008). Theoretical accounts on deinstitutionalization and the reform of mental health services: A critical review. *Medicine, Health Care, and Philosophy, 11*(3), 303–14.

Olmstead *v.* L. C. (98-536) 527 U.S. 581 (1999).

Pandiani, J.A., Banks, S.M., & Schatt, L.M. (1997). An examination of variation in long-term community tenure after psychiatric hospitalization in eight states. *Evaluation & The Health Professions, 20*, 131–45.

Passamanic, B., Scarpiti, F.R., & Dinitz, S. (1967). *Schizophrenics in the community: An experimental study in the prevention of hospitalization.* New York: Appleton-Century-Crofts.

Perlin, M.L. (2011). Abandoned love: The impact of *Wyatt v. Stickney* on the intersection between international human rights and domestic mental disability law. *Law & Psychology Review, 35*, 121–42.

Primeau, A., Bowers, T.G., Harrison, M.A., & XuXu (2013). Deinstitutionalization of the mentally ill: Evidence for transinstitutionalization from psychiatric hospitals to penal institutions. *Comprehensive Psychology, 2*(2), 1–10.

Prins, S.J. (2011). Does transinstitutionalization explain the over representation of people with serious mental illness in the criminal justice system. *Community Mental Health Journal, 47*, 716–22.

Raphel, S., & Stoll, M. A. (2013). Assessing the contribution of the deinstitutionalization of the mentally ill to growth in the U.S. incarceration rate. *The Journal of Legal Studies, 42*(1), 187–222.

Rissmiller, D.J., & Rissmiller, J.H. (2006). Evolution of the anti-psychiatry movement into mental health consumerism. *Psychiatric Services, 57*(6), 863–6.

Salisbury, I.T., & Thornicroft, G. (2016). Deinstitutionalization does not increase imprisonment or homelessness. *British Journal of Psychiatry, 157*, 412–3.

Schiffman, J., LaBrie, J., Carter, J., Cannon, T., Schulsinger, F., Parnas, J., & Mednick, S. (2002). Perception of parent-child relationships in high risk families, and adult schizophrenia outcome of offspring. *Journal of Psychiatric Research, 36*(1), 41–7.

Segal, S.P., & Jacobs, L.A. (2013). Deinstitutionalization. In *Encyclopedia of Social Work.* National Association of Social Work and the Oxford University Press.

Sisti, D.A., Segal, A.G., & Emanuel, E.J. (2015). Improving long-term psychiatric care: Bring back the asylum. *Journal of the American Medical Association, 313*, 243–4.

Slate, R. N. (2017). Deinstitutionalization, criminalization of mental illness, and the principle of therapeutic jurisprudence. *Southern California Interdisciplinary Law Journal, 26*(341), 341–56.

Sosowsky, L. (1980). Explaining the increased arrest rate among mental patients: A cautionary note. *American Journal of Psychiatry, 1602, 137*.

Stelovich, S. (2006). From the hospital to the prison: A step forward in deinstitutionalization? *Hospital and Community Psychiatry, 30*(9), 618–20.

Stroup, A. L., & Manderscheid, R.W. (1988). The development of the state mental hospital system in the United States, 1840–1980. *Journal of Washington Academy of Science, 78*(1), 59–68.

Susnick, L., & Belcher, J.R. (1995). The chronically mentally ill in Washington, D.C.: Why are they homeless? *International Journal of Mental Health, 24*, 70–84.

Sutherland, E. (2015). Shifting burdens: The failures of the deinstitutionalization movement from the 1940s to the 1960s in America. *Constellations: History and Classics, Undergraduate Student Journal, 6*(2), 35–42.

Talbot, J.A. (1980). Toward a public policy on the chronically mentally ill patient. *American Journal of Orthopsychiatry, 50*, 45–53.

Taylor, T.L., Kilaspy, H., Wright, C., et al. (2009). A systematic review of the international published literature relating to quality of care for people with longer term health problems. *BMC Psychiatry, 9*, 1–30.

Thornicroft, G., Deb, T., & Henderson, C. (2016). Community mental health care: Current status and further developments. *World Psychiatry, 15*, 276–86.

Torrey, E.F., Kennard, A.D., Eslinger, D., Lamb, R., & Palve, J. (2010). *More mentally ill persons are in jails and prisons than hospitals: A survey of the states.* Treatment Advocacy Center, National Sheriff's Association.

U.S. Department of Health and Human Services (USDHHS). (2012). Serving people with disabilities in the integrated setting: Community living and Olmstead. Retrieved May 7, 2020 from http://www.hhs .gov/ocr/civilrights/understanding/disability/serviceolmstead/index.html

Warner, R. (1989). Deinstitutionalization: How did we get where we are? *Journal of Social Issues, 45*(3), 17–30.

White, P., & Whiteford, H. (2006). Prisons: mental health institutions of the 21st century? *The Medical Journal of Australia, 185*(6), 302–3.

12. Psychiatric rehabilitation and continuity of care
Eva Dragomirecká, Jaap van Weeghel and Ondřej Pěč

In connection with profound changes in the care for people with mental illness in recent decades, psychiatric rehabilitation had become particularly important as a way of helping people with serious psychiatric disabilities to live and work in their communities as independently as possible. The perception of psychiatric rehabilitation gradually evolved from that of a nonessential supplement to biological treatment, through recognition that rehabilitation represents "one of the triumvirate of mental health initiatives: prevention, treatment, and rehabilitation" (Anthony et al., 2002, p. 1) to understanding it as a mental health approach or public health strategy aimed at promoting the human right to full inclusion and effective participation in society (Madianos, 2006; WHO, 1997). Psychiatric rehabilitation can therefore be seen as a procedure different from medical treatment in terms of both its goals and the theoretical models on which it rests. The difference between treatment and rehabilitation was defined as treatment being focused primarily on controlling or "minimizing illness," while rehabilitation interventions are aimed primarily on improving functioning, quality of life, and "maximizing health" (Anthony & Liberman, 1986; Drake et al., 2003).

DEFINITION

The basic elements of psychiatric rehabilitation were formulated 40 years ago. At that time, its goal was formulated as ensuring that persons with a psychiatric disability have the physical, emotional, social, and intellectual skills and abilities needed to live, learn, and work in the community with the least amount of support necessary from agents of the helping professions (Anthony & Liberman, 1986). In parallel, two main paths to this goal were formulated: developing the specific skills a person needs to function effectively and providing the support needed to strengthen that person's level of functioning (Anthony et al., 2002).

Since the 1990s, *psychiatric rehabilitation* has often been replaced by the term *psychosocial rehabilitation*. The terms are used interchangeably. The term "psychosocial" is used to imply the shift from illness to social functioning as stated in the Consensus Statement on Psychosocial Rehabilitation produced by the World Health Organization (WHO) and the World Association for Psychosocial Rehabilitation. The WHO also emphasized the role of the environment when defining psychosocial rehabilitation as "a process that facilitates the opportunities for individuals who are impaired, disabled, or handicapped by a mental disorder to reach their optimal level of independent functioning in the community" (WHO, 1997, p. 78).

Nowadays, psychiatric rehabilitation is often understood in a broader sense, as encompassing more than just a set of specific interventions. It is viewed as a process, a field with a defined set of values, techniques, program practices, and relevant outcomes (Farkas & Anthony, 2010) or as a strategy operating at the interface between an individual, his or her interpersonal network, and the wider social context (Barbato, 2006). In the broadest sense of the term, psychiatric rehabilitation is an approach intended to enhance the emancipation of people with severe mental disorders. Rehabilitation is strongly associated with such notions as hope, perspective, and progress. This reflects a kinship with ideals of the recovery movement (Davidson & Roe, 2007; Deegan, 1988; Slade et al., 2012), since recovery involves the personal processes and efforts of people who are trying to lead a good life, that is, a life not dominated by their illness. The aim of rehabilitation is to help ensure that recovery is also expressed in terms of results related to housing, income, work, as well as daily activities, learning, and social relationships (Van der Meer & Wunderink, 2019).

THE TARGET POPULATION

Psychiatric rehabilitation focuses on people who suffer from a severe mental illness and require a high level of support. Most definitions specify severe mental illness in terms of diagnosis of psychotic or personality disorder, prolonged duration, and marked disability (Anthony et al., 2002; Farkas & Anthony, 2010; Rössler, 2006; Van der Meer & Wunderink, 2019). Ruggeri and colleagues (2000) presented two alternative definitions suited to research into prevalence of severe mental illness: (1) a narrow three-dimensional definition which included (i) a diagnosis of any nonorganic psychosis, (ii) duration of treatment of two years or more, and (iii) a severe psychosocial dysfunction as measured by the Global Assessment of Functioning (GAF $\leq$ 50), and (2) a broader definition based only on the latter two criteria. Research conducted in London and Verona showed that over one-third of patients with a diagnosis of psychosis have a severe mental illness and from the totality of patients who do have a severe mental illness, 40 percent were affected by a nonpsychotic mental disorder, most frequently some personality disorder and alcohol or drug misuse (Ruggeri et al., 2000). In practice, the target group is very heterogeneous regarding their needs and can include people suffering from psychoses, severe affective disorders, personality disorders, addictions, and combinations of any of the above. Regardless of diagnoses, such individuals are substantively limited in their role functioning and can benefit from psychiatric rehabilitation.

Specification of the target group also depends on the main goals of psychiatric rehabilitation: in the process of deinstitutionalization, it was necessary to enable long-term inpatients to return to community life, while in the phase of developed community care, rehabilitation care can be provided to a wider range of people.

THEORETICAL FRAMEWORK

Modern mental healthcare has undergone a fundamental transformation. The Austrian social psychiatrist Heinz Katschnig (1998) succinctly described these changes as follows: "Institutionalization, depersonalization and removal of the psychiatric patients from their social network were the characteristics of asylum psychiatry at the turn of the last century. One hundred years later, deinstitutionalization, personalization and re-insertion of the patient into the community are the declared aims of official mental health policy."

Multidisciplinarity

The practice of psychiatric rehabilitation evolved in tandem with the shift from a biological to a *biopsychosocial model of health*. The definition of health as "a state of complete physical, mental and social wellbeing and not merely the absence of disease or infirmity" implied that mental illness affects not only the biological system, and that the path to health therefore requires interventions in all three of the above-mentioned systems. The stress theory specified the links between the course of an illness and interactions between the affected individuals and their surroundings, which opened room for interventions aimed at modifying various external factors to increase the wellbeing of people with mental health disabilities. The involvement of other disciplines, such as sociology, psychology, special education, and humanistic phi-losophy, led to the adoption of approaches, methods, and values that transcend the narrow focus of biological mental healthcare. The goal of rehabilitation, that is, recovery, has been specified on different levels, from clinical and functional recovery to social, psychological, and personal recovery. The corresponding outcomes include objective criteria (e.g., the number of rehospitalization days, time spent in paid job, or the number of social contacts per week), clinical assessments of symptomatology or indexes of functional impairment, but also subjective outcomes, such as quality of life, life satisfaction, need assessment, recovery scales, self-efficacy, and so on.

Continuity of Care

Bachrach (1981) introduced *continuity of care* as one of the seven main dimensions of care for persons with long-term mental health disorders (continuity of care, individuality, compre-hensiveness, flexibility, familiarity, accessibility, and communication) and specified that the process involves an orderly, uninterrupted movement of patients between the diverse elements of the service delivery system. As Adair et al. (2003) documented in their review, the concept had since the 1980s developed in connection with changes in the delivery of services.

Thornicroft and Tansella (1999) define continuity of care as the ability to provide both coherent interventions within and between care teams (*transversal continuity*) and as an uninterrupted series of contacts over a longer period of time (*longitudinal continuity*). Burns et al. (2009) distinguish even more aspects of continuity of care: subjectively experienced continuity, relational continuity, care coordination (long-term continuity), flexible continuity (tailored to changing care needs), consolidation and well-regulated transitions (cross-border continuity), and sheltered or supported housing (contextual continuity). The different aspects of continuity constitute a strong case for structural cooperation between mental healthcare providers, social service providers, and informal caregivers who care for people with severe mental illness. It is in the best interest of the client that all providers at least take notice of each other's expertise, activities, and working methods. A good tool for this can be Anthony's service outcome model (1993), in which each component shows how the client can benefit from it.

Person-Centered Care

Another important feature of current psychiatric rehabilitation is *person-centered care*, an approach that ensued from a change in the position of the ill in mental healthcare systems.

Patients, who were previously in a passive position and deprived of their usual social roles and choices, gradually became club members, clients, consumers of services, students, and finally people with experience. In addition to training clients to adapt to their environment, the emphasis is now on emancipation, normalization, and participation. Clients are supported in their efforts to restore their social roles, to integrate into the community regardless of disabilities, and to participate in the decision-making process until full autonomy is achieved (Wilken & den Hollander, 2013). The key process for achieving autonomy is empowerment. According to the WHO, empowerment is a process of taking control and responsibility. As such, it has four dimensions, namely, self-reliance, participation in decisions, dignity and respect, and belonging and contributing to a wider community, and can be characterized as referring "to the level of choice, influence and control, that users of mental health services can exercise over events in their lives" (WHO, 2010, p. 2). Active involvement of people with severe mental illness in the rehabilitation process led to a significant broadening and enrichment of the concept of recovery with the dimension of personal recovery.

Recovery-oriented Practice

Since the 1990s, people who experienced a severe mental illness (Davidson & Roe, 2007; Deegan, 1988; Fisher & Carling in Torrey & Wyzik, 2000) described recovery as a unique personal path to a meaningful life in spite of limitations. The term *rehabilitation* means literally restoring of functioning, a return to the pre-illness condition. However, in the case of a serious mental illness this is often not possible, and a person overwhelmed by the illness needs more than learning how to adjust and cope. According to Deegan, the skills and support which people with disabilities receive from the various services refer to successful adapting in the world, that is, to the *world pole*, while the recovery process refers to a *self pole*, "the lived or real-life experience of persons as they accept and overcome the challenge of the disability" (Deegan, 1988, p. 11).

Within the framework of this orientation, recovery is then defined as a personal process of finding the meaning and purpose of an individual experience with aspiration to living a satisfying life that contributes to the lives of others. A shift from despair to a new sense of integrity involves hope, courage, optimism, self-esteem, confidence, self-determination, and a sense of control (Deegan, 1988; Ralph, 2000; Torrey & Wyzik, 2000). Based on subjective reports, Ralph (2000) found four dimensions of personal recovery: recognition of the need to change, self-managed care, support from others, and empowerment. The importance of therapeutic alliance and peer support for recovery has been documented by other researchers (Liberman & Kopelowitz, 2005; Rössler, 2006; Van Weeghel et al., 2019) and summarized by Fisher (2018): "No compliance but alliance."

The principles of recovery have been expressed by an acronym, CHIME. Although the phraseology differs from the above, the importance of the CHIME approach to recovery (Leamy et al., 2011; Slade et al., 2012) is widely recognized (Van Weeghel et al., 2019). According to this framework, the processes relevant to recovery are: Connectedness (peer support, relationships, being part of society), Hope and optimism (motivation, positive thinking, having aspirations), Identity (positive sense of self), Meaning in life (having goals, meaningful living), and Empowerment (being responsible and focusing on strength).

At present, recovery is understood as a philosophy based on the values of self-realization, process of recovering, and outcomes that measure changes in the various aspects of recovery.

All these levels guide a successful rehabilitation practice. Recovery orientation, a term often used in current strategic documents on mental health, refers to the recognition of values of recovery and acceptance of recovery as the core mission of mental health services. The conviction that positive health can coexist with psychopathological symptoms is also anchored in the WHO definition which says that mental health is "a state of well-being in which the individual realizes his or her abilities, can cope with the normal stressors of life, can work productively and fruitfully, and is able to make a contribution to his or her community" (WHO, 2001, p. 1).

REHABILITATION PROGRAM

Hospital-based rehabilitation programs strove to protect patients from the negative effects of institutional care and to train patients in the skills they needed to live independently outside mental institutions. Since deinstitutionalization, a process which started in the 1960s but proceeded at different speed in different parts of the world, various rehabilitation models have emerged to help people live successfully in their communities. The one shared goal of these models was social inclusion.

Models

Psychosocial Clubhouses originated in activities of former patients of the Rockland State Hospital (New York) who founded a self-help club called Fountain House in 1947. Nowadays, the Clubhouse Model of psychosocial rehabilitation has spread all over the world and developed a system of accreditation and training. The program is based on ideas of therapeutic community and democratic decision-making. People with mental illness are referred to as "members" and work together with staff on operation of their club in a continuous, 24/7 fashion. The emphasis is on developing work skills and job opportunities for members and their mutual support. The program is setting-specific, separated from mental healthcare services, and it does not include treatment. The Clubhouse Model exemplifies the rehabilitative potential of transferring power from treatment providers to individuals with mental illnesses.

The *Boston Psychiatric Rehabilitation Approach* (BPR) was developed at Boston University's Center for Psychiatric Rehabilitation by William Anthony and his team. The program is not setting-specific and does not require a particular team composition or an integrated network of services. The emphasis is on supporting and teaching persons with mental illness how to choose, achieve, and keep a preferred role in order to achieve maximum autonomy. The choose–get–keep model of rehabilitation offers, for example, techniques for developing readiness, illness management, or specific interventions for substance misuse issues (Anthony et al., 2002; Farkas & Anthony, 2010). This model has been applied in many countries and its effectiveness has been repeatedly verified (Rogers et al., 2006; Van Busschbach & Wiersma, 2002; Van der Meer & Wunderink, 2019).

In the Netherlands, two multisite randomized controlled trials of this model showed mixed results. The more recent of the trials (Sanches et al., 2020) compared the Boston Psychiatric Rehabilitation Approach with an active control condition and found that clients improved under both sets of conditions. They improved significantly in social participation, quality of life, and social functioning, but the Boston Psychiatric Rehabilitation Approach was not any more effective than the control on any of the outcome measures. These results differ from those of a previous multisite randomized control trial, also conducted in the Netherlands, in which clients participating in the Boston model self-reported that they were more likely to realize their goals and were more successful in promoting social participation than clients who had other forms of counseling (Swildens et al., 2011).

The Program for Social and Independent Living Skills (SILS), developed at the University of California in Los Angeles by Robert Liberman, consists of specific modules with individualized assessment and skill training techniques that can easily be used in different types of services. Within this program, pharmacotherapy and psychiatric rehabilitation are understood as inseparable. A module for disease management (Medication and Symptom Management Module) includes psychoeducation, self-directed use of medication, development of relapse prevention, and an emergency plan (Drake et al., 2003; Liberman, 2006).

The *Case Management* (CM) approach consists of individual work with people with mental illness and focuses on developing formal and informal environmental resources according to a plan based on individual needs. The original idea, which was to link individuals to the services they needed and then coordinate the delivery of services, was extended so as to provide services in the individual's natural environment. This latter model came to be known as *Intensive Case Management* (ICM). It is a recovery-oriented practice aimed at ensuring a continuity of care while working with and relying on individuals' internal and external strengths. The model is tied to the multidisciplinary community team. Part of the case management of people with a high level of disability is assertive intervention. This model, which involves at-home psychiatric care, is known as *Assertive Community Treatment* (ACT). It is based on the Program of Assertive Community Treatment (PACT) designed in the 1970s by Stein and Test (1980) in Wisconsin as a community-based alternative to hospital treatment for persons with a severe mental illness. The Assertive Community Treatment model is classified as an evidence-based intervention with a documented decrease in the length of hospitalization and homelessness rates (Vita & Barlati, 2019). Its effectiveness has been linked to smaller caseloads, regular visits at home, and inclusion of psychiatrists in multidisciplinary teams (Rössler, 2006). While this approach was developed for the most severely ill people with a severe mental illness, its Dutch variant, the *Flexible Assertive Community Treatment* (FACT), is intended for all people with a severe mental illness in an area. Multidisciplinary community teams switch between the "normal" mode of care for people who are currently stable (individual case management with home visits) and an intensive mode for people in a worse mental health condition (Van Veldhuizen, 2007). Research studies comparing Assertive Community Treatment and Flexible Assertive Community Treatment have so far shown mixed results (Drukker et al., 2013; Nordén & Norlander, 2014; Nugter et al., 2016).

The chief objective of the *Comprehensive Approach to Rehabilitation* (CARe) approach was to improve the quality of life of persons with mental illness. To this end, it adopted three guiding principles: identification of clients' needs, teaching them to cope with their vulnerability, and improving the quality of the social environment. Priority is assigned to clients' goals; in case a client does not formulate any goals, the initiative rests with the care provider. This approach has been strongly influenced by the recovery movement, the presence approach, and the "strengths model" of case management. The results of a cluster of randomized control trials on the Comprehensive Approach to Rehabilitation were published in 2017 (Bitter et al., 2017). The study was conducted in organizations for sheltered and supported housing ($N = 263$). Teams in the intervention group were trained in the comprehensive approach, while teams in the control group continued to work as usual. The quality of life improved in both groups and no differences were found between the two settings. The study also found no differences in recovery or social functioning, and the number of unfulfilled needs for care decreased equally in both groups. No significant differences were found with regard to hope, empowerment, or the clients' confidence in their own abilities (Bitter et al., 2017).

Respect for the autonomy of people with a severe mental illness and their active engagement is emphasized in the *Active Recovery Triad* (ART) model developed for mental health inpatient facilities and supported housing. Active, recovery-oriented process gives people with a severe mental illness more autonomy through cooperation between the subjects, their families or friends, and the staff (Van der Meer & Wunderink, 2019; Zomer et al., 2020).

The *Resource Group* (RG) method builds upon the traditions of family intervention and integrated care. It is an effective way of establishing and maintaining continuity of care by providing a structure to ensure that family, friends, and caregivers remain fully involved in routine services, thus becoming collaborative partners in the recovery process. An RG includes individuals from the client's informal and formal networks and meets quarterly in order to discuss the patient's recovery goals and to jointly develop a plan for achieving them. By being part of an RG, significant others acquire skills to contribute to the goals and attention is paid to their needs and the burden they cope with as well as those of the client. Because the RG method places clients in the position of directors of their RGs, they are encouraged to assume command of shaping the support that meets their needs and aspirations. The origins of the RG method lie in the optimal treatment model, which integrates biomedical, psychological, and social strategies in the management of severe mental illness (Nordén & Norlander, 2014).

A randomized clinical trial carried out in the Netherlands (Tjaden et al., 2021) documented the effectiveness of the FACT approach combined with the RG compared with FACT as it is commonly used for improving empowerment and other psychosocial outcomes. In Sweden, the optimal treatment model was further developed into an RG Assertive Community Treatment (RACT) (Nordén & Norlander, 2014). A meta-analysis showed outcomes in favor of RACT for patients with psychosis with respect to social functioning, wellbeing, and symptoms (Nordén et al., 2012).

Interventions

The main domains of psychiatric rehabilitation are housing, work, education, relationships, and community participation. Farkas and Anthony (2010) suggested a categorization of interventions, or their elements based on the choose–get–keep process. The choosing phase includes building partnership between the provider and the client, motivational techniques, a sense of connection (such as in clubhouses), and psychoeducation or peer support. The getting phase consists of interventions focused on reduction of the stigma and improvement of opportunities, for example, via job development services. The keeping phase involves skill development interventions, cognitive remediation training, and a range of support interventions.

Since evidence-based practice is one of the core values of psychiatric rehabilitation, interventions can be evaluated based on scientific evidence, where a hierarchy of reliability goes from randomized controlled trials to observational or longitudinal studies to single case studies. Interventions are then categorized as evidence-based practice, experience-based practice, promising practice, or emerging methods (Farkas & Anthony, 2010; Pathak & Chaturvedi, 2015).

Several reviews have shown that the following interventions can be considered evidence-based practice for people with a severe mental illness in the sense that their effectiveness has been demonstrated in randomized controlled trials: Assertive Community Treatment (Bond & Drake, 2015), family psychoeducation (Sin & Norman, 2013), illness self-management training (Lean et al., 2019; Mueser et al., 2002), integrated dual diagnosis treatment (Kikkert et al., 2018), social skill training (Kurtz & Mueser, 2008; Turner et al., 2018), supported employment (Modini et al., 2016; Mueser et al., 2016), and supported housing (Harrison et al., 2020). There are also a number of good-quality randomized controlled trials on recovery-based interventions (Van Weeghel et al., 2019).

Individuals with severe mental illnesses often experience problems in cognitive functioning. Augmentation of psychiatric rehabilitation methods with elements of cognitive training may therefore further improve the outcomes. This suggestion has been confirmed by recent systematic reviews and meta-analyses focused on combinations of psychiatric rehabilitation with cognitive remediation (McGurk et al., 2007; Penadés et al., 2012; Van Duin et al., 2019). These studies had shown that augmentation of psychiatric rehabilitation with cognitive training significantly improved clients' employment rate, hours worked, quality of performance at work or in the education process, and social skills.

One of the best-researched evidence-based interventions is *Individual Placement and Support* (IPS), which focuses on helping clients find regular jobs or educational programs. Initial evidence on its effectiveness came from several studies conducted in the United States, with later studies coming from other countries, including the Netherlands (Bond et al., 2020; Michon et al., 2014). The core of this approach incorporates the following principles: client's preferences regarding work are decisive, quick search for the desired job ("first place, then train"), integration of mental health services and vocational guidance, and long-term support, including support from employers (Becker & Drake, 1994).

Still, psychiatric rehabilitation has its specifics which need to be taken into consideration when evaluating any kind of interventions. For instance, Mueser et al. (2002) pointed out that the results of effectiveness studies also depend on whether they focus on proximal outcomes closely related to the intervention, such as increasing knowledge about illness in psychoeducation, or on more distant outcomes, such as quality of life or reduced disability score. Moreover, identification of effective components can be complicated in the case of comprehensive programs where clients use various partial interventions as needed.

Farkas (2006, p. 161) spoke of value-based medicine as a twin concept to evidence-based medicine which respects the importance of a service recipient's perception of relevance of an intervention. It must be taken into account that this need not conform to the strict requirements of randomized clinical trials for assessing psychosocial intervention and the rehabilitation model.

Liberman referred to another important issue. The Individual Support and Placement Approach is the best evidence-based service for vocational rehabilitation but not all people with a severe mental illness are capable of participating in it. They still need other options, such as transitional employment or rehabilitation in day treatment centers (Liberman, 2006, p. 158). There are, moreover, ethical barriers to be considered in implementing randomized controlled trials when appropriate treatment as usual is not available for the control group.

RESEARCH BASE FOR PSYCHIATRIC REHABILITATION

Research findings have significantly contributed to the development of psychiatric rehabilitation by challenging the long-established therapeutic pessimism regarding schizophrenia. The assumption that schizophrenia necessarily has an unfavorable prognosis was contradicted by reports of documented improvement in long-term follow-up studies.

Longitudinal Studies of Schizophrenia

The outcome and course of a serious mental illness, mainly schizophrenia, has been investigated in longitudinal studies carried out in Germany (Huber at al., 1975; Marneros et al., 1992), Switzerland (Bleuler, 1978; Ciompi & Müller, 1976), and the United States (Breier et al., 1992; DeSisto et al., 1995; Harding et al., 1987). These studies produced varied outcomes, with the proportion of participants assessed as recovered or significantly improved ranging between 21 percent and 68 percent (Hopper et al., 2007, p. 35).

The most favorable results were described in a Vermont-based study (Harding et al., 1987) which found that inpatients from the Vermont State Hospital who had been provided with a comprehensive rehabilitation program achieved, after a 32-year-follow-up, significantly better functional and symptomatic outcomes than control inpatients in traditional care from a Maine sample (DeSisto et al., 1995).

The results of longitudinal studies show that the course of schizophrenia is not uniformly adverse, the degree of disability in patients varies in different areas of life, and rehabilitation programs can significantly improve functioning in the community even for people with severe symptoms of psychotic illness who have been hospitalized for a long time. On the other hand, the results were difficult to compare and generalize due to the inconsistent design of these studies. These methodological limitations were later overcome in international studies of schizophrenia organized by the WHO.

From 1967 to 1993, the WHO carried out a set of studies that involved over 20 research centers. The goal of the initial study was to determine whether the diagnostic entity "schizophrenia" exists in different parts of the world and whether the course of schizophrenia differs between countries. The results showed that using standardized criteria, schizophrenia can be found in all cultures. An unexpected and controversial finding was that patients in countries outside Europe and United States have a more favorable short- and medium-term course of the disease than patients in the developed countries do (Hopper et al., 2007; Sartorius et al., 1996).

Outcomes of a 25-year and a 15-year longitudinal cohort studies of multisite samples showed that over one-half of participants were assessed as "recovered." Nearly half experienced no psychotic episodes in the past two years and over half (three-quarters) worked in a paid job or household during this period (Harding, 2003, pp. 19–41; Hopper et al., 2007, pp. 27–8). Hopper et al. (2007, p. 37) pointed to the "mixed nature of recovery" demonstrated by the fact that over 20 percent of participants were able to work regularly despite persisting symptoms and disabilities. He concluded that symptoms, functioning, and social performance are relatively autonomous domains which require targeted interventions in treatment progress.

These results confirmed the differing outcomes and varying degrees of disability in different areas of patients' lives and highlighted the need for long-term support from community mental healthcare with interventions designed for specific domains.

PSYCHIATRIC REHABILITATION IN THE CZECH REPUBLIC

Basic Data about the Czech Republic

The territory of present-day Czech Republic is located in Central Europe and was historically part of multinational unions such as the Holy Roman Empire, the Austrian Empire, the Austro-Hungarian Monarchy, and most recently, Czechoslovakia, an independent democratic republic, that was established after the First World War (1918). As such, it existed until its occupation by Nazi Germany at the beginning of the Second World War. After the war, Czechoslovakia came under Soviet influence (1948), which lasted for four decades, until 1989, when the Communist government resigned, and democracy was restored. In 1993, Czechoslovakia split into a Czech Republic and a Slovak Republic. In 2004, the Czech Republic became a member state of the European Union (EU).

Development of Community Mental Healthcare

Until the mid-twentieth century, the development of psychiatric care and approaches to the mentally ill in principle did not differ from other European countries. The establishment of a totalitarian regime with a centralized economy and severe restrictions on democratic rights between 1948 and 1989 had fundamentally affected post-war development of mental healthcare compared with European countries with unbroken democratic traditions.

In the late 1980s, mental healthcare was provided exclusively by the health sector and there were hardly any community-based forms of care except for a network of outpatient psychiatric departments focused mainly on prescribing medications. It was only after 1990 that psychiatric rehabilitation began to develop in terms of overall support aimed at enabling people with severe mental disorders to integrate into society. The situation in Eastern European countries after the breakdown of the Soviet Bloc has been described elsewhere. Most briefly, let us just note that it was characterized by underfinancing of mental healthcare, reliance on institutional care, prevalence of the biological model, low cooperation between healthcare and social care systems, disempowerment of service users, and a high level of stigmatization (Alexa et al., 2015; Dlouhy, 2014; Höschl, Winkler, & Pěč, 2012; Hudson & Dragomirecka, 2019; Krupchanka & Winkler, 2016; Rössler & Drake, 2018). The Czech Republic had moreover a long tradition of large psychiatric institutions, with the highest average number of beds per institution in all EU countries (Dobiášová et al., 2016).

Over the past three decades, psychiatric rehabilitation was transformed from a nonessential occupational therapy to an important instrument of achieving independence and improving the quality of life of people with mental illness. Thanks to professional guidance from abroad, Czech psychosocial rehabilitation services are recovery-oriented and tend to apply the Dutch Flexible Assertive Community Treatment (FACT) model and the Individual Placement and Support (IPS) model for employment. Examples of rehabilitation programs provided in different types of facilities are presented in Table 12.1.

While community facilities offer a wide range of recovery-oriented rehabilitation interventions, inpatient rehabilitation care is changing relatively slowly. As an example, let us take the Bohnice Mental Hospital, the largest mental institution in the Czech Republic. In recent years, the hospital has opened to the outside world and cooperates closely with community services. Despite these efforts, the quality of psychiatric care in the Czech Republic is low, as shown

Table 12.1   Psychiatric rehabilitation interventions by type of facility

	Activities	Examples of interventions/programs
Mental hospital (MH) Bohnice, Prague[a]	• Living and social skill training • Cognitive training • Art therapeutic activities • Vocational activities and training • Recreational activities • Psychoeducation • Counseling • Peer support	Training of skills for independent living; 1–3-month stay in training apartments in mental health ward prior to discharge; everyday community sessions, individual planning based on need assessment (CANSAS), semi-structured day schedule
Day Hospital "Karlov," Prague[b]	• Aftercare and stabilization • Illness management • Lifestyle training • Cognitive training • Social skills training • Support with setting rehabilitation plan • Crises management	Wellness program; group program for physical health improvement consists of ten sessions; includes lifestyle education, both theoretical and practical including diet and exercise
ESET, Psychotherapeutic and Psychosomatic Clinic[c]	• Day treatment programs • Group psychotherapy • Individual psychotherapy • Occupational therapy • Mental health center • Home visits by psychiatric nurses	Day treatment program for patients with psychosis: a daily psychotherapeutic program in a half-opened group of 6–8 patients for nine months; 7.5 hours weekly of group psychodynamic psychotherapy; 2.5 hours of cognitive remediation; 1 hour of training of social competence; 1 hour of art therapy, 5 hours of practical training (shopping, cooking), 1 hour of occupational therapy, and half an hour of physical exercises
Focus Praha, NGO provider of community care[d]	• Case management • Housing (sheltered and supported housing) • Supported employment or study • Counseling and advocacy • Educational and training activities • Recreational activities • Illness and crisis management • Self-help activities and peer support	Community field teams operating in Prague districts; case management, support of independent living in the community based on respectful partnership and empowerment, advocacy, counseling, coordination of services

Notes:
a. Retrieved January 12, 2022, from https://bohnice.cz/lecba/centrum-krizove-intervence-a-resocializace/
b. Retrieved January 12, 2022, from https://psychiatrie.lf1.cuni.cz/denni-stacionar-pro-dospele
c. Retrieved January 12, 2022, from https://www.klinikaeset.cz/
d . Retrieved January 12, 2022, from https://www.fokus-praha.cz/

in a study which evaluated 12 psychiatric hospitals in the Czech Republic using the Quality Indicator for Rehabilitative Care (QuIRC). The results showed a low level of quality of care (< 50 percent) in all seven dimensions of care quality, with the lowest scores in the dimensions of self-management and autonomy and recovery-based practice (Kalisova et al., 2018).

Community mental healthcare in the Czech Republic is in many aspects similar to other Central and Eastern European countries (Dlouhy, 2014; Krupchanka & Winkler, 2016; Rössler, 2016; Winkler et al., 2017). Despite remarkable changes, a balance between community and hospital-based mental health services has not yet been achieved. Moreover, high-quality services which developed thanks to the enthusiasm of engaged individuals and organizations with support from international bodies often struggle with sustainability and integration into the general mental health system dominated by state-owned mental hospitals.

It seems that the current reform of psychiatric care which started in 2017 could overcome some of these limitations. Its aim is to complement the existing psychiatric inpatient facilities and outpatient departments with a network of community-based multidisciplinary mental health centers. These would provide systematic and comprehensive support to people with a serious mental illness because they would operate under both health and social sectors. The main services provided by them would include mobile case management, crisis interventions, and daycare services (MHCR, 2013; Pěč, 2019).

CONCLUSION

Since the turn of the century, literature on rehabilitation has substantially improved. The aim of psychiatric rehabilitation is clear: to enable full participation in society for as many clients as possible. This ambition has a variety of backgrounds, including deinstitutionalization, the rise of evidence-based treatment, the mission of the recovery movement, general societal expectations (living as independently as possible, with emphasis on participation) and socio-cultural trends ("People should be able to realize their dreams").

The target group has also gradually changed, which brings new tasks to rehabilitation programs. Rehabilitation now extends to various subgroups, such as young people with a history of multiple suicide attempts, persons with severe mental illness and substance abuse problems, homeless people, members of cultural minorities, or impoverished elderly with both physical and psychiatric disabilities.

Still, rehabilitation interventions or, more broadly, social interventions tend to have a low priority within mental healthcare services. This is also the case in British mental healthcare, leading Johnson (2017) to note that "the social" is the neglected child in the family of bio-psychosocial psychiatry.

We need to pay more attention to the implementation gap, that is, to the vast difference between what has been proven effective and its application in practice. Ensuring proper implementation and safeguarding of rehabilitation interventions will require a substantial investment in a clear, broadly supported vision, a project leader, a well-considered action plan, involvement of both internal and external collaborative partners, arranging for the necessary financial and organizational conditions, monitoring the progress and results, and integration of innovations in all the relevant team and organizational working processes (Van Duin et al., 2013).

It would also be wise not to implement rehabilitation solely as an independent working form. It would be better to collaborate closely with existing models of care and development which bring together large amounts of energy and try to create a suitable place for rehabilitation within them. This will require large investment in the growth points of the existing system of care for serious mental illness, including Flexible Assertive Community Treatment (FACT), Resource Groups, Peer-supported Open Dialogue (POD), Active Recovery in the Triad (ART), sheltered and supported housing, community teams, and recovery colleges.

More research should focus on finding effective interventions to combat stigmatization and self-stigmatization, and on ways of promoting social relations and activities other than just paid employment. In research, meaningful daily activities and unpaid work have so far received less attention than paid employment but many individuals with severe mental illnesses have goals in these areas. Setting and achieving personal goals has been identified as an important predictor of the quality of life. Moreover, goals are essential for experiencing life as meaningful and worthwhile.

Randomized controlled trials in rehabilitative research often yield ambiguous results and may not be the most suitable approach to assessing these types of interventions. When it comes to complex multicomponent approaches such as rehabilitative approaches, randomized controlled trials provide no information on which combination of elements is responsible for outcome and under what conditions. In the light of increasing demand of tailored care, methods investigating what works for whom may be particularly interesting. Adding a process evaluation to randomized controlled trials may be a good approach to gaining valuable insights on the implementation, reception, and setting of interventions.

ACKNOWLEDGEMENTS

The work was supported by the European Regional Development Fund Project "Creativity and Adaptability as Conditions of the Success of Europe in an Interrelated World" (No. CZ.02.1. 01/0.0/0.0/16_019/0000734).

We would like to thank Anna Pilátová, Ph.D., for proofreading and editing the manuscript.

REFERENCES

Adair, C.E., McDougall, G.M., Beckie, A., Joyce, A., Mitton, C., Wild, C.T. et al. (2003). History and measurement of continuity of care in mental health services and evidence of its role in outcomes. *Psychiatric Services*, *54*(10), 1351–6.

Alexa, J., Rečka, L., Votápková, J., van Ginneken, E., Spranger, A., & Wittenbecher, F. (2015). Czech Republic: Health system review. *Health Systems in Transition*, *17*(1).

Anthony, W. (1993). Recovery from mental illness: The guiding vision of the mental health system in the 1990s. *Psychosocial Rehabilitation Journal*, *16*(4), 11–23.

Anthony, W.A., & Liberman, R.P. (1986). The practice of psychiatric rehabilitation: Historical, conceptual, and research base. *Schizophrenia Bulletin*, *12*(4), 542–59.

Anthony, W., Cohen, M., Farkas, M., & Gagne, Ch. (2002). *Psychiatric rehabilitation*. Boston, MA: Center for Psychiatric Rehabilitation, Boston University.

Bachrach, L.L. (1981). Continuity of care for chronic mental patients: A conceptual analysis. *The American Journal of Psychiatry*, *138*(11), 1449–56.

Barbato, A. (2006). Psychosocial rehabilitation and severe mental disorders: A public health approach. *World Psychiatry*, *5*(3), 162–3.

Becker, D.R., & Drake, R.E. (1994). Individual placement and support: A community mental health center approach to vocational rehabilitation. *Community Mental Health Journal*, *30*(2), 193–206.

Bitter, N., Roeg, D., Van Assen, M., Van Nieuwenhuizen, C., & Van Weeghel, J. (2017). How effective is the comprehensive approach to rehabilitation (CARe) methodology? A cluster randomized controlled trial. *BMC Psychiatry*, *17*(1), 1–11.

Bleuler, M. (1978). *Long-term patient and family studies*. New Haven, CT: Yale University Press.

Bond, G.R., & Drake, R.E. (2015). The critical ingredients of assertive community treatment. *World Psychiatry*, *14*(2), 240.

Bond, G.R., Lockett, H., & Van Weeghel, J. (2020). International growth of individual placement and support. *Epidemiology and Psychiatric Sciences, 29*(e183), 1–3.

Breier, A., Schreiber, J.L., Dyer, J., & Pickar, D. (1992). Course of illness and predictors of outcome in chronic schizophrenia: Implications for pathophysiology. *The British Journal of Psychiatry, 161*(S18), 38–43.

Burns, T., Catty, J., White, S., Clement, S., Ellis, G. Jones, I.R. et al. (2009). Continuity of care in mental health: Understanding and measuring a complex phenomenon. *Psychological Medicine, 39*, 313–23.

Ciompi, L., & Müller, C. (1976). Lifestyle and age of schizophrenics. A catamnestic long-term study into old age. *Monographien aus dem Gesamtgebiete der Psychiatrie, 12*, 1–242.

Davidson, L., & Roe, D. (2007). Recovery from versus recovery in serious mental illness: One strategy for lessening confusion plaguing recovery. *Journal of Mental Health, 16*(4), 459–70.

Deegan, P.E. (1988). Recovery: The lived experience of rehabilitation. *Psychosocial Rehabilitation Journal, 11*(4), 11–19.

DeSisto, M.J., Harding, C.M., McCormick, R.V., Ashikaga, T., & Brooks, G.W. (1995). The Maine and Vermont three-decade studies of serious mental illness. I. Matched comparison of cross-sectional outcome. *British Journal of Psychiatry, 167*(3), 331–42.

Dlouhy, M. (2014). Mental health policy in Eastern Europe: A comparative analysis of seven mental health systems. *BMC Health Services Research, 14*(1), 42.

Dobiášová, K., Tušková, E., Hanušová, P., Angelovská, O., & Ježková, M. (2016). The development of mental health policies in the Czech Republic and Slovak Republic since 1989. *Central European Journal of Public Policy, 10*(1), 35–46.

Drake, R.E., Green, A.I., Mueser, K.T., & Goldman, H.H. (2003). The history of community mental health treatment and rehabilitation for persons with severe mental illness. *Community Mental Health Journal, 39*(5), 427–40.

Drukker, M., Visser, E., Sytema, S., & Van Os, J. (2013). Flexible assertive community treatment, severity of symptoms and psychiatric health service use, a real-life observational study. *Clinical Practice and Epidemiology in Mental Health, 9*, 202–9.

Farkas, M. (2006). Identifying psychiatric rehabilitation interventions: An evidence and value based practice. *World Psychiatry, 5*(3), 161–2.

Farkas, M., & Anthony, WA. (2010). Psychiatric rehabilitation interventions: A review. *International Review of Psychiatry, 22*(2), 114–29.

Fisher, D.B. (2018). *Heartbeats of hope: An empowerment way to recovery your life.* Keynote presentation in XXXV Social Psychiatry Conference, November 15–17, 2018, Loucna (the Czech Republic).

Harding, C.M. (2003). Changes in schizophrenia across time: Paradoxes, patterns, and predictors. In C.I. Cohen (Ed.), *Schizophrenia into later life: Treatment, research, and policy* (pp. 19–41). Washington, DC: American Psychiatric Publishing.

Harding, C.M., Brooks, G.W., Ashikaga, T., Strauss, J.S., & Breier, A. (1987). The Vermont Longitudinal Study of Persons with Severe Mental Illness. *American Journal of Psychiatry, 144*(6), 718–35.

Harrison, M., Singh Roy, A., Hultqvist, J., Pan, A.W., McCartney, D., McGuire, N. et al. (2020). Quality of life outcomes for people with serious mental illness living in supported accommodation: Systematic review and meta-analysis. *Social Psychiatry and Psychiatric Epidemiology, 55*, 977–88.

Hopper, K., Harrison, G., Janca, A., & Sartorius, N. (2007). *Recovery from schizophrenia: An international perspective.* Oxford: Oxford University Press.

Höschl, C., Winkler, P., & Pěč, O. (2012). The state of psychiatry in the Czech Republic. *International Review of Psychiatry, 24*(4), 278–85.

Huber, G., Gross, G., & Schüttler, R. (1975). A long-term follow-up study of schizophrenia: Psychiatric course of illness and prognosis. *Acta Psychiatrica Scandinavica, 52*(1), 49–57.

Hudson, C.G., & Dragomirecka, E. (2019). Decision making in psychiatric reform: A case study of the Czech experience. *Central European Journal of Public Policy, 13*(2), 15–27.

Johnson, S. (2017). Social interventions in mental health: A call to action. *Social Psychiatry and Psychiatric Epidemiology, 52*, 245–7.

Kalisova, L., Pav, M., Winkler, P., Michalec, J., & Killaspy, H. (2018). Quality of care in long-term care departments in mental health facilities across the Czech Republic. *The European Journal of Public Health, 28*(5), 885–90.

Katschnig, H. (1998). Quality of life for patients in the community. *European Psychiatry, 13*(S4), 180.

Kikkert, M., Goudriaan, A., De Waal, M., Peen, J., & Dekker, J. (2018). Effectiveness of integrated dual diagnosis treatment (IDDT) in severe mental illness outpatients with a co-occurring substance use disorder. *Journal of Substance Abuse Treatment, 95*, 35–42.

Krupchanka, S., & Winkler, P. (2016). State of mental healthcare systems in Eastern Europe: Do we really understand what is going on? *BJPsych International, 13*(4), 96–9.

Kurtz, M.M., & Mueser, K.T. (2008). A meta-analysis of controlled research on social skills training for schizophrenia. *Journal of Consulting and Clinical Psychology, 76*(3), 491.

Leamy, M., Bird, V., Boutillier, C., Williams, J., & Slade, M. (2011). Conceptual framework for personal recovery in mental health: Systematic review and narrative synthesis. *The British Journal of Psychiatry, 199*(6), 445–52.

Lean, M., Fornells-Ambrojo, M., Milton, A., Lloyd-Evans, B., Harrison-Stewart, B., Yesufu-Udechuku, A. et al. (2019). Self-management interventions for people with severe mental illness: Systematic review and meta-analysis. *The British Journal of Psychiatry, 214*(5), 260–8.

Liberman, R.P. (2006). Caveats for psychiatric rehabilitation. *World Psychiatry, 5*(3), 158–9.

Liberman, R.P., & Kopelowicz, A. (2005). Recovery from schizophrenia: A concept in search of research. *Psychiatric Services, 56*(6), 735–42.

Madianos, M.G. (2006). Psychiatric rehabilitation in the era of globalization. *World Psychiatry, 5*(3), 163–4.

Marneros, A., Deister, A., & Rohde, A. (1992). Comparison of long-term outcome of schizophrenic, affective and schizoaffective disorders. *The British Journal of Psychiatry, 161*(S18), 44–51.

McGurk, S.R., Twamley, E.W., Sitzer, D.I., McHugo, G.J., & Mueser, K.T. (2007). A meta-analysis of cognitive remediation in schizophrenia. *American Journal of Psychiatry, 164*(12), 1791–802.

MHCR. (2013). *Strategie reformy psychiatrické péče* [Strategy for the Reform of Psychiatric Care]. Ministry of Health of the Czech Republic.

Michon, H., Van Busschbach, J.T., Stant, A.D., Van Vugt, M.D., Van Weeghel, J., & Kroon, H. (2014). Effectiveness of individual placement and support for people with severe mental illness in The Netherlands: A 30-month randomized controlled trial. *Psychiatric Rehabilitation Journal, 37*(2), 129–36.

Modini, M., Tan, L., Brinchmann, B., Wang, M. J., Killackey, E., Glozier, N. et al. (2016). Supported employment for people with severe mental illness: Systematic review and meta-analysis of the international evidence. *The British Journal of Psychiatry, 209*(1), 14–22.

Mueser, K.T., Corrigan, P.W., Hilton, D.W., Tanzman, B., Schaub, A., Gingerich, S. et al. (2002). Illness management and recovery: A review of the research. *Psychiatric Services, 53*(10), 1272–84.

Mueser, K.T., Drake, R.E., & Bond, G.R. (2016). Recent advances in supported employment for people with serious mental illness. *Current Opinion in Psychiatry, 29*(3), 196–201.

Nordén, T., & Norlander, T. (2014). Absence of positive results for flexible assertive community treatment. What is the next approach? *Clinical Practice and Epidemiology in Mental Health, 10*, 87.

Nordén, T., Malm, U., & Norlander, T. (2012). Resource group assertive community treatment (RACT) as a tool of empowerment for clients with severe mental illness: A meta-analysis. *Clinical Practice and Epidemiology in Ment Health, 8*, 144–51.

Nugter, M.A., Engelsbel, F., Bähler, M., Keet, R., & Van Veldhuizen, R. (2016). Outcomes of FLEXIBLE assertive community treatment (FACT) implementation: A prospective real-life study. *Community Mental Health Journal, 52*(8), 898–907.

Pathak, A., & Chaturvedi, S.K. (2015). A systematic review of interventions in psychiatric rehabilitation. *International Journal of Medical Investigation, 4*(3), 272–81.

Pěč, O. (2019). Mental health reform in the Czech Republic. *BJPsych International, 16*(1), 4–6.

Penadés, R., Catalán, R., Pujol, N., Masana, G., García-Rizo, C., & Bernardo, M. (2012). The integration of cognitive remediation therapy into the whole psychosocial rehabilitation process: An evidence-based and person-centered approach. *Rehabilitation Research and Practice*.

Ralph, R.O. (2000). Review of recovery literature: A synthesis of a sample of recovery literature. *National Association for State Mental Health Program Directors (NASMHPD)*.

Rogers, E.S., Anthony, W.A., & Farkas, M. (2006). The choose-get-keep model of psychiatric rehabilitation: A synopsis of recent studies. *Rehabilitation Psychology, 51*(3), 247.

Rössler, W. (2006). Psychiatric rehabilitation today: An overview. *World Psychiatry, 5*(3), 151–7.

Rössler, W. & Drake, R.E. (2018). Psychiatric rehabilitation in Europe. *Epidemiology and Psychiatric Sciences, 26*, 216–22.

Ruggeri, M., Leese M., Thornicroft G., Bisoffi G., & Tansella M. (2000). Definition and prevalence of severe and persistent mental illness. *British Journal of Psychiatry, 177*, 149–55.

Sanches, S., Swildens, W., Schaefer, B., Moerbeek, M., Feenstra, T., Van Asselt, A. et al. (2020). Effectiveness of the Boston University approach to psychiatric rehabilitation in people with severe mental illness: A randomized controlled trial. *Frontiers in Psychiatry, 11*, 970.

Sartorius, N., Gulbinat, W., Harrison, G., Laska, E., & Siegel, C. (1996). Long-term follow-up of schizophrenia in 16 countries: A description of the International Study of Schizophrenia conducted by the World Health Organization. *Social Psychiatry and Psychiatric Epidemiology, 31*, 249–58.

Sin, J., & Norman, I. (2013). Psychoeducational interventions for family members of people with schizophrenia: A mixed-method systematic review. *The Journal of Clinical Psychiatry, 74*(12), e1145-62. doi: 10.4088/JCP.12r08308

Slade, M., Williams, J., Bird, V., Leamy, M., & Le Boutillier, C. (2012). Recovery grows up. *Journal of Mental Health, 21*(2), 99–103.

Stein, L.I., & Test, M.A. (1980). Alternative to mental hospital treatment. I. Conceptual model, treatment program, and clinical evaluation. *Archives of General Psychiatry, 37*(4), 392–7.

Swildens, W., Van Busschbach, J.T., Michon, H., Kroon, H., Koeter, M.W., Wiersma, D., & Van Os, J. (2011). Effectively working on rehabilitation goals: 24-month outcome of a randomized controlled trial of the Boston psychiatric rehabilitation approach. *Canadian Journal of Psychiatry. Revue Canadienne De Psychiatrie, 56*(12), 751–60.

Thornicroft, G., & Tansella, M. (1999). Translating ethical principles into outcome measures for mental health services research. *Psychological Medicine, 29*, 761–7.

Tjaden, C., Mulder, C.L., Den Hollander, W., Castelein, S., Delespaul, P., Keet, R. et al. (2021). Effectiveness of resource groups for improving empowerment, quality of life, and functioning of people with severe mental illness: A randomized clinical trial. *JAMA Psychiatry, 78*(12), 1309–18.

Torrey, W.C., & Wyzik, P. (2000). Recovery vision as a service improvement guide for community mental health center providers. *Community Mental Health Journal, 36*(2), 209–16.

Turner, D.T., McGlanaghy, E., Cuijpers, P., Van Der Gaag, M., Karyotaki, E., & MacBeth, A. (2018). A meta-analysis of social skills training and related interventions for psychosis. *Schizophrenia Bulletin, 44*(3), 475–91.

Van Busschbach, J., & Wiersma, D. (2002). Does rehabilitation meet the needs of care and improve the quality of life of patients with schizophrenia or other chronic mental disorders? *Community Mental Health Journal, 38*(1), 61–70.

Van der Meer, L., & Wunderink, C. (2019). Contemporary approaches in mental health rehabilitation. *Epidemiology and Psychiatric Sciences, 28*, 9–14.

Van Duin, D., Franx, G., van Wijngaarden, B., van der Gaag, M., van Weeghel, J., Slooff, C., Wensing, M. (2013). Bridging the science-to-service gap in schizophrenia care in the Netherlands: the Schizophrenia Quality Improvement Collaborative. International Journal of Quality in Healthcare 25(6), 626–632.

Van Duin, D., de Winter, L., Oud, M., Kroon, H., Veling, W., & Van Weeghel, J. (2019). The effect of rehabilitation combined with cognitive remediation on functioning in persons with severe mental illness: Systematic review and meta-analysis. *Psychological Medicine, 49*(9), 1414–25.

Van Veldhuizen, J.R. (2007). FACT: A Dutch version of ACT. *Community Mental Health Journal, 43*(4), 421–33.

Van Weeghel, J., Zelst, C. Van, Boertien, D., & Hasson-Ohayon, I. (2019). Conceptualizations, assessments and implications of personal recovery from mental illness: A scoping review of systematic reviews and meta-analyses. *Psychiatric Rehabilitation Journal, 42*(2), 169–81.

Vita, A., & Barlati, S. (2019). The implementation of evidence-based psychiatric rehabilitation: Challenges and opportunities for mental health services. *Frontiers in Psychiatry, 10*, 147.

WHO. (1997). Psychosocial rehabilitation: A consensus statement. *International Journal of Mental Health, 26*(2), 77–85.

WHO. (2001). *Strengthening mental health promotion*. Geneva: World Health Organization.

WHO. (2010). *User empowerment in mental health – a statement by the WHO Regional Office for Europe*. Copenhagen: WHO Regional Office for Europe.

Wilken, J.P., & den Hollander, D. (2013). *Rehabilitation and recovery: A comprehensive approach.* Uitgeverij SWP.

Winkler, P., Krupchanka, D., Roberts, T., Kondratova, L., Machů, V., Höschl, C. et al. (2017). A blind spot on the global mental health map: A scoping review of 25 years' development of mental health care for people with severe mental illness in central and eastern Europe. *The Lancet Psychiatry, 4*(9), e19.

Zomer, L.J., Voskes, Y., Van Weeghel, J., Widdershoven, G.A., Van Mierlo, T.F., Berkvens, B.S. et al. (2020). The Active Recovery Triad Model: A new approach in Dutch long-term mental health care. *Frontiers in Psychiatry,* 11.

PART IV

COUNTRY AND REGIONAL STUDIES

13. Australia. Good intentions – reviewing 30 years of mental health policy reform

Sebastian Rosenberg and Luis Salvador-Carulla

There needs to be greater accountability and visibility in reporting progress in implementing the new national approach to mental health services. Currently mental health data collection is inconsistent and would not be adequate to enable an assessment to be made of the relative stage of development of the Commonwealth and each State/Territory Government in achieving the objectives outlined in the National mental health policy. It is essential that such a consistent system of monitoring and accountability be created.

National Mental Health Policy, Commonwealth of Australia (1992)

The year 2022 marks 30 years since Australia's first National Mental Health Strategy, which included a policy and a plan. This strategy set Australia on a course to shut the old psychiatric institutions and "mainstream" mental health care.

Some achievements are clear and worthy of reflection. However, the trajectory of this reform has been far from straightforward. The past three decades have seen mental health in Australia subject to multiple reforms and overlapping policy goals. Key commitments to establish meaningful accountability for progress remain unfulfilled, leaving us outcome blind. Evidence of the impact of change is thin.

This chapter traces this history, across two national mental health policies, five national mental health plans, one national action plan, several other national documents, one roadmap and multiple statutory inquiries. There is merit in this kind of narrative review on the evolution of health systems (Greenhalgh et al., 2018). While perhaps lacking some of the protocol-based rigor of systematic reviews, narrative reviews such as this provide interpretation and critique of existing literature, deepening understanding and providing a synthesis of published literature to describe its current state-of-art (Pae, 2015).

Federal, state and territory governments have signed bilateral Mental Health and Suicide Prevention Agreements, in effect Australia's sixth national mental health plan.

Understanding Australia's historical approach to mental health planning can inform next steps and help drive the development of more robust processes designed to deliver national accountability. Australia's national approach to mental health reform offers lessons for other nations, for example in relation to the planning process, accountability and reporting on progress.

Of particular importance here is the need for better approaches to local or regional planning, supported by systems of accountability that facilitate quality improvement. This chapter describes some of the steps already taken in Australia (and elsewhere) to develop this new decision-support infrastructure and drive the next stage of mental health reform.

Table 13.1   Timeline of key mental health policies and plans

Year	Document
1992	First National Mental Health Strategy (and Policy)
1993–98	First National Mental Health Plan
1994	First National Mental Health Report
1995–2013	National Mental Health Report Series – 11 editions purporting to measure progress
1995	First Report on Government Services (ROGS) (Productivity Commission)
1997	Evaluation of the First National Mental Health Plan
1997	First National Survey of Mental Health and Wellbeing (Australian Bureau of Statistics)
1998–2003	Second National Mental Health Plan
2001	First Mental Health Services in Australia report (Australian Institute of Health and Welfare)
2001	International Mid-Term Review of the Second National Mental Health Plan
2003	Evaluation of the Second National Mental Health Plan
2003–08	Third National Mental Health Plan
2005	National Mental Health Report (9th)
2005	First National Mental Health Performance Framework
2006–11	Council of Australian Governments' (CoAG) National Action Plan on Mental Health
2007	Second National Survey of Mental Health and Wellbeing (Australian Bureau of Statistics)
2008	Evaluation of the Third National Mental Health Plan
2009	Second National Mental Health Policy
2009–14	Fourth National Mental Health Plan
2009	National Advisory Council on Mental Health
2010	Fourth National Mental Health Plan Implementation Strategy
2011	Fourth National Mental Health Plan Measurement Strategy
2012–22	Council of Australian Governments' (CoAG) National Roadmap for Mental Health Reform
2012	First National Report Card – A Contributing Life (National Mental Health Commission)
2014	National Mental Health Commission Review – Contributing Lives, Thriving Communities
2015	Australian Government Response to National Commission Review
2017	Fifth National Mental Health and Suicide Prevention Plan
2020	Productivity Commission Report into Mental Health
2020	National mental health and wellbeing pandemic response plan (Australian Government)
2020	CoAG process disbanded in favor of National Cabinet
2021	Victorian Royal Commission into mental health
2021	Prevention, Compassion, Care – National Mental Health and Suicide Prevention Plan
2021	National Child Mental Health and Wellbeing Strategy

METHOD

Key documents, policies, plans and strategies are reviewed in relation to the evolution of national mental health policy. Historical documents are cited. Table 13.1 provides a timeline of 30 years of key national mental health policies, plans and papers in Australia.

An initial $135 million investment made by the federal government to sponsor reform and under the First Plan was not repeated in subsquent plans (Whiteford, 1994). This meant each state and territory jurisdiction needed to find their own resources to implement change. This has never been easy, particularly when there are ceaseless demands being made on existing mental health services.

In addition to this plethora of papers, there would be few areas of public endeavor more investigated than mental health. In response to repeated concerns about safety and quality, there were 32 separate statutory, parliamentary or other inquiries into mental health between

2006 and 2012 alone (Mendoza et al., 2013). The findings of these inquiries typically characterize the Australian mental health system as being "in crisis."

Australia's health system operates in the context of our federal political system, which splits responsibility for health care. Simplistically, the federal (national) government is responsible for primary care, principally provided through our public health insurer, Medicare. The eight state and territorial jurisdictions are responsible for the provision of hospital-based services – inpatient and outpatient mental health care. National agreement-making, including in mental health, requires consensus across governments (Smullen, 2016). This chapter considers the strengths and weaknesses of Australia's approach, including implications arising from our federated system of government.

While this chapter focuses on national mental health reforms, it should be noted that much of this activity is then mirrored in each of the jurisdictions. Practically, this has meant that Australia ends up with nine mental health plans, or suicide prevention plans, or plans to improvement the social and emotional wellbeing of Indigenous peoples, and so on. This chapter also considers some of these jurisdictional plans. It is a curious feature of Australia's federated system of government that each state and territory has significant autonomy over its health policy and spending. The plans described here can be developed without approval from the federal government. On one hand this makes these documents more likely to reflect local needs and circumstances. On the other hand, it makes the task of identifying and fulfilling national priorities and goals more difficult.

One of the recurring themes of these reports has been the lack of independent, systematic evaluation of progress (Productivity Commission, 2020). The first two national plans were subject to evaluation and the third, a "summative" evaluation. But no other evaluation has occurred of either later plans or the reform process as a whole. More than $5 billion was spent on mental health under the CoAG National Action Plan, the impact of which has never been evaluated. We do not know the cost of the recent inquiries into mental health conducted by the Productivity Commission and the Victorian Royal Commissions, but it is likely to run to tens of millions of dollars. The impact of all this planning, inquiring and effort is unevaluated and unknown. This kind of evaluation is not simple. There is no agreed on, international set of indicators against which to evaluate Australia's performance.

While efforts to develop such indicators are gaining some momentum (http://unitedgmh .org/), they remain at a developmental level at best (Peitz et al., 2021). This kind of systemic assessment is also hampered by the partial view often afforded by the mental health indicators traditionally used which, at best, often focus on inputs and outputs of the health system and fail to properly reflect the broader mental health "ecosystem" (Furst, Bagheri, & Salvador-Carulla, 2021). Understanding budget trends and bed numbers is not unimportant. For example, the Australian Institute of Health and Welfare (AIHW) report that mental health represented 7.25 percent of total health expenditure in 1992–93, rising to 7.48 percent in 2018–19 (the latest year available) (AIHW, 2021a). The first National Mental Health Policy (Commonwealth of Australia, 1992) recognized that stigma against mental illness had led to a maldistribution of health resources. With mental illness representing around 12 percent of the burden of disease in Australia, the extent to which this stigma has been overcome is questionable (AIHW, 2021b).

Existing health focused data sets also fail to report on the matters of topmost concern to consumers and their families – such as stable housing, employment, education and social participation. This leaves any evaluation rather limited by the scope of the data available and limits opportunities for organizational learning.

On this basis, there is merit in focusing our attention on the original 1992 National Mental Health Policy, to explore the extent to which progress has been made against its stated goals. This chapter sets out evidence regarding Australia's progress on reform, against each of the key elements listed in the contents page under "Policies."

CONSUMER RIGHTS

The 1992 policy was innovative by world standards, placing strong emphasis on the rights of consumers. This was partly in response to repeated inquiries which had reported sub-standard care or even human rights abuses in Australia's long-term psychiatric institutions (Burdekin, 1993; Richmond, 1983). A key goal of the Policy was to support de-institutionalization across Australia. Again, the extent to which this has been successful is mixed. In 2018–19, Australia was still spending $580 million on 1,606 beds in psychiatric specialist hospitals, leaving the overall goal of "mainstreaming" mental health services incomplete.

The key agreement reached by all nine Australian governments in 1992 was to establish a National Community Advisory Group (NCAG) to be the voice of consumers and carers in the process of mental health reform. The NCAG recognized two key things: the powerlessness and human rights abuse often experienced by consumers and their families; and the intrinsic merit of drawing on lived experience to help drive reform.

The NCAG began in 1993. It was supposed to be supported by other CAG bodies established in each jurisdiction. However, the NCAG itself was disbanded by the federal government in 1996. Some of the jurisdictional CAGs also folded quickly but others staggered on (see here for example https://being.org.au/our-history/). Overall, the consumer and carer sector has not been provided with the resources necessary to build a sustainable, durable pool of expertise that can help drive national mental health reform. It remains a largely untapped resource. Despite some progress (AIHW, 2021c, d), Australia still lacks a national, validated collection of the experience of care. The data that is collected is not associated with any discernible process of service quality improvement.

Many consumers now focus their advocacy on the goal of establishing a peer workforce (Health Workforce Australia, 2014). This may address the woeful unemployment situation facing many people with mental illness (Rosenberg & Hickie, 2019a). It does not equip consumers with the skills and resources necessary to participate in systemic mental health planning.

Engaging mental health stakeholder groups, professionals, consumers, carers and academics in this planning would build understanding about the process and confidence in the results (Zabell et al., 2021). But so far, Australian mental health planning processes have largely been determined by bureaucrats working in federal and state governments.

The benefits of broadening this process have been recognized (Productivity Commission, 2020). Consumers and carers themselves have identified how far they are from being able to participate as skilled equals in co-design of mental health reform and will require considerable development (National Mental Health Consumer and Carer Forum, 2021).

With formal, organizational structures to enable co-design almost non-existent in Australia, the capacity of consumers and carers to meaningfully participate in detailed future planning about mental health is not evident. In relation to consumer rights involving services, one notable development has been the approach taken in Victoria to the establishment of its Mental Health Complaints Commissioner (https://www.mhcc.vic.gov.au). Several other Australian jurisdictions have established new mental health commissions over the past decade. With some variation, these new organizations have generally aimed at driving system-wide mental health reforms, through better services, more funding and so on (Rosen, Goldbloom, & McGeorge, 2010). Victoria's approach differed, in that it established its new commission specifically to identify and gather individual experiences and stories from consumers of mental health services, and then use these to look for patterns, trends, and engage with individual services about improvements. None of Australia's seven mental health commissions have been formally evaluated (Rosenberg & Rosen, 2012). However, Victoria's unique approach of using complaints to drive reform and uphold consumer rights may yet prove the most effective of them all.

THE RELATIONSHIP BETWEEN MENTAL HEALTH SERVICES AND THE GENERAL HEALTH SECTOR

Inequitable access to health care and related services for people with a mental illness manifest in various ways in Australia, including reduced average life expectancy (Roberts et al., 2018). In 2017, the National Mental Health Commission led the establishment of an initiative called Equally Well (2021), designed to improve the relationship between mental health services and the general health sector. While this problem persists, evidence of the impact of Equally Well is not yet available.

In recognition of the work Australia must do in relation to the health and welfare of its Indigenous peoples, the Australian Government established the "Closing the Gap" strategy (Closing the Gap, 2021), which provides regular reports on a very limited number of indicators to demonstrate progress towards equity in health outcomes with the general community. Despite a similar gap applying, there is no such overall strategy in relation to the general health of people with a mental illness in Australia. Even in areas of common overlap, for example the interface between mental health care and addictions, unhelpful divisions between services and practitioners prevent integration and foster poor quality care (Barrett, 2019). The general health of people with a mental illness in Australia remains a key area for future reform.

LINKING MENTAL HEALTH SERVICES WITH OTHER SECTORS

The 4th National Mental Health Plan (Department of Health, 2009) was in effect from 2009–14 and recognized the fundamental link between good mental health care and the social determinants of health. It sought to link health, housing, employment, education, justice and other areas into a broad discussion about how such linkages might be achieved. It is no coincidence perhaps that the National Mental Health Commission, established initially under the Department of Prime Minister and Cabinet (PM&C), published its "Contributing Life, Thriving Communities" framework during 4th Plan (2014).

However, by the 5th Plan (National Mental Health Commission, 2017), the Commission had been shifted out of PM&C into the Department of Health and the 5th Plan had narrowed its focus to health services. Links between sectors require the active engagement of the states and territories, given their role in the provision not just of health but also of related services such as drug and alcohol, housing, justice and education. While there are some exceptions (Rosenberg, Hickie, & Lawrence, 2021), in most cases government agencies and departments still operate as silos, with separate funding and reporting requirements.

And the same is true in relations between federally funded primary care and state hospital services. Recommendations from repeated inquiries (Productivity Commission, 2020) have called for joint planning, funding, commissioning and reporting. However, a profoundly unhelpful demarcation has emerged whereby the federal government has become associated with providing the care and treatment of high prevalence disorders such as depression and anxiety, while the states and territories respond to lower prevalence illnesses such as schizophrenia and bipolar disorder. With separate funding and separate clients, there seems little motivation for joint action. It is not clear whether the 4th Plan's goal of a more integrated approach to mental health care becomes part of the next phase of Australia's mental health reforms.

SERVICE MIX

As stated, one of the original premises underpinning the Strategy was to shift mental health care from long-term institutions to other settings. Despite this goal, the continued expenditure on beds in institutional settings has been noted earlier. But there is little doubt that "mainstreaming" has occurred, to the extent this means focusing the provision of mental health care in general public hospitals. Half of total spending on mental health in Australia was directed to psychiatric institutions at the start of the Strategy in 1992–93. This decreased to less than 10 percent by 2018–19. The vast majority of spending in Australia on mental health is now directed through inpatient or outpatient activity at general hospitals. We estimate that around 4 in every 5 dollars on mental health care is now directed towards hospital-based care.

What is demonstrated is that despite evidence supporting a balanced approach to mental health sector growth, with a prominent role for the community mental health sector, this model has failed to emerge in Australia (Rosenberg & Harvey, 2021). The community mental health teams, or assertive community outreach teams which characterized some of the key developments of mental health care in Australia during the 1980s and 1990s have largely retreated from the high street to the hospital campus (Rosen, Gill, & Salvador-Carulla, 2020). What is labeled "community care" is now often provided as an outpatient clinic on a hospital site. Psychosocial services, typically provided by non-government organizations (NGOs) in Australia were always a peripheral element of funding. They were 2 percent of total mental health funding in 1992 and were less than 6.5 percent in 2018–19. In New Zealand, by contrast, there are 240 NGO provider organisations that deliver 33.5 percent of all funded mental health services (Platform Trust, 2020). This provides many more community-based mental health service options than are available in Australia. The implications of Australia's failure go broader than the health system, with some suggesting that the psychiatric institution was merely replaced by public hospitals, and also by jails (White & Whiteford, 2006).

Australia has responded to evidence regarding the importance of structuring mental health care to meet needs as they emerge, particularly among adolescents. On this basis, led by a former Australian of the Year Professor, Patrick McGorry, Australia now has a network of more than 100 youth mental health centers. These "headspace" centers have been an important shift in the service mix. However, headspace has been affected by both patient waiting times (Rickwood et al., 2015) and workforce gaps impacting the model of care (Hilferty et al., 2016).

Recent inquiries have criticized state and federal governments for a lack of coordination, leading to gaps and duplication in services (Productivity Commission, 2020). A recent example of how this confusion continues involves community mental health centers. As a result of the recent Royal Commission Inquiry in Victoria, that state's government has committed to the establishment of several new adult and child community mental health centres (State of Victoria, 2021a). At the same time, but in response to the Productivity Commission inquiry, the federal government committed nearly $0.5 billion towards new adult "Head to Health" community centers (Australian Government, 2021b). There is no apparent coordination between these Victorian and federal initiatives.

PROMOTION AND PREVENTION

In accordance with the initial policy, the early days of the National Mental Health Strategy saw Australia invest in greater understanding of the role that promotion and prevention can play in effectively addressing mental illness in the community and lessening the burden of these issues on the health and welfare system (Commonwealth Department of Health and Aged Care, 2000). However, the Senate of the Australian Parliament in a 2006 inquiry (Australian Senate, 2006) not only found that resourcing in mental health was inadequate overall, but it was also overwhelmingly directed towards treatment for later stages of major mental disorders rather than prevention. Despite good evidence to justify this shift (Productivity Commission, 2020), successive National Mental Health Strategies have failed to fundamentally alter this balance, with states and territories struggling to manage ever rising demand for emergency and acute mental health care (Musker, 2021). The Productivity Commission (2020) estimates that activities focusing on promotion and prevention account for less than $0.5 billion of the $11.3 billion they identify as total expenditure on mental health in 2018–19. The National Mental Health Strategy has not driven a systemic shift towards promotion and earlier intervention overall, with perhaps the exception being in relation to headspace youth mental health centers (as discussed earlier).

PRIMARY CARE SERVICES

Established by the Australian Government as the key component of its contribution to the Council of Australian Government's (CoAG) National Action Plan on Mental Health in 2006 was the Better Access Program (Australian Government, 2021a). This Program saw the inclusion of services provided by psychologists included under Medicare, Australia's national public health insurance program. Importantly, access to these services was, at least initially, dependent on planning and review by general practitioners in primary care. The idea was that coordination of care, including both physical and mental health issues, could be managed by this group. Figure 13.1 demonstrates the colossal and largely uninterrupted growth of the program since its introduction.

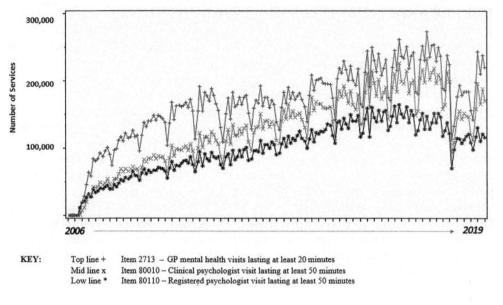

KEY: Top line + Item 2713 – GP mental health visits lasting at least 20 minutes
Mid line x Item 80010 – Clinical psychologist visit lasting at least 50 minutes
Low line * Item 80110 – Registered psychologist visit lasting at least 50 minutes

Source: Services Australia Medicare Item Reports.

Figure 13.1   Medicare Better Access Program 2006–19

The recent, evident, COVID-inspired dip in the graph has been compensated with other like services, particularly those provided via telehealth. In 2019–20, around 9.4 million services were provided to Australians by general practitioners and psychologists for mental health-related presentations at a cost of more than $900 million. Figure 13.1 shows the three main Medicare services provided:

1. Item 2713 – GP mental health visit lasting at least 20 minutes (top line).
2. Item 80010 – Clinical psychologist visit lasting at least 50 minutes (middle line).
3. Item 80110 – Registered psychologist visit lasting at least 50 minutes (low line).

The Better Access Program has only been evaluated once (Pirkis et al., 2011) and has been subject to various critiques (Jorm, 2019; Meadows et al., 2015; Rosenberg & Hickie. 2019b). Perhaps most significant in terms of the relationship between mental health and the general health sector, however, has been the failure of the Better Access Program in relation to accountability.

The predecessor to Better Access, called Better Outcomes, was a much smaller program and required the general practitioner to review each patient following their psychological interventions to trigger payment to the health professionals (Hickie & Groom, 2002). This mandatory review was removed under Better Access, from 2006. As a result, according to Medicare statistics, only half the mental health plans written by GPs are reviewed using the intended item. Doctors may monitor their patients in other ways, but from a systemic point of view, accountability is diminished.

CARERS AND NON-GOVERNMENT ORGANIZATIONS

Australia still relies very heavily on a medical model of mental health care, focusing on the role of clinical services. Other psychosocial services typically provided by NGOs and designed to help people with a mental illness live well in the community represented 2 percent of total mental health spending by the states and territories in 1992–93 and 6.5 percent in 2018–19. Neglect of the psychosocial sector deprives people with a mental illness of vocational support, educational opportunities, living skills and social connection. It also prevents psychosocial care from working as an effective partner to clinical care, reinforcing the latter and its associated medical model as the main, or only, form of treatment available to people in Australia seeking mental health care. A welcome change which has occurred over the life of the Strategy has been the establishment of legislation in each jurisdiction setting out the rights of mental health carers (Mental Health Carers NSW, 2021). Replicated in most jurisdictions, carers legislation is designed to strengthen the roles of carers/family members and involve them in the treatment and recovery of mental health consumers. While this change has been positive, as with consumer organizations (see earlier), funding for carer advocacy bodies has not been provided making it difficult for this voice to be heard in policy discussions.

MENTAL HEALTH WORKFORCE

Australia's last national mental health workforce strategy was published in 2010. This is despite repeated inquiries finding shortages of key professionals and maldistribution. Rural and remote mental health services struggle to operate at all, let alone provide quality (Royal Australian College of General Practitioners, 2018). There is no standard approach to measuring workforce needs, though this capacity is emerging (Furst, Salinas-Perez et al., 2021).

The way the workforce operates is affected by how it is paid. To a very great extent, Australia relies on payment systems, such as a fee for service, which discourage the multidisciplinary mental health care many people require (Hickie & McGorry, 2007). There are examples of sophisticated approaches to multidisciplinary training in other countries (see New Zealand for example, here https://www.tepou.co.nz/).

The impact of this lack of workforce organization, perpetuated by problematic models of funding, is role confusion and misallocation of resources (Australian Senate, 2006; Productivity Commission, 2020). The federal government has established a Taskforce to develop a Workforce Strategy, but long-term disorganization has perpetuated national problems in mental health service allocation and delivery. It should also be noted that unlike other countries, Australia has been very slow to adopt a model of peer support as a core element of our national mental health workforce, despite good evidence of the merits of such an approach (National Mental Health Commission, 2021a).

LEGISLATION

The 1992 Strategy acknowledged the benefits to consumers and their families that would arise from having consistent design and application of laws relating to mental health care across state and territory borders. Without mutual recognition of mental health orders, the capacity for states and territories to ensure seamless and safe care for individuals moving across borders is compromised (Productivity Commission, 2020). This has proved impossible. Australia continues to operate with eight different Mental Health Acts (Department of Health, 2021). From time to time, states have established bilateral agreements of mutual recognition of respective mental health laws. But these have been at best temporary arrangements.

In general, people's rights under the law still depend on where they live, meaning consumer experiences can vary significantly. This is not like other areas of health care. The inability of successive five-year national mental health plans, running from 1993 to 2015, to deal with this issue has been highlighted as emblematic of the limited effectiveness of Australia's mental health reform process (Productivity Commission, 2020).

RESEARCH AND EVALUATION

Funding for mental health research has been recognized as woefully inadequate both in Australia (Batterham et al., 2016) and internationally (Patel, 2020). This significantly hinders the evolution of new services and treatments, perpetuating pressure on existing services. The federal government's spending on research was 1.5 percent of total mental health expenditure in 1992–93, at the start of the Strategy. By 2018–19, it was 2.4 percent. The trend for expenditure on research was in decline between 2014 and 2019.

In terms of evaluation, recent reports have highlighted Australia's failure to establish an "evaluation culture," meaning most mental health programs and services are unevaluated or poorly evaluated (Productivity Commission, 2020). This leaves Australia vulnerable to waste and unable to identify the services or programs most likely to have a positive impact on people's lives. Australia has operated without a national strategy to guide and prioritize mental health research. The National Mental Health Commission is undertaking work to fill this gap now (National Mental Health Commission, 2021b).

STANDARDS

National Standards for Mental Health Services were first developed in 1996 and then a second edition produced in 2010 (Department of Health, 2010). The extent to which services adhere to these standards is now reported annually, as part of the Australia's overall system of accountability (Productivity Commission, 2021). In 2018–19, 95.8 percent of all services were assessed as meeting Level 2 of these Standards, with the remaining 4.2 percent at Level 1. However, this apparent success story does not tally with the repeated and contemporary stories of mistreatment and sub-standard quality of care reported by consumers and their families in repeated inquiries (State of Victoria, 2021b) and in the media (Australian Broadcasting Commission, 2018).

The process of developing the 2010 Standards was described as unclear and "diluted" (Miller et al., 2009). However, the disconnect between the very high rates of organizational compliance and the everyday reality for many consumers in the services they use illustrates the very limited utility of the Standards as a driver of systemic quality improvement in Australian mental health care. There have been calls to overhaul the process of standards accreditation (Duggan et al., 2020).

As part of executing the National Strategy, Australia has also invested around $50 million in establishing the Health of the Nation Outcome Score (HoNOS) reporting system (Australian Mental Health Outcomes and Classification Network, 2021). This instrument permits clinicians to rate the treatment outcomes of their patients in different mental health service settings, inpatients, outpatients and community care. This data has become part of regular national reporting on mental health care as part of the National Outcomes and Casemix Collection. However, and like the Standards, this data does not drive benchmarking or quality improvement (Productivity Commission, 2020).

MONITORING AND ACCOUNTABILITY

The 1992 National Mental Health Strategy, which included an overarching policy and a plan, had data and accountability at its heart. The 1997 Evaluation of the first national mental health plan, while noting the role of the National Mental Health Report, stated:

> Information in mental health is grossly undeveloped. The lack of nationally comparable data on service outputs, costs, quality and outcomes places major limitations on the extent to which the National Mental Health Strategy can achieve its objectives. (National Mental Health Strategy Evaluation Steering Committee, 1997)

A decade later, the "summative" evaluation of the 3rd National Mental Health Plan (2003–08) repeated concerns about national monitoring and reporting mechanisms, suggesting there was duplication, waste and an inability to measure appropriate outcome measures (Curie & Thornicroft, 2008).

The 4th National Mental Health Plan promised a "whole of government approach" so that:

> The public is able to make informed judgements about the extent of mental health reform in Australia, including the progress of the fourth plan, and has confidence in the information available to make these judgements. Consumers and carers have access to information about the performance of services responsible for their care across the range of health quality domains and are able to compare these to national benchmarks. (Department of Health, 2009)

These concerns about data and accountability processes in mental health were echoed in repeated statutory reports and inquiries, one of which found:

> The National Mental Health Strategy was developed over a decade ago to respond to obvious service failures and human rights concerns … we do not yet have a national process for translating the policy rhetoric into real increases in resources, enhanced service access, accepted service standards or service accountability. (Mental Health Council of Australia, 2005)

Unfortunately, and as affirmed by the Productivity Commission (2020) recently, this is perhaps the most significant failing of Australia's National Mental Health Strategy. Despite it being a core initial reform promise, Australian mental health remains largely outcome blind (Crosbie, 2009).

CONCLUSION

This chapter has provided a summary of progress against each of the key reform areas identi-fied in Australia's 1992 National Mental Health Reform Strategy. The story is mixed at best. There were broad aspirations with good intentions. Commitments to better accountability were made. Some additional resources provided to facilitate change and reform at the start of the process were discontinued. New plans emerged and the focus of mental health reforms shifted, seeking to consider issues beyond the health system.

Plans, reports, inquiries and recommendations appear very frequently. They overlap and confuse, rather than provide helpful guidance. An initial clarity of purpose in the Strategy has been lost. Key structures to enable the vibrant engagement of consumers, carers and the workforce would advance the evolution of the Strategy but have failed to emerge. The data infrastructure to support regular, independent monitoring and accountability for progress in mental health care is still largely absent. This is especially so in relation to data from outside the health system. There is no validated, national collection of the experience of care for mental health consumers and carers. No system of quality improvement in mental health services is identifiable.

The new National Mental Health and Suicide Prevention bilaterial Agreements between Australia's nine governments have been developed using the bureaucratic processes which have guided past plans and strategies, in isolation from people working in the mental health sector or using services.

COVID-19 has shed new light on the fragility of Australia's mental health service system. Telehealth services have been put in place as a response to the pandemic, providing some new evidence that it is possible to reverse Australia's hospital-centric approach to mental health care (Rosenberg et al., 2020). We have shown a capacity to do things differently.

A key consistent theme of current reports and recommendations is that mental health plan-ning in Australia must shift from historic, centralized approaches to more local or regional models of governance and decision-making (Productivity Commission, 2020).

There are new decision-support systems which can enable this local planning and mode-ling, but they are yet to be implemented in Australia (Atkinson et al., 2020; García-Alonso et al., 2019; Wong et al., 2018). Existing state and territory-focused mental health data collections cannot provide all the information these new models need to facilitate better local decision-making. Examination and resolution of these issues must be a key priority in Australian mental health reform going forward.

The Australian experience demonstrates the importance of establishing an accurate histor-ical account of the evolution of the core policy and planning processes underpinning mental health reform, giving context and meaning to the status of national and regional mental health systems. Our experience has shown how complicated this process can be, even in countries with significant resources.

Key steps in the mental health policy cycle remain missing in Australia, especially in rela-tion to evaluation and learning (Bridgman, 2003). Areas of public policy complexity such as mental health require effective knowledge-to-action plans, monitoring systems and independ-ent evaluation processes. The task is urgent.

REFERENCES

Atkinson, J.A., Skinner, A., Lawson, K., Rosenberg, S., & Hickie, I.B. (2020). Bringing new tools, a regional focus, resource-sensitivity, local engagement and necessary discipline to mental health policy and planning. *BMC Public Health*, 20, 1–9.

Australian Broadcasting Commission. (2018, May 11). Sweeping mental health reforms in NSW announced after Miriam Merten's death. Retrieved January 6, 2022 from https://www.abc.net.au/news/2018-05-11/nsw-government-announces-sweeping-mental-health-reforms/9750650

Australian Government. (2021a). Better Access Initiative. Retrieved January 6, 2022 from https://www.health.gov.au/initiatives-and-programs/better-access-initiative

Australian Government. (2021b). Federal Budget. Retrieved January 6, 2022 from https://budget.gov.au/2021-22/content/essentials.htm#two

Australian Institute of Health and Welfare (AIHW). (2021a). Mental Health Services in Australia. Retrieved January 6, 2022 from https://www.aihw.gov.au/reports/mental-health-services/mental-health-services-in-australia/report-contents/expenditure-on-mental-health-related-services

Australian Institute of Health and Welfare (AIHW). (2021b). Burden of Disease. Retrieved January 6, 2022 from https://www.aihw.gov.au/reports-data/health-conditions-disability-deaths/burden-of-disease/overview

Australian Institute of Health and Welfare (AIHW). (2021c). National Mental Health Committees. Retrieved January 6, 2022 from https://www.aihw.gov.au/reports/mental-health-services/mental-health-services-in-australia/national-mental-health-committees/mental-health-information-strategy-standing-committee/your-experience-of-service-survey-instrument

Australian Institute of Health and Welfare (AIHW). (2021d). Consumer Outcomes. Retrieved January 6, 2022 from https://www.aihw.gov.au/reports/mental-health-services/mental-health-services-in-australia/report-contents/consumer-outcomes-in-mental-health-care

Australian Mental Health Outcomes and Classification Network. (2021). Health of the Nation Outcome Scales (HoNOS). Retrieved January 6, 2022 from https://www.amhocn.org/publications/health-nation-outcome-scales-honos

Australian Senate. (2006, March). From Crisis to Community, Select Committee on Mental Health.

Barrett, E.L. (2019). Lived experiences of Australians with mental health and AOD comorbidity and their perspectives on integrated treatment. *The Australian Journal on Psychosocial Rehabilitation*, 38–42.

Batterham, P.J., McGrath, J., McGorry, P.D., Kay-Lambkin, F.J., Hickie, I.B., & Christensen, H. (2016). NHMRC funding of mental health research. *The Medical Journal of Australia*, 205(8), 350–1.

Bridgman, P., & Davis, G. (2003). What use is a policy cycle? Plenty, if the aim is clear. *Australian Journal of Public Administratio*, 62(3), 98–102.

Burdekin, B. (1993). National Inquiry Concerning the Human Rights of People with Mental Illness (Australia). Australian Government Public Service.

Closing the Gap. (2021). Retrieved January 6, 2022 from https://www.closingthegap.gov.au/

Commonwealth Department of Health and Aged Care. (2000). National Action Plan for Promotion, Prevention and Early Intervention for Mental Health. Canberra.

Commonwealth of Australia. (1992). National Mental Health Policy 1992. Canberra.

Crosbie, D.W. (2009). Mental health policy – stumbling in the dark? *Medical Journal of Australia*, 190(S4), S43–S45.

Curie, C., & Thornicroft, G. (2008). Summative Evaluation of the National Mental Health Plan 2003–2008. Canberra: Commonwealth of Australia.

Department of Health. (2009). 4th National Mental Health Plan. Retrieved January 6, 2022 from https://www1.health.gov.au/internet/publications/publishing.nsf/Content/mental-pubs-f-plan09-toc~mental-pubs-f-plan09-pla

Department of Health. (2010). National Service Standards. Retrieved January 6, 2022 from https://www.health.gov.au/sites/default/files/documents/2021/04/national-standards-for-mental-health-services-2010-and-implementation-guidelines-national-standards-for-mental-health-services-2010.pdf

Department of Health. (2021). What we're doing about mental health. Retrieved January 6, 2022 from https://www.health.gov.au/health-topics/mental-health-and-suicide-prevention/what-were-doing-about-mental-health#legislation

Duggan, M., Harris, B., Chislett, W.K., & Calder, R. (2020). Nowhere else to go: Why Australia's health system results in people with mental illness getting "stuck" in emergency departments. Mitchell Institute Commissioned report 2020. Victoria University.

Equally Well. (2021). Consensus Booklet. Retrieved January 6, 2022 from https://www.equallywell.org .au/wp-content/uploads/2018/12/Equally-Well-National-Consensus-Booklet-47537.pdf

Furst, M.A., Bagheri, N., & Salvador-Carulla,, L. (2021). An ecosystems approach to mental health services research. *BJPsych International*, 18(1), 23–5.

Furst, M.A., Salinas-Perez, J.A., Gutierrez-Colosia, M.R., & Salvador-Carulla, L. (2021). A new bottom-up method for the standard analysis and comparison of workforce capacity in mental health-care planning: Demonstration study in the Australian Capital Territory. *PLoS One*, 16(7). doi: 10.1371/journal.pone.0255350

García-Alonso, C.R., Almeda, N., Salinas-Pérez, J.A., Gutiérrez-Colosía, M.R., Uriarte-Uriarte, J.J., & Salvador-Carulla, L. (2019). A decision support system for assessing management interventions in a mental health ecosystem: The case of Bizkaia (Basque Country, Spain). *PLoS One*, 14(2), e0212179.

Greenhalgh, T., Thorne, S., & Malterud, K. (2018). Time to challenge the spurious hierarchy of system-atic over narrative reviews? *European Journal of Clinical Investigation*, 48(6), e12931. https://doi .org/10.1111/eci.12931

Health Workforce Australia. (2014). Mental health peer workforce study.

Hickie, I., & Groom, G. (2002). Primary care-led mental health service reform: An outline of the Better Outcomes in Mental Health Care initiative. *Australasian Psychiatry*, 10(4), 376–82.

Hickie, I.B., & McGorry, P.D. (2007). Increased access to evidence-based primary mental health care: Will the implementation match the rhetoric? *Medical Journal of Australia*, 187(2), 100–3.

Hilferty, F., Cassells, R., Muir, K., et al. (2016). Is headspace making a difference to young people's lives? Final Report of the independent evaluation of the headspace program. SPRC Report 08/2015. Sydney: Social Policy Research Centre, UNSW Australia.

Jorm, A.F. (2019). Impact of Australia's "Better Access" scheme on population mental health: Response to commentaries. *Australian & New Zealand Journal of Psychiatry*, 53(3), 184–6.

Meadows, G.N., Enticott, J.C., Inder, B., Russell, G.M., & Gurr, R. (2015). Better access to mental health care and the failure of the Medicare principle of universality. *Medical Journal of Australia*, 202(4), 190–4.

Mendoza, J., Elson, A., Gilbert, Y., et al. (2013). Obsessive hope disorder: Reflections on 30 years of mental health reform in Australia and visions for the future. *BJN Graphic Design*.

Mental Health Carers NSW. (2021). Carer rights. Retrieved January 6, 2022 from https://www.m entalhealthcarersnsw.org/carer-rights/

Mental Health Council of Australia. (2005). Not For Service: Experiences of Injustice and Despair in Mental Health Care in Australia, Mental Health Council of Australia. Canberra.

Miller, V., Rosen, A., Gianfrancesco, P., & Hanlon, P. (2009). Australian national standards for mental health services: A blueprint for improvement. *International Journal of Leadership in Public Services*, 5(3).

Musker, M. (2021, April 15). There's a mental health emergency happening in South Australia. We need a radical overhaul. Retrieved January 6, 2022 from https://theconversation.com/theres-a-mental -health-emergency-happening-in-south-australia-we-need-a-radical-overhaul-158961

National Mental Health Commission. (2014). A Contributing Life, Thriving Communities – The National Review of Mental Health Programmes and Services. Sydney: NMHC.

National Mental Health Commission. (2017). 5th National Mental Health and Suicide Prevention Plan. Retrieved January 6, 2022 from https://www.mentalhealthcommission.gov.au/monitoring-and -reporting/fifth-plan/5th-national-mental-health-and-suicide-prevention

National Mental Health Commission. (2021a). Mental Health Lived Experience Work Development and Promotion. Retrieved January 6, 2022 from https://www.mentalhealthcommission.gov.au/Mental -health-Reform/Mental-Health-Peer-Work-Development-and-Promotion

National Mental Health Commission. (2021b). National Mental Health Research Strategy. Retrieved January 6, 2022 from https://www.mentalhealthcommission.gov.au/Mental-health-Reform/National -Mental-Health-Research-Strategy

National Mental Health Consumer and Carer Forum. (2021). Co-design and Co-production. Retrieved January 6, 2022 from http://nmhccf.org.au/sites/default/files/docs/nmhccf_-_co-design_and_co-production_ab_-_final_-_october_2017_0.pdf

National Mental Health Strategy Evaluation Steering Committee. (1997, December). The Australian Health Ministers Advisory Council, Evaluation of the National Mental Health Strategy: Final Report, Mental Health Branch, Commonwealth Department of Health and Family Services.

Pae, C.U. (2015). Why systematic review rather than narrative review? *Psychiatry Investigation*, 12(3), 417–19. https://doi.org/10.4306/pi.2015.12.3.417

Patel, V. (2020). Mental health research funding: Too little, too inequitable, too skewed. *Lancet Psychiatry*.

Peitz, D., Kersjes, C., Thom, J., Hoelling, H., & Mauz, E. (2021). Indicators for Public Mental Health: A scoping review. *Frontiers in Public Health*, 1330.

Pirkis, J., Ftanou, M., Williamson, M., et al. (2011). Australia's Better Access initiative: An evaluation. *Australian & New Zealand Journal of Psychiatry*, 45(9), 726–39.

Platform Trust. (2020). Mental Health and Addiction Non-Government Organisation (NGO) Sector Policy briefing 2020–2023. Retrieved January 6, 2022 from https://www.platform.org.nz/assets/Briefing-to-incoming-Parliamentarians-FINAL.pdf

Productivity Commission. (2020). Mental Health, Report No. 95. Canberra.

Productivity Commission. (2021). Report on Government Services. Retrieved January 6, 2022 from https://www.pc.gov.au/research/ongoing/report-on-government-services/2021/health/services-for-mental-health

Richmond, D. (1983). Inquiry into Health Services for the Psychiatrically Ill and Developmentally Disabled State Health Publication No. (DP) 83–020. Department of Health, Sydney, NSW. ISBN 0 7240 3193 6.

Rickwood, D.J., Telford, N.R., Mazzer, K.R., Parker, A.G., Tanti, C.J., & McGorry,, P.D. (2015). The services provided to young people through the headspace centres across Australia. *Medical Journal of Australia*, 202(10), 533–6.

Roberts, R., Lockett, H., Bagnall, C., Maylea, C., & Hopwood, M. (2018). Improving the physical health of people living with mental illness in Australia and New Zealand. *Australian Journal of Rural Health*, 26(5), 354–62.

Rosen, A., Goldbloom, D., & McGeorge, P. (2010). Mental health commissions: Making the critical difference to the development and reform of mental health services. *Current Opinion in Psychiatry*, 23(6), 593–603.

Rosen, A., Gill, N.S., & Salvador-Carulla, L. (2020). The future of community psychiatry and community mental health services. *Current Opinion in Psychiatry*, 33(4), 375–90.

Rosenberg, S., & Harvey, C. (2021). Mental health in Australia and the challenge of community mental health reform. *Consortium Psychiatricum*, 2(1), 40–6. https://doi.org/10.17816/CP44

Rosenberg, S., & Hickie, I. (2019a). No gold medals: Assessing Australia's international mental health performance. *Australasian Psychiatry*, 27(1), 36–40.

Rosenberg, S., & Hickie, I. (2019b). Making better choices about mental health investment: The case for urgent reform of Australia's Better Access Program. *Australian & New Zealand Journal of Psychiatry*, 53(11), 1052–8.

Rosenberg, S., & Rosen, A. (2012). It's raining mental health commissions: Prospects and pitfalls in driving mental health reform. *Australasian Psychiatry*, 20(2), 85–90.

Rosenberg, S., Mendoza, J., & Tabatabaei-Jafari, H., The Pandemic-Mental Health International Network (Pan-MHIN), & Salvador-Carulla L. (2020). International experiences of the active period of COVID-19 – mental health care. *Health Policy and Technology*. https://doi.org/10.1016/j.hlpt.2020.08.011

Rosenberg, S., Hickie, I., & Lawrence, P. (2021, June 28). Who are the "missing middle" of mental health care? *MJA Insight*. Retrieved January 6, 2022 from https://insightplus.mja.com.au/2021/23/what-exactly-is-the-missing-middle-of-mental-health-care/

Royal Australian College of General Practitioners. (2018, December 7). Rural and remote mental health crisis needs national strategy: Senate report. Retrieved January 6, 2022 from https://www1.racgp.org.au/newsgp/clinical/rural-and-remote-mental-health-crisis-needs-nation

Smullen, A. (2016). Not centralisation but decentralised integration through Australia's National Mental Health Policy. *Australian Journal of Public Administration*, 75(3), 280–90.

State of Victoria. (2021a). Royal Commission into Victoria's Mental Health System, Final Report, Summary and recommendations, Parl Paper No. 202, Session 2018–21.

State of Victoria. (2021b). Royal Commission into the States Mental Health System. Retrieved January 6, 2022 from https://www.mhrv.vic.gov.au/recommendation-5-core-functions-community-mental -health-and-wellbeing-services

White, P., & Whiteford, H. (2006). Prisons: Mental health institutions of the 21st century? *Medical Journal of Australia*, 185(6), 302–3.

Whiteford, H. (1994). The Australian Health Ministers' Advisory Council (AHMAC) and the National Mental Health Reforms. *Australasian Psychiatry*, 2(3), 101–4.

Wong, Y.C., Davis, A., Hudson, P., Wright, E., Leitch, E., & Allan, J. (2018). National Mental Health Service Planning Framework – implementation of joined-up regional planning of mental health service delivery. *International Journal of Integrated Care* (IJIC).

Zabell, T., Long, K., Scott, D., et al. (2021). Engaging healthcare staff and stakeholders in healthcare simulation modeling for research translation: A systematic review. *Front Health Serv*ice. doi: 10.3389/frhs.2021.644831

14. European Union. Mental health care ecosystems

Mencía R. Gutiérrez-Colosía, Jose A. Salinas-Perez and Luis Salvador-Carulla

Europe is shaped by highly diverse mental health care systems, all countries have adopted action plans to ensure the shift from institutional psychiatry to community-focused care but the pace has been uneven. Standard methods for context analysis are essential to guide evidence-informed policy. In this chapter we provide an overview of the evolution of mental health care in Europe and introduce some methods for the analysis and comparison of care delivery systems.

EUROPEAN MENTAL HEALTH SYSTEMS OVERVIEW

Mental illness is the second major cause of morbidity in Europe after cardiovascular disease, representing 20 percent of disability adjusted life years and up to 45 percent of work absenteeism (Coldefy, 2012). One in four individuals will experience some type of mental disorder in their lifetime (OMS Europe, 2006 as cited in Coldefy, 2012). Wittchen et al. (2011) estimated that each year 38.2 percent of the European Union (EU) population suffers from a mental disorder, which adjusted for age and comorbidity would be 164.8 million affected people. In terms of costs, mental problems may amount to 3–4 percent of gross national product (GPN). Given the long-term nature of mental illness, the most evident economic burden is direct costs of treatment (e.g. hospitalization for the treatment of depression). However, indirect costs (unemployment, higher absenteeism, lower productivity, etc.) outweigh direct treatment costs by two to six times more in developed countries, and even more in developing countries where the expenditures for treatment tend to be lower (Funk et al., 2007).

Therefore, mental health care is a health policy priority in Europe and the reform and scaling-up of mental health services a key target (Salvador-Carulla, Costa-Font, et al., 2010). For that, a more balanced hospital-ambulatory approach is needed, as it has been recognized that community-based care has a positive impact on the quality of life of patients (Thornicroft & Tansella, 2004). Community mental health care is understood as the promotion of mental health for a target population, considering its needs and strengths, favoring social support, and highlighting evidence-based and recovery-oriented service (Thornicroft et al., 2011).

Deinstitutionalization and the Development of Community Mental Health

Until the first quarter of the twentieth century, large institutions were built outside the main cities, working as self-sufficient communities – this fact contributing to the isolation of patients and professionals. Segregation and social exclusion eventually led to the decline of asylums beginning in the mid-1950s, spawning a process of psychiatric deinstitutionalization which started in the 1960s (Coldefy, 2012; Tansella & Thornicroft, 1998), and led to the development of the community model based on the development of new treatment techniques and pharmacology outside the precincts of hospitals and closer to the living environment of the patient. In essence, the development of community mental health was highly influenced by models originated in the US. First, by the work of Adolf Meyer mainly before World War II; and then, by the development of the community psychiatry model following the report of the US Joint Commission and the Mental Retardation Facilities and Community Mental Health Centers Construction Act approved in 1963 (Salvador-Carulla, Costa-Font, et al., 2010). Curiously enough, this Act had a greater impact in Western Europe than in the US, as this model of care became the standard for organizing community care in many European countries. However, the pace of the psychiatric reform has been uneven in different countries. The history of social psychiatry in the first half of the twentieth century had complex interactions with psychoanalysis and medical hygiene, on the one hand, and with Marxism and Nazism, on the other.

Possibly, the main contribution to the development of "extramural" psychiatry prior to World War II was by Arie Querido in the Netherlands. Querido was the director of public mental health care for the city of Amsterdam in the 1930s. He was highly influenced by the mental hygiene movement promoted by the Swiss-American psychiatrist Adolph Meyer (Boenink & Huyse, 1997). The aim of Querido was to prevent the need for admission or readmission to institutions considering both a better care provision and a more efficient resource allocation and expenditure. His work continued in the development of social medicine and public health.

In Germany, Max Fischer advocated for psychiatric care outside the asylums as early as 1911 and called it "Soziale Psychiatrie" (Schmiedebach & Priebe, 2004). This framework gave rise to two models of social psychiatry in the 1920s that differed substantially from the therapeutical community model of the Tegel Hospital based on psychoanalysis. A model of "extramural" psychiatric care as a community extension to institutional care was developed by Gustav Kolb in Bavaria in the 1920s. Also, in this decade Friedrich Wendenburg promoted a psychiatric open care system which was an integral part of a community network. Unfortunately, the perspective of eugenics and "social pathology" adopted the use of the term social psychiatry and prevailed during Nazism. As a consequence, social psychiatry and its application to community services was abandoned in Germany until the 1960s in Western Germany, when this approach was reinstated following the path of the movement of psychiatric rehabilitation and social psychiatry in the US.

An interesting and less documented case occurred in Spain prior to the Spanish Civil War. In 1931, a law protecting the rights of psychiatric inpatients was approved and a national psychiatric council established. Services, including outpatient centers in the community, were developed within catchment areas called "comarques" in Catalonia between 1936 and 1939 (Salvador-Carulla, Costa-Font et al., 2010). However, the reform process was delayed until 1975 when a national plan for psychiatric care based on the French system was approved for the establishment of community centers in some regions. A major step forward for the integration of mental health care into the general health care system was accomplished with the formation of the Ministerial Commission for Psychiatric Reform in 1983 and the General Health Act of 1986 (Salvador-Carulla, Costa-Font, et al., 2010; Salvador-Carulla, Salinas-Perez, et al., 2010).

In France, the high death rates of inmates of psychiatric institutions during World War II revealed the inhumane living conditions of these patients, raising awareness of the need for a radical change of the mental health care system. In 1960, the government instituted the psychiatric sectorization policy that organized mental health care into geographic sectors "Psychiatrie de secteur" (Salvador-Carulla, Costa-Font, et al., 2010; Salvador-Carulla, Salinas-Perez, et al., 2010). The sector constituted the basic unit of provision of integrated care which pivoted in the general hospital. Therefore, the French system may be considered more hospital-based than other neighboring countries in Western Europe (Cetrano et al., 2020).

Italy was slower in initiating the reform, but it was more radical; the Law 180 of 1978 prohibited admission to asylums, leading to a firm process of closure of these institutions (Coldefy, 2012). The comparison of the Italian case with other Organisation for Economic Co-operation and Development (OECD) countries may indicate a benchmark performance of the community mental health model in this country (Barbui et al., 2018) . However, there has been a shift of part of long-term care to community-based residential care, even with substantial outsourcing to private for-profit and non-profit agencies with insufficient definition of standards of care (de Girolamo et al., 2002).

The transformation of mental health care in new Member States, especially those under previous communist regimes, has been late, and to some extent isolated from new developments (Caldas de Almeida & Killaspy, 2011). The more pronounced the role of traditional values in the regulation of communal, family, and professional life, the more likely they were to yield to authoritarian pressure. As a result, this psychiatric institutional culture has been difficult to overcome.

Mental Health Policy in Europe Today

Mental health care is part of complex dynamic systems where apparently confounding factors may in fact be part of the overall causal package which determines long-term outcomes (Salvador-Carulla, Costa-Font, et al., 2010). Western European regions such as Scandinavia, Benelux, Central Europe, France, and Southern Europe differ in culture, health literacy, legislation, financing, resource utilization, and intersectoral collaboration. However, there are also some commonalities that favor progressive harmonization and integration of care. For example, there is a common underlying model of community-oriented mental health care; that is supported by robust welfare systems and universal access coverage. There is increasing multisector coordination and consensus for harmonization of policies and practice with the development of guidelines and common culture of care. Improving international research cooperation, European harmonization, and patient mobility have been encouraged by multidisciplinary teams and knowledge transfer. England and Italy, pioneers of the deinstitutionalization process, are reference systems focused on providing as much community care as possible, while realizing that there will always be a need for a minimum of acute hospital beds. Also, they are aware that changes should be gradual and incremental.

The EU has influenced the development of the mental health reform throughout a series of programs. It certainly influenced the transformation of the mental health systems in Southern European countries such as Greece, Portugal, and Spain in the 1980s, and the reform in Eastern Europe with national mental health programs and action plans being developed since the 1990s. Eastern European countries have undergone a major social and economic transition in the last two decades. These reflect the direction of necessary reforms and know-how about modern mental health although this does not mean actual implementation (Dlouhy, 2014). Mental health services are funded from the public health insurance like any other health service in countries such as the Czech Republic, Hungary, Moldova, Romania, Poland, and Slovakia, where there is no specific budget allocation for mental health. Additionally, local experts inform of a lack of intersectoral cooperation between the social and health care systems in these countries, as well as a lack of specific goals for how much psychiatric hospitalization should be reduced. Apart from the EU, the World Health Organization (WHO), and large non-governmental organizations (NGOs) have served as a stimulus to care reform. This is particularly the case of Bulgaria and Romania, where EU membership led them to improve human rights and psychiatric reform. However, despite changes and efforts, a balanced mental health care system is not a reality yet (Cetrano et al., 2020; Dlouhy, 2014; Hudson & Dragomirecka, 2019).

The experience of the mental health reform in Europe indicates that despite differences in the mental health care systems, and the evolution to a community-based approach, there are some key elements for the transition to a successful balanced system, specifically for longer-term mental health care. Caldas de Almeida and Killaspy (2011) delineated these elements in Table 14.1.

Ecosystem Research

The generation and use of scientific knowledge for mental health policy and planning is essential on the path to a balanced system and requires a perspective broader than the one provided by traditional evidence-based medicine. There is growing interest in moving from evidence-based to evidence-informed planning. This acknowledges that policymaking is an inherently political process in which research evidence is only one of the elements that influences decision-making (WHO, 2018). Among other factors, it considers information on the local context, including service provision. Context analysis is part of "health-care ecosystem research," an emerging discipline that analyzes the complexity of care systems and interventions in a specific environment. It provides a framework for analysis which encompasses the diverse sectors, levels and types of services involved in the delivery of health care in an area as well as local characteristics and drivers of the system (socio-economic, demographic, legislative, and policy). From this, a picture of the structure of the whole ecosystem of care in a particular area can be built, showing the pattern of care delivery, gaps, and duplications in service availability, and providing a basis for comparison with other systems. The mental health ecosystem is a subset of the general system that focuses on the characteristics of the population with mental illness such as epidemiology, workforce and organizations providing care, and connections, meaning the relationship between users-services and users-professionals.

The different domains of the system can be translated into indicators to plan, design, and monitor the mental health care reform. In this regard, the Mental Health Care Matrix model developed by Thornicroft and Tansella (2006) set the ground for the current approach to mental health care ecosystems.

Table 14.1   *Elements that influence the development of balanced mental health care systems*

Element	Sub-element	Description
Mental health policy		Existence of a policy that sets the values and principles; defines objectives and determines areas for action.
Mental health plan		Defines the strategies and timeframe; sets the targets and indicators; determines activities, resources, and budget.
Coordination unit		Responsible for the implementation of the plan.
Strategies	Development of community services and psychiatric units in general hospitals	Community mental health services are responsible for the provision of outpatient and home interventions; essential for cooperation with primary care, general hospital units, and non-health services. General hospital units are essential for inpatient treatment of acute episodes and liaison with other services.
	Integration of mental health in primary care	For the early identification of new cases, monitoring of longer-term cases, and treatment of comorbid health problems.
	Psychosocial network	Services to promote social inclusion (e.g. occupational services, supported employment, etc.).
	Specialized institutional services	Forensic and inpatient and community residential units for complex cases in liaison with other non-institutional care.
	Training of staff	For effective, compassionate, and professional work.
	Reduce stigma and exclusion	Dissemination of information on mental disorders that fights against prejudice; programs promoting living in the community.
	Support to families	Measures for families coping with the problems of their relatives.
	Participation in all care aspects	Of users and families. It is essential to promote human rights and improve quality of care.
	Research	Epidemiological studies and service research contribute to increasing evidence-informed policies.
	Improvement of quality of care in psychiatric hospitals	Especially important in countries under institutionalized care, and in psychiatric hospitals of any other country.

METHODOLOGIES FOR ECOSYSTEMS RESEARCH

The system indicators that can be collected to complete the care matrix are essential for the development of tools for ecosystems research and decision support systems (DSS). This is crucial for improving the management of care systems and for policymaking (Furst et al., 2020). Our research network (Asociación Científica Psicost, Universidad Loyola Andalucía, Australian National University) has worked extensively in the development of practical tools for mental health care ecosystems research.

Taxonomies and Classifications of Mental Health Services

International mental health ecosystem comparison has largely failed to provide satisfactory information for health planning; this fact is mainly attributed to problems of terminological variability (e.g. services that perform different activities are named similarly and vice versa) and commensurability, where different units of analysis are compared like-with-like (e.g. community mental health services versus electroconvulsive therapy) (Salvador-Carulla et al., 2013). Meaningful international comparisons need a common consensus-based terminology to improve health, strengthen health systems, and provide essential health care for all (WHO, 2009, 2013). A common coding system, using a standardized method of assessment, is important to overcome these challenges.

Recently developed system tools are now providing standardized empirical data about service provision in an area, based on a taxonomy. The European Service Mapping Schedule (ESMS) was developed by the EPCAT group (European Psychiatric Care Assessment Team) in 1994 to facilitate the classification of mental health services and the standardized description of the care system for adults experiencing mental health problems (Beecham & Munizza, 2000; Johnson et al., 2000). Over time, it has been adapted to other populations, such as disabilities (DESDE) (Salvador-Carulla, Poole et al., 2006) and long-term care (DESDE-LTC) (Salvador-Carulla et al., 2011; Salvador-Carulla et al., 2013). The classification uses two units of analysis to code targeted services: the Basic Stable Input of Care (BSIC) which can be defined as a stable group of professionals providing care to a discrete group of users (service); and the Main Type of Care (MTC), which is defined as the basic activity carried out by the BSIC or service. BSICs are described operationally by the main characteristics of their service provision (users, staff, and management) as well as by their temporal and organizational stability. The most recent classification for mental health, the DESDE-LTC, is composed of more than 160 codes distributed among six main care branches (residential, day, outpatient, self-help, information, accessibility).

The DESDE-LTC system adopts a multiaxial code structure that is explained in Figure 14.1 using the example of a BSIC called "Assertive Community Treatment team" in the Basque Country (Spain). The first two letters of the code specify the care cluster in which the service is provided (SH = health care cluster). The next two letters define the age group of the target population, in this case AX refers to adults (18–65 years). The following code in parentheses identifies the target health condition for this service using the International Classification of Diseases – ICD-10 (WHO, 2004) (any mental health disorder F0-F9). Next, the main type of care that defines the service main function is represented with the taxonomy code (mobile outpatient care: O5.1), and finally, the additional qualifier that provides supplementary information on the service characteristics. In this example, "d" means that the mobile care is entirely provided at the home of the user.

By 2020, the ESMS/DESDE system is being used in 35 countries and has provided the basic information for producing local atlases of mental health care in America, Australia, and Europe. Metadata of aggregated codes of all published studies using ESMS/DESDE is collected and is being incorporated into a website developed within the GLOCAL project (2021). The use of the system for the analysis of local change and improvement has been tested in Catalonia (Spain). The evolution of the mental health care in this region was analyzed before and after the implementation of the regional mental health plan (2002–10) (Romero-Lopez-Alberca et al., 2019). The REsearch on FINancing systems' Effect on the quality of MENTal health care (REFINEMENT) project integrated the DESDE-LTC classification in a battery with other tools for analyzing the context of care at national and local levels (Salvador-Carulla et al., 2015). A semi-automated version of the system, the DESDE-AND, was developed to obtain a standard directory of the health and social services in Andalusia (Alonso-Trujillo et al., 2021).

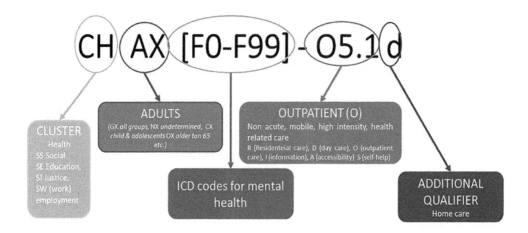

Figure 14.1   Basic structure of the multiaxial system of DESDE

Glossary of Terms for Health Systems Research

Terminology is defined as "a set of designations belonging to one special language" and aims at eliminating ambiguity from technical languages through standardization (Roche, 2012). However, a common terminology is lacking in health care: for example, even the terms "service" and "hospital" encompass a range of definitions. Different types of ambiguity and vagueness have been the subject of considerable attention in general ontology, linguistics, information technology, and health care. Ambiguity exists when a term can be interpreted in more than one way. The definition is imprecise and cannot be translated to a unique code of the reference classification system. Vagueness occurs when a word is imprecise and admits borderline cases or relative interpretation. The definition requires several codes of the classification system (Castelpietra et al., 2020). "Disambiguation" refers to the resolution of both vagueness and ambiguity and requires the development of international taxonomies, related glossaries, vocabularies or dictionaries, and the semantic mapping of the international taxonomy to national listings, directories, and classifications. Meaningful international comparisons need a common consensus-based terminology to improve health, strengthen health systems, and provide essential health care for all.

Several recent projects and initiatives have provided grounds for a consensus-based terminology on mental health care (Montagni et al., 2018), including the REFINEMENT project which compared differences in financing mechanisms to understand their impact on the quality and efficiency of European mental health systems. A consortium developed the REFINEMENT glossary of terms that covered mental health care services, their utilization and quality and related financing issues (Montagni et al., 2018). The glossary was built with the aim of producing a comparable terminology for countries with different cultures, languages, health, and social care systems to address the above-mentioned problems.

More recently, the Global Impact Analytics Framework (GIAF) in development by the Australian National University and Psicost, includes a taxonomy, a glossary, and an assessment toolkit to support the impact analytics of health and social services implementation research. The glossary produces operational definitions across research settings and derives recommendations for future work on the impact analysis of implementation research.

Mental Health Atlas

Health care ecosystem research follows a bottom-up approach that intends to include local evidence of mental health care systems to overcome the usual limited top-down perspective. The analysis of local context is comprehensive, including geographic, demographic, and socio-economic factors, the provision and utilization of services, legislation, and costs (Furst et al., 2019). This approach requires multidisciplinary teams and the involvement of experts, stakeholders, and decision-makers for external validation across the research process (Salinas-Pérez, Gutiérrez-Colosía, Romero López-Alberca. et al., 2020).

Atlases comprise information on the local characteristics of the health care system, geographical availability of resources collected with a standard instrument and their use. They use a toolkit composed of a standard classification of mental health services (ESMS/DESDE system) a basic set of indicators on mental health systems agreed first with mental health planners in Spain and later in Australia (Salvador-Carulla, Salinas-Perez, et al., 2010), and Geographic Information Systems to analyze and to map georeferenced information, as well as other visualization tools.

The typical process to carry out a mental health atlas includes:

1. **Information collection:** selection of the study areas (usually health districts), identification of relevant organizations, stakeholders, and services, and data collection through interviews or online questionnaires to service managers or local agents. This stage also includes the search for socio-economic information in public statistics organizations.
2. **Standardized coding of services:** a multiaxial code is assigned to describe the coverage area, the target population (age group and diagnosis), and the characteristics of the service (DESDE-LTC code and other descriptors or qualifiers).
3. **Analysis of the context:** analysis and display of socio-economic indicators, service provision, and utilization indicators by using thematic maps and graphs.
4. **Analysis of care patterns and comparisons:** mapping of the services, analysis of the provision of services using radial graphs with the rates of availability of services, beds and professionals per inhabitant.
5. **Co-design:** involvement of stakeholders across the study from the preparation of the initial service and contact lists to the review of drafts until the released version.

Mental health atlases are intended to be helpful for service planning and policy since they allow detecting care gaps and duplications in care provision, monitoring changes of the system over time, and carrying out national and international comparisons. In addition, the knowledge provided by the atlases can be incorporated into decision support systems for effective planning of mental health services based on informed evidence.

Mental Health Analytics and Modeling

Atlases support advanced modeling tools for decision-making in mental health service planning and policy (Salinas-Pérez, Gutiérrez-Colosía, Romero López-Alberca et al., 2020). Modeling techniques improve knowledge on the health ecosystem, resource allocation, and management in regional mental health planning. There are previous experiences on the assessment of relative technical efficiency of mental health areas and management interventions in the Basque Country, as well as the design of mental health community care models through Bayesian networks in Spain (Figure 14.2).

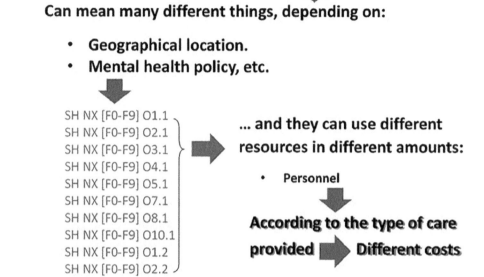

Figure 14.2   DESDE-LTC and technical efficiency as decision support systems in mental health care policy

Relative Technical Efficiency (RTE) techniques analyze the relationship existing between the inputs consumed (e.g. health care, beds/places, and professionals provided) and the outputs produced (e.g. service utilization and outcomes) by a set of comparable Decision Making Units (DMU) (e.g. health services, small catchment areas, and health districts) (Charnes et al., 1978). The analysis of the RTE is typically carried out through Data Envelopment Analysis (DEA). Its application to the mental health field has been limited (García-Alonso, Almeda, Salinas-Pérez, Gutiérrez-Colosía, Uriarte-Uriarte, et al., 2019).

The EDeS-MH (Efficient Decision Support – Mental Health) was specifically created to analyze the RTE of mental health care systems overcoming the limitations of the classical DEA and taking into account the complexity, uncertainty, non-linearity, dimensionality, and multiscalarity of the mental health care systems (Salvador-Carulla et al., 2006). The model is hybrid combining Monte-Carlo simulation, artificial intelligence, DEA, basis statistics, and measures of stability and entropy (García-Alonso, Almeda, Salinas-Pérez, Gutiérrez-Colosía, & Salvador-Carulla, 2019).

The EDeS-MH was used for the assessment of the global performance, as well as specific management interventions, in the health care system of Bizkaia in the Basque Country (García-Alonso, Almeda, Salinas-Pérez, Gutiérrez-Colosía, Uriarte-Uriarte, et al., 2019). The analysis of the initial situation of this mental health system showed that there was a relevant opportunity for improving the system performance from both input (resources) and output (outcomes) management points of view. The planners and managers of the Bizkaia district approved the feasibility of the model for supporting decision-making processes and resource allocation.

Other analytics applied in the study of the mental health system, although to a limited extent, are causal models (Almeda et al., 2019). These models are formal approaches for displaying knowledge by using graphical structures called Bayesian networks. These graphics identify and describe the domains or constructs (nodes in the graph) needed to understand the structure of the system and its cause-effect causal relationships (connections between nodes) (Constantinou et al., 2016). A Bayesian network can be tested by using statistics, such as structural equations (Pearl, 2009).

Mental health systems can be modeled through Bayesian networks since they work as a subsystem with relationships with other subsystems such as social, employment, justice, and other sectors (Salvador-Carulla et al., 2020). Bayesian networks allow the creation of complex indicators to quantify the status of the domains and constructs. It is especially interesting to analyze the levels of service provision for different types of care and community care levels, and to identify the potential effects of policies on both indicators.

Analytics and modeling, despite their limited use thus far, can be combined with expert knowledge in decision support systems for designing evidenced-informed decisions in mental health planning and policy.

NATIONAL AND CROSS-NATIONAL COMPARISONS BASED ON ECOSYSTEMS RESEARCH TOOLS

European-funded projects have played a major role in the development of the current mental health ecosystem knowledge base. They have contributed substantially to service research, making, and development of innovative tools.

REMAST Study – REFINEMENT Project

A comparison of representative study areas in eight European countries with diverse mental health systems was conducted within the REFINEMENT Mapping services Tool (REMAST) as part of the REFINEMENT project (Gutiérrez-Colosía et al., 2019). Information was collected on Industrieviertel in Austria, Hampshire in England, Helsinki and Uusimaa in Finland, Loiret in France, Verona in Italy, Sør-Trøndelag in Norway, Jud-Suceava in Romania, and Girona in Spain for the reference years (2008–11). A total of 857 services (BSICs) were identified and coded using the DESDE-LTC classification system, resulting in 1,018 main types of care or codes. Findings were useful to detect differences in the deinstitutionalization status of the evaluated countries. Hampshire was one of the areas with greatest diversity of care, which could be the result of the major transformation of the care delivery system in England. Together, Verona and Girona were the areas with the strongest community approach. They included health residential care in the community as an alternative to hospitals and mobile outpatient care teams for crisis situations. In Loiret, the sector model of care implemented in the 1960s in France could explain the high rates of acute hospital services and the consequential impact in the development of community services. Scandinavian countries presented high availability of community, residential, and hospital services. In particular, the pattern of service provision in Helsinki and Uusimaa was more hospital based than other areas. There has been a remarkable development of community facilities, but most resources are still allocated to residential care, which may represent a trans-institutionalization (a shift from hospitals to other institutions). Mental health care in Romania was not organized in catchment areas and care was still concentrated in large psychiatric hospitals available for the whole nation. This country is still at a very early stage in the psychiatric reform.

REMAST data was also used to analyze the balance of care among study areas. "Core health care" (understood as direct clinical treatment provided by health professionals) and "other care" services were compared according to types of care (residential, outpatient, and day care), target group (mental health and general health), and characteristics (workforce and capability) (Cetrano et al., 2020). The distinction between health and other care overcomes the traditional division between health and social services based on governance. Hampshire showed a predominance of community mental health teams with multidisciplinary staff being highly prevalent in most services. Verona was the area with the highest percentage of services identified as not providing core health care including non-acute residential services with various levels of support, home care teams, and day services in the community. Sør-Trøndelag presented the highest bed rate in residential units providing health care, represented by both acute and non-acute hospital-based services, and Loiret the highest rate in acute hospital beds. Conversely, Girona registered the lowest number of beds in health care services. This study confirmed that in Europe, mental health is predominantly delivered in "other care" services, which play different roles depending on the country, meaning heterogeneous configurations of mental health care provision.

In a later study, the areas of Girona and Helsinki-Uusimaa were analyzed in an attempt to compare Northern and Southern Europe patterns of care (Sadeniemi et al., 2018). Both systems relied on tax-funded mental health, and care was delivered primarily through care teams rather than single-handed professionals. Girona presented higher rates of unemployment and immigrant population and Helsinki-Uusimaa was higher in education level, single households, and suicide rates, and both were economically developed areas within their countries. The rate of health professionals was six times higher in Helsinki-Uusimaa than in Girona and residential hospital and non-hospital availability of services and beds was also significantly higher. In Mediterranean countries it is culturally acceptable for young adults to live with their parents, unlike other European countries, which could explain the high number of people living alone in Finland. The connection of socio-economic indicators such as single households with the use of residential services has been supported by previous research in this country (Sadeniemi et al., 2014). The spider graph in

Health Care Provision in Remote Areas: Lapland

In any health reform, rural and remote care requires a separate analysis, as the context (geography, population characteristics, service provision, workforce including shortage and turnover of professionals) and performance indicators differ substantially from urban areas.

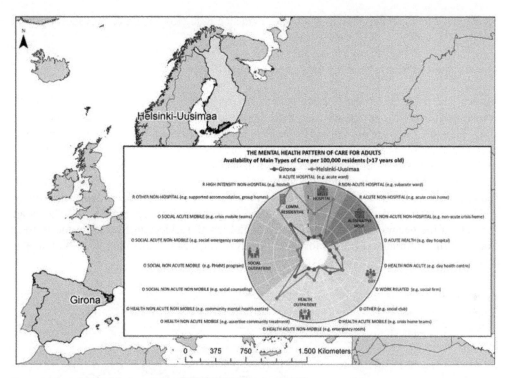

Source: Adapted from data recorded by REFINEMENT project (2013).

Figure 14.3   *Mental health care patterns in the health districts of Girona (Spain) and Helsinki-Uusimaa (Finland)*

Models of care, interventions, and services need to be culturally specific, adapted for example to the typical patterns of lower service utilization, poorer mental health and higher suicide rates present in Indigenous peoples (Perkins et al., 2019). Effectively integrated mental health systems must be based on the analysis of local evidence. In this regard, comparisons with remote areas in other regions are more informative than with the country itself. The development of international tools for health care ecosystem research allowed the comparative analysis of the mental health systems of eastern Lapland (Finland), Nunavik (Quebec), and the Kimberley (Western Australia) (Salinas-Pérez, Gutiérrez-Colosía, Furst et al., 2020). The three areas differed in their service availability, but they shared comparable characteristics of remoteness and a community mental health care that reflected the bias of urban care and the lack of adaptation to remote territories. Lapland was the most diverse and self-sufficient area. Its care pattern was like other Finnish non-remote areas. However, it lacked specific services for Indigenous peoples. Nunavik and Kimberly relied partly on services located outside their boundaries for the treatment of severe and complex cases. This study failed to get information from western Lapland as has happened before in previous national health provision studies in Finland (Romero-Lopez-Alberca et al., 2019). Lack of access to information and transparency of service provision has been highlighted as a major problem in health care planning and accountancy and hampers building a strong evidence base (Rosenberg & Salvador–Carulla, 2017).

Development of Mental Health Atlases in Europe

Atlases have been developed for the study of areas from several European mental health systems, although it is in Spain where their development has been longer and greater. Since 2005, Integrated Atlases of Mental Health have been carried out for nine regions comprising over 65 percent of the Spanish inhabitants. So far, the impact on service planning of the mental health atlases has been only measured in Spain, where they were commissioned by health agencies. The impact has been unequal for the different regions. Catalonia, Bizkaia, Gipuzkoa, and Andalusia reached the highest impact as in these areas, health advisors have been actively involved in their co-design and implementation in service planning. Figure 14.4 shows an example of the geographical distribution of mental health services in Bizkaia in the Basque Country. This information is used for spatial analysis regarding availability, distribution, and accessibility to mental health care.

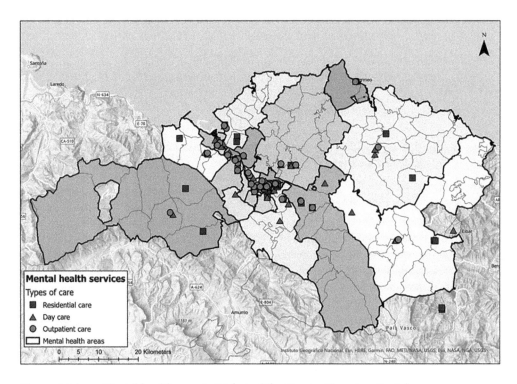

Figure 14.4   Mental health care in Bizkaia (The Basque Country, Spain)

In other European countries, atlases were developed in the framework of the REFINEMENT project (2011–13) by using the REMAST data (REFINEMENT project, 2013). In Finland the original service mapping of the Helsinki-Uusimaa district (Sadeniemi et al., 2018) was later updated and extended nationwide (Pirkola et al., 2009). The findings of the REFINEMENT project have led to an extensive bibliography of comparative studies on service provision worldwide (Romero-Lopez-Alberca et al., 2019).

The informed evidence obtained from atlases and local comparisons has impacted in areas such as Girona (Spain) and Helsinki-Uusimaa (Finland), where local planners and decision-makers have incorporated changes in the system and organization of resources (Gutiérrez-Colosía et al., 2019). Findings led to a change in the pattern of residential care in the region of Helsinki- Uusimaa representing one of the first documented cases of the usability of quantitative international comparisons for priority setting and resource allocation in mental health policy.

CONCLUSION

Differences in the deinstitutionalization process and the structure of European mental health care systems highlight the importance of incorporating the context in evidence-informed research for building effective policies and planning, on the path to balanced systems. The European experience reveals the coexistence of services and models of care and the importance of effective tools such as the mental health atlas and local comparisons for monitoring the systems changes.

REFERENCES

Almeda, N., García-Alonso, C.R., Salinas-Pérez, J.A., Gutiérrez-Colosía, M.R., & Salvador-Carulla, L. (2019). Causal modelling for supporting planning and management of mental health services and systems: A systematic review. *International Journal of Environmental Research and Public Health*, *16*(3), 332. https://doi.org/10.3390/ijerph16030332

Alonso-Trujillo, F., Almenara-Abellán, J., Salinas-Pérez, J., Gutiérrez-Colosía, M., Romero-Lopez-Alberca, C., & Salvador Carulla, L. (2021). Maturity of a semi-automated classification system for producing service directories in Social and Health Care. *Journal of Medical Internet Research*, *23*(3). https://doi.org/10.2196/24930

Barbui, C., Papola, D., & Saraceno, B. (2018). Forty years without mental hospitals in Italy. *International Journal of Mental Health Systems*, *12*(43). https://doi.org/10.1186/s13033-018-0223-1

Beecham, J., & Munizza, C. (2000). Introduction: Assessing mental health in Europe. *Acta Psychiatrica Scandinavica. Supplementum*, *s405*, 5–7.

Boenink, A.D., & Huyse, F.J. (1997). Arie Querido (1901–1983): A Dutch psychiatrist: His views on integrated health care. *Journal of Psychosomatic Research*, *43*(6), 551–7.

Caldas de Almeida, J.M., & Killaspy, H. (2011). Long-term mental health care for people with severe mental disorders. Retrieved February 1, 2021 from https://ec.europa.eu/health//sites/health/files/mental_health/docs/healthcare_mental_disorders_en.pdf

Castelpietra, G., Simon, J., Gutierrez-Colosía, M., Rosenberg, S., & Salvador-Carulla, L. (2020). Disambiguation of psychotherapy – a search for meaning. *British Journal of Psychiatry*, epub.

Cetrano, G., Salvador-Carulla, L., Tedeschi, F., Rabbi, L., Gutiérrez-Colosía, M.R., Gonzalez-Caballero, J.L., et al. (2020). The balance of adult mental health care: Provision of core health versus other types of care in eight European countries. *Epidemiology and Psychiatric Sciences*, *29*(e6). https://doi.org/10.1017/S2045796018000574

Charnes, A., Cooper, W.W.W., & Rhodes, E. (1978). Measuring the efficiency of decision making units. *European Journal of Operational Research*, *2*(6), 429–44. https://doi.org/10.1016/0377-2217(78)90138-8

Coldefy, M. (2012). The evolution of psychiatric care systems in Germany, England, Fance and Ialy: Similarities and differences. *Questions D'économie de La Santé, 180*, 1–8.

Constantinou, A.C., Fenton, N., & Neil, M. (2016). Integrating expert knowledge with data in Bayesian networks: Preserving data-driven expectations when the expert variables remain unobserved. *Expert Systems with Applications, 56*, 197–208. https://doi.org/10.1016/j.eswa.2016.02.050

de Girolamo, G., Picardi, A., Micciolo, R., Falloon, I., Fioritti, A., Morosini, P., & Group, P. (2002). Residential care in Italy. National survey of non-hospital facilities. *British Journal of Psychiatry, 180*, 220–5. https://doi.org/10.1192/bjp.181.3.220

Dlouhy, M. (2014). Mental health policy in Eastern Europe: A comparative analysis of seven mental health systems. *BMC Health Services Research, 14*(42). https://doi.org/10.1186/1472-6963-14-42

Funk, M., Drew, N., & Saraceno, B. (2007). Global perspective on mental health policy and service development issues: The WHO angle. In M. Knapp, D. McDaid, E. Mossialos, & G. Thornicroft (Eds.), *Mental health policy and practice across Europe: The future direction of mental health care. European observatory on health systems and policies series* (pp. 426–40). McGraw-Hill. Open University Press.

Furst, M.A., Gandré, C., Romero López-Alberca, C., & Salvador-Carulla, L. (2019). Healthcare eco-systems research in mental health: A scoping review of methods to describe the context of local care delivery. *BMC Health Services Research.* https://doi.org/10.1186/s12913-019-4005-5

Furst, M. A., Bagheri, N., & Salvador-Carulla, L. (2020). An ecosystems approach to mental health services research. *BJPsych International.* https://doi.org/10.1192/bji.2020.24

García-Alonso, C.R., Almeda, N., Salinas-Pérez, J.A., Gutiérrez-Colosía, M.R., & Salvador-Carulla, L. (2019). Relative technical efficiency assessment of mental health services: A systematic review. *Administration and Policy in Mental Health and Mental Health Services Research*, 1–16. https://doi.org/10.1007/s10488-019-00921-6

García-Alonso, C.R., Almeda, N., Salinas-Pérez, J.A., Gutiérrez-Colosía, M.R., Uriarte-Uriarte, J.J., & Salvador-Carulla, L. (2019). A decision support system for assessing management interventions in a mental health ecosystem: The case of Bizkaia (Basque Country, Spain). *PLoS One, 14*(2), e0212179. https://doi.org/10.1371/journal.pone.0212179

GLOCAL project. (2021). Retrieved April 5, 2021 from https://rsph.anu.edu.au/research/projects/glocal-global-and-local-observation-and-mapping-care-levels

Gutiérrez-Colosía, M.R., Salvador-Carulla, L., Salinas-Pérez, J.A., García-Alonso, C.R., Cid, J., Salazzari, D., et al. (2019). Standard comparison of local mental health care systems in eight European countries. *Epidemiology and Psychiatric Sciences.* https://doi.org/10.1017/S2045796017000415

Hudson, C.G., & Dragomirecka, E. (2019). Decision making in psychiatric reform: A case study of the Czech experience. *Central European Journal of Public Policy, 13*(2), 15–27. https://doi.org/10.2478/cejpp-2019-0007

Johnson, S., Kuhlmann, R., & Group, E. (2000). The European Service Mapping Schedule (ESMS): Development of an instrument for the description and classification of mental health services. *Acta Psychiatrica Scandinavica. Supplementum, 405*, 14–23. Retrieved from http://www.ncbi.nlm.nih.gov/pubmed/11129094

Montagni, I., Salvador-Carulla, L., Mcdaid, D., Straßmayr, C., Endel, F., Näätänen, P., et al. (2018). The refinement glossary of terms: an international terminology for mental health systems assessment. *Administration and Policy in Mental Health and Mental Health Services Research, 45*(2), 342–51. https://doi.org/10.1007/s10488-017-0826-x

Pearl, J. (2009). *Causality: Models, reasoning and inference.* 2nd ed. Cambridge University Press.

Perkins, D., Farmer, J., Salvador-Carulla, L., Dalton, H., & Luscombe, G. (2019). The Orange Declaration on rural and remote mental health. *Australian Journal of Rural Health, 27*(5), 374–9. https://doi.org/10.1111/ajr.12560

Pirkola, S., Sund, R., Sailas, E., & Wahlbeck, K. (2009). Community mental-health services and suicide rate in Finland: A nationwide small-area analysis. *www.Thelancet.Com, 373*. https://doi.org/10.1016/S0140

REFINEMENT project. (2013). *Refinement Atlas.* Retrieved February 12, 2021 from http://www.psychiatry.univr.it/refinement/atlas/atlas.html

Roche, C. (2012). Ontoterminology: How to unify terminology and ontology into a single paradigm. *Proceedings of the 8th International Conference on Language Resources and Evaluation, LREC.* Retrieved from http://www.lrec-conf.org/proceedings/lrec2012/pdf/567_Paper.pdf

Romero-Lopez-Alberca, C., Gutierrez-Colosia, M.R., Salinas-Pérez, J.A., Almeda, N., Furst, M., Johnson, S., & Salvador-Carulla, L. (2019). Standardised description of health and social care: A systematic review of use of the ESMS/DESDE (European Service Mapping Schedule/Description and Evaluation of Services and DirectoriEs). *European Psychiatry, 61*, 97–110.

Rosenberg, S., & Salvador–Carulla, L. (2017). Perspectives: Accountability for mental health: The Australian experience. *The Journal of Mental Health Policy and Economics, 20*(1), 37–54.

Sadeniemi, M., Pirkola, S., Pankakoski, M., Joffe, G., Kontio, R., Malin, M., Ala-Nikkola, T., & Wahlbeck, K. (2014). Does primary care mental health resourcing affect the use and costs of secondary psychiatric services? *International Journal of Environmental Research and Public Health, 11*, 8743–54. https://doi.org/10.3390/ijerph110908743

Sadeniemi, M., Almeda, N., Salinas-Pérez, J.A., Gutiérrez-Colosía, M.R., García-Alonso, C., Ala-Nikkola, T., et al. (2018). A comparison of mental health care systems in northern and southern Europe: A service mapping study. *International Journal of Environmental Research and Public Health, 15*(6), 1133. https://doi.org/10.3390/ijerph15061133

Salinas-Pérez, J.A., Gutiérrez-Colosía, M.R., Furst, M., Suontausta, P., Almeda, N., Sadeniemi, M., & Salvador-Carulla, L. (2020). Patterns of mental health care in remote areas: Kimberley (Australia), Nunavik (Canada), and Lapland (Finland). *The Canadian Journal of Psychiatry/La Revue Canadienne de Psychiatrie.* https://doi.org/10.1177/0706743720944312

Salinas-Pérez, J., Gutiérrez-Colosía, M., Romero López-Alberca, C., Poole, M., Rodero-Cosano, M., García-Alonso, C., & Salvador-Carulla, L. (2020). Todo está en el mapa: Atlas Integrales de Salud Mental como herramientas para la planificación de servicios de salud mental. *Gaceta Sanitaria, 34*(Suppl. 1), 11–19.

Salvador-Carulla, L., Poole, M., Gonzalez-Caballero, J.L., Romero, C., Salinas, J.A., & Lagares-Franco, C.M. (2006). Development and usefulness of an instrument for the standard description and comparison of services for disabilities (DESDE). *Acta Psychiatrica Scandinavica, 114*(Suppl. 432), 19–28. https://doi.org/10.1111/j.1600-0447.2006.00916.x

Salvador-Carulla, L., Haro, J.M., & Ayuso-Mateos, J.L. (2006). A framework for evidence-based mental health care and policy. *Acta Psychiatrica Scandinavica, 111*(Suppl. 432), 5–11.

Salvador-Carulla, L, Costa-Font, J., Cabases, J., McDaid, D., & Alonso, J. (2010). Evaluating mental health care and policy in Spain. *The Journal of Mental Health Policy and Economics, 13*(2), 73–86. Retrieved from http://www.ncbi.nlm.nih.gov/pubmed/20919594

Salvador-Carulla, L, Salinas-Perez, J.A., Martin, M., Grane, M.S., Gibert, K., Roca, M., & Bulbena, A. (2010). A preliminary taxonomy and a standard knowledge base for mental-health system indicators in Spain. *International Journal of Mental Health Systems, 4*(1), 29. https://doi.org/10.1186/1752-4458-4-29

Salvador-Carulla, L, Dimitrov, H., Weber, G., McDaid, D., Venner, B., Sprah, L., et al. (Eds.). (2011). *Evaluation and classification of services for long term care in Europe. Edesde-ltc project.* PSICOST and Catalunya Caixa.

Salvador-Carulla, L, Alvarez-Galvez, J., Romero, C., Gutiérrez-Colosía, M.R., Weber, G., McDaid, D., et al. (2013). Evaluation of an integrated system for classification, assessment and comparison of services for long-term care in Europe: The eDESDE-LTC study. *BMC Health Services Research, 13*, 218. https://doi.org/10.1186/1472-6963-13-218

Salvador-Carulla, L., Amaddeo, F., Gutiérrez-Colosía, M.R., Salazzari, D., Gonzalez-Caballero, J.L., Montagni, I., et al. (2015). Developing a tool for mapping adult mental health care provision in Europe: The REMAST research protocol and its contribution to better integrated care. *International Journal of Integrated Care, 15*(e042). https://doi.org/10.5334/ijic.2417

Salvador-Carulla, L, Almeda, N., Álvarez-Gálvez, J., & García-Alonso, C. (2020). En la montaña rusa: breve historia del modelo de atención de salud mental en España. Informe SESPAS 2002. *Gaceta Sanitaria.* https://doi.org/10.1016/j.gaceta.2020.06.009

Schmiedebach, H.P., & Priebe, S. (2004). Social psychiatry in Germany in the twentieth century: Ideas and models. *Medical History, 48*(4), 449–72. https://doi.org/10.1017/s0025727300007961

Tansella, M., & Thornicroft, G. (1998). A conceptual framework for mental health services: The matrix model. *Psychological Medicine, 28*(3), 503–8. http://files/283/displayAbstract.html

Thornicroft, G., & Tansella, M. (2004). Components of a modern mental health service: A pragmatic balance of community and hospital care. Overview of systematic evidence. *British Journal of Psychiatry.* https://doi.org/10.1192/bjp.185.4.283

Thornicroft, G., & Tansella, M. (2006). *The Mental Health Matrix: A manual to improve services.* Cambridge University Press. http://books.google.es/books?id=XXkSxXL0fVgC

Thornicroft, G., Szmukler, G., Mueser, K.T., & Drake, R.E. (2011). *Oxford textbook of community mental health.* Oxford University Press. https://doi.org/10.1093/med/9780199565498.001.0001

WHO. (2004). *International statistical classification of diseases and related health problems 10th revision (ICD-10).* Retrieved February 1, 2021 from http://www.who.int/classifications/icd/ICD10Volume2_en_2010.pdf

WHO. (2009). *Improving health systems and services for mental health.* World Health Organization.

WHO. (2013). *The European Mental Health Action Plan 2013–2020.* World Health Organization. Retrieved February 1, 2021 from http://www.euro.who.int/__data/assets/pdf_file/0004/194107/63wd11e_MentalHealth-3.pdf

WHO. (2018). *European Health Report 2018: More than numbers – evidence for all.* World Health Organization.

Wittchen, H.U., Jacobi, F., Rehm, J., Gustavsson, A., Svensson, M., Jönsson, B., et al. (2011). The size and burden of mental disorders and other disorders of the brain in Europe 2010. *European Neuropsychopharmacology: The Journal of the European College of Neuropsychopharmacology, 21*(9), 655–79. Retrieved August 2022 from http://www.ncbi.nlm.nih.gov/pubmed/21896369

15. Mental health policy in Israel's community-based mental health services

Liron David, Max Lachman, Hilla Hadas and Sylvia Tessler-Lozowick

ISRAEL MENTAL HEALTH SYSTEM DEVELOPMENT AND THE ISRAELI CONTEXT

Background, Demographics, and Data

Israel is a relatively young, multicultural state, with considerable national, religious, and ethnic diversity. Since its establishment in 1948, Israel has been in a constant state of emergency, including a long-standing conflict with the Palestinian population. It has also had to contend with the complex issue of nationality among its Palestinian Arab citizens. The state, established in the wake of the immensely collective trauma of the Holocaust, immediately faced the challenge of taking in millions of Jewish refugees from all over the world, mainly from Europe and the neighboring Arab States, in a very short period of time (Haj-Yahia, Nakash, & Levav, 2019).

The current population of Israel amounts to some 9,291,000, of which 6,870 million are Jews (73.9 percent of the overall population), 1.956 million Arabs (21.1 percent), and 465,000 other ethnicities (5.0 percent) (Central Bureau of Statistics, 2020). This cultural diversity is attributable, among other things, to waves of immigration over the years; some 25 percent of today's population was not born in Israel. The last waves of immigration arrived in the 1990s with a mass influx from Russia and Ethiopia. According to current data, 75 percent of the Jewish population was born in Israel, 17 percent in Europe and the former USSR, and 8 percent are from Africa (Central Bureau of Statistics, 2020). Added to this complexity is, of course, Israel's precarious security situation, both external and internal, as mentioned above.

It is in this complex and challenging environment that Israel's mental health system, reflecting both Western psychiatry and more traditional systems (Levav & Grinshpoon, 2004), must operate. The health system is based on the National Health Insurance Law, 5754 (1994), according to which all residents are entitled to medical insurance coverage via the Health Tax according to their level of income. Most of the population receives treatment via one of the four Health Maintenance Organizations (HMOs) that were established by trade unions even prior to the state itself (Aviram, 2019; Levav & Grinshpoon, 2004).

There is a lack of precise data in Israel as to the number of people diagnosed with Serious Mental Illness (SMI), or people contending with psychosocial disabilities. The health system estimates that about 130,000–150,000 people in Israel cope with SMI. If we add to this the family members taking care of them, we arrive at a number closer to 400,000 people who are affected by mental health problems, out of a total population of 9 million people. In fact, people with psychosocial disabilities in Israel represent the large proportion of people with disabilities, amounting to 41 percent of those receiving disability pensions (about 115,000 men and women) (Aviram, 2019; Aviram & Azary-Viesel, 2015, 2018a, 2018b; Ministry of Health, 2022; David, 2020a; National Council on Rehabilitation, 2021).

In terms of data on psychiatric hospitalization, in 2019 there were 58,641 visits to the psychiatric emergency rooms (ER) at both the general and psychiatric hospitals, 63 percent of which were at government hospitals; 40 percent of those visits ended in hospital admissions, -third of those under the age of 25 were hospitalized compared with 44 percent of those 25 years or above. As of 2022 A total of 3,482 of the 3,560 beds in Israel's psychiatric hospitals are located in public hospitals (Ministry of Health, 2021, 2022).

As is the case with other countries too, in Israel mental health is a sphere that has long been sorely neglected, both in terms of the response and services provided for the unique needs of those with psychosocial disabilities and mental illness, and also in terms of the professional aspect of developing innovative practices (Aviram, 2019; David, 2020a; WHO, 2021).

The Early Days

As noted above, the State of Israel evolved as a multiethnic immigrant state. In its early days, government authorities had to focus their efforts on developing and establishing the very institutions of the state, including systems to help accommodate millions of immigrants arriving in the aftermath of the Holocaust. Even in the early days of the state, a mental health system had to be developed to provide a relevant response to those affected by the traumatic events of that period, including the numerous cases of Holocaust survivors, immigrants, and even the state's founders, who required psychiatric treatment (Aviram, 2019; Aviram & Shnit, 1981). At that time, there was an urgent need to provide a psychiatric response for many suffering from mental illness, and emphasis was placed on separating them from the general population and placing them in psychiatric institutions. This usually involved involuntary commitment, and the quality of treatment was vastly inferior to the treatment of physical illnesses (Mark & Siegal, 2009).

While mental health policy in the early days of the state may be considered somewhat minimal, or even primitive, social welfare legislation in Israel was much more significant. Even from its inception, the State of Israel enacted broad social legislation (Gal & Benish, 2018; Hovav, Lawental, & Katan, 2012). Thus, the health and mental health systems were less developed, separate from the social welfare and education structures. To this day, the health and mental health services are still operated via the central government at the Ministry of Health through outsourcing through HMOs, and private service providers, rather than via local government and municipalities (David, 2020a; Galnoor, Paz-Fuchs, & Zion, 2015).

The mental health system in the early days of the state was based mainly on the mental health services that were developed during the British Mandate that ruled in the country between 1917 and 1948. As such, it existed in hospitals, non-profit organizations, and private profit organizations, alongside institutions of the pre-state HMOs that provided medical treatment within the community. At the time, belonging to one of these HMOs was based on affiliation to one of the trade unions, and these HMOs gave marginal attention to mental health at best. The mental health system also provided a mental health response for people who did not belong to the HMOs, and consequently it began to allocate budgets for the various psychiatric institutions (both the public and private ones) (Aviram, 2019). The health system was based on the independence and power of its physicians, the Government Hospital Directors' Forum, who had a monopoly in the field of mental health. Their power and bias in favor of hospitalization often delayed and even prevented the implementation of changes toward more community-based solutions (Aviram, 1991b, 2019; Ginath, 1992).

Mental health legislation, especially the enactment of the Treatment of the Mentally Ill Law, 5715 (1955) (which has since been amended on several occasions) in the early years of the state, reflected the medical approach. Consequently, the budgetary sources originating from contributions of philanthropists and various funds were mainly used in support of hospital beds and inpatient days (Aviram, 2019). Until the mid-1960s, emphasis was placed on increasing the number of hospital beds and providing a response to those in need of hospitalization. During the 1960s, attention began to be paid to the serious problems of mental health hospitalization. Already at that early stage, calls were heard for a change in the existing arrangements and for reorganization of the mental health services to reduce long-term hospitalization, along with initial discussions on prevention and rehabilitation instead of hospitalization (Aviram, 1991a). In the early 1970s, there were more than 8,000 hospital beds for psychiatric patients in all hospitals. This represented 2.7 beds for every 1,000 residents (compared with 1.3 in 1948 and 0.4 in 2016) (Aviram, 1991a, 2019).

The First Steps in the Reform of the Mental Health System

The lack of hospital beds, together with social and professional developments, led to a change in the early 1970s, at first mainly involving the dialogue on the required changes. This appeal emanated both from a bottom-up approach by social change organizations in the civil society calling for changes in the field, along with expansion of the approach advocating integration within the community and forces from within the government. One example is that of the State Comptroller's Office, which in the early 1970s examined the psychiatric and mental health system and commented on the lack of community-based solutions to provide support (State Comptroller, 1971). The first attempt to effect a change in mental health policy and reform arrived in the form of the Ministry of Health's 1972 reorganization program plan. The plan was based on understanding the new trends, mainly in the United States, which advocated transferring the focal point of the mental health system from the psychiatric hospitals to community mental health services, mainly by downsizing the number of hospital beds, reducing the number of inpatients and the length of hospital stays, along with developing community mental health services to the population (Aviram, 2019; Ministry of Health, 1972). The plan proposed enhancing community mental health service centers (based on the model of the Kennedy administration in the United States), whose objectives were providing therapeutic services in the vicinity of the patient's home and providing preventive services to counter the development of individual, family, and social pathology (Aviram, 2019; Tramer, 1975). The plan emphasized the fundamental concepts of the community approach to mental health: regionality (accessibility), comprehensiveness, and continuity of care (the constancy and variety of the services). The original plan proposed establishing a district community center in each geographical area to serve the community and provide hospitalization and emergency services, outpatient clinics, partial hospitalization, along with counseling, and education services. This was based on the understanding that coordinated work with the various health and welfare agencies would be a prerequisite for implementation of the proposed plan. The main argument in favor of the deinstitutionalization plan was a significant decline in the number of inpatients that would reduce hospitalization costs and enable the closure of lesser quality private hospitals. (Aviram, 2019).

Aviram (2019) states that despite the inherent promise in this plan of reducing hospitalizations, it was not implemented, due both to the positions of various pressure groups and to the budgetary method/approach that tended to prefer hospitalization. Added to these impediments was the fact that community mental health was still at an embryonic stage. Hospitals were allocated budgets directly as independent units based on the number of beds and their occupancy (Aviram, 2019; Aviram & Levav, 1981). The initial community centers established were located around the psychiatric hospitals, which reinforced the medical hospitalization establishment, thereby influencing the social perception of mental illnesses and the mental health services (Aviram, 2019). An additional attempt to change the funding of the mental health services and the division of responsibility between the state and the HMOs in 1977 following the political power shift in Israel from a left-wing social democratic government to a right-wing administration also met with failure. The actual state of mental health service funding was something of an anomaly – people who came to hospitals, the mental health centers, and the government-sponsored community services received free service, while those patients referred to a general hospital by the HMOs for psychiatric treatment were charged. This state of inequality had an adverse effect on those in need of treatment and led to problems in the development of the psychiatric services that continued to be dependent on the state budget (Aviram, 2019; Elizur, 1998).

The National Health Insurance Law and the Mental Health Insurance Reform

In the 1990s, changes in this field were planned as part of the National Health Insurance Law, 5754 (1994), which established universal health insurance in Israel. The planned changes for the mental health system were intended to improve the availability and accessibility of the services, streamline them economically, tailor the services for the needs of the consumers, and release individuals from institutionalization and integrate them into the community. This reform included a number of components, among them: the inclusion of mental health services in the basic health services basket provided by the HMOs, thereby essentially transforming the government apparatus into one that relied more on market forces; organization of the mental health services into district administrations; establishment of a fund for the treatment of the chronically ill; and reorganization of the Department of Mental Health Services, thereby effectively releasing it from any direct responsibility for the provision of services (Aviram, 2019; Aviram & Rosen, 1998; Mark & Shani, 1995).

The planned move reflected a shift to a multi-dimensional integrative perception of individuals removing the artificial separation between the physical and the mental; promoting equal rights for people with mental health conditions, reducing stigma and bolstering normative attitudes towards mental health conditions. It also constituted an incentive for streamlining and developing the system, building community services, and better deploying services. This move dovetailed economically with the processes of privatization and outsourcing of the health and welfare systems, which began to gain momentum during the 1980s, driven by the perception that the alternative of community treatment would reduce hospitalization costs (Aviram, 2019; Benish, 2012; State Commission of Inquiry into the Operation and Efficiency of the Health Care System in Israel, 1990).

The proposed National Health Insurance Law stipulated that within three years of the law taking force, the responsibility for mental health would pass over to the HMOs, as these services were to be included in the state health services basket (Aviram, 2019). This was supposed to help promote mental health treatments, make them available, equal, and accessible to residents close to their homes (Mark et al., 1996; Shemer & Vienonen, 1995). The proposed reform was based on the principles of mainstreaming and integration, representing the approach that there should be no separation between physical and mental problems (Aviram, 2019; Mechanic, 1994).

Despite the substantial work to include mental health within the law, this move was delayed for several years. The delay in introduction of the insurance reform in this area was the result of a number of factors, above all, economic and conceptual aspects of mental health. It is important to understand that there are multiple players in the mental health sector in Israel: HMOs, state psychiatric hospital directors, trade unions, and especially the unions representing the psychiatric hospitals, representatives of the various professional disciplines within the field of mental health and within civil society, including the members of the family organizations, non-profit organizations and legal defense organizations, as well as the contractors providing mental health services in the community. The delay in the reform resulted from the reluctance of the policy makers and the HMOs to move ahead with this initiative. Moreover, the delay was also affected by the slow growth of the consumer organizations in Israel, along with the limited influence of civil society organizations at that time on the policy makers, and their limited ability to promote the reform against the power of the Ministry of Finance, the hospitals, and HMO directors, along with the systemic and public perceptions of mental health, which were heavily infused with stigma towards the issue (Aviram, 2019; Aviram, Guy, & Sykes, 2007; Mark, 2011). This trend was also reflected in the budget that was largely granted to the psychiatric hospitals over the years (Aviram, 2019).

The Advocacy Efforts for a Mental Health Reform

In the decades that have elapsed since enactment of the National Health Insurance Law in 1994, civil society organizations began a more serious effort to push for change and for transferring the insurance responsibility for mental health to the HMOs. Within the civil society organizations themselves, there were those who favored delaying the reform, mainly the public psychology organizations who were afraid of the reform's implications on the state of public mental health and treatment availability. Nevertheless, a coalition was formed of relevant mental health organizations, including the organizations of the families and persons with lived experience, organizations representing the rights of people with disabilities, and service providing organizations that espoused promoting the reform and regarded it as the key to a conceptual change in relation to mental health. The State Comptroller also pointed to the country's growing mental health needs, and thus the resulting need to move ahead with the reform, and transfer responsibility to the HMOs, while dealing with those factors preventing such progress (State Comptroller, 2010, 2016).

An additional factor involved in formulating and promoting mental health policy is the courts. The courts in Israel play a significant role, both in the development of legal rulings and the defense of the rights of patients in psychiatric hospitals under the Treatment of the Mentally Ill Law, as well as in the defense of their constitutional rights as part of hearings in the High Court of Justice (Mark, 2011). The Supreme Court of Israel also accompanied this process over the years, hearing petitions filed by civil society organizations, the coalition of mental health organizations and family organizations that called for the implementation of the government decision from 2003 to transfer responsibility for the mental health services to the

HMOs (HCJ 5777/05 Bizchut – The Israel Human Rights Center for People with Disabilities et al. v. Minister of Health, 2011). To a certain extent, this case served as a catalyst for state decision-making between 2005 and 2012. In 2012, the government stipulated in a governmental order (National Health Insurance Order, 2012) to implement the reform, defining a period of three years to prepare for the change.

After numerous postponements, in 2015 the insurance reform in Israel was launched, and outpatient treatment was transferred to the HMOs that provide medical services within the community. The insurance reform supplemented the hospitalization reform (downsizing the number of hospital beds) and the rehabilitation reform that included enactment of the Rehabilitation in the Community of Persons with Mental Health Disability Law – 2000, and the establishment of the rehabilitation system, and thus represented a substantial step in reducing stigma and promoting the approach of linking physical and mental needs (Government decision 4611, dated May 10, 2012).

COMMUNITY-BASED MENTAL HEALTH SERVICES – REHABILITATION IN THE COMMUNITY OF PERSONS WITH MENTAL DISABILITIES LAW

This section presents the material change that came in the form of the Rehabilitation in the Community of Persons with Mental Health Disability Law in 2000 (hereinafter: Community Mental Health Law) which prescribes an innovative national level model of psychiatric rehabilitation in the community, regulated by the central government and administered on a national basis.

Psychiatric rehabilitation took time to develop in the world. The theories of Bill Anthony and others helped to formulate a different practice based on a number of principles (Anthony & Farkas, 2012; Corrigan et al., 2008):

1. The belief in people's ability to recover and integrate within the community. Every person coping with psychiatric disabilities has "strengths" alongside "disabilities" that should enable that person to gain independence and control of the course of their life.
2. Recognition of the importance of the ability of a person to choose what is important for him or herself to create a meaningful life for themselves.
3. The importance of equipping a person with new skills to facilitate better self-management.
4. A person's readiness for change and ability to generate motivation are related to setting personal goals, which that person chooses independently.
5. Everybody lives within and belongs to their surroundings and community; the community's involvement and the use of natural community resources will improve a person's ties with the community.
6. Experience-based knowledge based on lived experience is important to create a rehabilitation treatment setup based on co-production.
7. Social, self, and professional stigmas constitute a significant barrier to promoting these objectives and the efforts of any person on the way to recovery. Therefore, intervention is necessary to reduce stigma.

Psychiatric rehabilitation in the community helps in the effort to adopt strategies for coping better with the mental health state and placing integration in the community as a key to independent life. Rehabilitation, which evolves from a social, community approach, seeks to change the focus from symptoms and diagnoses to the strengths and goals of the individual as part of the recovery process (Lachman, 1998; Hadas-Lidor & Lachman, 2007; Roe, Garber-Epstein, & Khatib, 2019; Roe, Lachman, & Mueser, 2009). The recovery movement stressed the ability to help people with SMI to live a meaningful life in the community, based on personal choice, despite the disability with which they cope, using practices proven to be effective (Davidson et al., 2010; Deegan, 1993; Drake at al., 2001).

The models of psychiatric rehabilitation and the importance of the community services began to be developed in Israel in the 1960s, and the psychiatric institutions also developed rehabilitation services in the community, mainly for patients who tended to be hospitalized for drawn-out periods or who were subject to repeat hospital stays (Mark & Siegal, 2009). Some of the growth in the development of rehabilitation was based on family community initiatives along with the activity of non-profit organizations (NPOs) such as Enosh, the Israeli Mental Health Association, founded in 1978. Enosh began as an organization of family members seeking to advance mental health policy and to develop services in the community for people with SMI, dealing with living accommodations, employment, social life, and leisure (Enosh website[1]; Sykes, 2003; WHO, 2003, 2021). The development of the variety of community responses and their professional establishment enabled the creation of a substantial basis to include the field of rehabilitation in both legislation and policy in Israel, such as in the early stages of the supplement to the National Health Insurance Law, and later on as part of the enactment of the Rehabilitation in the Community of Persons with Mental Health Disability Law (Mark & Siegal, 2009).

The changes in attitude to people with disabilities took placed against the backdrop of additional trends, mainly the efforts to promote legislation of the Equal Rights for Persons with Disabilities Law, 5758-(1998), and the ensuing regulations (Feldman, 2008).[2] The Equal Rights Law, which was advanced by civil society organizations, and above all by *Bizchut* – The Israel Human Rights Center for People with Disabilities, formulated a new language in relation to people with disabilities and marked the beginning of the public discourse on the subject of disability. The official representatives of the State of Israel together with civil rights organization like Bizchut were among those who later drafted the Convention on the Rights of Persons with Disabilities (CRPD) and introduced insights into it garnered from the process of enacting the Equal Rights Law.

Moreover, a professional organizational framework began to be established in the Ministry of Health, which started to develop a nationwide network for rehabilitation in the community, stressing the need of the individual person for maximum ties to and integration within the community in all walks of life (Shershevsky, 2006). Initially, the responses focused chiefly on housing and employment services, alongside processes for the deinstitutionalization of chronic patients in both state and private hospitals, with the aim of reducing the number of hospital beds, and these also focused on the community centers located alongside the hospitals.

The need for rehabilitation services led to the introduction of new practices and new psychiatric developments in accordance with the Treatment of the Mentally Ill Law, which enabled the duration of hospital stays to be reduced. However, due to the delay in introducing the insurance reform and the transfer of responsibility for the provision of the mental health services to the HMOs, the rate of development of these new services slowed down and budgetary allocations to the rehabilitation system were held back, based on the argument that it was necessary to wait for clarification regarding the demarcation of responsibilities between the government and the HMOs (Mark & Siegal, 2009).

It is for this reason that in the late 1990s, M.K. Tamar Gozansky initiated the Rehabilitation in the Community of Persons with Mental Health Disability Law. The law defined a new range of community rehabilitation services for people with psychosocial disabilities. The objective of the law is "to enable *rehabilitation and integration in the community* of persons with a mental health issue so as to enable them to attain a maximum possible level of functional independence and quality of life, while maintaining their respect in the spirit of the Basic Law: Human Dignity and Liberty." The rehabilitation basket or the services to which an individual is entitled are defined in the first supplement to the law, which specifies "help with referral and funding" of the following services: employment, housing, completing education, social life and leisure, dental treatment, short vacations and consultation, training, and guidance for family members of people with psychosocial disabilities. It also prescribed the appointment of a treatment coordinator or case-manager to be responsible for implementation and coordination of all the services provided to an individual with a psychosocial disability. The law also stipulates the establishment of a National Council for Rehabilitation in the community of persons with psychosocial disabilities, and many of the law's various clauses touch upon this. The council has considerable importance in terms of advising the Minister and the Ministry in relation to multiannual national rehabilitation policy decisions, planning the rehabilitation services and improving them, development of broad programs of public awareness through education, changes in the rehabilitation services basket, and setting standards for the rehabilitation service providers. The council is supposed to receive reports and data on the implementation of the law and to initiate studies on rehabilitation. This council has been given precedence in discussions on changes to the law and how they are to be implemented. It also has an important role to play in relation to the potential issues of involvement and visibility of people with mental health concerns and their families in their interaction with the government ministry. The council, which convenes on a regular basis include representatives with lived experience, professionals from the rehabilitation field, family members, and representatives of civil society and advocacy organizations (Aviram, 2019; David, 2020a; Rehabilitation in the Community of Persons with Mental Disabilities Law).

The service-organizational and ministerial responsibility, the budgetary and funding element, as well as the supervision and oversight, remained under state control, while the service itself is delivered by service providers, some of them NPOs and some commercial corporations (Aviram & Azary-Viesel, 2015; David, 2020a).

The legislative model was based on determining the individual's eligibility and receiving approval from a professional rehabilitation committee. Besides determining eligibility rehabilitation services, the task of the rehabilitation committee is to ensure that the services are tailored for the individual's needs, and to examine the specific rehabilitation programs along with the auxiliary services from the service basket defined in the law. The law also defines monitoring committees as a supervisory mechanism of the rehabilitation program that is comprised together with the individual, and to examine changing needs and apply changes to the program accordingly. The individual appears before the committee to present his or her program, and generally should be accompanied by his or her family and main treating practitioner. Once a person is found to be eligible for the rehabilitation basket, and the application is approved, the person is expected to conduct a "market survey" together with the referring authority, and select the appropriate framework or service, often more than one, designed to meet the needs of the rehabilitation program. Examination of the manner in which these services are supplied has shown that failure to realize these rights to be extremely prevalent due the numerous barriers (Benish & David, 2018; David, 2020a; Eden-Baruch et al., 2015; Khatib, 2015; State Comptroller, 2016).

THE DEVELOPMENT OF LEGISLATION FOR THE RIGHTS OF PEOPLE WITH PSYCHOSOCIAL DISABILITIES

In order to understand the overall development of legislation, we present here a number of legislation items laid down over the years that have affected the rights of people with psycho-social disabilities in Israel.

The Treatment of the Mentally Ill Law, 5715 (1955), reflected the classic psychiatric medical model, helping to bolster the trend of institutionalization (Aviram & Shnit, 1981). Between 1970 and 1980, draft amendments were proposed on five occasions, but none of them included any reference to the community mental health services policy. Amendment No. 4 to the law in 1977 actually reinforced the status of the district psychiatrist, once again bolstering the trend of institutionalization (Aviram, 2019).

Mental health has always been perceived by politicians in Israel as a marginal social issue, as it has traditionally been associated with an excluded and essentially invisible population. Consequently, any effort to address the area was deemed to lack any political gain, and there was therefore no real incentive to focus attention on it. To this, we might add the lack of public, civil forces supporting the efforts to advance these topics as well as the lack of media attention to them (Aviram, 2019).

The Treatment of the Mentally Ill Law was amended in 1991 and it stipulates the requisite conditions for hospitalization, evaluation, and involuntary psychiatric treatment. There are two tracks for application of the law – a civil track regarding an order for psychiatric evaluation by the district psychiatrist, and a criminal track via court order. The law enables an individual to receive legal representation at the psychiatric committees both by the Ministry of Justice's Legal Aid Department and the Public Defense in cases of criminal proceedings (Feldman, 2008).

As observed above, the investment of resources and the focus of Israeli legislation over the years, mainly in the field of institutionalization, combined with the inequality in the division of resources between the hospitalization institutions and the community mental health services, has created a social climate that encouraged involuntary commitment and a resulting breach of human rights (Feldman, 2008). In 1992, the following Basic Laws were enacted in Israel: Human Dignity and Liberty and Freedom of Occupation, which led to a more in-depth discourse on the topic of rights, and in 1996, the Patient's Rights Law was enacted, which defines the rights of an individual who seeks medical treatment, including the right to available, proper medical care, without discrimination, and to be treated with respect and consideration along with the right to privacy. This law also regulates the issue of informed consent (Feldman, 2008; Melamed et al., 1999). There has been a significant discourse on the reciprocal relations and tension between the Patient's Rights Law and the Treatment of the Mentally Ill Law, 5751 (1991), which imposes treatment for mental disability (Mark, 2011).

The Equal Rights for Persons with Disabilities Law, enacted in 1998, provided an additional safeguard to guarantee the rights of people with psychosocial disabilities. The law aims to defend the dignity and freedom of a person with disabilities, to prescribe the person's right to equal and active participation in society in all walks of life, as well as providing an appropriate response to the person's special needs, in order to enable them to live an independent life, as far as possible, in privacy and dignity, while enhancing the person's inherent capability. The law stipulates the establishment of a Commission for Equal Rights of Persons with Disabilities, stating that its functions shall include advancing the fundamental principles of the law; promoting equality and preventing discrimination of people with disabilities; and fostering the integration and active participation of people with disabilities within society. The law advocates that the rights of people with disabilities and the commitment of Israeli society to those rights are based on acknowledgement of the principle of equality, recognition of the value of all humans who are created in the image of God and the principle of human dignity. In addition, the law defines the right of persons with disability to make decisions regarding their own life and encourages affirmative action for them. In terms of employment, the law determined that it is prohibited to discriminate against an individual due to his or her disability in relation to being accepted for work, and the terms of work and promotion, provided that the individual is fit to function. In order to facilitate the principle of equality, the workplace must make relevant modifications for the worker (for example, equipment, training, and working hours) as long as such an effort does not impose an unreasonable burden on the employer.

In 2006, Israel signed the International Convention on the Rights of Persons with Mental Disabilities, ratified in 2012. Since then, the State of Israel has been involved in implementing the principles of the convention, both via internal legislation and by promoting an inclusive climate for people with psychosocial disabilities to express their views in various forums and to formulate policy. In Israel, there are still many barriers limiting the access of people with psychosocial disabilities and there is an animated discourse on implementation of the convention and how to assimilate it within the civil society organizations (CRPD, 2020).

THE POSITIVE EFFECT OF THE COMMUNITY MENTAL HEALTH LAW ALONG WITH THE CHALLENGES IN ITS IMPLEMENTATION

Rehabilitation is a field based on principles focused on the individual and the personal process created between that person and the surroundings in order to further advance his or her rehabilitation in the community. The Rehabilitation Law in general regards rehabilitation as

> a process within the community designed to develop the capabilities and skills of people with psychosocial disabilities, in order to guarantee the achievement of the greatest possible level of functional independence and quality of life accompanied by medical oversight, including each of the following: realization of the rights of people with psychosocial disabilities to housing, employment, education and professional training; as well as training in the development of social skills and use of leisure time. (Section 2 of the Rehabilitation Law)

The underlying professional approach to the field of psychiatric rehabilitation is one of recovery. The professional practices and the services that developed, referred to as "rehabilitation services," include recovery-oriented interventions, focusing on the individual process, processing the mental crisis, coming to terms with the illness and managing it, early identification of para-psychotic symptoms, enhancing social skills, self-identity and esteem, and coping with social stigma and empowerment of strengths, skills, and hopes, in a different manner to the clinical definitions (Fawcett, 2012; Kleinman-Balush, Gerber Epstein, & Roe, 2018; Knaifel & Mirsky, 2015).

Psychiatric rehabilitation includes a variety of basic principles, some detailed here. Above all, working together with the recipient of the service, including joint decision-making between the professional staff and that individual; supporting the decision-making process and access to learning; integration within the community to ensure full use of rights; recognition of the importance of fulfilling obligations; conveying a message of hope and dignity by the staff, based on the belief that each individual is equipped with the ability to learn and grow; enabling self-definition and empowerment; developing social networks for such individuals in their own communities and surroundings; promoting initiatives for support by colleagues and self-help groups; and attributing importance to the development of evidence-based practice together with innovative, promising practices as effective tools for promoting recovery processes. These principles focus on the accessibility and availability of the service, together with the holistic combination and coordination of the therapeutic services, and the individual's interface with their various activities of daily living (United States Psychiatric Rehabilitation Association).

The rehabilitation process is a personal one, which can be judged, first and foremost, by the individual himself or herself; and is not necessarily connected to a reduction in the psychiatric symptoms or a result of professional intervention. This is a long-term, multidimensional process, which constantly varies, and the idea of a personal process is an essential component, as is the involvement of that individual in managing the process (Hadas-Lidor & Lachman, 2007; ISPRA website; Roe et al., 2007).

The rehabilitation process is accompanied by professional teams including treatment coordinators, social workers, psychologists, and therapists, as well as staff who are not required to have professional certification, such as rehabilitation counselors, or people with lived experience who work as supporters, or counselors, and group moderators. The rehabilitation process is supported by these teams in accordance with the individual's needs at various points in time.

The professional guidelines that apply to these professionals are defined in the ethical codes and the legislation that regulates this field of activity, as well as in Ministry of Health regulations. Rules laid down in the ministry's regulations apply to teams operating via service providers subject to outsourcing contracts with the Ministry of Health (David, 2020a).[3]

Since enactment of the Rehabilitation Law, the rehabilitation services have significantly expanded, and this field has become well established and developed (Goldman & Frank, 2012; Hornik-Lurie, Zilber, & Lerner, 2012). Nonetheless, there are a number of challenges preventing the rehabilitation services from fulfilling their role in terms of integration within the community, as expressly stipulated in the purpose of the law. The number of people in need of this service is much greater than those who actually exercise their right to it. Although the group of those entitled to the service is extremely broad and includes some 115,000 who have been recognized by the National Insurance Institute as persons with a 40 percent level of psychosocial disability, which is a condition for eligibility to enter the rehabilitation services, the actual number of persons receiving rehabilitation services amounts to 30,000 (Ministry of Health, 2022). In fact, the State Comptroller has stated that, on average, only 50 percent of those eligible actually exercise their rights (David, 2020a; State Comptroller, 2016). Many more do not even come within the bounds of the law, due to, among other reasons, the heavy stigma involved, bureaucratic barriers, the lack of accessibility of the process, and the requirement of recognition of 40 percent mental health disability. The majority of applications for the rehabilitation basket are made a long time after an individual has already been coping with his or her state of mental health. The preconditions for entry into the rehabilitation program are complex. People who come into contact with the rehabilitation system suffer from prejudice that is very difficult to change. We have seen that the motivation for change is extremely low and the belief that a significant recovery process can be built requires much support (Meidaos, 2021).

First, rehabilitation is a separate field to that of other community systems provided as part of the government social services. It neither strongly shares the professional medical approach in the Ministry of Health nor does it directly belong to the field of welfare but is located somewhere on the spectrum between the two of them. As there is no real integrative work between the systems in Israel, it is extremely difficulty to create a coordinated, integrative, community-based response. The explanation for this is rooted in the historical state structure of the provision of the services. From the very early days of the state, the welfare and education services have been provided at the local government level. While the health system was in part provided in the community via the HMOs, which acted as an extension of the Ministry of Health's "long arm," the mental health reform, instituted in 2015, has not yet succeeded to combine provision of outpatient services and rehabilitation in the community. This problem weakens the integration within the community.

Second, there has been considerable budgetary erosion over the years. The population in Israel is constantly growing, the professional field has been making substantial headway, but the budgets are not sufficient to meet the needs of the population (Aviram, 2019; Mark & Siegal, 2009). This clearly leads to erosion of manpower, and difficulty in developing new services and placing new focus on the services in the community.

Third, there is a lack of continuous treatment and rehabilitation. The system is organized according to discrete disciplines rather than systemically, so that somebody in need of assistance or somebody who turns to the health services for help with an acute case might receive help and guidance from the system for the acute phase, but with no sufficient oversight of the whole treatment process which may include, besides hospitalization, also rehabilitation in the community along with general realization of rights, as is required according to the rehabilitation law.

Fourth, the lack of tailoring services to unique populations and the division among the various government ministries impede the ability to facilitate tailor-made responses for diverse communities. For certain population groups, this division creates a lacuna in the field of mental health care, including: the elderly; children and youth; people with multiple disabilities; LGBTQ; people with co-occurring disorders (mental health and addiction). More innovative practices need to be developed to support the specific needs of these populations. (Hornik-Lurie, Zilber, & Lerner, 2012). Additional impact is the limited adaptations of services to the needs of minorities such as Israeli-Arab citizens, Bedouins, Palestinians within Israel itself, and immigrants who are not citizens (Haj-Yahia, Nakash, & Levav, 2019).

Although this field is beginning to develop, and interesting initiatives are being generated within it that create specially tailored responses, there is still no overall advanced approach of personally customized services, together with the relevant budget required to support such development.

An issue of critical importance for the system is the lack of resources and insufficient development of quality mental health manpower in general, and, in particular, in the field of rehabilitation. Clearly, it is impossible to implement any reform without the requisite manpower. There is an inherent lack of human resources within the system and many of the reforms that have occurred in Israel have not generated a change in the training of mental health professions which include social work, psychology, medicine, and psychiatry – in parallel with the weakening trend of public psychology due to the lack of resources (Meidaos, 2021). The fact that the field of rehabilitation is organized via outsourcing also exposes it to contractual engagements that make it difficult to introduce changes, increase budgets, and support development.

CURRENT MENTAL HEALTH POLICY – THE NEED FOR CONTINUITY OF TREATMENT AND REHABILITATION

In October 2021, the Ministry of Health presented a strategic vision program designed to position the issue of mental health at the focus of the discussion, to fight stigma and grant people with mental health concerns appropriate and timely conditions of treatment. Transferring the focus to the community was to be achieved by strengthening the community and expanding the clinic services; developing a community that genuinely provides benefit for people who have been in hospital all their lives; and considering integrating the psychiatric hospitals within the general hospitals. The emphasis in the program was placed on models of medical treatment and hospitalization in the community – shortening the waiting list for psychotherapy, releasing people with SMI from hospitals and transferring them to community based 24/7 treatment services; and establishing an alternative to psychiatric hospitalization (Systemic Program for Mental Health, Ministry of Health, 2021).

An analysis of the program underscores the fact that the focus has actually been placed on psychiatric hospitalization with very little emphasis on rehabilitation within the community. Although the term community does appear, it refers to hospitalization alternatives in the community and not support systems that can implement community inclusion. The plan focuses on allocating budgets for renovation of psychiatric hospitals, which clearly reflect the desire to strengthen psychiatric hospitalization within the recognized hospital system. The promise within the program is to incorporate these hospitals in the future within general hospitals. The second level is that of alternative hospitalization services in the community, including home hospitalization, respite homes, and rehabilitation communities, whose role is crucial in taking people with severe psychiatric conditions out of the government hospital system. This approach is designed to bolster those models that focus on the continuity of hospital care as previously mentioned, rather than budgets for prevention, early treatment for the young and adolescents, and rehabilitation and integration in the community. This move appears to be connected to the Ministry of Health's historical trend that is based on the field of conventional medicine and the majority of its resources are channeled into this (Aviram, 2019). Investing the major parts of strategy and development in hospitalization does not correspond with the trend of focusing the main effort on services in the community. In addition, deeper scrutiny of the statistics reveals that people in an acute state who really need to be hospitalized are the minority of people in need of mental health support and the associated therapeutic and rehabilitation services (Ministry of Health, 2020).

Related to the trends that we have identified, it appears that community medicine is on the wane and turning more and more into a digital service, and the face-to-face meeting between the patient and the physician is reduced to barely a few moments. As this approach to medicine refrains from in-depth treatment, we are now seeing an increasing number of people requiring longer hospitalization, as they arrive at the hospital too late for more efficient interventions.

The mental health system in Israel does not currently contain sufficient preventive components to deal with the general population. The insurance reform might offer some degree of promise here, but the gap is still extremely large to be able to provide accessible and available mental health services to all residents across the country.

As far as continuity of care and rehabilitation is concerned, the access to appropriate and integrative rehabilitation-focused treatment is extremely limited. The load on the community clinics is also problematic when trying to prioritize the population in need of such services, and there is a lack of sufficient training for the professional practitioners in the clinical-treatment array who are able to provide supportive care for psychiatric rehabilitation, apart from drug-based treatment.

THE COVID-19 PANDEMIC CRISIS IN ISRAEL AND REHABILITATION IN THE COMMUNITY

Throughout its history, the State of Israel has often faced emergency situations, mainly emanating from security threats. The need to contend with significant, intense, and often drawn-out emergencies, taking place within the civilian heart of the State of Israel, has called for well-oiled systemic organization of a number of entities, along with the optimal use of national resources. Over the course of time, various governments in Israel have made a number of decisions to regulate the issue of the responsibility and authority for dealing with the civilian home front during times of emergency and to improve its readiness for such eventualities. However, this has still not led to a complete and optimal solution, and numerous problems have repeatedly emerged both in terms of preparing the home front and actually dealing with it during times of emergency. One of the more substantial and complex issues is the fact that people with mental health issues are under the responsibility and supervision of the Ministry of Health, while the responsibility for dealing with special sectors of the population during times of emergency is that of the local authorities and the welfare services, which on many occasions neither recognize nor provide treatment for this special population (David, 2020b; Sela, David, Cohen, & Hadas, 2022).

The global outbreak of the COVID-19 virus created an entirely different reality. This situation required unusually extensive physical isolation and had a direct impact on the mental health of the general public. People who prior to the current COVID-19 crisis experienced great mental difficulty or who were coping with mental health challenges were found to be at a higher degree of risk for deterioration in their mental state due to isolation (WHO, 2021). This was mainly due to the lack of routine treatment and rehabilitation processes as well as personal interaction, combined with a shift from fixed routine patterns including sports and social activity. The mental health community rehabilitation services include support of people in the process of recovery in a variety of walks of life. Usually, these services are provided almost exclusively on a face-to-face basis, via home visits, various group sessions, and coordination of treatment by a professional mental health specialist worker. The new reality that developed due to the COVID-19 pandemic forced many organizations to rethink how they could provide services, requiring serious systemic work to generate viable alternatives for the continued rehabilitation and therapeutic work (Sela, David, Cohen, & Hadas, 2022).

Following the outbreak of the coronavirus, the main challenge for the organizations was how to provide stability and certainty for the recipients of the service and the professional staff in a situation of great uncertainty, as a result of the daily changing situation, the lockdowns, and mandatory isolation. As a result of the frequent changes in the regulations and guidelines, there was a need to make rapid decisions, changes in the working environment, together with a demand for continued support of the rehabilitation processes. Due to the need to maintain physical distancing and closely adhere to the Ministry of Health regulations relating to COVID-19, the Mental Health Division, Rehabilitation Department provided clear working guidelines, tailored for the employment, housing, and hostels services. The ability of organizations to pave the way for alternative services would not have been possible without the support and the ongoing instructions of the Ministry of Health's Mental Health Division, Rehabilitation Department, both at the head office and in the various regions, which updated the instructions on a regular basis, made them accessible to service providers, maintained daily contact, and supported the opening of alternative frameworks by making the bureaucratic processes much more accessible (for example, conducting the rehabilitation basket committee hearings via video), and so on (Ministry of Health Guidelines during the COVID-19 Pandemic; Sela, David, Cohen, & Hadas, 2022).

On the one hand, the COVID-19 crisis underscored the importance of having the rehabilitation services operate under the central government, constantly issuing regulations to keep pace with the developments. On the other hand, the COVID-19 pandemic exposed the lack of coordination and integration of the welfare services as a whole. One of the issues that emerged quite clearly during the crisis was the lack of familiarity of people with mental health concerns with the welfare system, and, consequently, many resources did not reach people who really needed them, the organizations providing rehabilitation services had to serve as a social safety net (distribution of food, purchase of medications, assistance with obtaining pension allowances, and more) (David, 2020b; Hamilton et al., 2020). Throughout this challenging period, the government tried to promote round-table sessions as part of its efforts to encourage public participation, attended by representatives of the organizations of people with psychosocial disabilities, the various government ministries and authorities, the philanthropic foundations, and so on. The objective of this effort was to create a dedicated platform to raise the issue of the barriers affecting people with disabilities (Israel Commission for Equal Rights of Persons With Disabilities, 2020).

REHABILITATION – THE PATH AHEAD AND REQUISITE REFORMS

Mental health policy in Israel is beginning to assume a more central position within the public and political discourse in Israel. Policy makers have started realizing the importance of mental health to the state's future growth and the State of Israel's ability to meet international standards in relation to public spending on mental health services. The considerable, growing exposure to the field of integrating people with psychosocial disabilities in the community now calls for renewed thinking on the related resources and their distribution, both due to the importance of this issue and the need to comply with the provisions of the International Convention on the Rights of Persons with Disabilities (CRPD). The State of Israel has made progress and introduced a reform to reduce the amount of hospitalization in Israel, a reform to establish rehabilitation services in the community for people with mental health problems, and the insurance reform, which are by no means without any difficulty. Nonetheless, they constitute the basis of a significant catalyst to strengthen the overall mental health system, and in our opinion, now is the time to move ahead with a community reform. Such a reform needs to be based on preventive mental health services and community-based work to reduce public stigmas in relation to mental disability and mental disorders. In parallel with increasing the requisite level of public expenditure for mental health as a whole, it is important to bolster and increase the resources for services in the community, and thus to affect a shift in momentum and reform the two key parts of this field: prevention and rehabilitation.

In addition, an effort is required to expand the accessibility and availability of the services in the community and to bolster treatment models and services that do not reinforce stigma but contend with it, as well as reducing the entry barriers into the system. The interface between the various services needs to be shored up, in order to further the continuity of care and boost the responses given to an individual based on specific needs when dealing with various government ministries, especially for people coping with complex needs.

One of the solutions is to bolster treatment coordination. This investment must be based on the development of professional staff and the reinforcement of the community-based peer-support groups, as well as recognition of this field as a professional sphere. People living with SMI are in real need of ongoing, stable, and humane support. There is a need for policy that supports the creation of this link and prevents too much staff turnover; thus, enabling the minimal conditions for the therapists and caregivers. The wages of social workers and their professional promotion paths are also a requisite component of such an effort.

It is also important to expand the efforts to measure and study the impact of these responses to mental health needs. Such measurement is usually based on the medical psychiatry model that includes quantifying the number of people admitted for psychiatric hospitalization along with the duration of their hospital stay. However, when formulating mental health policy, it is actually no less important to establish the models on criteria that examine additional elements such as independence, ability to cope and lead an independent life via a variety of personally tailored practices.

All this together provides an overview of Israel's mental health policy developments and achievements, and can provide some directions to the future investment on mental health in Israel and other countries.

NOTES

1. http://www.enosh.org.il
2. Equal Rights for Persons with Disabilities Law, 5758-1998, *Sefer Ha-Chukkim* (Book of Laws) 1658; Equal Rights for Persons with Disabilities (Service Accessibility Adjustments) Regulations, 5763-2013, *Kovetz Ha-Takanot* (Collection of Regulations) 7240; Equal Rights for Persons with Disabilities (Accessibility Adjustments for a Public Place which is an Existing Building) Regulations, 5772-2011, *Kovetz Ha-Takanot* (Collection of Regulations) 7062; Equal Rights for Persons with Disabilities (Accessibility Adjustments for a Public Place which is not a Building) Regulations, 5774-2013; *Kovetz Ha-Takanot* Collection of Regulations 7304; Feldman (2008, p.195).
3. See ethical codes of therapeutic professions, Ministry of Health Director General Guidelines for Rehabilitation: Ministry of Health Director General Guideline 80.001 "Hostel services – standards and service operation regulations" (September 1, 2009), Ministry of Health Director General

Guideline 80.002 "Sheltered accommodation – standards and service operation regulations" (September 1, 2009), Ministry of Health Director General Guideline 80.003 "Sheltered (rehab) facility: standards and service operation regulations" (September 1, 2009), Ministry of Health Director General Guideline 81.005 "Sheltered (rehab) facility: standards and service operation regulations" (September 1, 2009), Ministry of Health Director General Guideline 82.002 "Social club: standards and service operation regulations" (September 1, 2009), Ministry of Health Director General Guideline 80.050 "Opening and closure of rehabilitation framework regulation" (January 1, 2006), Ministry of Health Director General Guideline 88.001 "Community rehabilitation program management service" (January 1, 2004), Ministry of Health Director General Guideline 81.005 "Financial auditing in rehabilitation frameworks" (September 1, 2011), Ministry of Health Director General Guideline 75.004.01 "Regulation for treatment of public inquiries/complaints in the rehabilitation system" (October 1, 2015), Ministry of Health Director General Guideline 85.001 "Regulation for treating an unusual incident in the rehabilitation services" (February 1, 2016). Rerieved August 18, 2022 from https://www.health.gov.il/UnitsOffice/HD/MHealth/mental/Pages/regulations.aspx

REFERENCES

Anthony, W.A., & Farkas, M.D. (2012). *The essential guide to psychiatric rehabilitation practice.* Boston University Center for Psychiatric Rehabilitation.

Aviram, U. (1991a). Mental health policy and programs in Israel: Trends and problems of a developing system. *The Journal of Sociology & Social Welfare, 2,* Special Issue on Mental Health Services: An International Perspective, 89.

Aviram, U. (1991b). Mental health policy and services in Israel: Stagnation or progress. *Bitachon Soziali (Social Security Journal), 37,* 71–99. (Hebrew).

Aviram, U. (2019). *Mental health policy and services in Israel: Stagnation or progress.* (Hebrew).

Aviramm, U., & Azary-Viesel, S. (2015). Mental health reform in Israel: Challenge and opportunity. Taub Center for Social Policy Studies in Israel. Policy Paper 2015; 2015.02;1-48 (English and Hebrew).

Aviram, U., & Azary-Viesel, S. (2018a). Mental health reform in Israel: Challenge and opportunity. Part I: Fundamentals of the reform and the mental health service system on the eve of the reform. *Israel Journal of Psychiatry, 55*(3), 45–54.

Aviram, U., & Azary-Viesel, S. (2018b). Mental health reform in Israel: Challenge and opportunity. Part II: Implementation of the reform – issues and problems. *Israel Journal of Psychiatry, 55*(3), 55–64.

Aviram, U., & Levav, I. (1981). Trends and issues in community mental health in Israel. In U. Aviram & I. Levav (Eds.), *Community mental health in Israel* (pp. 13–23). Tel-Aviv, Israel: Cherikover. (Hebrew).

Aviram, U., & Rosen, H. (1998). Mental health policy and services in Israel – the planned reform following enactment of the National Health Insurance Law. *Hevra Verevaha (Society and Welfare), 18*(1), 161–89. (Hebrew).

Aviram, U., & Shnit, D. (1981). *Psychiatric treatment and civil liberties: The involuntary hospitalization of the mentally ill in Israel.* Zmora, Bitan, Modan Publishers. (Hebrew).

Aviram, U., Guy, D., & Sykes, I. (2007). Risk avoidance and missed opportunities in mental health reform: The case of Israel. *International Journal of Law and Psychiatry, 30*(3), 163–81.

Benish, A. (2012). Welfare services in the 21st century: Trends and challenges. *Bitachon Soziali (Social Security Journal), 90,* 5. (Hebrew).

Benish, A., & David, L. (2018). The right of access to the administration in the welfare state: The (non-) take-up of social rights and the duty to make social rights accessible. *Mishpat Umimshal (Law & Government), 19,* 395–427. (Hebrew).

Central Bureaus of Statistics in Israel. (2020, December 31). Population of Israel on the Eve of 2021. Rehabilitation in the Community of Persons with Mental Health Disability Law, 5760-2000. *Sefer Ha-Chukkim* (Book of Laws) 1746.

Civilian Forum Report on Promoting the Convention on the Rights of Persons with Disabilities (CRPD). (2020).

Corrigan, P.W., Mueser, K.T., Bond, G.R., Drake, R.E., & Solomon, P. (2008). *Principles and practice of psychiatric rehabilitation – an empirical approach.* The Guilford Press.

David, L. (2020a). Governmental procurement for social services as relationship regulation – Israel community mental health services as a test case. *Mekharei Mishpat (Law Studies), 32,* 989. (Hebrew).

David L. (2020b). Enosh: Supporting people with psychosocial disabilities in Israel during COVID-19. The Mental Health Innovation Network. Retrieved from https://www.mhinnovation.net/blog/2020/may/3/enosh-supporting-people-psychosocial-disabilities-israel-during-covid-19

Davidson, L., Rakfeld, J., & Strauss, J. (2010). *The roots of the recovery movement in psychiatry: lessons learned.* John Wiley & Sons.

Deegan, P. (1993). Recovering our sense of value after being labeled mentally ill. *Journal of Psychosocial Nursing and Mental Health Services, 31*(4), 7–9.

Drake, R.E., Essock S.M., Shaner, A., et al. (2001, April). Implementing dual diagnosis services for clients with severe mental illness. *Psychiatric Services, 52*(4), 469–76.

Eden-Baruch, Y., Moran, G., Azaiza, F., & Lachman, M. (2015). "This rehabilitation plan is not mine" – why individuals do not implement the decisions of the rehabilitation committee. *Hevra Verevaha (Society and Welfare), 35*(1), 7–32. (Hebrew).

Elizur, A. (1998). Institutionalization and deinstitutionalization. Regional organization of mental health services as an alternative. *Hevra Verevaha (Society and Welfare), 18,* 13–32. (Hebrew).

Equal Rights for Persons with Disabilities Law, 5758-1998. *Sefer Ha-Chukkim* (Book of Laws).

Fawcett, B. (2012)/ Mental health. In M. Gray, J. Midgley, & S.A. Webb (Eds.), *The SAGE handbook of social work* (pp. 515–30). SAGE.

Feldman, D. (2008). Human rights of people with mental disabilities in Israel. In N. Hadas-Lidor & M. Lachman (Eds.), *Recovery and rehabilitation readings in the mental health field from different perspectives: Practice, Policy & Research* (p. 207). Resling.

Gal, J., & Benish, A., Eds. (2018). *For the welfare state: Selected essays by Abraham Doron.* Resling. (Hebrew).

Galnoor, I., Paz-Fuchs, A., & Zion, N., Eds. (2015). *Privatization policy in Israel: State responsibility and the boundaries between the public and the private.* The Van Leer Jerusalem Institute and Hakibbutz Hameuchad, Jerusalem. (Hebrew).

Ginath, Y. (1992). Organization of psychiatric services in Israel and their financing. *Harefuah (Medical Journal), 123,* 264–8. (Hebrew).

Goldman, H.H., & Frank, R.G. (2012). Beyond the trends: Policy considerations in psychiatric rehabilitation. *Israel Journal of Health Policy Research, 1*(1), 1–3.

Hadas-Lidor, N., & Lachman, M. (2007). *Recovery and rehabilitation readings in the mental health field from different perspectives: Practice, policy and research.* Kfar Yona, Israel: Litom. (Hebrew).

Haj-Yahia, M.M., Nakash, O., & Levav, I., Eds. (2019). *Mental health and Palestinian citizens in Israel.* Indiana University Press.

Hamilton, A., Sala, G., Qureshi, O., & Eaton, J. (2020). Stories from the field: Mapping innovation in mental health during the COVID-19 pandemic. *Intervention (Journal of Mental Health and Psychosocial Support in Conflict Affected Areas), 18*(2), 159–65.

HCJ 5777/05 *Bizchut – The Israel Human Rights Center for People with Disabilities et al. v. Minister of Health.* (2011).

Hornik-Lurie, T., Zilber, N., & Lerner, Y. (2012). Trends in the use of rehabilitation services in the community by people with mental disabilities in Israel; the factors involved, *Israel Journal of Health Policy,* 1–24.

Hovav, M., Lawental, E., & Katan. J., Eds. (2012). *Social work in Israel.* Hakibutz Hameochad (Hebrew).

ISPRA wesbite. The Israel Psychiatric Rehabilitation Association.

Israel Commission for Equal Rights of Persons with Disabilities. (2020). Report of the Sub-table on People with Disabilities during the COVID-19 Crisis. Retrieved from https://www.gov.il/he/departments/publications/reports/multisector_committee_recommendations_corona

Khatib, A. (2015). Trust level among individuals with severe mental illnesses in mental health care providers. *Hevra Verevaha (Society and Welfare), 35(1),* 33–46. (Hebrew).

Kleinman-Balush, V., Gerber Epstein, P., & Roe, D. (2018). Psychiatric rehabilitation interventions recovery oriented into the psychiatric rehabilitation system – paths in the recovery journey, Part I and II. In N. Hadass-Lidor & M. Lachman (Eds.), *Against all odds – from rehabilitation and recovery to community inclusion in mental health* (pp. 200–18). Ono Academics College. (Hebrew).

Knaifel, E., & Mirsky, J. (2015). Rehabilitation in the context of migration: Immigrants from the former Soviet Union in psychiatric rehabilitation in Israel. *Hevra Verevaha (Society and Welfare), 35*(1), 63–4. (Hebrew).

Lachman, M. (1998). Psycho-social rehabilitation in the State of Israel: A turning point? *Hevra Verevaha (Society and Welfare), 18(1)*, 45–63. (Hebrew).

Levav, I., & Grinshpoon, A. (2004). Mental health services in Israel. *Bulletin of the Board of International Affairs of the Royal College of Psychiatrists, 4.*

Mark, M. (2011). Therapeutic jurisprudence perspective on Israel's mental patients' rights: A view through a modern psycho-therapeutic-legal lens on an old dilemma. *Kiryat Hamishpat, Ono Academic College Law Journal, 9*, 83–166. (Hebrew).

Mark, M., & Shani, M. (1995). The implementation of mental health care reform in Israel. *Israel Journal of Psychiatry and Related Sciences, 32*(22), 80–5.

Mark, M., & Siegal, G. (2009). The rights to mental health services and their operational policy in Israel: Between medicine, law and society. *Journal of Health Law and Bioethics, 26*, 71–3. (Hebrew).

Mark, M., Rabinowitz, J., Feldman, D., Gilboa, D., & Shemer, J. (1996). Reform in mental health services in Israel: The changing role of government, HMOs, and hospitals. *Administration and Policy in Mental Health and Mental Health Services Research, 23*, 253–9. https://doi.org/10.1007/BF02108323

Mechanic, D. (1994). Integrating mental health into a general health care system. *Hospital and Community Psychiatry, 45*, 893–7.

Meidaos, Journal of the Association of Social Workers of Israel, 97 (2021). (Hebrew).

Melamed, Y. et al. (1999). Clinical assessment of competency to consent to psychiatric hospitalization. *International Journal of Law and Psychiatry, 22*(1), 55–64.

Ministry of Health, Information and Evaluation Department. Mental Health in Israel. Statistical Yearbook, 2020 (Hebrew).

Ministry of Health, Information and Evaluation Department. Mental Health in Israel. Statistical Yearbook, 2021 (Hebrew).

Ministry of Health, Information and Evaluation Department. Mental Health in Israel. Statistical Yearbook, 2022 (Hebrew)

Ministry of Health, Mental Health Department Guidelines to face to face meetings with service users during the COVID-19 pandemic. (2020, April 26). Reference: 214481620.

Ministry of Health, Mental Health Services. (1972). *A Proposal for a Reorganization of the Mental Health Services: A Comprehensive Integration Plan.*

National Council on Rehabilitation. (2021, October 27). Protocol of the National Council on Rehabilitation discussionu. Ministry of Health.

National Health Insurance Law, 5754-1994. *Sefer Ha-Chukkim* (Book of Laws) 1469.

National Health Insurance (Change in the Second and Third Supplements to the Law) Order, 5772-2012. *Kovetz Ha-Takanot* (Collection of Regulations) 7154. (May 29, 2012).

Roe, D., Rudnick, A., & Gill, K.J. (2007). The concept of "being in recovery". *Psychiatric Rehabilitation Journal, 30*(3), 171–3.

Roe, D., Lachman, M., & Mueser, K.T. (2009). The emerging field of psychiatric rehabilitation. *Israel Journal of Psychiatry and Related Sciences, 46*(2), 82–3.

Roe, D., Garber-Epstein, P., & Khatib, A. (2019). Psychiatric rehabilitation in the context of Palestinian citizens in Israel. In M. Haj-Yahia, O. Nakash, & I. Levav (Eds.), *Mental health and Palestinian citizens in Israel* (pp. 380–91) Indiana University Press.

Sela, C., David, L., Cohen., A., & Hadas, H. (2022). Emergency preparedness and advancing resilience in Enosh community-based mental health services. *Disability & Society, 1*, 101–20. (Hebrew).

Shemer, J., & Vienonen, M. (1995). *Reforming health care systems.* Jerusalem: Gefen.

Shershevsky, Y. (2006). Community rehabilitation of persons with mental disabilities in Israel. In U. Aviram & Y. Ginath (Eds.), *Mental health services in Israel: Trends and issues* (pp. 357–87). Cherikover. (Hebrew).

State Commission of Inquiry into the Operation and Efficiency of the Health Care System in Israel. (1990). Majority Report. Jerusalem.

State Comptroller. (1971). Annual report 21 for 1969/70 financial year. Jerusalem

State Comptroller. (2016). Israel State Comptroller. Annual report No. 66c for the year 2015 and 2014 budget year accounts. Jerusalem: The State Comptroller and Ombudsman, 2016.

State Comptroller, Mental Health Issues. (2010). *Annual report 60b for 2009 and the 2008 financial year accounts*. Jerusalem.

Sykes, I. (2003). *The use of data in the effort to transfer mental health services in Israel from the Ministry of Health to the health plans. A case study: 1995–1996*. JDC Brookdale.

Systemic Program for Mental Health, Ministry of Health. (2021). Presented at the Knesset Health Committee (October 12, 2021).

Tramer, L. (1975). A proposal for a reorganization of the mental health services: A comprehensive integration plan, *Public Health, 18*, 1–12. (Hebrew).

Transfer of Full Mental Health Insurance Responsibility from the State to the Health Maintenance Organizations. Government Decision 4611. (May 10, 2012).

Treatment of the Mentally Ill Law, 5715-1955. *Sefer Ha-Chukkim* (Book of Laws) 167.

Treatment of the Mentally Ill Law, 5751-1991. *Sefer Ha-Chukkim* (Book of Laws) 1339.

United States Psychiatric Rehabilitation Association. Retrieved from http://www.psychrehabassociation .org/who-we-are/core-principles-and-values

World Health Organization (WHO). (2003a). Advocacy for Mental Health (Mental Health Policy & Service Guidance Package).

World Health Organization (WHO). (2021). Guidance on community mental health services: Promoting person-centered and rights-based approaches.

16. United Kingdom. An overview of its mental health policies and services

Christopher G. Hudson

The United Kingdom (UK) has developed a wide range of mental health policies and services. Yet, its historic advantages have in recent years been severely tested due both to economic retrenchment and the growing diversity of its population. The nation has had the advantage of a particularly long history of mental health services, dating back to the twelfth century. It has also had the advantage of a National Health Service (NHS), allowing for the development of nationwide mental health policies and standards, centralized administration, and in general, accountability on the part of its providers. Given the system's long history and its centralized administration, some observers have pointed out its overly cautious approach and lack of innovation in developing community mental health services evidencing a "less dramatic rash of consequences compared with the United States" (Gawron, 2019, p. 100), which has often been precipitous in such developments. Given the UK's advantages and ongoing challenges, the nation has clearly been prioritizing mental health, struggling to "create a genuinely whole person, whole population mental health service" (Bell, 2017, p. 2). This has continued in the face of severe disruptions of the COVID-19 pandemic and the exit from the European Union (EU).

The UK's geographic, cultural, and demographic context has served to amplify both the advantages and challenges noted above. The UK, situated in northwest Europe, occupies one large island that includes England, Wales, Scotland, and Northern Ireland, a smaller part of Ireland, and several small islands scattered around the coasts. It is classified as a high-income country, and in 2019 consisted of a population of 55.9 million, with the second highest population density in Europe at 407 people per square kilometer, just behind Malta. A major advantage is its high literacy rate, at 99 percent of those above age 15, which is attributable to its universal state education system, introduced in 1870 (and in Scotland in 1872), and at the secondary level in 1900. Its health care system is also quite well developed, despite recent retrenchment, with per capita expenditure on health care standing at 12.8 percent of Gross Domestic Product (GDP) in 2020, up from 10.2 percent in 2019. The NHS's budget for mental health stood at £12.2 billion in 2018/19, just about 10 percent of all expenditures by the Department of Health and Social Care. These no doubt contribute to an above average life expectancy of 81.0 in 2020 (World Bank, 2020).

The diversity of the nation, presenting both opportunities and challenges, has been formed by successive waves of immigration, including that of the Vikings, Normans (eleventh century), Huguenots (sixteenth century), Eastern European (twentieth century), and the various newly independent colonies in the West Indies and India. Although English is the predominant language, other languages include Welsh, Scots, Gaelic, and various South Asian languages. The diversity of this nation has been a continuing political challenge for what is a parliamentary democracy, with remnants of a system of government through hereditary succession. Its House of Commons serves as the elected democratic branch of its Parliament, whereas the House of

Lords consists of appointed hereditary lords and peers. In contrast, Scotland passes legislation through its own Scottish Assembly, as well as electing Members of Parliament to the House of Commons. Other challenges include split allegiances between the United States and the EU, as well as large-scale reductions in state support for public services such as health, welfare, education, and transport (Goldie & Sayce, 1993).

BACKGROUND

The Era of Institutionalization

The nation's extensive history of treating the mentally ill dates back to the establishment of the Bethlem Royal Hospital in London, in 1247, by a monastic priory at the location where Liverpool Street station now stands (Table 16.1). The priory's services also included those for the sick and infirm, and beginning in 1330, was referred to as a hospital. During its early years development was slow and ripe with reports of malpractice, scandals, and embezzlement, such that King Henry IV established a Royal Commission to investigate them. Its report provides the first clear evidence that the hospital attempted to treat men suffering from "insanity" (Killaspy, 2006).

At a time when madness became a source of income for some medical practitioners (Parry-Jones, 1972), the era of institutionalization proceeded very slowly, with an important development being the establishment of the York Retreat in 1796, where William Tuke pioneered the application of the humane approach to the mentally ill known as "moral treatment." At the turn of the nineteenth century, King George III developed severe depression, focusing attention on the mentally ill, and reinforcing the development of asylums for the mentally ill. This newfound interest in the well-being of those suffering from mental illness was incorporated in the charitable social and political policy of the Victorians. County asylums were recommended by a House of Commons select committee, which had been set up in 1807, "to enquire into the state of lunatics." Legislation in support of the establishment of asylums followed, including Wynn's Act of 1808, "for the better care and maintenance of lunatics, being paupers or criminals" as well as the Shaftesbury Acts of 1845 "for the regulation of the care and treatment of lunatics" (Killaspy, 2006, p. 247).

During this period of institutionalization, the mental health histories of the UK and United States largely paralleled one another. For example, with the increases in state regulation and growth, there came about increasing specialization in the treatment of the insane, developmentally disabled, and those with neurological conditions such as Alzheimer's. The movement toward private services continued to develop, along with the emergence of alienists, or early community psychiatrists.

By the end of the nineteenth century, the Lunacy Act of 1890 established standards for admission to mental hospitals, providing a legal framework in which a patient had to be certified as insane to be admitted to an asylum. Under this Act, asylums became "a last resort for the insane rather than a means to their recovery" (Killaspy, 2006, p. 247). No psychiatric opinion was required prior to admission. The parish doctor declared the patient insane and they were then placed on a compulsory reception order by a local magistrate and taken to the asylum (p. 247). These changes in admission standards contributed to a dramatic rise in the asylum populations. For example, the Colney Hatch Asylum, the largest in Europe, was

Table 16.1   Key dates in the history of mental policy and services in the United Kingdom

1247	Founding Bethlem Royal Hospital in London
1796	William Tuke establishes the York Asylum ("The Retreat")
1807	House of Commons select committee, appointed to "enquire into the state of lunatics"
1808	*Wynn's Act of 1808* & other legislation enacted in support of the establishment of asylums
1845	*Shaftesbury Acts of 1845* enacted "for the regulation of the care and treatment of lunatics"
1890	*Lunacy Act of 1890* established mental hospital standards
1930	*Mental Treatment Act of 1930* extended the voluntary admission procedure to asylums
1948	National Health Service established
1954	Percey Commission appointed
1959	*Mental Health Act* enacted, repeals 1890 Act
1961	Enoch Powell's Water Tower Speech proposes policy of closing asylums
1963	"Health and Welfare: The Development of Community Care"
1968	*Report of the Commission on Local Authority and Allied Personal Social Services* leads to creation of integrated social work profession
1971	Creation of the *Royal College of Psychiatrists*
1974	NHS reorganizes and integrates mental health with general medical and hospital services in districts coterminous with Local Authorities
1975	Report of the *Committee on Mentally Abnormal Offenders* (Butler Report)
1983	*Mental Health Act* enacted to protect civil rights of mentally ill patients
1988	Community Care: Agenda for Action (Griffiths Report), leading to –
1990	Enactment of *NHS and Community Care Act*
1991–96	Establishment of NHS Trusts, including Mental Health Trusts
1992	*Modernising Mental Health Services* White Paper
1992	*Health of the Nation* sets forth mental illness targets
1999	National Service Framework for Adult Mental Health
2001	*Health and Social Care Act*
2002	*NHS Reform and Health Care*
2004	New GP contract implemented
2006	Establishment of the Increasing Access to Psychological Therapies (IAPT) program
2007	*Mental Health Act*
2019	Issuing of the *Mental Health Framework Document for Adults and Older Adults*

originally built to accommodate 1,250 patients but was enlarged within ten years to take 2,000 and in 1937 (when it was renamed Friern Hospital), it had grown to 2,700 patients. In order to address the burgeoning asylum population, the Mental Treatment Act of 1930 extended the voluntary admission procedure to asylums, and supported the establishment of outpatient departments "for the examination of applicants as to their fitness for reception as voluntary patients into asylums" (Hunter & MacAlpine, 1974). By 1925, there were 25 psychiatric outpatient departments in the UK, and by 1935, this figure had grown to 162 (Killaspy, 2006, p. 248). These are among the origins of community mental health services.

The UK has seen considerable academic interest in the history of its mental health services, spawning much debate as to the underlying social dynamics. Goldie and Sayce (1993, p. 395) identify two major interpretations of this history. On one hand, the Whiggish tradition has been adopted by many historians who see "unfolding progress as severely challenged by a view that contends that the history of madness reflect[s] little in the way of increasing understanding of mental illness." On the other hand, there are those who emphasize "the role of institutions of control with an evolving capitalist society" (Miller & Rose, 1986; Goldie & Sayce, 1993). Still others have often been surprised at how little impact the psychoanalytic movement has had on mainstream psychiatry in the UK and the development of community mental health, to which we will now turn (Ramon, 1985).

Deinstitutionalization and Community Mental Health

The development of post-war mental health policies – specifically psychiatric deinstitutional-ization and community mental health – followed the earlier pattern evident in many nations, that of institutionalization and subsequent stagnation. Before mid-century, methods and practices were antiquated, mental health was ripe with stigma, and hospitals were dramatically overcrowded. The primary treatment took place in austere Victorian asylums, secluded from home communities. A newfound interest in mental health had begun to emerge during World War II, as service men and women returned home with severe symptoms of conditions such as post-traumatic stress disorder (PTSD). This resulted in the establishment of the National Health Service in 1948, and the development of antipsychotic medications in the 1950s.

Beginning in 1954, the Churchill government had established the Percey Commission which established the principle that people should be treated in their home communities when-ever possible (UK-NHS, 2008). Then, in 1959, the Mental Health Act was the first legislation to clarify the reasons why an individual might need to be hospitalized and treated against their will (Turner et al., 2015). Under the 1959 Act, admission to mental hospitals was to be decided on medical rather than legal terms. This Act also introduced review tribunals and eliminated prior legislation and acts of magistrates regarding mental illness.

An important turning point in the development of community mental health services was the renowned "water tower" speech by Enoch Powell in 1961 that advocated for the closure of the asylums (Gawron, 2019). This speech was followed by the Ministry of Health implementing the policies, "A Hospital Plan for England and Wales" in 1962 and the "Health and Welfare: The Development of Community Care" in 1963. Thus, it was in the 1960s that psychiatric deinstitutionalization in the UK began, although even then closures were slow, with services still dominated by institutions, led by psychiatrists, who established a distinct professional identity under the Royal College of Psychiatry.

By 1971 a government White Paper on "Hospital Services for the Mentally Ill" recom-mended the complete abolition of the mental hospital system, with all inpatient services being delivered by district general hospitals in collaboration with General Practitioners (GPs) and social services (UK-DHHSC, 1971). At that time there were 120 mental hospitals paid for by local authorities and ratepayers, most of which were closed in the 1970s and 1980s (OECD, 2011). By 2014, psychiatric deinstitutionalization in the UK had advanced so substantially that one comparative international study concluded that the UK had fallen short of its need for psychiatric beds, whether in specialty or general hospitals, which that year stood at 34.1 per 100,000 population, whereas estimated bed need was between 53.7 and 81.7 (Hudson, 2020).

By the early 1980s, the first manifestations of the service user movements were evident (Turner et al., 2015). This movement demanded civil and economic rights for patients in the community, along with advocacy groups such as the National Association of Mental Health (Mind) which promoted changes in the 1959 Act, all of which propelled both psychiatric dein-stitutionalization and the development of community care. This included the increasing use of psychological treatments in the community.

The 1980s also saw several critical developments, in parallel with those in the United States. One was the implementation of the Care Programme Approach (CPA) which involved the assignment of care managers to all patients in need of them to coordinate their services (Turner et al., 2015). In 1983, Parliament passed the Mental Health Act (Goldie & Sayce, 1993) that changed procedures for compulsory detention and treatment. It defined an enhanced role for GPs who increasingly referred people detained to multi-disciplinary Community Mental Health Teams which delivered more specialized services, a development also supported by the CPA initiative. Two Griffith reports during the 1980s sought to strengthen the role of regional and district managers into the health service. In particular, the second of these reports in 1988, as well as the National Health and Community Care Act of 1990, aimed to further increase levels of managerialism, creating a purchaser-provider split in the NHS and a clearer allocation of responsibility for community care to local authorities (Turner et al., 2015). Also, by the late 1980s, the government made its policy explicit not to further close hospitals until community services were established (Goldie & Sayce, 1993).

The National Health and Community Care Act of 1990 served not only to further solidify the shift of responsibility for community care to local authorities, rather than the NHS, but also signaled a shift from medical to psychosocial treatment approaches (Goldie & Sayce, 1993). Local authorities were expected to provide social care services for ex-patients such as home support, day centers, hostels, and supported housing. These developments set the stage for the 1999 National Service Framework (NSF) for Mental Health which called for the development of several new modalities of community services, including early intervention services and crisis resolution teams, as well as assertive outreach teams. Additional spending by the late 1990s for such new services was in part stimulated by the plan defined in the Modernizing Mental Health Services Report in 1998, with the 1999 NSF Act setting specific objectives, but only for adults of working age. The shift to psychosocial services received a major boost in 2006 with the implementation of the Increasing Access to Psychological Therapies (IAPT) program in which people suffering from common forms of mental distress could refer themselves to such services without their GP's intervention. Such changes are among the defining features of contemporary mental health policy and services in the UK since the early 2000s, which will be discussed following a review of the prevalence and incidence of mental disorders in the next section.

MENTAL ILLNESS AND HEALTH IN THE UK

Integral to any well-planned mental health system is a source of data on the psychiatric epidemiology of the area of concern. Fortunately, the UK undertakes an in-depth assessment of the nation's mental health every seven years through its Adult Psychiatric Morbidity Survey (APMS) (see Baker, 2020). This study has most recently reported that an estimated one in six adults in the UK have experienced a "common mental disorder" (CMD), such as depression and anxiety, in the previous week, with little change in the proportion of people with a severe CMD (CIS-R score of 18+) between 2007 and 2014.

Available data permits breakdowns of prevalence rates based on demographic characteristics, diagnoses, and for positive mental health as well. Whereas one-fifth of adult women had a CMD (20.7 percent), only one-eighth of men did (13.2 percent) (Baker, 2020). Similarly, one-eighth of children aged 5 to 19 were estimated to have at least one mental health problem. As in the case of various studies around the world, social isolation and fragmentation were found to be strong predictors for prevalence (see Hudson & Doogan, 2019), particularly for depression in the UK. For example, rates are higher in people who are single or divorced, and increasingly, as people live alone, the 2014 APMS survey identified them as having higher rates of most mental disorders, including CMD, PTSD, psychosis, personality disorder, and bipolar disorder (Baker, 2020). People who live in regions with high deprivation and fragmentation were more likely to be diagnosed with serious mental illness (Grigoroglou et al., 2019). This same study found a clear distinction between rural and urban areas, with the exception of London. Urban areas, in general, were found to have greater recorded levels of depression. For serious mental illness (SMI), the study reported greater variability across and within regions, with similar patterns for depression and SMI, with the exception of London. Increased levels of SMI were found in urban areas in the South East and North West regions of the nation, but London had by far the greatest recorded levels for SMI across regions. Grigoroglou et al. (2019) emphasize the geographic distribution of mental illness, especially as it is correlated with social fragmentation and isolation, and argue that in the UK the distribution of mental health resources should be informed by data on such conditions.

The APMS data also permits breakdowns according to diagnosis, and shows that the most prevalent diagnoses, beyond "Other or not specified" which stood at 7.8 percent of adults, was for generalized anxiety disorder, at 5.9 percent. Next in prevalence were depressive episodes, at 3.3 percent; phobias, at 2.4 percent; obsessive compulsive disorders, at 1.3 percent; and panic disorder, at 0.6 percent. Of particular importance are drug abuse and alcohol use disorder. Based on the Alcohol Use Disorders Identification Test (AUDIT), 16.6 percent of adults drank at hazardous levels (AUDIT scores of 8 to 15), 1.9 percent were harmful or mildly dependent drinkers (AUDIT scores of 16 to 19), and 1.2 percent were probably dependent drinkers (AUDIT scores of 20 or more) (McManus et al., 2016). And, about one in 33 adults, or 3.1 percent, showed signs of dependence on drugs. Overall, 35.4 percent of men and 22.6 percent of women had taken an illicit drug at least once in their life.

Less prevalent are the psychotic disorders which affected almost one adult in 150 (0.7 percent) in 2014, up from 0.4 percent in 2007. Also of increasing prevalence is self-harm, with such reports doubling in both men and women and across age groups between 2007 and 2014 (Baker, 2020).

Rarely have psychiatric researchers investigated the prevalence of the manifestations of positive mental health which have traditionally been found to be only weakly correlated with specific mental health diagnoses and symptoms. Jacobi (2017) examined the association of all-cause mortality and positive mental health in the UK using the new Warwick-Edinburgh Mental Well-being Scale (WEMWBS). He found that the better the positive mental health (PMH), the greater was the protective effect against mortality, and somewhat uncorrelated with negative mental health. He found that PMH was not directly protective against the effects of negative mental health for people who are already suffering from mental disease. Instead, it is reported, PMH had an independent protective effect for people who are not suffering from mental illness (Jayawickreme et al., 2012; Jacobi, 2017).

CURRENT POLICY, SERVICES, AND ORGANIZATION

Current Policies

Since the early 2000s, the focus of policy in the UK has shifted to one of refinement, balancing, and fine-tuning the current system. Its broad outlines are determined by the central government, through the NHS, and continues to be one of community care being offered to all who are "ordinarily resident" in preference to institutional care (Goldie & Sayce, 1993). As such, it aims to be universal and comprehensive, with the major components of the policy consisting of advocacy, promotion, prevention, treatment, and rehabilitation (WHO, 2005). Lynchpins of the policy were established by the National Service Framework for Mental Health in 1999 and the NHS Plan of 2000: (i) All people in crisis will have access to crisis resolution and home treatment teams by 2005; (ii) All people with a first episode of psychosis will have access to intensive treatment for the first three years, by 2006, and; (iii) All people with intensive needs will have access to service outcome teams, by 2004. Similar to the United States, there have been systematic efforts to mainstream mental health and give it parity with physical health, a policy that is sometimes referred to as "no health without mental health" (WHO, 2005).

The contemporary period has also seen an attempt to counterbalance a historical focus on rights, particularly the right to health care, with a new managerial and cost-saving focus. New themes in service provision, such as person-centered care, the promotion of well-being and recovery, the involvement of service users and increased access to psychological therapies, represent a departure from the earlier medical and maintenance focus. According to Turner et al., "a historical narrative structured around rights (the right to health and the right to liberty) is now complicated by the rise of new organising categories such as 'costs', 'risks', 'needs', 'inclusion' and 'equality', which contemporary actors use to define competing visions of mental health services" (2015, p. 622). He argues that its effect has been the rise of risk avoidance and heightened concerns for public protection, and less so with humanitarian concerns for the welfare of afflicted individuals.

An important focus on efforts to refine contemporary mental health policies has been the development of new standards of care. Three initiatives exemplify this development. One is the recent National Institute of Clinical Excellence (NICE) guidelines on schizophrenia which includes a series of clinical practice recommendations regarding primary practice, the development of advance directives, and guidelines for referrals from primary to specialized care (England & Lester, 2005). Another initiative of the NHS is the introduction of waiting time standards for mental health services in 2016. And very important was the introduction in 2006 of the *Improving Access to Psychological Therapies* (IAPT) program involving people with common mental health conditions (CMDs), such as anxiety and depression, meant to enhance access to a range of treatments including face-to-face therapy and digital therapists including apps and online programs (UK-NICE, 2008).

Another policy initiative for fine-tuning the current system has been continued efforts to enhance the integration of care. These efforts have reportedly been piecemeal and ineffective:

> while the central thrust of a raft of recent Government policies in England has been towards integration of different parts of the health care system, policy waterfalls and implementation failures, the adoption of ideas before they have been thoroughly tried and tested, a lack of clarity over roles and responsibilities and poor communication have led to an integration rhetoric reality gap in practice. (England & Lester, 2005, p. 1)

Efforts at integration have often focused on improving the role of the GP in primary care. General medical practitioners are encouraged to decide on whether to offer services at one of three levels: (i) essential services for people with acute and chronic illnesses and which have to be provided by all practices; (ii) additional services such as maternity and contraceptive services which are being offered by most practices; and (iii) enhanced services (which are optional) including specialized care for people with depression. This also included referral to hospitals and to the Community Mental Health Teams noted earlier (England & Lester, 2005).

Current Services

While the UK mental health system offers a comprehensive array of services, its precise scope is not defined by statute or by legislation, and there is no absolute right for patients to receive particular treatments. Treatments offered by physicians and mental health specialists, including the Community Mental Health Teams, are intended to be guided by the NICE recommendations for particular conditions. These standards are to be based on published evidence, expert contributions, and real-life experiences, and are officially used in England, but may also be used in Wales and other parts of the UK. Among the most common types of treatment potentially available are talking treatments and psychiatric medication, as well as supportive employment and housing options, and other alternatives, such as arts, creative therapists, and complementary and alternative therapies. Some services can be provided or arranged directly by the GP, but others are offered through hospitals, non-governmental organizations (NGOs), and the Community Mental Health Teams. These teams typically include a community psychiatric nurse (CPN), a psychologist, and occupational therapist, counselor, and a community support worker, as well as a specialist social worker. Often one of these are appointed to be the service coordinator for a given consumer.

The provision of talking therapies, such as the psychotherapies, changed after 2006 with the introduction of the IAPT program which, as stated earlier, made it possible for patients to access such services without a recommendation from their GP. One of the most common of such therapies has been some version of cognitive behavioral therapy (CBT). Whether CBT, or other psychological or counseling interventions are considered, research in the UK has shown little significant difference in client outcomes (see England & Lester, 2005).

One of the most common treatments has involved the prescription of psychiatric medications, which, while rarely curing mental health problems, serve to ameliorate many symptoms of mental illness, often with significant side effects. These medications typically include antidepressants, antipsychotics, sleeping pills and minor tranquilizers, and mood stabilizers such as lithium. McManus et al. (2016) report that one person in three in the UK with a common mental disorder was in receipt of either a psychotropic medication and/or counseling.

For those with acute or severe mental health problems, inpatient hospital care continues to be provided in both public and private facilities. Most hospital admissions are voluntary, but as is the case in many nations, if the individual is adjudged to be at risk of harming self or others, he or she may be involuntarily detained; in the UK, this is under the Mental Health Act of 1983 (in England and Wales). Publicly owned hospitals are provided either as part of NHS Trusts (currently 64) or as part of foundation trusts. In total there are an estimated 515 private hospitals in the UK, some for-profit and non-profit. Private hospitals with psychiatric services provide a variety of services, including treatments either unavailable in the NHS or subject to long waiting lists, such as bariatric surgery and fertility treatment, and generally do not have emergency, trauma, or intensive-care facilities. Such private providers must be registered with the Care Quality Commission and with NHS Improvement, but their charges to private patients are not regulated, and there are no public subsidies. Supplementing some hospital and community services are adult day units (ADUs). One recent study (Lamb et al., 2019) identified 45 such ADUs in England, including such atypical programs as drop-in "crisis cafes." Such programs remain the exception as only a third of the NHS Trusts have access to ADUs. These programs typically offer a variety of services such as medication, physical checks, psychological interventions, group sessions, and peer support, with a median treatment period of 30 days.

A critical service for many of the seriously mentally ill are housing supports (see Killaspy, 2016). These are typically provided through various NGOs, and include hostels, which are short-term accommodations with supervision; residential care homes, which provide longer-term and more intensive services; therapeutic communities, which involve short stays, with various group or individual therapies; and supported housing schemes, which enable greater independence but with visits by mental health support workers when help is needed. In addition, a range of modalities of social or community care is available, as is crisis intervention (Mind, 2017).

Current Management and Organization

In the UK, mental health policy and services are considered an integral part of the NHS, a single payer national agency (Figure 16.1). Nonetheless, silos exist that split the ways that physical and mental health care are organized and paid for (Stanton, 2014). Through the NHS, the government owns the hospitals and providers of NHS care, including ambulance, mental health services, district nursing, and various other community services, through providers referred to as NHS Trusts (Durand-Zaleski, 2020). Other important public agencies include NHS Improvement, responsible for licensing providers; the Commonwealth Fund, which includes the NICE, the main standard-setting agency for new health care treatments; the local authorities, charged with providing social care; Health Education England, responsible for workforce planning; and the Care Quality Commission (CQC), charged with assuring basic standards of safety and quality. The CQC performs a particularly critical function in that all providers, including institutions, partnerships, and sole practitioners must be registered with this Commission which monitors performance, using nationally set quality standards, and surveys and rates each provider. When necessary, it can close services that do not meet its standards (Durand-Zeleski, 2020). These public agencies are supported by a wide range of private NGOs, the largest of which is Mind, which sponsors supported housing, employment, advocacy, befriending schemes, counseling centers, and social support programs (Goldie & Sayce, 1993).

Funding

The UK mental health system is essentially a single payer system, with the nation spending 12.8 percent of its GDP on health care (World Bank, 2020). Public expenditures for NHS services account for 79.4 percent of this amount, with the majority originating from general taxes, and a small portion (20 percent) from national insurance. This insurance is supported by a payroll tax shared by employees and employers. A considerably smaller portion of the NHS budget

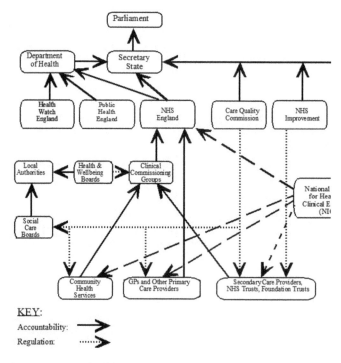

Figure 16.1   *Organization of public mental health services in the UK*

Source: Adapted from Thorlby, 2020.

originates from copayments and people using NHS as private patients (Durand-Zaleski, 2020). In 2015, just over 10 percent of the UK population had private voluntary health insurance, accounting for 3.3 percent of total health expenditures. Some of the private insurance plans are offered directly by employers, but some individuals also purchase policies so as to obtain more rapid access to care, greater choice of specialists, and enhanced access to elective procedures. Most of these policies, however, exclude mental health, maternity services, emergency care, and general practice. An important feature of health care funding in the UK is that there is very limited cost-sharing for any publicly covered services which are free at the point of consumption for both outpatient and inpatient services. However, out-of-pocket payments for GP visits are required only for provision of certifications for insurance purposes and travel vaccinations.

As is the case in many nations, strategies of cost containment in UK health care have been a challenge. The primary strategy in the UK involves the use of a fixed national budget, instead of cost-sharing requirements. These budgets are typically established at the national level on three-year cycles. Other strategies used include the freezing of staff pay increases, expansion in the use of generic drugs, reduction in Diagnostic Related Group (DRG) payments for certain hospital services, managing demand, and control of administrative costs. Also, outcome-based payment systems are used for somatic disorders, and are increasingly being used to control mental health care costs through what is referred to as "Care Clusters" for payment. This has been made possible by the extensive work in the UK on development of the National Outcome Scales (HoNOS) framework, similar to that in Australia and New Zealand. The nation has a well-developed mix of quality and outcome indicators (OECD, 2011). Costs for outpatient prescription drugs are controlled by a copayment requirement of £8.80 per prescription, whereas those prescription in NHS hospitals have no such requirement. Similarly, NHS dentistry services are subject to a copayment of up to £256.50 per course of treatment, a charge set by the NHS. In total, out-of-pocket health expenditures by household represented about 15 percent of total expenditures in the UK in 2016 (Durand-Zaleski, 2020).

PUBLIC POLICY PROCESS AND DECISION MAKING

In contrast to the US federal system with its divided and often conflicting powers, the UK's parliamentary system is considerably more centralized with its various health and social services ultimately reporting to the Parliament, through its Secretary of State (Gawron, 2019). Day-to-day responsibility for the NHS – which is responsible for mental health policy – lies with NHS England, which serves as an "arm's-length-government-funded body" which is run independently from the Department of Health. It, however, does not define the specific parameters, but rather only the general outlines of what is developed by local health and social service departments (Goldie & Sayce, 1993). The administration of health and social services policies is undertaken by the Department of Health, the Welsh Office, the Scottish Office, and the Northern Ireland Office. At the local level, these authorities are accountable to appointed boards; the local authorities are elected entities that develop local policy. It is particularly important to note that each of these local authorities decide what proportion of its budget to devote to mental health, as well as the particular mix of mental health services that it provides (Goldie & Sayce, 1993).

System Outcomes

The term "outcome" has historically had a variety of meanings, despite efforts on the part of many to restrict it to matters involving the actual resolution or minimization of target problems. Nonetheless, mental health system outcomes have commonly included the degree of service access, various intermediate outcomes involving quality of care and how well patients feel that they are treated, as well as progress in resolving or minimizing the target problem and enhancing functioning. In the UK and elsewhere, the first two of these have historically been the easiest to assess, and for that reason more data is available in these areas.

In recent years, the UK has made concerted attempts to reduce waiting times for access to NHS psychological therapies, particularly those in the IAPT program. In 2020, Baker reported that such waiting times have varied from 4 to 61 days in different parts of the nation (Baker, 2020). There have been 3.5 referrals for every 100 adults in England, about 11 percent more than the previous year. Just over a million of these entered treatment in 2018/19, with just over half (582,000) finishing their treatment, and 473,000 failing to begin treatment, a referral success rate not dissimilar to that in many nations. Some of the greatest wait times were for people referred to specialist mental health teams (OECD, 2011). One report suggests that,

> The majority of people who do come to mental health services get well looked after. But there are many, many people who could and should get through but don't, and who either have to cobble together different bits of care from the voluntary sector, the private sector, and from friends and

family to try to compensate for what the NHS should be doing to help them. (Molodynski, cited in Spence, n.d., p. 4)

Perhaps the most extensive data available on the quality of mental health services in the UK originates from the annual inspections that the Care Quality Commission conducts each year for the nation's mental health services. As of May 31, 2017, this Commission's inspectors rated two-thirds (68 percent) of core services provided by NHS Trusts, and a greater number (72 percent) of those provided by independent providers as "good," with an additional 6 percent of NHS and 3 percent of independent services rated as outstanding. The Commission reinspected 22 of those programs that were initially rated as inadequate or requiring improvement and found that 16 managed to improve these ratings. Only a very small number were rated as inadequate: seven core services (1 percent) in NHS Trusts and three core services (1 percent) among independent services (UK-CQC, 2017). In their report, the Commission identified several areas of concern (UK-CQC, 2017): (i) The safety of services; (ii) persistence of restrictive practices; (iii) access and waiting times; and (iv) poor information systems. Those that performed highly tended to be community mental health services for people with learning disabilities or autism, as well as community-based mental health services for older people.

Published data on recovery and improvement rates is less readily available, but what is available indicates some positive outcomes. Baker (2020) reports that about two-thirds of people see an improvement in their condition after finishing IAPT therapy. NHS England has a benchmark target that 50 percent of those finishing a course of treatment should "move to recovery," meaning that the patient has improved from having a clinical case of depression or anxiety to not having a clinical case. In 2018/19, 52.1 percent of those finishing a course of treatment moved to recovery, up from 50.8 percent in 2017/18. Recovery rates were reported greater for anxiety-related disorders (54.2 percent) than depression (50.3 percent), in contrast to conditions with the lowest recovery rates, which include agoraphobia (39.8 percent), PTSD (41.8 percent), and social phobias (43.5 percent). These rates may well be a function of the greater severities of these conditions. Only very modest improvement rates have been reported for those with schizophrenia. For example, employment rates for those with this condition have fallen over the last 50 years, and now stand at between 5 percent and 15 percent. In addition, those with schizophrenia have been found to die 20 to 25 years earlier than average (Stanton, 2014), a rate similar to that found in other nations.

DISCUSSION AND CONCLUSIONS

The UK's mental health system is arguably one of the better developed systems in the world. It provides a wide range of community and hospital services and is effectively managed using well-developed standards. The extent of the system's development is no doubt a function of the nation's wealth, its well-educated populace, and its culture. These advantages have been only realized over a particularly extended history of mental health policy, one characterized by considerable caution, and even minimal innovation. Many of the unmet needs and problems in the system reflect continuing limitations in the development of mental health treatments and other interventions. Psychiatric deinstitutionalization and the development of community mental health services have, likewise, proceeded slowly. As noted earlier, the nation is now at the stage of fine-tuning and attempting to integrate its community services. This effort has at once demonstrated some emerging innovations, such as the efforts to move from a medical to a psychosocial model and to open up access to a wide range of therapies through the IATP program, and yet has been limited by a lack of integration of traditional community services with a broader array of social welfare services, which have fallen outside the traditional purview of mental health. Most notable has been a lack of innovation in respect to mental health services for mentally disordered offenders. Other areas requiring attention are consumer rights, research and evidence-based practice, and workforce needs that have been exacerbated given the nation's exit from the EU.

It has been pointed out that the UK's risk adverse approach to mental health has not only slowed the process of psychiatric deinstitutionalization, but has severely limited the UK's adoption of therapeutic jurisprudence models, particularly mental health courts, in contrast to the wider range of diversion policies evident in the United States (Gawron, 2019). Wolff (2002), likewise, argues that a low tolerance for risk in the UK has led many mental health providers to limit their risk exposure by avoiding complex and difficult-to-treat patients. This has often meant providers restricting access to multi-problem patients through the use of service denials based on residency and other eligibility requirements, or the conclusion that they may be untreatable.

The risk adverse approach has also served to slow efforts to protect consumer rights in the UK. It has been pointed out that advocacy in the UK has developed more slowly than in many other nations. In the UK, modern advocacy and service-user groups, which have embraced greater choice and freedoms on the part of patients and ex-patients, did not emerge until the 1980s. It has only been in recent years that groups such as *Rethink Mental Illness* and *Time to Change* have brought mental health concerns to the attention of the public and advocated for better programs (Gawron, 2019).

As is the case in many nations, the UK has in recent years struggled with the push for evidence-based practice, originating in medicine in the early 1990s. On one hand, the integration of psychological therapies into practice through the IAPT program has been driven by NICE guidelines which have emphasized randomized controlled trials, and various versions of cognitive behavioral therapies. Turner et al. (2015) have questioned the extent to which such guidelines have actually been integrated into day-to-day practice. In addition, the growing importance of the neurosciences, especially those that incorporate behavioral genetics and psychopharmacology, may have been missed by many practitioners, especially given the extent to which subscription to such contrasting practice models may be hamstrung by professional silos. These issues highlight the importance of workforce development, especially the need for non-medical practitioners, such as social workers, to be clinically trained on the post-graduate (post-bachelors) level.

The continued need for fine-tuning of both the professional workforce and the community mental health system has been severely exacerbated by mental health staffing shortages created by the exit from the EU. The NHS has been particularly reliant on overseas workers; as of 2016, the NHS workforce in England included almost 60,000 staff with an EU nationality, including 10,000 doctors and 20,000 nurses and health visitors (Zanon, 2016). Over a third (41 percent) of psychiatrists in training in the UK were non-UK graduates. The EU also has traditionally provided considerable supplementation to the UK's mental health research budget, a resource which will not be easily compensated for.

Many of the items of unfinished business noted above have been recognized by NHS planners and have recently stimulated new initiatives to address them. Most important, in

September 2019, NHS England issued a new framework document that outlines changes it anticipates in community mental health services over the next five years. This framework supplements the NHS Long Term Plan, also published in 2019. Significant new funding – £2.3 billion – is planned for mental health over this time period. The plan emphasizes increased access to psychological therapies, improved physical health care, employment support, personalized and trauma-informed care, and support for services to address self-harm and coexisting substance use (Bell, 2017). Specifically, it envisions "a new place-based community mental health model … to shift to whole person, whole population approaches." It marks the end of the Care Program Approach (CPA), a system which has been in use for almost 30 years. Instead, the Framework states that anyone requiring support in the community "should have a co-produced and personalised care plan," including their Care Act and Mental Health Act Section 117 aftercare rights (Bell, 2017, p. 2). It seeks to remedy the discontinuities between primary and secondary care and place less emphasis on assessments, service thresholds, and risk assessments (Bell, 2017).

The initiative also seeks to reform the Mental Health Act, enabling individuals to take greater control over their treatment, providing enhanced individualization of care, as well as tackling the continuing lack of parity between physical and mental health care. It includes a renewed emphasis on treatment in the least restrictive environment. Four principles are specifically identified that will guide the reform of the Mental Health Act: (i) Choice and autonomy, ensuring that service users' views and choices are respected; (ii) least restriction, ensuring the use of new powers in the least restrictive manner; (iii) therapeutic benefit, ensuring that patients are supported in their recovery and discharged from the Act in a timely manner; (iv) individualization, ensuring that patients are treated as rounded individuals. The realization of such pivotal principles of mental health care will no doubt be ongoing challenges for policy makers, administrators, and practitioners in the UK mental health system, who are in an excellent position to make progress on them in coming years.

REFERENCES

Baker, C. (2020). *Mental health statistics: Prevalence, services and funding in England.* Briefing paper number 6988. House of Commons Library, UK Parliament (6988). Retrieved August 17, 2022 from http://researchbriefings.files.parliament.uk/documents/SN06988/SN06988.pdf

Bell, A. (2017). *The mental elf. NHS England's new framework for community mental health services,* 2676(2016), 1–9.

Durand-Zaleski, I. (2020). *International health care system profiles.* The Commonwealth Fund, 1–22.

England, E., & Lester, H. (2005). Integrated mental health services in England: A policy paradox? *International Journal of Integrated Care,* 5(October), 1–8.

Gawron, C.R. (2019). Funding mental healthcare in the wake of deinstitutionalization: How the United States and the United Kingdom diverged in mental health policy after deinstitutionalization, and what we can learn from their differing approaches to funding mental healthcare. *Notre Dame Journal of International & Comparative Law,* 9(2), 85–115. Retrieved August 17, 2022 from https://scholarship.law.nd.edu/ndjicl/vol9/iss2/6/

Goldie, N., & Sayce, L. (1993). United Kingdom. In D.R. Kemp (Ed.), *International handbook on mental health policy* (pp. 292–411). Westport, CT: Greenwood.

Grigoroglou, C., Munford, L., Webb, RT., Kapur, N., Ashcroft, D.M., & Kontopantelis, E. (2019). Prevalence of mental illness in primary care and its association with deprivation and social fragmentation at the small-area level in England. *Psychological Medicine,* 50(2), 293–302. https://doi.org/10.1017/S0033291719000023

Hudson, C.G. (2020). Benchmarking psychiatric deinstitutionalization: Development, testing, and application of a model through predictive analytics. *Best Practices in Mental Health*, 16(1), 13–32.

Hudson, C.G., & Doogan, N. (2019). The impact of geographic isolation on mental disability in the United States. *SSM: Population Health*, 8, 1–10.

Hunter, R., & MacAlpine, I., (1974) *Psychiatry for the poor: 1851 Colney Hatch Asylum-Friern Hospital 1973. A medical and social history*. Dawsons of Pall Mall.

Jacobi, C. (2017). *Positive mental health and mortality in the United Kingdom literature and theory.* Oxford, UK: Nuffield College, University of Oxford.

Jayawickreme, E., Forgeard, M.J.C., & Seligman, M.E.P. (2012). The engine of well-being. *Review of General Psychology*, 16(4), 327–42.

Killaspy, H. (2006). From the asylum to community care: Learning from experience. *British Medical Bulletin*, 79–80(1), 245–58. https://doi.org/10.1093/bmb/ldl017

Lamb, D., Davidson, M., Lloyd-Evans, B., Johnson, S., Heinkel, S., Steare, T., & Osborn, D. (2019). Adult mental health provision in England: A national survey of acute day units. *BMC Health Services Research*, 19(1), 1–11. https://doi.org/10.1186/s12913-019-4687-8

McManus, S., Bebbington, P., Jenkins, R., & Brugha, T., Eds. (2016). *Mental health and wellbeing in England: Adult Psychiatric Morbidity Survey 2014*. Leeds: NHS Digital. Retrieved Augusy 17, 2022 from https://assets.publishing.service.gov.uk/government/uploads/system/uploads/
attachment_data/file/556596/apms-2014-full-rpt.pdf

Miller, P., & Rose, N. (1986). *The power of psychiatry*. Oxford: Polity Press.

Mind. (2017). *Mental Health Problems*. www.Mind.Org.Uk, 1–25. Retrieved August 17, 2022 from https://www.mind.org.uk/information-support/types-of-mental-health-problems/mental-health-problems-introduction/#.XCUs8mT7R1M

Organisation for Economic Co-operation and Development (OECD). (2011). One of the most innovative mental health systems in the OECD, spending cuts in the UK risk undermining progress, 0–1. Paris.

Parry-Jones, W.L. (1972). *The trade in lunacy*. London: Routledge & Kegan Paul.

Ramon, S. (1985). *Psychiatry in Britain*. Bechenham: Croom Helm.

Spence, A. (n.d.). NHS patients want privacy, not privatisation. *OurNHS*.

Stanton, E. (2014). The case for change for British mental healthcare. *Journal of the Royal Society of Medicine*, 107(4), 135–7. https://doi.org/10.1177/0141076814522144

Thorlby, R. (2020). InternationalHealth Systems Profiles (n.p.), Commonwealth Fund.

Turner, J., Hayward, R., Angel, K., Fulford, B., Hall, J., Millard, C., & Thomson, M. (2015). The history of mental health services in modern England: Practitioner memories and the direction of future research. *Medical History*, 59(4), 599–624. https://doi.org/10.1017/mdh.2015.48

United Kingdom, Care Quality Commission (UK-CQC). (2017). *The state of care in mental health services: 2014 to 2017*. Retrieved August 17, 2022 from https://www.cqc.org.uk/publications/major-report/state-care-mental-health-services-2014-2017

United Kingdom, Department of Health and Social Security (UK-DHHSC). (1971). *Hospital services for the mentally ill*. London: HMSO.

United Kingdom, National Institute for Health Care and Excellence (UK-NICE). (2008). *Mental health and the NHS: What has changed and what's to come?* Retrieved August 13, 2022 from https://indepth.nice.org.uk/mental-health-and-the-nhs/index.html

United Kingdom, NHS Employers (UK-NHS). (2008). *Mental health and employment in the NHS*. October, 1–39. Retrieved August 17, 2022 from http://www.nhsemployers.org/publications

Wolff, N. (2002). Risk, response, and mental health policy: Learning from the experience of the United Kingdom. *Journal of Health Politics, Policy and Law*, 27(5), 801–32. https://doi.org/10.1215/03616878-27-5-801

World Bank. (2020). *Data*. Retrieved August 17, 2022 from https://data.worldbank.org/country/united-kingdom?view=chart

World Health Organization (WHO). (2005). *Mental health atlas*. Revised Edition. United Kingdom (pp. 486–8). Geneva: World Health Organization.

Zanon, E. (2016). Brexit and NHS mental health services. *Health Business UK*, 1–5. Retrieved 8/17/2022 from https://healthbusinessuk.net/features/brexit-and-nhs-mental-health-services" https://healthbusinessuk.net/features/brexit-and-nhs-mental-health-services

17. United Kingdom. The place of shared decision making in UK mental health services

Shulamit Ramon and Echo Yuet Wah Yeung

The United Kingdom's Shared Decision Making (SDM) policy is located within its National Health Service (NHS) system. The UK's highly centralized health system entitles all citizens in need of mental health service to use all services regulated by the Department of Health and Social Care (DHSC). SDM is a recommended practice (see National Institute of Clinical Excellence (NICE) guidelines, 2021), but the implementation of this policy is in its infancy, especially in the case of mental health inpatient services.

Mental ill health and infectious diseases are the only two health areas where it is possible to admit and treat people against their will, on the assumption that they are unable to make reasonable decisions due to either their mental health state or their physical health state, and that refusing treatment may endanger either themselves and/or others. According to the Office of National Statistics, 50,893 people were detained under the Mental Health Act 2007 in 2019–20 in England. Table 17.1 indicates some key inequalities in the current mental health system.

The length of hospital stays in the twenty-first century is lower than it was previously, due to a de-institutionalization policy enacted in the UK between 1990 and 2010 (Ramon, 2018). Most mental health wards are based in a general hospital and have a small number of beds (often no more than 20). It is legally allowed to put patients in a seclusion room within the ward, and to treat them against their will (inclusive of injections), while it is not allowed to use physical means of coercion. This experience is perceived by many of those detained as a highly undesirable intervention, and the fear of it may make people accept interventions they would not wish to have (Shashidaran et al., 2019). People can also be detained in secure units, most of which are privately owned, but paid for by the NHS.

Community Treatment Orders (CTOs) and Guardianship are additional legal forms of a lower level of compulsion while people live in the community with their mental ill health condition, even though the evidence for the usefulness of the CTOs is unpromising (Rugkasa & Burns, 2018). The UK has wide-ranging community services, most of which are either provided by the health and social care statutory services or by the voluntary non-profit sector. The processes of policy making and legislation in this field are lengthy in the time they take to complete, partly due to the consultation process which accompanies any major change and partly as they tend to be the result of a compromise between more than one option. Service users are consulted alongside professionals working in the statutory sector, as well as voluntary sector organizations. By regulation, service users have to be consulted on proposed policy and legislation changes, and research applications have to demonstrate that service users and lay people have been consulted about their usefulness. Both of these requirements are systematically implemented. Most mental health trusts employ peer support workers who are by definition people with lived experience of mental ill health (Gillard et al., 2017).

Currently, a new Mental Health Act is being consulted about, formally justified by the wish to improve service users' degree of choice while decreasing compulsory measures (DHSC,

Table 17.1   Rates of adults detained for mental ill health in England

Age	Rate (per 100,000)
18–34	129.8
50–64	92.5
BAME (Black Asian and Minority Ethnic)	321.7
White people	73.4
Community treatment orders (CTOs): males	10.5
CTOs: females	6.1
CTOs: BAME	61.3
CTOs: White people	6.0

Source: Office of National Statistics, 2019–20, Mental Health Statistics, HMSO.

2018). It is stated that the new Act will be designed to tackle the complex balance between respecting a person's autonomy and the duty of a civilized society and its government to protect vulnerable people, recognizing the fear by patients, the public, and the professionals involved in the system of negative outcomes due to having a mental illness condition.

The consultation aims to "improve choice and decision making both prior to and within a setting of compulsion" (DHSC, 2018, p. 6). The review recognizes that the current system is not good enough in providing either choice or support for decision making. While the concept of SDM is absent from the review, enabling service users to have a say in decisions about their lives is recognized as a way of enhancing their dignity. Existing evidence demonstrating that the active engagement of service users in decision making about their lives is more effective than when they are not engaged is left unmentioned, as are the necessary conditions for successful SDM, which include mutual respect and trust (Morant et al., 2015). The emphasis is on advanced directives prepared when service users are not in a crisis situation, even though there is convincing evidence that most patients in an acute ward are capable of participating in SDM shortly after a crisis (Hamman et al., 2011). Yet both the DHSC and NICE have published calls for the application of SDM in mental health (as well as in physical health) since 2009; the latest of which appeared in 2021 (NICE, 2021), which is looked at below.

The proposed new Act has been criticized for insufficient attention to the over-representation of Black people detained under the Mental Health Act (as highlighted in Table 17.1), and under-represented in being provided with psychological intervention (The Mental Health Foundation, 2021).

WHAT IS SHARED DECISION MAKING?

SDM is a process that aims to secure the engagement of both service users and providers in jointly making intervention decisions (Charles et al., 1999). This objective is justified by acknowledging that experiential knowledge is as important as scientific knowledge, given that a person is usually an expert about their own experience and that sharing this type of knowledge would constitute an important addition, one often unknown to the service provider. Furthermore, existing evidence indicates that people who are active in decision making concerning themselves are more motivated to follow these decisions than those who are not engaged (Stovell et al., 2016).

There are significant variations in the type and degree of involvement in SDM each approach provides, such as whether the process is led by a practitioner alongside a service user, or only by a professional (Figure 17.1). Initially the focus of SDM in mental health was on medication management, but now psychosocial issues are also included, such as employment (Hutchinson et al., 2018), housing, parenting, and other close relationships, such as informal caring (Weiss et al., 2021).

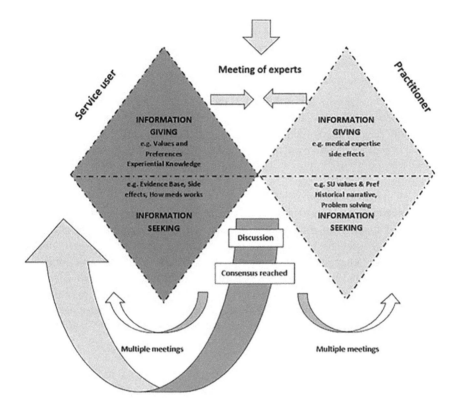

Figure 17.1   *The ideal relationships between the two key partners to the process of SDM*

SDM was introduced into the mental health setting following research evidence from SDM in the context of physical illness, which originated at the end of the twentieth century in both the UK and the US, as well as in other Western countries (Légaré et al., 2018: Ramon et al., 2017b). Existing research highlights the usefulness of SDM in mental health, both at the level of one-to-one interaction (Stovell et al., 2016) as well as at a hospital ward level (Crawford et al., 2021). The regime of SDM in the Springbank Ward in Cambridge's Fulbourn Hospital began by revoking the compulsory admission the patient had, a symbolic – yet risky – gesture towards returning responsibility to the person (UH and CPFT, 2018). Patients have to make decisions concerning leaving the ward and coming back, planning their discharge in detail, and attending all individual and group Dialectical Behavior Therapy (DBT) sessions.

The results of an evaluation of this program indicate progress from a high level of self-harming to almost no self-harming episodes, with a high number of women succeeding to leave the ward and leading a meaningful life in the community. The video from UH and CPFT talked about the experience of a patient Jazmine that highlights this process; Jazmine is now a peer support worker on the Springbank Ward (UH and CPFT, 2018). SDM is also closely aligned to the mental health recovery conceptual and practice framework, developed towards the end of the twentieth century, which is based on the belief that people experiencing mental ill health can lead a meaningful life with their illness and beyond it (Anthony, 1993; Davidson, 2003).

Practitioners' voices concerning the usefulness of SDM focus on questioning whether people experiencing mental ill health have valid insight, and the validity of experiential knowledge versus that of scientific knowledge. On the whole, service users and most mental health practitioners such as nurses, occupational therapists, psychologists, and social workers tend to be supportive of SDM, while more dissenting voices come from psychiatrists (Kaminskiy et al., 2021; Shepherd et al., 2014).

The changing attitudes towards the role of service users comes from a history of considerable shift in mental health policy and services that took place towards the end of the twentieth century, which continue to unfold. Similar to other countries, the UK also has moved from reliance on hospitalization as the main mode of intervention to community care and to adhering to mental health recovery and strengths-based approaches (Rapp & Goscha, 2012). While the recovery approach has been introduced initially by service users (Chamberlin, 1979) and psychologists, the strengths approach has been created by social work academics and is practised in relation to all types of disabilities, including mental health (Saleeby, 1992). This approach is aligned to the social model of disability, created by researchers with physical disabilities (Oliver, 1990) who argued that being disabled should not imply lack of capacity to function socially and to contribute meaningfully to communal life. Rapp and Goscha's work (2012) applies the strengths approach to mental ill health, and focuses on changing attitudes of service providers and the general public in reducing existing stigma, as well as on finding ways to enable the fulfilment of service users' potentials and minimizing their internalized stigma.

While the physical barriers to the integration of people with physical disabilities are easy to recognize, those exercised in the context of mental illness are more complex and subtle to identify and to change. A key barrier is the notion of insight, where service providers argue that many people experiencing mental ill health do not have the ability to reach rational decisions due to their illness. While insight in the sense of self-reflexivity may be reduced in acute psychosis and requires an integrated approach to improve it (Lysaker et al., 2018), the possibility that they may have insight that differs from that of the professionals working with them, or their family members, is often negated by both lay people and mental health professionals (Roe & Davidson, 2005).

Service users' decisions to stop taking psychiatric medication are usually perceived by clinicians as lacking insight, and not as due to reaching such a decision based on calculating the balance between the negative and positive effects of the medication (Katz et al., 2018). Deegan's (2005) concept of personal medicine highlights an alternative perspective of weighing such a balance, which indicates the existence of a well-constructed insight framework, but one that has a different end objective to that of medical practitioners. In a more recent publication, Zisman-Illani et al. (2021a) justifiably call for applying Shared Risk Making as key to ensuring the viability of SDM, focusing on intersubjective knowledge and its application. Yet the issue of the need for a positive risk-taking policy and practice, viewing SDM as an example of such a risk-taking position, is not raised by those who write about risk avoidance and lack of insight, though it has already been raised by those who promoted de-institutionalization and recovery (Mezzina, 2005; Ramon, 2006). The existing UK legislation and policy concerning mental capacity in mental health (excluding neurologically caused illness, such as dementia) provides a high level of safeguarding in case of lack of capacity (Mental Capacity Act, 2021 update), and too little recognition that in reality the lack of such capacity is often of very short duration (Hamman et al., 2006).

Slade (2017) asserts the needs for a cultural change and the use of relevant SDM tools if the government is committed to support the implementation of SDM. It is disappointing that the Royal College of Psychiatrists (2017) in its recent publications on risk and on job requirements of consultant psychiatrists focuses primarily on risk to others. The publications do not mention SDM, but declare that their role is to support patients "to develop a set of realistic recovery goals and a care plan" (Royal College of Psychiatrists, 2018, p. 8). This declaration implies that consultant psychiatrists do not need to change anything in order to promote SDM.

Unlike traditional psychiatry, SDM is based on accepting the value of experiential knowledge as a necessary component alongside scientific knowledge as the key assumption underlying SDM. Interestingly, the need for both types of knowledge is rejected not only by mental health professionals who believe that professionals know best, but also by service users who follow the Mad Studies Approach to mental ill health (Beresford, 2020). The latter group believes that only service users have the right knowledge and hence should have the sole right to make decisions for themselves. This argument is rooted in Western parliamentary democracies' human rights agenda, in which full independence and autonomy is assumed to exist. However, SDM is based on the assumption that we are interdependent on other people, and hence the use of the knowledge others bring with them needs to be taken into account alongside our own preferences when a major decision is called for. In this sense, SDM is "reactionary" from the perspective of Mad Studies, and "ignorant" from the perspective of professionals who think they know best due to being trained to follow scientific knowledge principles. The claim to interdependency has considerable evidence in any aspect of our lives, including in health and social care (Ramon, 2018). Furthermore, following the intersectional approach (Crenshaw, 1991) there are a number of structural factors which either limit or enhance our degree of independent decision making, such as living in poverty, prevailing social attitudes to ethnicity, gender and sexuality, and the impact of natural disasters or human-made disasters. This does not mean that we should not aim to pursue our preferences during decision making, but it means that the degree of autonomy we have is limited, and that interdependence has both positive and negative aspects to it.

FAMILY GROUP CONFERENCES

Key variations of mental health SDM have been the introduction of Family Group Conferences (FGC), which have been practised mainly in the context of child protection (Manthorpe and Rapaport, 2020; Ramon, 2021), and the Open Dialogue in the UK and elsewhere (Putnam & Martindale, 2021). In these types of interventions, it is the family unit that is given the power to make decisions within a specific legal brief.

The role of the family in SDM is not self-evident. Informal carers in the UK are encouraged to participate in care reviews alongside the index service user, provided the service user does not object to their participation. However, the periodical care reviews (about once per six months) do not focus on following SDM principles or processes. FGC represent a system in which key care issues of an individual are sorted out by calling a family meeting to reach jointly relevant decisions and an implementation plan. This strategy was developed initially in New Zealand, based on the Maori's problem-solving strategy that employs a meeting of their elders, to which relevant others are invited too (Love, 2000). FGC is practised in social care across English-speaking countries and the Netherlands, including child protection (Normantov et al., 2020), mental health (Schout et al., 2017), restorative justice (Fox, 2008), adults of working age and older people's domestic abuse (Edwards & Parkinson, 2018; Parkinson & Rogers, 2018).

Adult mental health is the largest area of FGC practice at the level of adult services, though only ten English local authorities are currently registered as doing so (Manthorpe & Rapaport, 2020). The process differs considerably from SDM in health. To start with, the request for FGC usually comes from a social worker who has a legal role towards the service user, and at times towards other members of their family (e.g. children, partner). An independent coordinator is then appointed, whose role it is to discuss the participation in the FGC meeting with each participant, beginning with the index service user. The key social worker provides more than one potential scenario for decisions to be consulted by the family, each of which meets the key legal requirements. This discussion, which also needs to be concluded with an implementation action plan, takes place without the social worker or the coordinator. Existing research highlights that most participants are pleased with the initial meeting, including those who had considerable doubts prior to attending the meeting as to whether the family network is able to work together effectively in FGC, given a history of previous disagreements and increasing distancing between the index service user and the family network (Ramon, 2021). However, outcomes at the end of the implementation phase are inconclusive, in that some objectives are met, but others are left unmet (De Jong et al., 2016; Normantov et al., 2020).

It is likely that meeting the requirements of the implementation phase is either not receiving the attention it deserves or that the underlying tensions have not been resolved. Hence, rigorous evaluation that includes the implementation phase is a necessity, inclusive of cost-effectiveness. In addition, Randomized Control Trials (RCT) were not used as a method of selecting a sample for evaluation, and hence existing research evidence is perceived as not meeting systematic review conditions. Evaluation with experimental and control group designs have been applied, and did demonstrate the usefulness of FGC in working with adults experiencing mental ill health (De Jong et al., 2016; Tew et al., 2017).

THE OPEN DIALOGUE

The Open Dialogue is an adaptation of a systemic family therapy approach in which practitioners declare from the outset that decisions are made by the non-professional participants, consisting usually of the index service user diagnosed as having a mental illness and family members (Putnam & Martindale, 2021). It is practised in at least six mental health and social care trusts in the UK, and it is popular among both participating staff members and family members.

Experimented with initially in Lapland in Finland, the research follow-up demonstrated good outcomes in terms of considerable reduction of the acute phase of mental illness and return to ordinary living (Alakare & Seikkula, 2021). Some updated follow-up research highlighted less successful outcomes (Freeman et al., 2019). Currently, a randomized control study is being conducted in six different NHS Trusts funded by the UK government (Osborne, 2021; Razzaque, 2021). Although SDM is practised in this model, there are no publications which focus specifically on this aspect.

SDM PILOT PROJECTS

Two pilot SDM training projects for service providers and service users have been delivered. The first took place between 2012 and 2018 in the Cambridgeshire and Peterborough NHS Foundation Trust (CPFT) funded by the Research for Patients Benefits (RfPB) project. The second one took place between 2019 and 2022 in Hertfordshire Partnership Foundation Trust (HPFT). It is a service improvement project, focusing on training both service users and service providers to be co-leaders of SDM. The CPFT project has published a number of articles in peer-reviewed journals (Morant et al., 2015; Ramon et al., 2017a; Ramon et al., 2017b; Stead et al., 2017).

There are different decision-making aids that aim at reducing the decisional conflict that may be encountered when making decisions between alternative interventions, each with its advantages and disadvantages. Some have been well validated, such as the Decision Conflict Scale, developed by O'Connor et al. (2009). The Three Talk Approach is a much shorter decision-making aid, which reduces the number of questions that need to be asked, and has been validated internationally (Joseph-Williams et al., 2021). Simmons et al. (2017) have developed a decision-making aid with the active involvement of young people who have experienced mental ill health, demonstrating the value of co-production of the aid. The young people have also been trained to act as peer supporters in the process of SDM.

Developed specifically for mental health SDM, Patricia Deegan, who is a service user activist and a qualified clinical psychologist, promoted the SDM Common Ground Framework (Deegan et al., 2008). This approach recognizes the centrality of personal medicine (Deegan, 2005), alongside medical and psychological approaches, and provides peer support securing computerized communication between service users and professionals. This approach differs from Elywn et al.'s (2012) three-talk model which focuses more on the service user's perspective. A network of provider champions was added later, when it became clear that focusing only on service users is insufficient for the implementation of SDM (MacDonald-Wilson et al., 2016).

DEVELOPMENT OF NICE SDM GUIDELINES

SDM is driven by the duties of NHS England set out in the NHS Act 2006 and amended by the Health and Social Care Act 2012, to promote individual participation in decision making about health and social care. NICE formally adopted SDM in 2015 as an important aspect in healthcare practice and research. It developed the first SDM guidelines in December 2018 and launched a working draft of the guidelines in December 2020. After a six-month consultation with stakeholders, the refined guidelines were published in 2021. The guidelines emphasize that SDM should be part of everyday care in all healthcare settings. It promotes partnership working between healthcare professionals and people using services as well as their families, to make decisions about treatment and care. There are four recommendations in the guideline, they are:

- **Embedding shared decision making at an organizational level.** To ensure that SDM becomes standard practice, leadership, planning, and commitment from the organization's highest level is required. Organizations should develop an improvement plan to implement SDM by identifying existing good practice, developing training for staff, reviewing and monitoring implementation of SDM.
- **Putting shared decision making into practice.** As SDM is a process necessitating collaborative working between service users and healthcare professionals, service users should be encouraged and supported to engage in the whole consultation process, to enable them to reach an informed decision about their healthcare. Where appropriate, efforts should be made to ask service users if they want to involve families, friends, or any other advocates to support them.
- **Decision aids.** Decision aids should be used as part of toolkits to engage service users throughout the decision-making process. Healthcare professionals are encouraged to use the three-talk model developed by Elwyn et al. (2012), including the team, option and decision talk stages during consultation. The model is based on practice experience with people with physical ill health when they use primary care services. Healthcare professionals should be familiar with particular decision aids that are relevant to the needs, preferences, and values of their service users.
- **Communicating risks, benefits, and consequences.** Healthcare professionals should discuss risks, benefits, and possible consequences of different options. Professionals should make an effort to provide personalized information, utilizing relevant decisions aids so that people are supported to engage in the process of SDM.

We acknowledge the positive step taken by NICE to promote participation in the decision-making process, to enable service users, as well as their families, to move away from the periphery to the core of the planning and decision-making process. NICE's guidelines underline the importance of training service users to become trainers and appointing "service user champions" at the highest organizational level to make sure their voices are heard. To support implementation of SDM, NICE and Keele University, UK, worked in partnership to develop an online learning package. The package is mainly for all healthcare professionals and aims to equip them with the skills and knowledge to have good-quality shared decision-making conversations with the people they care for. The learning package is made up of six modules, takes approximately four hours to complete and is free to access.

However, most of the guidelines and tools that facilitate SDM are mainly for physical healthcare and generic physical health issues; the resources available on the NICE and NHS website that are designed specifically for people with mental health issues are very limited. No specific guidance has been developed as yet to disseminate information to promote and support this group in applying SDM. Furthermore, as highlighted by Zisman-Ilani et al.'s (2021b) article, only RCT research was included to inform the development of the NICE guidelines. Other studies, including non-randomized quasi-experimental design, which are the preferred methodologies to understand SDM mental health research, were excluded as sources of information. This means that most studies measuring the ethos underpinning SDM in mental health, such as empowerment, participation, hope, and recovery, were not included in the resources available during the consultation process (e.g. Kaminskiy et al., 2021; Ramon et al., 2017a; Stovell et al., 2016).

Looking at the membership of the Advisory Committee of NICE's Board that developed the guidelines on SDM, and the 409 stakeholders who signed up for the consultation exercises, only a very small number of stakeholders had a clear connection to charitable mental health organizations, for example, Mind, the Mental Health Foundation, and Rethink Mental Health. The limited representation of people with mental health issues and mental health service providers taking part in the consultation process casts doubts on the relevance of the tools and resources used to implement SDM for people with mental health issues. Leading charitable organizations that campaign for the improvement of mental health services and to raise community awareness about mental health have developed some helpful resources to empower people with mental health issues to be involved in SDM (The Mental Health Foundation, 2015; Mind, 2017). However, these resources do not cover specific guidance for individuals and their families living with mental health issues on how to apply SDM. Also, they do not provide training in SDM to either their staff groups or to the people using their services. Deegan et al.'s (2008) SDM Common Ground Approach which was developed specifically for people with mental health issues is not mentioned in the NICE guidelines.

CHALLENGES AND OPPORTUNITIES

Commitment to embed the SDM within organizations is required in order to implement SDM successfully. NICE is advocating making SDM mandatory in day-to-day practice as the way forward, stipulating clearly the need to identify key staff and service users to attend "train-the-trainer" workshops so that these champions can deliver training to key stakeholders. Existing studies, left unmentioned by NICE, demonstrate the potential benefits of training for different stakeholders in mental health settings (MacDonald-Wilson et al., 2016; Ramon et al., 2017a; Ramon et al., 2017b). Service users found that the training can help to reduce decisional conflict, make them feel more informed and in control of the decision-making process (Kaminskiy et al., 2021). Feedback from different practitioners, including CPNs, occupational therapists, clinical psychologists, social workers, and recovery workers, highlights that training helps them gain more confidence to initiate the dialogue about possible interventions with service users. SDM is more likely to facilitate alliances between professionals with service users (Metz et al., 2018), better working relationship with them and hence to reduce the likelihood of a relapse.

However, feedback from psychiatrists involved in SDM training tended to focus on the management of risk avoidance, while omitting the need for calculated positive risk taking, and assuming a lack of insight by service users of their mental health conditions and needs (Zisman-Ilani et al., 2021a). The tensions between having responsibility for medication prescription and the belief that SDM will lead to reducing medication taking by service users is a key reason as to why many psychiatrists may not be fully supportive of the drive for SDM (Kaminskiy et al., 2021; Katz et al., 2018; Ramon et al., 2017a). Other mental health professionals believe that not all people want to be involved in SDM and would rather have decisions made for them (Shepherd et al., 2014), disregarding the long socialization most people have of believing that doctors know best. Stovell et al. (2016) assert that an approach positioned in the middle-ground between paternalism and autonomy, such as SDM, can potentially yield more positive outcomes for therapeutic relationships, service users' empowerment, and decision-making abilities. Training for psychiatrists, as well as for other mental health disciplines, is imperative to address the tensions and discomfort, so that they are more aware of these potential positive outcomes of SDM.

Individuals and communities who traditionally experience health inequalities are likely to be excluded from having a SDM conversation. Table 17.1 has highlighted that people of racial and ethnic minority communities are more likely to be treated via compulsory admission. Zisman-Ilani et al. (2021b) also voice their concern that the NICE guidelines fail to address cultural differences in SDM practice. The model has not been validated among people with mental health issues from different racial and cultural backgrounds. It fails to address the challenges in practice because of language difference. Some people may not have proficient language skills in English and hence will not be fully informed of their rights and options during an SDM conversation. The preferred "three-talk model" highlights the importance of communication during choice, option, and decision talk (Elwyn et al., 2012). However, when language difference is an issue, it is difficult to communicate the message of choice, options, risks, benefits, and consequences effectively and accurately (Yeung et al., 2017). Additionally, due to language difficulties among newcomers from ethnic minorities, medication may be the only treatment alternative because "talking therapy" is not a viable option for them (Yeung, 2013).

Moreover, all the information and resources made available for the public on the website of the NICE and NHS are written only in English, it is difficult to reach the "seldom heard groups" during the consultation exercise and yet again their voices concerning the possible challenges they may experience in the preparation for, and during the process of SDM, will not be heard. The NICE recommendation rightly points out the need to involve interpreters. However, for those seeking community language support, there is no guidance and resources to inform them where and how to reach language support. Finally, there is a training issue for interpreters so that they are equipped with the knowledge of SDM and mental health literature to facilitate a meaningful SDM conversation.

Social and family support are very important during the recovery journey of people with mental health issues. In the NICE guidelines, healthcare professionals are encouraged to explore if people want their family, friends, and advocates to be involved in the SDM process. This approach may work well with people from certain ethnic and cultural backgrounds. For example, people from Asian and Chinese communities often involve their families in healthcare decision making including matters relating to mental health issues (Yeung et al., 2013). However, it is important to respect service users' rights, as some service users may not want their families to be involved in decision making. There could be conflicts between rights and needs of service users and their families and carers. This conflict could be exacerbated if the relatives of the service user cared for live in the same household. Some service users may not want to share their mental health issues with their families because of feeling ashamed of their situation (Ramon, 2021). Detailed guidelines to resolve this dilemma are essential, but these are absent in the SDM guidelines.

Finally, there is a lack of coordination in relation to dissemination of information about SDM among different stakeholders. In September 2016, NICE showed its commitment to work in collaboration with different stakeholders to develop a single point of online access to up-to-date and relevant SDM tools. However, to date little effort has been made to develop this single point of access. This has created many challenges for service users, mental health practitioners, and anyone who wants to find information and resources to support the implementation of SDM. Users have to navigate across different sites to search for information and resources about SDM. It is concerning that although a number of charitable organizations have developed resources to support SDM, they have not made strenuous efforts to champion its cause. Resources related to SDM have not been updated on their sites in the past few years.

SUMMARY

In conclusion, it seems that SDM is encouraged to develop further, and be applied at present in the UK as a policy and practice model, but without a sufficient commitment to actually implement it from the policy-making organizations. Although organizational support is called for by the policy makers, it is unspecific, and does not include an equal role for service users as for providers. The need for attitudinal change among providers, service users, and family carers is left largely unrecognized in the proposed policy. Attention to ethnic minorities is lacking, as is attention to recent and ongoing pilot projects, and updated articles published in international peer-reviewed journals.

REFERENCES

Alakare, B., & Seikkula, J. (2021). The historical development of open dialogue in Western Lapland. In Putnam, N. & Martindale, B. (Eds.), *Open dialogue of psychosis. Organizing mental health services to prioritise dialogue, relationship and meaning* (pp. 35–51). London: Routledge.

Anthony, W. (1993). Recovery from mental illness: The guiding vision of the mental health service system in the 1990s. *Psychosocial Rehabilitation Journal*, 16(4), 11–23.

Beresford, P. (2020). "Mad", mad studies and advancing inclusive resistance. *Disability and Society*, 35(8), 1337–42.

Charles, K., Gafni, A., & Wheelan, T. (1999). Decision-making in the physician-consumer encounter: Revising the shared treatment decision making model. *Social Sciences and Medicine*, 49(5), 651–61.

Chamberlin, J. (1979). *On our own: Patients controlled alternatives to mental health services*. New York: Haworth Press.

Crawford, P.A., Khan, T.S., & Zimbron, J. (2021). Rethinking risk assessment in a borderline personality unit: Patient and staff perspectives. *Cureus*, 13(2), e1357. doi: 10.7759/cureus.13557

Crenshaw, K. (1991). Mapping the margins: Intersectionality, identity politics and violence against women of color. *Standford Law Review*, 43(6), 1241–99. doi.org.10.2307/1229039

Davidson, L. (2003). *Living outside mental illness: Qualitative studies of recovery in schizophrenia*. New York: New York University Press.

De Jong, G., Schout, G., Meijer, E., Mulder, C.L., & Abma, T. (2016). Enabling social support and resilience: Outcomes of family group conferencing in public mental health care. *European Journal of Social Work*, 19, 731–48. doi: 10.1080/13691457.2015.1081585

Deegan, P. (2005). The importance of personal medicine: A qualitative study of resilience in people with psychiatric disabilities, *Scandinavian Journal of Public Health*, Supplement, 33(s56), 29–35.

Deegan, P.E., Rapp. C.A., Holter, H., & Riefer, M. (2008). A program to support shared decision making in an outpatients psychiatric medication clinic. *Psychiatric Services*, 59(6), 603–5.

Department of Health and Social Care (DHSC). (2018). *Modernizing the Mental Health Act*. London: HMSO.

Edwards, D., & Parkinson, K., Eds. (2018). *Family group conferences in social work*. Bristol: Policy Press.

Elwyn, G., Elwyn, G., Forsch, D., Thomson, R., Joseph-Williams, N., Lloyd, A., & Kinnersley, P. (2012). Shared decision making: A model for clinical practice. *Journal of General Internal Medicine*, 27(10), 1361–7.

Fox, D. (2008). Family group conference and evidence-based practice: What works. *Research, Policy and Planning*, 26(3), 157–67.

Freeman, A.M., Tribe, R.H., Stott, J.E., & Pilling, S. (2019). Open dialogue: A review of the evidence. *Psychiatric Services*, 70(1), 46–59.

Gillard, S., Foster, R. Gibson, S., Goldsmith, L, Marks, G., & White, S. (2017). Describing principled-based approach to developing and evaluating peer workers roles as peer support moves into mainstream health services. *Mental Health and Social Inclusion*, 21(3), 133–43. doi: 10.1108/MHRSI-03-2017-0016

Hamman, J., Langer, B., Winkler, V., Busch, R., Cohen, R., Lechut, S., & Kissling, W. (2006). Shared decision making for in-patients with schizophrenia. *Acta Psychiatrica Scandinavica*, 114(4), 265–73.

Hamman, J., Mendel, R., Meier, A., Asani, F., Pausch, E., Lecuht, S., & Kissling, W. (2011). "How to speak to your psychiatrist": Shared decision-making training for inpatients with schizophrenia. *Psychiatric Services*, 62(10), 1218–21.

Hutchinson, J., Gilbert, D., & Papworth, R. (2018). Implementing employment: Lessons for the making individual placement and support (IPS) work project. *International Journal of Environmental Research and Public Health*, 15(7), 1507–45. doi: 10.3390/ijerph15071545

Joseph-Williams, N., Abhyankar, P., Boland, L., Bravo, P., Brenner, A., Brodney, S., et al. (2021). What works in implementing patient decision aids in routine clinical settings? A rapid realist review and update from the International Patient Decision Aid Standards Collaboration. *Medical Decision Making*, 41(7), 907–37. doi: 10.1177/0272989x20978208

Kaminskiy, E., Zizman-Ilani, Y., & Ramon, S. (2021). Barriers and enablers to shared decision making in psychiatric medication management: A qualitative investigation of clinician and service users' views. *Frontiers Psychiatry*, 12. doi.org/10.3389/fpsyt.2021.678005

Katz, S., Goldblatt, H., Hasson-Ohayon, I., & Rose, D. (2018). Retrospective account of the process of using and discontinuing psychiatric medication. *Qualitative Health Research*, 29(2), 1–13. doi: 10.1177/1049732318793418

Légaré, F., Adekpedjou, R., Stacey, D., Turcotte, S., Kryworuchko, J., Graham, I.D., et al. (2018). Interventions for increasing the use of shared decision making by healthcare professionals. *Cochrane Database of Systematic Reviews*. doi:10.1002/14651858.CD006732.pub4

Love, C. (2000). Family group conferences: Cultural origins sharing appropriation. In G. Burford & J. Hudson (Eds.), *Family group conferences* (pp. 15–30). London: Routledge.

Lysaker, P.H., Pattison, M.L., Leonhadt, N.L., & Phelps, S. (2018). Insight in schizophrenia spectrum disorders: Relationship with behaviour mood and perceived quality of life, underlying causes and emerging treatments. *World Psychiatry*, 17(1), 12–23.

MacDonald-Wilson, K.L., Hutchinson, S.L., Karpov, I., Wittman, P., & Deegan, P.E. (2016). A successful implementation strategy to support adoption of decision making in mental health services. *Community Mental Health Journal*, 53(3), 251–6.

Manthorpe, J., & Rapaport, J. (2020). *Researching family group conferences in adult services: Methods review*. London: NIHR School for Social Care.

Mental Capacity Act. (2021). Retrieved from https://www.hra.nhs.uk/planning-and-improving-research/policies-standards-legislation/mental-capacity-act/

The Mental Health Foundation. (2015). Thinking ahead: A planning guide for families. Retrieved from https://www.mentalhealth.org.uk/sites/default/files/thinking-ahead-planning-guide-23042013 D2143.pdf

The Mental Health Foundation. (2021). Black, Asian and minority ethnic communities. Retrieved from https://www.mentalhealth.org.uk/a-to-z/b/black-asian-and-minority-ethnic-bame-communities

Metz, M., Elfeddali, l., Verbeek, M., de Beurs, E., Beekman, A., & van der Feltz-Cornelis, C.M. (2018). Effectiveness of a multi-facetted blended eHealth intervention during intake supporting patients and clinicians in Shared Decision Making: A cluster randomised controlled trial in a specialist mental health outpatient setting. *PLoS One*, 13(6), e0199795-e0199795. https://doi.org/10.1371/journal.pone.0199795

Mezzina, R. (2005) Paradigm shift in psychiatry: Processes and outcomes. In S. Ramon & J.E. Williams (Eds.), *The promise of the psychosocial approach* (pp. 81–94). Aldershot: Ashgate.

Mind. (2017). Seeking help for a mental health problem. Retrieved from https://www.mind.org.uk/media-a/2900/seeking-help-for-a-mental-health-problem-2017.pdf

Morant, N., Kaminskiy, E., & Ramon, S. (2015) Shared decision making for psychiatric medication management: Beyond the microsocial. *Health Expectations*, 19(5), 1002–14.

National Institute of Clinical Excellence. (NICE). (2021, 17 June). Shared Decision Making NICE Guidelines. Retrieved August 17, 2022 from http://www.nice.org.uk/guidance/ng197

Normantov, B.U., Foster, C., Bezeczky, A., Owne, J., El-Banna, A., & Mann, M. (2020). *Impact of shared decision-making family meetings on children's out-of-home care, family empowerment and satisfaction: A systematic review*. Cardiff: What Works for Children Social Care Centre, Cardiff University.

O'Connor, AM, Stacey, D. Bennettt, C.L. (2009) decision Aids for people facing health treatment or screening decisions. Cochrane Database of Systems Review, 10, CDOO1431.

Oliver, M. (1990). *The Politics of disablement*. London: Macmillan Education.

Osborne, J. (2021). Research into peer-supported open dialogue service in the UK. In N. Putnam & B. Martindale (Eds.), *Open dialogue of psychosis. Organizing mental health services to prioritise, dialogue, relationship and meaning* (pp. 252–4). London: Routledge.

Parkinson, K., & Rogers, M. (2018). Addressing domestic abuse through family group conferences. In D. Edwards & K. Parkinson (Eds.), *Family group conference in social work: Involving families in social care decision making* (pp. 123–40). Bristol: Policy Press.

Putnam, N., & Martindale, B., Eds.) (2021). *Open dialogue for psychosis: Organizing mental health service to prioritise dialogue, relationships and meaning.* Abingdon: Routledge.

Ramon, S. (2006). Risk avoidance and risk taking in mental health social work. In L. Sapouna (Ed.), *Knowledge in mental health: Reclaiming the social* (pp. 101–22). New York: Nova.

Ramon, S. (2018). The place of social recovery in mental health and related services. *International Journal of Environmental Research and Public Health*, 15, 1–14. doi:0.33900/ijerph15061052

Ramon, S. (2021). Family group conferences as a shared decision-making strategy in adult mental health work. *Frontiers Psychiatry*, 12.663288. doi: 10.3389/fpsyt.2021.663288

Ramon, S., Brooks, H., Rae, S., & O'Sullivan, M.J. (2017a). Key issues in the process of implementing shared decision making in mental health practice. *Mental Health Review Journal*, 22(3), 257–74. doi: 10.1108/MHTR-O1-2017

Ramon, S., Morant, N., Stead, U., & Perry, B. (2017b) Shared Decision making for psychiatric medication: a mixed methos evaluation of a UK training programme for service users and clinicians. *International Journal of Social Psychiatry*, 63(8), 763–78. Doi:10.1100/0020764017733764

Rapp, C.A., & Goscha, R.G. (2012). *The Strengths Model: A recovery oriented approach to mental health Services.* New York: Oxford University Press.

Razzaque, R. (2021). The UK ODDESSI trial. In N. Putnam & B. Martindale (Eds.), *Open dialogue of psychosis. Organizing mental health Services to prioritise, dialogue, relationship and meaning* (pp. 248–51). London: Routledge.

Roe, D., & Davidson, L. (2005). Self and narrative in schizophrenia: Time to author a new story. *Journal of Medical Ethics*, 31(2), 89094. doi: 10.1136/jmh.2005.000214

Royal College of Psychiatrists. (2017). *Rethinking risk to others in mental health services*. London: Royal College of Psychiatrists, CR201.

Royal College of Psychiatrists. (2018). *Safe patients and high quality services: Jobs description of consultant psychiatrists*. London: Royal College of Psychiatrists, RC207.

Rugkasa, J., & Burns, T. (2018). Community treatment orders: Are they useful? *British Journal of Psychiatric Advances*, 23, 222–30. doi: 10.1192/aptop.115.015743

Saleeby, D. (1992). *The Strengths Perspective in social work practice.* New York: Longman.

Sashidharan, S.P., Mezzina, R., & Puras, D. (2019). Reducing coercion in mental healthcare. *Epidemiology and Psychiatric Sciences*, 28, 605–12. https://doi.org/10.1017/ S2045796019000350

Schout, G., van Dijk, M., Meijer, E., & Laneweer, E. (2017). The use of family group conference in mental health: Barriers for implementation. *Journal of Social Work*, 17, 52–70. Doi:10.177/ 4668017316637227

Shepherd, A., Shothouse, O., & Gask, L. (2014). Consultant psychiatrist' experiences of an attitudes towards shared decision making in antipsychotic prescribing: A qualitative study. *BMC Psychiatry*, 14(1), 127. https://doi.org/10.1186/1471-244X-14-127

Simmons, M., Batchleor, S., Dimpoulos-Bic, T., & Howe, D. (2017). The Choice Project: Peer workers promoting shared decision making at a youth mental health service. *Psychiatric Services*, 68(8), 764–70.

Slade, M. (2017). Implementing shared decision making in routine mental health care. *World Psychiatry*, 16(2), 146–53.

Stead, U., Morant, N., & Ramon, S. (2017). Shared decision making in medication management: Development of a training intervention. *British Journal of Psychiatric Bulletin*, 42, 221–7.

Stovell, D., Morrison, A., Panyayiotou, M., & Hutton, P. (2016). Shared treatment decision-making and empowerment related outcomes in psychosis: Thematic review and meta-analysis. *The British Journal of Psychiatry*, 209(1), 23–8.

Tew, J., Nicholls, V., Plumbridge, J., & Clarke, H. (2017). Family inclusive approaches to re-ablement in mental health: Models, mechanisms and outcomes. *British Journal of Social Work*, 47, 863–84. doi: 10.1093/bjsw/bew106

Weiss, P., Redlich-Amirav, D., Daas-Iraqi, S., & Hadas-Lidor, N. (2021). Aspects of shared decision making in a cognitive-educational intervention for family members of persons coping with severe mental illness. *Frontiers Psychiatry*, 12, 681118. doi: 10.3389/fpsyt.2021, 681118

Yeung, E.Y.W. (2013). *Role of social networks in the pathway to care of Chinese people living with a diagnosis of severe mental illness in England*. Ph.D. thesis, The University of Hong Kong.

Yeung, E.Y.W., Irvine, F., Ng, S.M., & Tsang, K.M. (2013). Role of social networks in the help-seeking experiences among Chinese suffering from severe mental illness in England: A qualitative study. *British Journal of Social Work*, 43(3), 486–503. https://doi.org/doi: 10.1093/bjsw/bcr199

Yeung, E.Y.W., Ng, S.M., Tsang, S., & Irvine, F. (2017). How people from Chinese backgrounds make sense of and respond to experiences of mental distress: Thematic analysis. *Journal of Psychiatric and Mental Health Nursing*, 24(8), 589–99.

Zizman Ilani, Y., Lysaker, P.H., & Hasson-Ohayon, I. (2021a). Shared risk taking: Shared decision making in mental illness services. *Psychiatric Services*, 72(4), 461–3. https://doi.org/10.1176/appi.ps .202000156

Zisman Ilani, Y., Chemilowska, M., Dixon, L., & Ramon, S. (2021b). NICE shared decision making guidelines and mental health challenges for research, practice and implementation. *British Journal of Psychiatry Open*, 7(5).

Video Material

University of Hertfordshire and Cambridgeshire and Peterborough NHS Foundation Trust (UH and CPNFT). (2018, October). Jasmin: Learning from success in shared decision making. Retrieved from https://www.youtube.com/watch?v=PT9LrrPCy_I

Community Care Studies https://www.youtube.com/watch?v=YEDgOFPqGZE the text refers to the mother's video

18. United States. The development of integrated mental health policy

Ronald W. Manderscheid and Amy Ward

National mental health policy in the United States (US) is critical because it sets the context and framework for action. Thus, it brings focus to issues confronting our field, and it marshals organizational, human, and financial resources in the service of desired goals, the same being true internationally. Both developed and developing countries are struggling with some of the same policy issues that will be discussed in this chapter. Several distinctions are necessary regarding mental health policy:

- First, the difference between policy content and process. In the US, most of the focus is on the content of policy, and, unfortunately, very little attention is placed upon the process of policy development and implementation. Most documents on mental health policy address the specific content of a policy and its likely effect, not the process through which the policy was created in the first place (Srole et al., 1962). Much more attention is needed on the process of policy development if we are to achieve more positive consumer outcomes in the field.
- Second, the difference between "de facto" and "de jure" policy. Mental health policy functions in two different ways. The first is "de facto mental health policy," in which the goal and means are common practice in the field but are not specified by regulations or law (Srole et al., 1962). The second is "de jure mental health policy," in which the goal and means are codified in law and public policy (Srole et al., 1962). Much of our current service practice in the mental health field reflects de facto mental health policy. De jure mental health policy is used to bring change to our current practices. For example, as we will discuss below, integrated care is a very good example of how de jure mental health policy currently is influencing practices in the field.
- Third, the significant disconnect between research, policy, and practice. Ideally, research would be conducted and would inform policy and practice; policy would be developed based upon research findings and would influence practice, and the three areas would operate in synchrony. However, disconnects among the three are exacerbated by the extreme time gap between availability of research findings and field implementation, and the virtual lack of connection of either of these with de jure mental health policy.

KEY HEALTH SERVICE PROBLEMS AND MENTAL HEALTH POLICY

The mental health field is confronted by several key service problems that have a deep and significant linkage to both de facto and de jure mental health policy. These issues are prevalence and incidence of disorder and disability; implementation of integrated care systems; inpatient and community-based services; movement toward recovery; and assessing systems and outcomes. Below, we describe these issues and their relationship to public policy.

Prevalence and Incidence of Disorder and Disability

Why is epidemiology so important to mental health policy? Mental health epidemiology is a key component of developing policy around the scope and response to mental health issues. This is the case because it provides estimates of the magnitude of the problem, the number of new cases, predictors of rates of new and existing cases, and, in some instances, information on services and outcomes, including issues of recidivism. Therefore, at all levels, national, state, county, and city, epidemiological findings can provide important guidance to policy makers who are charged with creating policy around mental health issues and care, and who also are charged with developing appropriate budgets for these areas. What has happened in this area? How has it developed over time?

There is a long history of development of American epidemiology of mental health conditions. Until the late 1970s, there was no major national community epidemiological survey that was diagnostically based. There were various national health and wellbeing surveys (Srole et al., 1962), but nothing that was based upon diagnostic criteria. In the late 1970s, the National Institute of Mental Health (NIMH) undertook a project called the Epidemiological Catchment Area (ECA) Project which was a major survey effort in six American cities to develop good information on the number of people in the adult community population (age 18 and older), as well as institutionalized populations, who were experiencing mental health conditions at the time of the survey and the number of people who had these conditions over the course of their lifetime. Hence, this work provided both prevalence estimates (annual and lifetime) and incidence estimates. (Prevalence reflects the total number of cases for some period of time; incidence reflects the number of new cases for some period of time.) The finding of this survey indicated that approximately 25 percent of the adult population of the US experienced a mental disorder significant enough to receive a diagnosis in a one-year period, had a diagnostic assessment been carried out. Incidence numbers varied considerably by type of diagnosis; the incidence of schizophrenia was very low; the incidence of depression was very high. The ECA study represented the standard of American mental health epidemiology into the 1990s. Study data from the ECA governed discussions of national mental health policy issues for more than ten years.

In the 1990s, a second major survey effort study was undertaken, the National Comorbidity Survey (NCS), which again covered persons from age 18 to death. As earlier, this survey was based upon clinical diagnostic criteria, like the ECA survey. However, the scope of the survey was a national probability sample of the US community population, not a sample from six cities. In addition, the 1990s survey only included measures of prevalence, and no information on incidence. In general, the results from the NCS reconfirmed the prevalence findings from the ECA; no major differences were observed.

Ten years later, the NCS was repeated on a national probability sample of persons in the community, 18 to 64 years of age. Once again, results remained very similar to the two previous efforts, despite the trend toward greater severity in the more recent data. However, in this third effort, a secondary sample was added for adolescents ages 12 to 17 from a sample of 400 schools. This latter work provided the first national look at mental health epidemiology for children ever conducted in the US.

Today, a new effort is underway, funded by the Substance Abuse and Mental Health Services Administration (SAMHSA), to collect national data from a community probability sample of adults 18 to 65, also to include a probability sample of people residing in group quarters, such as hospitals and other group living arrangements. This survey effort has been delayed by COVID-19 because the intent was to conduct an in-person survey, which cannot be completed until the issue of COVID-19 has been abated. At present, what is being piloted is a telephonic survey in the event that the in-person survey cannot be conducted.

What are the specific implications of this area for policy actions?
Clearly, these epidemiological data have strong implications for policy development and funding of mental health services. They can provide estimates of the magnitude of the overall problem, and they can provide estimates for specific diagnostic categories ranging from schizophrenia and other psychoses, all the way to depression and anxiety. Hence, it is critical that these data be made available to policy makers in a form that is useful to them for developing national policy and funding services. However, it also has been shown to be possible to use these data in conjunction with small area estimation methods to generate estimates for cities and counties through statistical regression techniques (Hudson, 2012).

These data also have other implications. For example, these data can tell national policy makers the distribution of these problems in the US population. For example, what are the rates of particular disorders for minority populations, as opposed to Caucasians? What are the rates of disorders in specific geographical locations, as opposed to other areas? What are the rates of disorders by various age groups, including other co-morbidity such as chronic physical illnesses? Such information also is very useful to policy makers in targeting policy and financial resources.

Finally, such data also are important to policy formulation around research because they can tell us in a better way how people with certain diagnoses fare when they are provided with different types of treatment. Hence, the data can provide important benchmarks for assessing how well our research effort is proceeding at all levels of research: basic research, clinical research, and services research.

Assessment of success: how well have we fared in this area?
Over the past 40 years, several major landmark studies have been conducted on the prevalence and incidence of mental disorder and disability. The first is the Epidemiologic Catchment Area (ECA) study; the second, the National Comorbidity Survey (NCS); the third. the National Comorbidity Survey Replication (NCS-R) and, the fourth, a new study currently being implemented by SAMHSA, which focuses on updating the 16-year-old data used to formulate policy today. This new study will update the NCS-R that was completed in 2004 (Kessler et al., 2004).

The survey results were congruent in each cycle of epidemiological findings, meaning that a high rate was found for a one-year prevalence of about 20–25 percent, with a lifetime prevalence of 57 percent (Kessler & Merikangas, 2004; Harvard Medical School, 2007). Because of how legislators were approached with these epidemiological data, much of this research has yet to be translated into sound policy and effective practice. A related issue is lack of national incidence data ever since the original ECA study, a deficit that is being remedied in the current work. However, in another study, partly based on the NCS-R data, Hudson showed how it is possible to compute incidence rates from the data, and reported a few such incidence rates (Hudson, 2012).

The overall numbers for diagnoseable conditions have been very large and as a result have had limited effect upon policy development. However, the specific information on diagnoses and groups has been extremely helpful to the field, including with respect to policy development. The overall prevalence figures, about 25 percent of adults in a one-year period and 57 percent of adults over a lifetime, although very important to know, have not easily been translated into policy (Kessler & Merikangas, 2004; Harvard Medical School, 2007). The likely reason is that the numbers are so large that the typical policy maker is unable to fathom a problem so large and come up with effective solutions.

By contrast, the specific information on particular diagnoses, such as depression and bipolar disorder, has been very useful in guiding the formulation of national policy for the care of individuals with these disorders and also in increasing funding for services and research for these particular subpopulations.

The contrast between these two assessments is stark. There are clear implications for future efforts in the field to present such information to the Congress and to State Legislatures and to County Councils. Such information will need to be broken down into smaller aggregations, with clearly articulated steps that policy makers can take to address these sub-problems as opposed to simply presenting overall prevalence and incidence estimates.

Implementation of Integrated Care Services

Why is the implementation of integrated care services important to policy? A second major area of policy concern is implementation of integrated care services. Beginning approximately 35 years ago, and continuing down to the current day, care integration has been a topic for policy development. Early work showed that mentally ill persons get chronic diseases earlier, and that these illnesses are more severe than for other people (McCarrick et al., 1986). Much later research showed that public mental health clients die 25 years earlier than other Americans because they do not receive basic primary care (McCarrick et al., 1986). Policy attention to these issues culminated in the passage of the Affordable Care Act (ACA) in 2010, which set forth de jure policy for care integration strategy and practice.

Integrated care is critical for persons with mental illness because the vast majority of people with mental illness also suffer from chronic physical conditions (Barreira, 1999; Colton & Manderscheid, 2006). It also must be pointed out that integrated care is less expensive to provide because of lower overall administrative costs. Finally, the majority of persons receiving mental health care now receive that care in a primary care setting (Kessler, et al., 2004). This is an important setting where integrated care is currently developing at a rapid rate.

What has happened in this area? How has it developed over time?

In US Surgeon General David Satcher's 1999 *Report on Mental Health*, the importance of the finding that the research base of the mental health field is sound cannot be overestimated. It is exactly what gives great credence to the primary recommendation in this Report that the next decade of work must focus on integration of mental health and primary care. More than two decades later, its effects are still reverberating across the field, via its impact upon the ACA.

Several models are available to deliver integrated care: collaborative care in which a primary care and a mental health entity work together to deliver the care; integration of primary care into the mental health entity; and integration of mental health care into the primary care entity. Recently, these models have been extended from actual integration of organizations to virtual integration of care. Considerable work is currently underway in the US to test these different models and their effects.

What are the specific implications of this area for policy actions?
Although the ACA took huge steps in promoting the integration of mental health and primary care into integrated service systems, it did not consider other needs that were equally important. In the interim, we have learned that our concept of integration needs to be broadened to include not only behavioral health and primary care, but also social services. This has come about as more work has been done to develop our understanding of the role of the social and physical determinants of health, which lead to trauma and behavioral health conditions, and physical health conditions as well. The work on the social and physical determinants of health also has underscored the importance and need for much more work on implementing disease prevention and health promotion protocols as part of integrated care efforts. A need exists for further policy development in this area to incorporate social services and prevention and promotion into the array of services that we have more traditionally conceptualized as integrated care.

Integration is a very good specific instance in which a careful policy development process, carried out over several decades, culminated in good national policy content that now is guiding the evolution of practice in the field. All the key steps to good policy development were followed (SOREL). Now, attention can turn to improving integrated care practice in the field.

Assessment of success: how well have we fared in this area?
Integrated care is a notable area of success in the national policy arena because of its incorporation into the broad-reaching ACA. Subsequent to this important step, the field has begun moving into implementation of integrated care, which has been much more challenging. This has occurred because integrated care involves not only change in clinical protocols, but also major changes in how organizations are configured and operated, and major changes in payment protocols. The development of virtual care has been one of the important tools in facilitating more rapid implementation in integrated care in the mental health field. However, much more remains to be done in fully implementing integrated care, especially integrated care that now also will involve social services broadly throughout the US.

Inpatient and Community-based Mental Health Services

Why is the implementation of inpatient and community services important to policy? At the time of the founding of the National Institute of Mental Health in 1949, if you were mentally ill, you typically received care in an inpatient unit of a mental or general hospital. In subsequent years, this standard of care changed dramatically, and, later, most persons with mental health conditions were cared for in community-based settings.

Today, mental health services are provided primarily in community settings through four sectors (Regier et al., 1993): specialty care, primary care, care in the human services, and self-care. More recently, service delivery has begun in a fifth sector, criminal justice (Manderscheid et al., 2019).

Policy development around the settings of care for mental health services has been guided since 1999 by the Olmstead Supreme Court Decision, which requires that care be delivered in the least restrictive setting possible. The fact that a Supreme Court decision was required indicates the issue of care settings has been and continues to be a policy area that is fraught with considerable controversy.

What has happened in this area? How has it developed over time?
The issue of the duality of inpatient and community care is a very persistent problem that the field has been grappling with since the mid-1950s. At that time, we witnessed the initial development and implementation of modern psychotropics for psychosis that made possible the deinstitutionalization of people from state hospitals, private psychiatric hospitals, and veterans' administration hospitals. At approximately the same time, the then director of NIMH Dr. Robert H. Felix went to the Congress and told members that he was going to eliminate state mental hospitals and replace them with community-based services.

In earlier years, initial work had been done in some states to begin developing community-based systems of care, including Minnesota. This initial work created momentum around building more community-based systems and this effort culminated in the passage of the 1963 Mental Retardation and Community Mental Health Centers Act. That Act called for the construction of 1,500 community mental health centers throughout the US, each serving a community population between 75,000 to 150,000 people, and with a full range of services including prevention, treatment, and rehabilitation. By 1980, 804 of these community mental health centers had been built.

The major deinstitutionalization that occurred prior to 1980 fostered a counter reaction organized by family members that eventuated in the founding of the National Alliance on Mental Illness. These families expressed great concern over their family members not having access to needed services. This opposition between deinstitutionalization and the desire of family members to have access to inpatient care for their loved ones has continued down to the present time. At the same time, the NIMH created a new program called the Community Support Program that was based in a case management model and coordinated a series of essential services including mental health, substance use, primary care, social services, and several others.

Deinstitutionalization accelerated with the passage of the 1963 Act; the major bulk of deinstitutionalization occurred between that time and 1980. However, as deinstitutionalization occurred, those patients that entered the community were not picked up by the community mental health centers, because the latter had the requirement of becoming financially independent within seven years. This meant that they had to focus on people who had health insurance, including Medicaid, which most recent state hospital patients did not have.

At about the same time, the Carter administration had completed the Carter Presidential Commission on Mental Health that culminated in the Mental Health Systems Act that became law in 1980. This law was intended to remedy the lack of community services associated with deinstitutionalization. Immediately upon election in 1980, President Ronald Reagan instituted the dismantling of that law and its replacement with a block grant to the states including a 25 percent reduction in funding. This change had a huge impact on the future of community mental health centers.

After 1980, the community mental health centers program did not grow further, and the financing of community-based services became problematical for the next quarter century.

Hence, not only had the community mental health centers developed an orientation to a different care population, but they subsequently also did not have the resources to serve the people being deinstitutionalized, even if they had chosen to do so.

In 1999, the US Supreme Court issued a determination called the Olmstead Decision that found that mental health care must be provided in the least restrictive setting possible. Thus, if clients could fare better in a community setting than in residential setting, they must be provided that opportunity.

After 1989, deinstitutionalization continued, but at a much reduced rate, so that by the early 2000s, there were only about 50,000 people receiving inpatient care in state mental hospitals, most of whom were committed involuntarily or were forensic patients. That approximate level of inpatient care has continued down to the present. During the past four years, larger numbers of people who were or would have been served in state mental hospitals have become enrolled in Medicaid as a result of the ACA. Thus, these individuals were able to receive care in community mental health centers, often renamed as behavioral mental health centers.

Thus, the major threads of deinstitutionalization and building a community system of care have persisted throughout the past 70-year period. The only thing that is different at present is the relative balance of residential and inpatient care versus community-based care. Some of the fundamental problems that existed in the 1950s such as lack of adequate housing, jobs, and social support networks continue to persist down to the present day.

What are the specific implications for policy actions?
A major need for policy reform still exists in the area of deinstitutionalization. Within the past three years, the Congress has funded demonstration sites for comprehensive community behavioral health clinics (CCBHCs) in eight original states and now eight additional states. These CCBHCs are well equipped to serve the full range of the population that traditionally would have been served in the state mental hospitals. This is true because they offer a full range of services including inpatient, residential, and integrated care. Ideally, this effort would continue to expand this program so that every single state could configure CCBHCs to serve all communities. That will require considerably more funding from the Congress to bring this new system up to scale. If these steps were taken, the duality between inpatient care and community care would gradually disappear over time because everyone would receive the care that they need.

Assessment of success: how well have we fared in this area?
Overall, community-based services have grown dramatically in the period that has just been discussed. The inability of this growing system to incorporate an adequate level of community-based and residentially based care has caused a persistent duality between these two modes of care. The problem created by this duality caused the formation of NAMI and the Olmstead Supreme Court Decision, as well as considerable discussion in recent years about the availability and adequacy of inpatient and residential care beds. It is only with the development of the CCBHC demonstration that a bridge has been created that has the potential to resolve this duality. Hence, much more funding and service development will be necessary before we will be able to say that this problem has been solved successfully.

Movement toward recovery

Why is the implementation of a recovery orientation important to policy? Undoubtedly, there is no more important concept for the mental health field than that of recovery from illness. Recovery can make possible a complete and full life in the community for someone who has suffered from mental illness in the past. Thus, for persons who have been afflicted by mental illness, recovery is really the holy grail that all seek. Unfortunately, the concept of recovery did not enter the mental health field until very recently.

What has happened in this area?

The concept of recovery did not emerge in the mental health field until almost the year 2000. Prior to that time, the standard assumption of providers and researchers was that once a person had a serious mental disorder, that person would always have that mental disorder and always would need care. Further, in many instances, providers were able to convince persons with mental illness that this was to be their reality moving forward.

A few years before 2000, reports began circulating from primary consumers that they had experienced the process of recovery. For them, this meant that they had made a personal decision that they wanted to recover and that they needed to find a way to achieve recovery. Those who undertook this difficult road learned that a major part of recovery is regaining one's own voice and one's own roles in the community. They also discovered that recovery for most people is a lifelong process.

The recovery movement generated by these insights is tethered to direct client experience in the field. This movement challenges the way of thinking that once mentally ill, always mentally ill, and holds out the opportunity of recovery. It is based upon the concept of a personal journey, in which the client seeks to regain his or her personal life. The recovery movement has eventuated in the development in major changes in the mental health field, including the development of trauma-informed care, recovery-oriented systems of care, and a strong peer support movement, all of which are still evolving.

Over the past 20 years, the concept of recovery has been embraced by the field and is now an expectation that primary consumers have when they enter care. The introduction of this concept also has facilitated a broader understanding of the causes of mental illness, including trauma experienced because of the operation of the social and physical determinants of health in a community, and the role of trauma-informed care in promoting recovery. Today, it is assumed that almost all mental illness occurs because of trauma experienced either in childhood or adulthood.

What are the implications for policy action?

Policy regarding recovery is found principally in the 2010 ACA. Fortunately, the ACA was prepared and implemented in the modern era in which recovery is promoted as a major goal. For the ACA, a major underlying philosophical goal is to promote person-centered care, which makes the person focal to illness remediation and moves away from a simple focus on diagnosis.

In the most recent decade, the ACA concept of person-centered care has continued to evolve to a point at which the major correlates of person-centered care include self-direction in care and self-determination in life. Self-direction in care is akin to the recovery concept of regaining one's own personal life. Self-determination in life is a logical extension of this. Thus, this transition has taken the form of person-centered care in which the person rather than the illness becomes the center of attention, and recovery becomes a key goal. These concepts now are gradually beginning to find their way into national public policy (Diener & Seligman, 2004; Diener et al., 2009).

Assessment of success: how well have we fared in this area?

Related to the concept of recovery, work has been underway at SAMHSA and the Centers on Disease Control and Prevention (CDC) on developing key approaches to wellbeing and its assessment. At SAMHSA, that work has progressed to defining eight dimensions of wellbeing and developing key recommendations for how patients can improve these eight dimensions of wellbeing in their personal lives. These eight dimensions are: Mental/Emotional, Spiritual, Intellectual, Physical, Environmental, Financial, Occupational, and Social. This work has helped us to unbundle the concept of wellbeing and to make it more operational, specifically in relationship to improving personal recovery.

In parallel work at the CDC, an effort also has been underway to unbundle different dimensions of wellbeing and to measure these dimensions. Most of these dimensions are coextensive with the dimensions defined by SAMHSA. The CDC work has resulted in a series of wellbeing measures that are in the process of being incorporated into national initiatives, such as Healthy People 2030, and major national data collection systems, such as the National Health Interview Survey.

Operationalization of approaches to wellbeing and their measurement as an outcome of mental health and health interventions can represent a huge step forward in our understanding of illness and recovery. This work should be pursued further. We have known for more than 70 years that health is a complete state of physical, mental, and social wellbeing and not merely the absence of disease, as was noted in the preamble to the Constitution of the World Health Organization in 1948.

Work also has been underway for much more than a decade to actually measure recovery itself and to determine how far a person has proceeded on his or her recovery journey. SAMHSA has been developing these measures and has been incorporating such measures into the National Outcomes Measurement System (NOMS). This work continues down to the present day.

Assessing outcomes and performance

Another feature of care in the modern recovery era is the need to assess care outcomes and provider performance. Like care itself, the outcomes and performance area has been evolving over the last several decades. We have gone from simple measures of process, such as how many people with what diagnoses are under what care, to measures of performance in the community. What recovery does is allow us to move to the next step in this work to examine the relationship between the process of recovery and wellbeing as an outcome.

During the time of the Clinton health reform efforts in the 1990s, it became obvious that better work was needed in assessing performance and care outcomes. Most places lacked outcome and performance measures.

Developments during this period included a consumer-oriented report card, which included a consumer survey focused on access to care, quality of care, and outcome (AMBHA, 1995). The survey was implemented nationally in 1995 and is still used by the federal government;

it reflects the consumer's view. Since that time, relatively little progress has been made. We still lack performance and outcomes measures at the points in which services are delivered.

National policy continues to promote the use of outcome and performance measures, but implementation has been poor at the national and state levels.

PROGRESS ACROSS DOMAINS THROUGH INTEGRATION OF POLICY

As can be noted, in each of the sections above, every major area of policy development has shown some progress in the last few decades. However, it is also obvious that progress has been very uneven across the major focal areas. Part of the reason for this is that different groups in the field focus on different pieces of these areas with different outcomes for the policy process. Thus, if we are to increase the evenness of policy development across these areas, it is important that we develop an integrated policy framework that incorporates all of them.

Integrated policy refers to a framework that includes all areas discussed in this chapter from epidemiology through outcomes. It is only through full integration of policy that it will be possible to more fully address the problems of mental illness experienced by the US population. In effect, integrated policy will link problem definition, solution specification, and outcome assessment together rather than treating them separately, as has been done in the past.

To begin to make the case for this effort toward integrated national policy, one can start by examining the interrelationship among these five areas. Let us begin with the work on prevalence and incidence of disorder. Obviously, what we do in integrated care is contingent upon what we learn about the prevalence and incidence of disease. Where we place service systems, how big they are, how they are staffed, all depend on prevalence and incidence of disorder. Similarly, as we come to understand the importance of integrated care, we have also learned that the relative balance between inpatient and community services needs to continue to evolve in favor of community services because good integrated care actually can prevent the need for inpatient services. Consumers are most interested in recovery, therefore, for each of these areas it is important that we examine the relationship with recovery. For example, prevalence and incidence should also include prevalence and incidence of those in the process of treatment and recovery, which is currently not the case. The effectiveness of integrated care depends upon whether structures and interventions are actually leading to recovery or not. The balance between inpatient and community services depends upon how each modality of care relates to recovery and what role it plays in that process. Finally, it is important that in each of these dimensions we do good methodological work on outcomes and performance measures, led by recovery measures, but including other measures as well. This brief overview of the five policy areas documents how interrelated they are and the importance of integrated policy that encompasses all of them.

The development of integrated policy will not be something that occurs overnight. It will require careful consideration and work. Some of the key features will include collaboration among the organizations that advocate for each of the five areas. That collaboration will be essential if we are to bridge the chasm that now exists among these areas. Another dimension of this work will be a detailed examination of current legislation and policy in each of the areas that has direct relevance to each of the other areas. For example, a policy on integrated care, which is covered by Section 2703 of the ACA, needs to relate to our work on trauma-informed care and the role that it plays on recovery. The question becomes: how does the configuration of integrated care arrangement relate to the delivery of trauma-informed care and recovery as an outcome?

With the accession of the Biden Harris administration, a potential opportunity may arise to initiate this work on development of integrated mental health policy. One strategy could be the convening of a President's commission on mental health with the explicit mission of convening key representatives from the field to develop a strategy through which integrated mental health policy could be developed and implemented. Several recent presidential commissions have had a significant role in advancing work in the mental health field, most recent was the presidential commission convened by President George W. Bush, entitled the President's New Freedom Commission on Mental Health.

Clearly, to be effective, once this policy framework is developed, it should be shared broadly in the mental health field to build consensus around the work that is being done here, so that there is broad political support for moving the integrated policy framework forward.

Once consensus is formed around its utility, it will be important to continue working with the Biden Harris administration and the US House and Senate, about the importance of moving this agenda forward, yet doing so in a way that does not do violence to the current good work being done in the field and is financially viable as a strategy. Like the actual construction of the integrated policy framework itself, it will take some time to build understanding and support in these various constituencies. At the same time, it will be important to work with the other national-level entities such as the National Governor's Association and the National Conference of State Legislators, the National Association of Counties, and the National League of Cities, so that the states, counties, and cities can play a role in this as well.

THE PROCESS OF INTEGRATED POLICY

The process of developing policy is as important as its content, and integrated policy can be developed in the same way that any policy is developed (Manderscheid, 2012). There are a number of key steps in this process. First, it will be important to build consensus and support that integrated policy is actually needed. This will involve forming collaborations among groups that have not necessarily collaborated in the past, and, in some instances, have been in conflict around particular mental health policy issues. This may be across different levels of government, the public and private sector, and the not-for-profit community. These may include peers, providers, managers, administrators, policy makers, and researchers. In essence, it will be important to have all key groups involved.

Second, it will be important to identify national champions for integrated policy. These national champions may include leaders in the mental health field, as well as other types of leaders in health and social welfare. The role of the champion will be to communicate the need for integrated policy beyond the confines of the mental health field. The purpose will be to enable others to understand the importance of integrated policy and why action needs to be taken to bring it into existence.

Operationally, the national champions could form an initial group to take leadership in developing national integrated mental health policy. This would serve the purpose of bringing together leaders from different areas of the mental health field, as well as leaders with different policy concerns. The field has experienced similar efforts in the past. For example, when the leadership of the mental health field collectively advocated for the ACA.

Third, allies need to be fostered at the legislative and executive levels of government at the national level. Within the mental health field, there already are leaders who work in these areas everyday with key leaders and staff from each of these other arenas. In this process, it also will become clear that some of these leaders already support key elements of integrated policy for different reasons – program, political, financial, or other reasons. Addressing those needs should be part of this process.

Fourth, it also will be important to develop the language that will be necessary for integrated policy. This can best be done by practitioners and researchers from the field who understand integrated policy on an operational basis and why it is necessary.

In any legislative work, each of these process steps is necessary in order to be successful. In many instances where the field has not been successful in a legislation effort, it often is true that one or more of these steps has been omitted.

IMPROVING THE BRIDGE AMONG POLICY PRACTICE AND RESEARCH

There can be numerous benefits to integrated policy, some of which will be briefly described here. Undoubtedly, primary among these benefits will be a more appropriate balance between the nature of the problem and the effort we are spending to address it. As should be obvious from what has been stated above, currently our problem far outstrips our capacity to address it. Poor linkages among research, policy, and practice have contributed to this problem.

In good integrated policy, prevention has a role, which is not fully the case at present in mental health. We did not include a section on prevention and prevention policy in this chapter because there currently is very little to say about prevention. However, it should be obvious to all that prevention is always to be preferred over treatment and is especially needed at this time of COVID-19. Specifically, if we are to address some of the mental health consequence of COVID-19 and its mitigation efforts, we must move upstream to address the social and physical determinants of health that are generating those mental health problems. Integrated policy will include a specific role for prevention efforts of this type.

With good integrated policy we also should be able to develop a much clearer understanding of how our entire effort leads to better personal outcomes and improved system performance. If we have integrated policy, we then can put together models that will show how prevention relates to intervention, rehabilitation, and recovery. This cannot be done unless we have integrated policy.

Finally, with good integrated policy there will be fewer unanticipated consequences of actions that we take because we will have a better understanding of antecedents and consequences of these actions. At the present time, many policy actions are taken with little understanding of the consequences they will have. With good integrated policy and models developed from this policy, this problem should be greatly reduced in the future.

CONCLUSION

It has been the privilege of the authors to prepare this chapter on national mental health policy. We hope that it is clear from what we have written that progress is being made in each of the areas that we have covered here – prevalence and incidence, integrated care, inpatient and community services, movement toward recovery, and assessing systems and outcomes. Therefore, granted current efforts, there is reason to be somewhat optimistic about the future. However, we also hope that we have made a sufficient case that our current lack of integration in policy will not produce the same desirable effects as would a more fully integrated national mental health policy. This national mental health policy will include content and process elements. In this era of COVID-19, there is great urgency that we work on this integrated policy for national mental health. Thus, this chapter also is a call to action.

REFERENCES

American Managed Behavioral Healthcare Association (AMBHA). (1995). *PERMS 1.0: Performance measures for managed behavioral healthcare programs.* Washington, DC: AMBHA.

Barreira, P. (1999). Reduced life expectancy and serious mental illness. *Psychiatry Services,* 50(8), 995.

Colton, C.W., & Manderscheid, R.W. (2006). Congruencies in increased mortality rates, years of potential life lost, and causes of death among public mental health clients in eight states. *Prevention of Chronic Disease,* 3(2), A42. Retrieved July 16, 2021from http://www.cdc.gov/pcd/issues/2006/apr/05_0180.html

Diener E., & Seligman, M.E. (2004). Beyond money. Toward an economy of well-being. *Psychological Science in the Public Interest,* 5(1), 1–31.

Diener E., Lucas R., Schimmack U., & Helliwell J. (2009). *Well-being for public policy.* New York: Oxford University Press.

Harvard Medical School. (2007). Lifetime prevalence of DSM-IV/WMH-CIDI disorders by sex cohort. Retrieved July 16, 2021 from https://www.hcp.med.harvard.edu/ncs/ftpdir/NCS-R_Lifetime_Prevalence_Estimates.pdf

Hudson, C.G. (2012). Declines in mental illness over the adult years: An enduring finding or methodological artifact? *Aging and Mental Health,* 16(6), 735–52.

Kessler, R.C., & Merikangas, K.R. (2004). The National Comorbidity Survey Replication (NCS-R): Background and aims. *The International Journal of Methods in Psychiatric Research,* 13(2), 60–8.

Kessler, R.C., Koretz, D., Merikangas, K.R., & Wang, P.S. (2004). The epidemiology of adult mental disorders. In B.L. Levin, J. Petrilia, & K.D. Hennessy (Eds.), *Mental health services: A public health perspective.* 2nd ed. New York: Oxford University Press.

Manderscheid, R.W. (2012). Formulation of mental health policy in the United States, with comparative case studies of South Africa and Thailand. In E.S. Sorel (Ed.), *21st century global mental health* (pp. 351–64). Burlington, MA: Jones and Bartlett Learning.

Manderscheid, R.W., Green V.R., Everett, A., Leaf P., & Barry, C. (2019). American mental health services after the Affordable Care Act: Perspective through care patterns for 100 adults, with aggregate facility, service, and cost estimates. In W.W. Eaton & D. Fallin (Eds.), *Public mental health.* 2nd ed. (pp. 403–16). New York: Oxford University Press.

McCarrick, A.K., Manderscheid, R.W., Bertolucci, D.E., Goldman, H.H., & Tessler, R.C. (1986). Chronic medical problems in the chronically mentally ill. *Hospital and Community Psychiatry,* 37(3), 289–91.

Regier, D.A., Narrow, W.E., Rae, D.S., Manderscheid, R.W., Locke, B.Z., & Goodwin, F.K. (1993). The de facto US Mental and Addictive Disorders Service System: Epidemiologic catchment area prospective 1-year prevalence rates of disorders and services. Archives of General Psychiatry, 50(2), 85–94. doi:10.1001/archpsyc.1993.01820140007001

Srole, L., Lagner, S.T., Micheal, S.T., Oplers, M., & Rennie, T. (1962). Mental health in the metropolis:

The Midtown Study. *Social Work*, 7(4). https://doi.org/10.1093/sw/7.4.121
United States, Public Health Service, Office of the Surgeon General. (1999). *Dispelling the myths and stigma of mental illness: The Surgeon General's report on mental health*. US Department of Health and Human Services. Office of the Surgeon General.

PART V

CONCLUSION

19. Conclusion – key lessons and emerging directions in the integration of research into mental health policy and practice

Christopher G. Hudson

This Handbook has been designed as both a guide and a resource for the conduct and use of research designed to support the development of balanced mental health systems. It has explored the complex and often problematic interface of research and policy, considering policy issues that drive research, and new research methods that inform policy. In doing this, the book has brought together a diverse array of perspectives from the chapter authors on the conduct and methods of such research, as well as some of its most important findings. These range from the qualitative to the quantitative, along with combinations of such methods. Very importantly, it identifies key issues and decisions involved in design and use of policy research. This concluding chapter will, therefore, review these themes, discuss some recommendations for new policy directions, and identify lessons for integrating research into the development of mental health policy and services.

CROSSCUTTING THEMES

One of the crosscutting topics reviewed by several authors has been psychiatric deinstitution-alization, its causes and consequences, which is treated as an essential part of the backdrop of contemporary policies. Even in developed nations, deinstitutionalization continues to have an impact, although the primary focus has shifted from reducing hospital use toward continued development of community mental health systems and their fine-tuning. In contrast, many middle- and low-income nations (MLINs), some of those in Eastern and Central Europe, are actively seeking to deinstitutionalize, and others in developing nations are seeking to further develop their inpatient services. Just as many nations have simultaneously sought to dismantle their hospitals and implement community services, the controversies have typically involved the disparate forces that have driven this megatrend. Both the ideals of social reformers and the financial considerations of social conservatives have often clashed, leading to alternating periods of innovation and retrenchment. The recovery movement and the growing voices of mental health consumers, ex-patients, and their families have also clashed and resulted in a tightening of the criteria of commitment laws, as well as several versions of outpatient commitment, leading to both lower hospital censuses, and growing pressures for improved community services.

While not minimizing its successes, Belcher (Chapter 11) documents several of the failures of deinstitutionalization, such as homelessness, and trans-institutionalization involving shifts of mentally ill individuals to nursing homes, shelters, and prisons. He argues that "Clinically, we know that many people with SMI [serious mental illness] would be treated better in the community than in the hospital; however, other people with SMI will at times need hospitalization. Thus, it makes little sense to close state hospitals, but to better integrate them with community care." Often the lack of development of community services has involved criticisms that they have not been funded sufficiently to incorporate practical supports needed by ex-patients. For example, Mandersheid and Ward (Chapter 18) comment that "the inability of this growing system to incorporate an adequate level of community-based and residentially based care has caused a persistent duality between these two modes of care." Whereas none of the authors argue that there is a need to reinstitute psychiatric hospitals as they once existed, most advocate for continued development of community services to provide the flexibility, outreach, and practical supports that are needed in the community. A range of ideas have been advanced along these lines, including development of better standards for community care, shared decision making, and systems for monitoring their progress.

Along with psychiatric deinstitutionalization, there has been the devolution, privatization, and decentralization of mental health services. While this has been a particularly difficult issue in federated systems such as the United States, it is also noted as a problem elsewhere. Advocates for the shift of authority from national to local, and from public to private providers, argue that decision making should be closer to where the need is to permit greater flexibility and responsiveness. Yet, numerous authors have lamented the resulting service fragmentation, duplication, service gaps, and lack of continuity of care, especially as patients need to transition between inpatient and community mental health care. Rosenberg and Salvador-Carulla (Chapter 13) observe that, in Australia, "in most cases government agencies and departments still operate in silos, with separate funding and reporting requirements." They also point out that inequities in service provision have resulted from the devolution of decision authority from federal to the state level. Similarly, the authors of the chapter on US mental health policy (Chapter 18) argue for the development of a national mental health policy. Several of the chapters, particularly those on the Czech Republic's (Chapter 12) and on the Israeli mental health systems (Chapter 15) have explored some of the ways that planners in these nations have sought to overcome problems with assuring the continuity of care.

Given the numerous problems of service system fragmentation that have developed as a result of deinstitutionalization, it is not surprising that various researchers, both those featured in this book and those from elsewhere, have advocated for the further system building of mental health services, often using the terminology of "balanced mental health systems," "integrated care," and the like. Hudson (Chapter 1) highlights the notion of balanced mental health care, which requires the discovery of the optimal mix of service modalities and their systematic linkages, an ideal that has also been emphasized by a variety of other authors (Gerhard, Miles, & Dorgan, 1981; Thornicroft & Tansella, 2013). Several have cited the example of the Community Service System initiative in the United States, one feature of which has been the simultaneous attention paid to the development of multi-level mechanisms of coordination on the policy, program, and client levels, the last of which is typically sought through the use of case management.

In their chapter on the US mental health system, Manderscheid and Ward (Chapter 18) have emphasized the needed development of an integrated mental health policy. They explain that their "concept of integration needs to be broadened to include not only behavioral health and primary care, but also social services." Important progress has been achieved, they note, given the recent achievements of the Affordable Care Act (ACA), a national multi-payor health care policy advanced by Obama in 2012, in introducing new integrated structures, such as medical homes and accountable care organizations (ACOs), often on the local level. They suggest that, in the end, "The balance between inpatient and community services depends upon how each modality of care relates to recovery and what role it plays in that process." Continued progress, they conclude, will be contingent upon identifying "national champions for integrated policy," and, operationally, forming an initial group to take leadership in developing national integrated mental health policy.

Rather than addressing needs for changes in policies and organizations, several authors – most notably Schutt (Chapter 6) and Rochefort and Hirschfield (Chapter 7) – emphasize evidence-based practice and policy, as well as the development of implementation science in achieving the carry-over of research results into services. Schutt (Chapter 6) points out that, "Difficulties in implementing new approaches in public and mental health services and increased institutional attention to improving the research-to-practice pipeline fueled development of Implementation Science." Such a science has, among other things, led to the recommendation of Hudson (Chapter 2) related to the importance of the timing of introducing research into the policy development progress. For example, Rochefort and Hirschfield (Chapter 7) advise that "For evidence to be successfully translated into policy, it must not merely be available, but available 'at a certain time and in a particular form, to solve a very specific problem' (Cairney, 2016, p. 60). Evidence not disseminated during such a window may easily escape policymakers' attention."

While the history of mental health policy, especially that involving deinstitutionalization, and the efforts to implement integrated care and enhance patient recovery have been essential to planning research in the field, the authors of the various chapters have identified a range of other considerations in this regard. The initial chapter on research methods (Chapter 2), that covering research formulation and planning, is based on the observation that how problems are defined and conceptualized may sometimes determine the findings and their implications for policy. For this reason, researchers have struggled to assure that their research is relevant to policy makers, especially given the extent that so much of it falls by the wayside. In this chapter (2), Hudson reviews several approaches to the integration of research and policy, and highlights what has come to be termed a "multiple streams" approach in which work must often proceed in parallel lines with policy development, involving a kind of multi-tasking or juggling of tasks that have traditionally been split off from one another. The chapter characterizes this as one involving the coordination of two sets of decisions, one involving the policy development process, and the other, of research conceptualization and planning.

Chapter 2 on research problem formulation is followed by that on qualitative and exploratory research methods, by Hugo Kamya (Chapter 3), who emphasizes the importance of explicitly identifying the underlying assumptions of one's research, even those of a philosophical nature. Kamya discusses the epistemological and ontological dimensions of research, emphasizing the extent that policy research is inherently value-laden. Such insight, he argues, leads to a recognition of "the importance of decentering dominant voices and allowing the centering of marginalized voices ... Decentering hegemonic voices in mental health policy research is key." To the extent that such decentering is achieved, Kamya points out that "Qualitative research methods help to address the disconnect between the goals and language of policy makers and researchers." As such, qualitative and exploratory methods can be regarded as invaluable tools for the formulation and planning of policy-relevant research.

Also, of central importance in the planning of mental health research is the study of the environmental context of mental health problems and interventions. This is investigated often through epidemiological research, in addition to other qualitative and quantitative methods. Data on the etiology, incidence, and prevalence, as well as patterns of progression of and recovery from mental disorders are all invaluable for planning services. The use of such methods and data is explored in several chapters, especially those on quantitative and emerging methods. Ihara, Lee, Karavatas, and Wolf-Branigan, in Chapter 5 on emerging research methods, present developments in the use of geographic information systems that have expanded dramatically in recent years. These permit not only to the targeting of particular services to various localities, but also the generation of invaluable information on risk factors and the etiology of various mental disorders. The authors argue that "Spatial methods provide the foundation for computational and predictive methods because location matters." Each of the chapters on national or regional services provide examples of applications of spatial methods in policy development. Chapter 14 on European developments, in particular, illustrates a rich array of applications such as mental health atlases, the ESMS/DESDE system, and the Efficient Decision Support – Mental Health (EDeS-MH) to improve knowledge on the health ecosystem, resource allocation and management in regional planning. The authors report that "Findings led to a change in the pattern of residential care in the region of Helsinki Uusimaa representing one of the first documented cases of the usability of quantitative international comparisons for priority setting and resource allocation in mental health policy." Similarly, the authors of the US chapter (18) note that geospatial "data can provide important benchmarks for assessing how well our research effort is proceeding at all levels of research: basic research, clinical research, and services research."

The importance of the study of environmental context is perhaps most dramatically illustrated in the study of those groups who experience oppressed or marginalized social statuses, particularly when they are intersectional, or combine with one another. Kamya (Chapter 3) illustrates this in his discussion of research on gang-affiliated adolescents: "intersectionality of race, socioeconomic status, gender, and ethnicity, all must be considered when thinking about where and how research findings would be of the most benefit ..." One such group consists of children. Yvonne Vissing argues in Chapter 8 that research about children's mental health is skewed because it relies so heavily upon parent and adult perceptions of the children's experiences and points out that "The position of the child rights field is that much of what we know *about* children comes from information written *by* adults, *for* adults, using *adultified* theoretical assumptions and *adult-based* methodologies."

Along these same lines, Chapters 10 and 17 – those on psychiatric commitment and on shared decision making, respectively – advance strong arguments for improving the protection of patient rights. Ramon and Yeung, in Chapter 17 on the policy of shared decision making (SDM) in the United Kingdom, analyze the challenges that have been involved in the development of this policy, one involving the officially recommended collaboration between patients and their providers in regard to treatment decisions, in both medical and mental health care. They discuss the attitudinal barriers that have complicated this development, pointing out that the policy is still in its infancy, despite the considerable progress that the United Kingdom has made in this area compared with many nations. They also note practices and policies in other nations, using different terminology such as advanced directives and family conferencing that share some of the features of SDM.

In Chapter 10 on psychiatric commitment, Lukens and Solomon review the extended efforts to protect the human rights of patients, particularly those involving the undue deprivation of liberty as a result of psychiatric commitment. They note that although considerable progress has been made in this regard, for example, with efforts to implement outpatient psychiatric commitment, progress remains very incomplete. They explain that "consumers continue to resist such policies as being little more than coercive practices and mechanisms of social control." Alternatives that they review and consider to be promising include advanced directives with which patients, while functioning competently, execute legal documents specifying how they wish to be treated should they become incompetent due to severe mental breakdown. Another alternative that is being increasingly implemented is the separation of psychiatric commitment decisions from decisions regarding the right to consent to treatment. For example, in many parts of the United States, patients can be committed if they are deemed imminently dangerous to self or others, but still regarded as competent to refuse specific treatments such as psychotropic medications given the recognition that commitment and treatment decisions involve very different criteria. The notion is an important one that such decisions are not all or nothing, and that opportunities for the enhancement of patient decision making may exist even when protective measures are required.

Several of the chapters, ranging from the introduction to those on particular geographic areas, have emphasized the importance of considering global context in mental health policy and planning. International comparisons as well as the identification of the outcomes of various solutions to policy dilemmas, all are invaluable in policy development. Hudson notes (Chapter 1) the unique challenges that developing nations are facing in regard to their limited resource base and available workforce. The movement, led by the World Health Organization, to develop programming approaches for such environments is one that directly addresses the needs of marginalized and oppressed populations. One such initiative has been advocacy for enhancing the mental health preparation of primary care physicians in such environments. But as important as this is, this should not minimize the longer-term needs for systems of community care that integrate both traditional specialist care with indigenous approaches.

Service system development has been an emerging theme in this Handbook, nonetheless, issues with various intervention and service models have also been reviewed in its various chapters. One such theme has involved the need to broaden the array of available approaches beyond the traditional medical and psychiatric methods, to encompass psychosocial models and talk therapies. For example, a review of the recent development of mental health in the United Kingdom (see Chapter 16) noted that the shift to psychosocial services received a major boost in 2006 with the implementation of the Increasing Access to Psychological Therapies (IAPT) program in which people suffering from common forms of mental distress could refer themselves to such services without their General Practitioner's (GP) intervention. In general, the expansion in community mental health has brought with it an interdisciplinary approach that has featured the clinical services of psychologists, social workers, and other allied professionals who have focused on the delivery of psychotherapeutic and other talk therapies. A particularly popular clinical approach has been the use of various versions of cognitive behavioral therapy (see Chapter 7), which is often short-term, easily taught, and evidence-based.

Another approach commonly featured in the community mental health systems of many nations has been case management, particularly, versions known as Assertive Community Treatment (ACT). This more comprehensive model of case management, which combines treatment, advocacy, education, and outreach in a team approach with a high patient-staff ratio, is generally used only for those with some of the most serious mental disorders, as Rochefort and Hirschfield (Chapter 7) advises that "The ratio of benefits to costs for providing ACT are only favorable for mental health services if its use is limited to patients who tend otherwise to be frequently hospitalized (50 or more days annually) and if the cost of that hospitalization is included in the calculation."

Many observers of contemporary mental health systems, including several of this Handbook's authors, have highlighted gaps in primary prevention and early intervention services. Although strong arguments are repeatedly made on both ethical and empirical grounds for such approaches, instituting them has often received less than enthusiastic support from payers and from many professionals, given pressures to target services to those with the most urgent and distressing symptoms of mental illness. For example, Rosenberg and Salvador-Carullo note in Chapter 13 that the National Mental Health Strategy in Australia has, in general, failed to pursue a shift toward promotion and early intervention. Such approaches are often central in addressing problems involving the stigmatization of mental illness. In Chapter 9 on stigma involving mental illness, Kundert and Corrigan argue that "Education, protest, and contact-based interventions can reduce [the] stigma of mental illness."

Given the urgency to target services to the needs of severely mentally ill individuals, there has been considerable activity in implementing psychiatric rehabilitation services in many nations, ranging from the Czech Republic, Israel, the United Kingdom, to the United States. Dragomirická and her colleagues (Chapter 12) note that its aim is to help ensure that recovery is also expressed in terms of results related to housing, income, work, as well as daily activities, learning, and social relationships. Some of its essential elements include multidisciplinarity, continuity of care, person-centered care, recovery-oriented practice. It is an approach that is consistent with the ideals of many treatment professionals and consumers and one that can be implemented in a variety of contexts, both inpatient and outpatient, and as part of case management and other programs, and in general, has a strong empirical foundation.

Mental health policy makers have often struggled with the problem of engaging those who are not motivated, for whatever reason, into treatment. Whereas efforts are periodically made, often to an insufficient degree, to make services as attractive and relevant as possible, through such means as outreach, low-demand (drop-in) services, psychosocial clubhouses, use of staff with "lived experience" of mental illness, and the like, these have not always been sufficient. Thus, many nations have developed various coercive legal measures to assure service provision. Lukens and Solomon (Chapter 10) discuss several of these that are variously referred to as outpatient commitment, assisted outpatient treatment (AOT), or community treatment orders (CTOs). While they question the wisdom of these approaches, they conclude that the "ethical justification for involuntary outpatient treatment hinges not only on issues of right and wrong, but also the practical considerations of treatment access and effectiveness." They also note that the question of whether they unduly restrict consumers' liberties or expand them, in part, hinges on the criteria that are used for inpatient commitment: to the extent that the outpatient commitment criteria fails to reduce the need for inpatient commitment and simply replaces commitment in the hospital with that in the community, then it is less defensible. They also point out that psychiatric advance directives (PADs) may sometimes serve as an antidote to coercive interventions such as psychiatric hospital commitment and AOT since they also provide a means to build on a patient's own decisions while they are fully competent.

A critical area that mental health planners need to consider are workforce needs, one that is discussed by several of the chapter authors (see Chapters 12, 13, 16), but overlooked by many in the field. The development of community mental health has brought with it an expansion in the numbers and responsibilities of allied health professionals such as psychologists and social workers, especially given the shortage of traditional medical staff in most jurisdictions.

The focus on multidisciplinarity is discussed by Eva Dragomirecká and colleagues (Chapter 12) as an essential feature of the rehabilitation approach, and is pointed out as a policy in such nations as Australia, the United Kingdom, and the United States (Chapters 13, 16, 18). Part of this trend has been the expansion in the use of peer supports, typically involving the employment of ex-patients with "lived experience" of various forms of mental illness. In Australia, for example, Rosenberg and Salvador-Carullo point out that many consumers now focus their advocacy on the goal of establishing a peer workforce (Chapter 13). These same authors report that although there has been no standard approach to measuring workforce needs, this capacity has been under development in Australia.

Questions of leadership in mental health policy development are also particularly salient. In some nations such as the United States, Mandersheid and Ward (Chapter 18) argue that a critical lack has been leadership in the development of a national mental health policy. These authors comment that "we also hope that we have made a sufficient case that our current lack of integration in policy will not produce the same desirable effects as would a more fully integrated national mental health policy." Such a policy, they recommend, should include both content and process elements. Both the US system of federalism involving the sharing of powers between localities, states, and the federal government, and between the executive, judicial, and legislative branches, has no doubt been a significant factor in the paralysis of national policy decision making that has hamstrung the effort to develop national mental health policy. Manderscheid and Ward specifically recommend the identification of policy champions and a national council dedicated to this purpose. In contrast, Rosenberg and Salvador-Carullo (Chapter 13) recommend that Australia requires some strengthening in mental health policy in its states. They conclude that "A key consistent theme of current reports and recommendations is that mental health planning in Australia must shift from historic, centralized approaches to more local or regional models of governance and decision-making" and suggest that "Australia's national approach to mental health reform offers lessons for other nations. Of particular importance here is the need for better approaches to local or regional planning, supported by systems of accountability that facilitate quality improvement."

As noted at the beginning of this chapter, the integration of research into mental health policy development has been one of the most pivotal themes of this Handbook. Each author has emphasized different dimensions of this need. Initial chapters by Hudson (1 and 2) and also Kamya (3) have explored various process issues in the conduct of research and how it needs to be coordinated with that of policy development, perhaps even in a fashion akin to juggling. It is one that Mandersheid and Ward (Chapter 18) comment on in respect to US needs, noting that "very little attention is placed upon the process of policy development and implementation." Hudson comments that in order for the aims of evidence-based practice and policy to be realized, it will be necessary to better understand, and thus research, various models of decision making that will better allow for such integration. Several authors (see Chapter 13) have discussed the importance of using research in the development of mental health standards and benchmarks, to permit better monitoring of mental health policy outcomes.

The chapters on research methods (Part II) have examined the pros and cons of various qualitative and quantitative methods, as well as emerging and mixed methods research strategies. Chapter 5 on emerging methods highlighted geospatial methods and predictive analytics, which Chapter 14 on Europe has built upon, especially in respect to its presentation of the development of mental health atlases and decision support systems that can in real time support both practitioners and planners. This chapter's authors emphasize the understanding of relevant ecosystems, involving both the mental health epidemiological study of mental health problems as well as care systems.

Reginald York, in Chapter 4, emphasizes the importance of quantitative methods, such as random controlled trials (RCTs), which are not only essential in the exploration and description of population-level problems, but in the identification of etiology and, thus, possible interventions through conventional evaluative designs that are invaluable in identifying both causes and consequences. So, although RCTs may be an important ideal, Rochefort and Hirshfield (Chapter 7) point out that only a small minority of treatments in active use had been validated by RCTs. Thus, while RCTs can be expanded in certain areas, this is also an argument for expanding the use of quasi-experimental designs, some of which, like the Two Stage Least Squares-IV design (Rose & Stone, 2011), can be equally powerful in identifying causal patterns when random assignment in experiments cannot be ethically justified. Rochefort and Hirshfield (Chapter 7) mention that "As early as the mid-1990s, the case for evidence-based medical practice was being advanced with increased frequency. The consequence was not merely prioritization of controlled experiments for existing and proposed treatments, but also initiation of a new field of Implementation Science that adopted a mixed-methods approach for studying the spread of beneficial practices." While mixed methods are in principle optimal ways for combining the best of qualitative and quantitative methods, it is not always clear how results from diverse methods can be meaningfully combined, especially when they conflict with one another.

CONCLUDING RECOMMENDATIONS

This Handbook has been based on the notion that the continued development of mental health policy and services requires improvements in the content and process of research, and especially in its integration into policy-making processes. Such improvements are needed on multiple levels, including fundamental research on the etiology and course of various mental illnesses; on various service models, involving effectiveness, efficiency, responsiveness among other considerations; and on the leadership, financing, and organization of local and national service systems. Research on the etiology and course of various mental illnesses should involve not only biological and ecological factors, but also psychological, sociological, and larger system dimensions, most notably, causes and patterns of stigmatization of mental illness, and responses. Mental health research is a very broad field, an important subset of which involves local and national governmental policies, whether they involve leadership, financing, or organization. Mental health policy research must maintain a focus on system interventions, while at the same time be grounded in psychiatric epidemiology and the broader biopsychosocial problems that surround it.

Beyond questions of content in mental health policy research, attention to its process is also of paramount importance. This involves the process of its formulation and planning, as well as the ways that researchers decide on and implement various methods in particular environments. Given the complexity and many unknowns inherent in most policy topics, it is usually critical that researchers assume a multi-perspectival and multi-method approach. This will often involve emphasizing and eliciting the perspectives of clients, families, observers, as well as providers and other stakeholders, whether research involves mental health problems, services, or policies. Strategies for doing this may involve exploratory methods such as semi-structured interviews, focus groups, or observational studies, as well as large-scale surveys, experiments, data mining, and predictive analytical studies, involving both qualitative and quantitative sources of data. Continued attention needs to be paid to examining patterns of error and bias in such data, and resolving conflicts between such diverse sources.

Many opportunities would best be pursued for the improved integration of research into policy development. These involve the ways that professionals are trained and educated, as well as the ways that researchers are employed and develop their topics in collaboration with policy makers. While incentives need to be created for both researchers and policy makers to collaborate more closely, standards also need to be defined to protect the autonomy of researchers vis-à-vis political processes and protect the integrity of the research from political co-optation, a delicate balancing act. Particularly important processes that cannot be assumed and need to be systematically pursued are those involving the dissemination and implementation of research results, including decommissioning of some antiquated programs and practices or instituting new and improved ones. Just as research formulation may involve carefully linked preliminary studies, dissemination and implementation may also involve systematically linked follow-up studies. Research incentives and funding opportunities need to systematically allow for such integrated programs of research, often involving multiple researchers.

Finally, successful research processes involve building research into the design of decision support and policy development systems. Examples include the need for the continued development of common process and outcome indicators, or benchmarks, that can be transparently reported to support both the fine-tuning as well as the reform of service and policy systems. The design of these need to include multiple systems of care so as to address the many trade-offs in their design and avoid the crippling limitations of service siloing and resulting fragmentation.

Those engaged in mental health policy research need to consider how their work can be used in the public arena, to minimize stigma and educate the public regarding mental health services and build confidence in them. By doing so, political support will be built, and its resource base will be provided for, especially to the degree that such confidence-building enhances demand for and utilization of such services. To the extent that the success of services can be demonstrated, such demand will follow and mental illness and mental health services will be normalized, similar to services for many physical health conditions.

Researchers need to also consider how their work might be used to improve the leadership and organization of mental health service systems. While the means considered will to some extent be contingent on the socio-political context, in most nations there are several levels of national, regional, and local organization that require leadership and a coherent means of organization. Typically, the national level involves policy development, funding, and standard setting and regulation, often as a part of health care and/or social services. An important function often consists of the equitable distribution of resources between constituent localities, a task for which it is essential to negotiate competing demands with the help of convincing data on relative levels of need.

Research is also needed on establishing standards and benchmarks of care, and facilitating service access across localities and service modalities. Regional and local mental health authorities require research results that will support their numerous operational decisions regarding resource deployment, services that need to be expanded or eliminated, and manpower development. Both within and between each of the organizational levels, issues involving the means of linkage are critical. How can autonomy be respected at the same time that the various organizational units are incentivized to be maximally responsive to others – to consumers, workers, and to other relevant organizational units?

Mental health policy researchers, thus, need to be attuned to a wide range of questions that at their core involve the task of building balanced and integrated mental health systems that employ evidence-based practices. There are always many decisions to be made regarding the optimal balance between inpatient and community services, between various modalities of each, as well as decisions on their management and staffing, and the establishment of standards and incentives for their coordination. It is assumed that these involve ongoing dynamic decision processes that often will call for data on needed incremental adjustments for progressively approximating the values and goals established. Ideals involving understanding, transparency, engagement, recovery, community, and caring are among those that need to be at the heart of both the design of mental health research and systems of care.

REFERENCES

Gerhard, R.J., Miles, D.G., & Dorgan, R.E. (1981). *The balanced service system: A model of personal & social integration.* Clinton, OK: Responsive Systems Associates.

Rose, R.A., & Stone, S.I. (2011). Instrumental variable estimation in social work research: A technique for estimating causal effects in nonrandomized settings. *Journal of the Society for Social Work Research*, 76(2), 76–88.

Thornicroft, G., & Tansella, M. (2013). The balanced care model: The case for both hospital- and community-based mental healthcare. *British Journal of Psychiatry*, 202(4), 246–8.

Index

academic literature 16
accountability 6, 10, 98, 190, 197, 199, 200, 293
accountable care organizations (ACOs) 289
Active Recovery Triad (ART) model 178
acute crises 139, 140
Adair, C. E. 174
ADAMHA Reorganization Act (1992) 78
Administration and Policy in Mental Health and Mental Health Services Research 101
adult day units (ADUs) 251
adultified theoretical assumptions 122, 290
Adults with Severe Mental Illness 99
Advancing Correctional Excellence (ACE) 66
adverse life experiences (ACES) 117
Advisory Committee of NICE's Board 266
Advocacy Coalition Framework 18
Affordable Care Act (ACA) (2010) 275, 279, 288
African-American males 48
Agency for Health Care Policy and Research (AHCPR) 79
agency-level coordination 10
agenda-setting policy formulation 17
agent-based models (ABM) 61, 63, 64
Alcohol, Drug Abuse, and Mental Health Administration (ADAMHA) 78
alcohol-related disorders 49
Alcohol Use Disorders Identification Test (AUDIT) 248
Alderson, P. 122
American Medical Association 73
American Psychological Association 46
American School Counselor Association (ASCA) 115
Anna Freud Center (2021) 122
Anthony, B. 228
Anthony, W. A. 176, 178
    service outcome model 174
Anti-Drug Abuse Act (1988) 78
anti-psychiatric movement 161
Anti-Stigma Project 141
anxiety 249
    administer 49
    CBT for 77
    depression 127
    disorders 49
    symptoms of 75
Archer, J. 165
Arie Querido, in Netherlands 207
Arizona School Counselors Association 115

Assertive Community Treatment (ACT) 74, 76–7, 96, 177, 179, 291
    high-risk persons 77
    team 211
Assisted Outpatient Treatment (AOT) 153, 292
    community treatment orders 153
    lack of capacity 154
    psychiatric hospital commitment 155
    surveillance 154
attention deficit hyperactivity disorder (ADHD) 117
Australia
    health system 192
    long-term psychiatric institutions 193
    National Mental Health Strategy 200
    National Strategy 200
    non-government organizations 195
Australian Institute of Health and Welfare (AIHW) report 192
Aviram, U. 226
avoidance behaviours 135
Azrin, S. T. 94

Bachrach, L. L. 163, 174
Baker, C. 254
Banks, S. M. 100, 166
Basic Stable Input of Care (BSIC) 211
Becker, H. 122
behavioral challenges 34
behavioral implications 35
behavioral psychology 73
Belcher, J. R. 166, 287
beliefs
    negative 134
    positivists 30
benzodiazepines 75–6
Better Access Program 196, 197
Better Outcomes 197
Bickman, L. 90
Biden, J. 94
biopsychosocial model of health 174
Black/Hispanic youth 35
Boktor, S. W. 50
Bossert, T. 9
Boston Psychiatric Rehabilitation Approach (BPR) 176
Boston University's Center for Psychiatric Rehabilitation 176
British Medical Journal 94